MW00851286

THE BATTLE OF LIBERTY PLACE

SEPTEMBER 14th, 1874

The Louisiana Outrages — Attack upon the Police in the Streets of New Orleans
(From Harper's Weekly, Oct. 3, 1874 — Courtesy Leonard V. Huber)
Note the Iron Building in the distance at the right

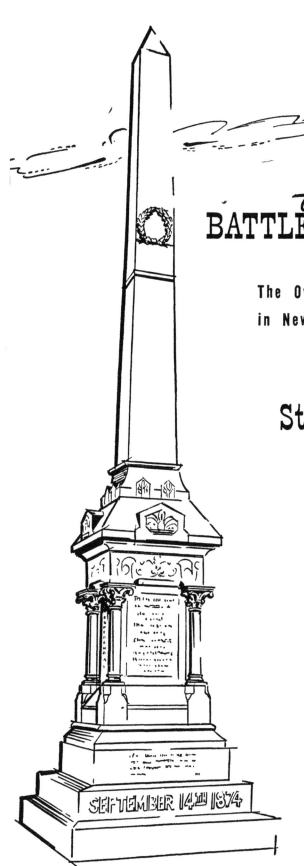

BATTLE *the* OF LIBERTY PLACE

The Overthrow of Carpet-Bag Rule
in New Orleans - September 14, 1874

by
Stuart Omer Landry

A FIREBIRD
PRESS
BOOK

OMPANY

Gretna 2000

......U.S.A.

Manufactured in the United States of America
Published by Pelican Publishing Company, Inc.
1000 Burmaster Street, Gretna, Louisiana 70053

To

The Memory of the Heroes of the Fourteenth of September, whose Patriotism should be an Inspiration, not only to their Descendants, but to all Louisianians of Good Intent.

NOTE

Acknowledgement is due the following members of the Board of Commissioners of Liberty Place, who have assisted in the financing of the production of this book and who underwrote part of the expense:

Charles P. Carriere	Bernard J. McCloskey
Arthur A. de la Houssaye	Frank J. McLoughlin
Dr. Roy E. de la Houssaye	Fred N. Ogden
Hughes Jules de la Vergne, II	Dr. Henry D. Ogden
William B. Dreux	Charles J. Smith
William A. Feiullan, Jr.	Walter J. Stauffer
Richard R. Foster	Hughes P. Walmsley
Rene J. LeGardeur	Hugh M. Wilkinson
Judge Richard T. McBride	William B. Wisdom

CONTENTS

LIST OF ILLUSTRATIONS

PREFACE

The idea of writing a book about the Battle of the Fourteenth of September, 1874 is not a new one.

In the *Picayune* of September the Twenty-second there was published under the heading of "A Suggestion," the following letter written from St. John the Baptist Parish, dated Sept. 20, 1874 and signed, "Respectfully, PLANTER":

> Allow me to make the following suggestion: Why would not some competent person set to work, gather up all the correct statements of the different events that have, and that will yet occur during this eventful month, and publish the whole in a book form, under the title of "September, 1874, in Louisiana." Such a publication would sell readily. Profits derived from the sale, turned over to the widows and orphans of our martyred fellow-citizens of last Monday's (14th inst.) engagement, would go far towards relieving those that so nobly deserve relief. Besides, the publication going North and West, would go far towards giving them correct views of our brilliant *coup d'etat*, and of the immediate cause that brought things to a focus much sooner than Kellogg has expected.

For all these many years Planter's idea for a book has lain dormant. Now it has at last reached fruition — too late to do complete justice to all the participants, but not too late to relate in sequence and in the right perspective the story of an almost forgotten chapter in the annals of the Crescent City.

Intrigued by the drama of the Reconstruction period and imbued with admiration for those who strove for Liberty by resisting the oppressor's wrongs, I have attempted to piece together fading and crumbling papers found in the pigeon holes of History's desk to make a design, created out of the testimony of actors and onlookers, that will enable us to experience and feel again the surge of patriotism which was the Spirit of '74.

In accordance with the suggestion of the Planter of St. John Parish I have "gathered" the statements of various persons who were active in the affair of the Fourteenth of September, as well as the opinions and testimony of men of prominence concerning conditions in Louisiana and New Orleans before the event.

My book, then, is more or less an editorial job. The method employed has an advantage in that we read the actual words of the narrators of the events chronicled, told sometimes forcibly, sometimes piquantly, and often in the quaint journalistic style of the Victorian age.

Although to some extent repetitious, the accounts of the events of the Fourteenth as published in the various newspapers are given in full, as well as the official reports of Gen. Ogden, reports of the company commanders of the

White League, Gen. Longstreet's report to Gov. Kellogg and other accounts. Newspaper comments and the testimony of witnesses before Congressional Committees are quoted verbatim. There are excerpts of considerable length from Nordoff's book — unknown to most readers — which throw much light on the conditions that brought on the September *emeute,* as Gov. Kellogg calls it, and which makes interesting reading.

The employment of actual quotations and the use of original accounts of witnesses and commentators makes for historical accuracy, lessens the number of footnotes and permits the reader to draw his own conclusions after having reviewed the evidence itself. On the other hand this method of rendering history has its disadvantages. It tends towards diffuseness, takes up more space and is sometimes dull reading.

But the author's idea is to include all the material relating to the Battle of the Fourteenth that he could find. He is not trying to condense it, to describe the day's events in a few words or to paraphrase or digest the words of others. His aim is to "gather" the writings and statements made by the participants and the journalists of the time, and to let the story tell itself.

In spite of the lack of dramatic concentration I believe this history on the whole is very readable, and that the inclusion of many details will make it a record of permanent value.

One of the difficult problems that confronted me was the checking of the names of the participants in the Battle of the Fourteenth. The muster rolls of companies are missing. Mr. W. O. Hart, who wrote of the Battle in the Louisiana Historical Quarterly in 1924 on the occasion of the fiftieth anniversary, said that they could not be found. Several lists are available. One, printed in 1877, which included all members of the White League, the Louisiana Field Artillery and the First Louisiana Regiment, lists all those who served from September, 1874 to April, 1877. Another, the roster of Col. W. T. Vaudry's First Crescent City Regiment, covers the same period. In both these pamphlets those members who took part in the battle of the Fourteenth had a star or asterisk after their names. Several thousand joined the White League and affiliated military companies after the 14th of September. These companies drilled and were active as watchers in the elections of 1874 and 1876. As the election of 1876 brought on another dispute between Nicholls and Packard over the governorship, in January 1877 the League turned out in full force to support the claims of Gov. Nicholls. For 100 days the White League patrolled the Vieux Carré, while Packard and his officials were "bottled up" in the State House, until President Hayes withdrew the Federal troops and recognized Nicholls as the governor. Thus many who were active White Leaguers and served patriotically did not participate in the affray of the 14th of September, 1874.

This has led to much confusion. The families or descendants of White Leaguers sometimes claim that ancestors or relatives were in the Battle of the 14th when it is possible they are confusing the battle service with service at the polls or in the Spring of 1877. Also, some fought on the 14th whose names were not on the rolls, or whose names were inadvertently omitted, or who belonged to no organized troop but who went home after the mass meeting on Canal Street, grabbed a gun and joined in the meleé. Several persons have written that their ancestors were participants and I have accepted their word.

For easy reference I have arranged the names of those in the printed lists who fought on the Fourteenth in alphabetical order.

Although there are some still alive who were born before 1874, I cannot find anyone who took part in the battle. If alive he would have to be at least ninety-eight years old provided he was seventeen years old in September 1874.

In preparation for the writing of the book, advertisements were placed in the personal columns of New Orleans' newspapers. These resulted in much information as well as contacts with older persons who remember vividly the excitement of the times, but no veteran of '74 was located.

I have assembled many illustrations of the affair of September 14th, but I have not been able to find photographs or pictures of all of the captains of the various companies of the White League, the Louisiana Field Artillery or the First Louisiana Regiment. This is to be regretted, but to locate all these pictures at this late date is an almost insuperable task. For instance, I was able to find a picture of Gen. Angell by writing to his grand-nephew, an Army officer, who sent it to me from Turkey.

The task of gathering information, editing it and writing the history of the Battle of Liberty Place has been an arduous but pleasant one. I have read through three volumes of Congressional Committee reports containing over three million words. For instance, the Senate Report of February 20, 1875 on the condition of affairs in Louisiana has over 1100 pages of testimony, much of it set in 8 point type, averaging 1,000 words to the page. I have likewise read hundreds of columns of newspaper matter — news, editorials and "letters from the people." In additon I read some ten books and numerous pamphlets, magazines and issues of the Louisiana Historical Quarterly.

I have had assistance from many persons in compiling this history and wish to thank particularly the following:

Leonard V. Huber; Thomas Harrison, Military Historian, Office of Adj. Gen., La. State Militia; John Hall Jacobs, Librarian, New Orleans Public Library; Dr. Garland Taylor, Librarian, Howard-Tilton Library; Mrs. Frances Moore and Mrs. Shirley Hayem of the Louisiana State Museum; Mrs. Rosa M. Oliver, Librarian, State Museum Library; Mrs. Poole and Mrs. Fortier of the Confederate Memorial Hall; William B. Wisdom, Dr. Henry Ogden, J. J. Meunier, E. L. Harris, William Nott, Miss Louise Guyol, Morgan D. Hite, Mrs. Matilda Francis, Miss Texada Carter, Mrs. Georgie H. Regan, Albert Lieutaud, Arthur de la Houssaye, Walter J. Stauffer, Frank H. Allen, Mrs. Beatrice McHale, Mrs. Arthur S. Bliss of Wheeling, W. Va., Lt.-Col. A. George Bliss, USA., Miss Emily Hosmer, I. V. Shannon, Mrs. Sidney M. Pelayo, and Merwin J. Angell.

S. O. L.

BIBLIOGRAPHY

THE TRAGIC ERA: Claude A. Bowers. — Houghton Miflin Co., N. Y. 1929.

The best history of the Reconstruction Period in the South. Besides picturing the deplorable conditions of the times, Bowers comes to conclusions, suggested by the title of his book, based on numerous facts, the sources of which are carefully authenticated. Both in its details and in its generalizations it is a comprehensive work and should be in every library. "The Tragic Era" includes a chapter or so on Reconstruction in Louisiana, but as it covers the whole South its discussion of affairs in Louisiana is necessarily limited.

HISTORY OF RECONSTRUCTION IN LOUISIANA THROUGH 1868: John R. Ficklen. — John Hopkins University Press, Baltimore, 1910.

An important book on the early years of Reconstruction.

RECONSTRUCTION IN LOUISIANA AFTER 1868: Ella Lonn. — Putnam, N. Y. 1918.

Takes up where Ficklen leaves off. Probably the authoritative work on the Reconstruction Era in Louisiana, yet contains errors of fact such as careless statements about Governor Penn.

LOUISIANA REDEEMED: Garnie W. McGinty. — Pelican Pub. Co. New Orleans, 1941.

Covers the period of Reconstruction from 1876 to 1880, and the overthrow of carpet bag rule. A carefully documented study.

THE UNCONQUERED: Ben Ames Williams. — Houghton Miflin Co. Boston. 1953.

A novel of the Reconstruction Period with the scene laid in New Orleans. While fictional, it contains much factual material with good descriptions. The Battle of the Fourteenth is told about in detail.

WAR, POLITICS AND RECONSTRUCTION: Henry C. Warmouth. — McMillan Co. N. Y. 1930.

Gov. Warmouth's defense of his activities during the post-war era. An interesting, readable and informative book.

HISTORY OF NEW ORLEANS: John S. Kendall. — Lewis Pub. Co. Chicago. 1922.

The chapter describing the affair of September the Fourteenth is excellent. It is the best succinct description of the events of that day and those that lead up to it.

CREOLE CITY: E. L. Tinker. — Longmans Green & Co. 1951.

Chapter on post Civil War days is interesting.

CARPET BAG MISRULE IN LOUISIANA: James J. A. Fortier. — Publication of La. State Museum, New Orleans. 1938.

A pamphlet containing much information about the Battle of September the 14th, 1874. Well illustrated.

THE COTTON STATES IN THE SPRING AND SUMMER OF 1875: Charles Nordoff. New York. 1875.

Written by an abolitionist, a Republican and a "Yankee." A splendid picture of affairs in the South during the Tragic Era. The chapter on Louisiana is especially pertinent.

AFTER THE WAR — A SOUTHERN TOUR: Whitelow Reid, Cincinnati, Ohio. 1866.

Anti-Southern but interesting.

A HISTORY OF LOUISIANA: Alcee Fortier, Goupil & Co. Parish. 1904.

LOUISIANA HISTORICAL QUARTERLY

HARPER'S MAGAZINE

FRANK LESLIE'S ILLUSTRATED WEEKLY

SCRIBNER'S MAGAZINE

NEW YORK GRAPHIC

NEW YORK WORLD

NEW YORK HERALD

NEW YORK TRIBUNE

NEW ORLEANS PICAYUNE — Contemporary

    "   "   BULLETIN   "

    "   "   REPUBLICAN   "

    "   "   TIMES   "

    "   "   BEE (L'Abeille)   "

    "   "   TIMES-DEMOCRAT

    "   "   STATES

    "   "   ITEM

    "   "   MORNING TRIBUNE

    "   "   TIMES-PICAYUNE

REPORTS OF CONGRESSIONAL COMMITTEES,

    Investigating condition of affairs in Louisiana.

INTRODUCTION

Eighty years have now passed since the Battle of Liberty Place at the foot of Canal Street on September 14, 1874. Thus three generations are included in the span of time that reaches back to that fateful day.

A fourth generation is now here and the stirring events of those times are not only unremembered, but are almost unheard of by the young people of today. A newspaper man, born in Louisiana, when asked about the Battle of Canal Street, had never heard of it and did not know why there was a monument at Liberty Place. So soon are the heroes of yesteryear forgotten!

One of the reasons for the lack of knowledge about and the lack of interest in the terrible days of Reconstruction is the tendency of human nature to forget. Events crowd in upon us so that it is difficult even to keep up with current history. And not much is printed today about the difficulties that beset the people of New Orleans during the Tragic Era.

Furthermore, a revisionist school of historians is now endeavoring to show that the Reconstruction period was not as bad as it has been painted, and that the South did not suffer as the Southern people have said it did. An effort is made to palliate the enormity of the outrages that occurred in the Southern States, and to discount the hardships imposed upon a defeated people by a carpetbag-rule maintained in power by Federal troops.

There is another reason for overlooking the historical significance of the Battle of the 14th of September. The present attitude towards colored people, entertained not only by Northerners but by Southerners too, is inimical to the idea of "white supremacy." And because the Battle of the 14th was fought on one side by the "White League," it is assumed by some that it was a struggle between the races, and as such the White League participants are not only not worthy of commemoration, but that their actions should even be branded as reprehensible.

The Battle of Liberty Place was not a race riot nor a struggle between whites and Negroes. It was the effort of freedom-loving Americans to throw off the shackles of a dictatorship of sordid politicians, illegally elected and holding office with the aid of Federal bayonets. As such it deserves more than passing consideration, for it was evoked by a desire for freedom, liberty and justice, and the motive was a patriotic one.

It is easy, then, to forget the principles involved in the conflict which came to a climax at the foot of Canal Street on the Fourteenth of September, 1874, or to be apathetic towards the participants in what some would term a trivial affair.

It is unfair, too, not to try to understand the point of view of the Southerner of Reconstruction days. Surely, by his courage, his dignity in defeat and his resolution to adapt himself to the new order of things, he has won our respect and deserves our sympathy. His country ravaged by armies, his wealth — invested principally in slaves — taken from him, his sons killed and maimed in battle, he found himself governed by "carpetbaggers," scalawags, ignorant freedmen and rascally Southerners,* who joined in with these others to direct and control the newly enfranchised colored people for plunder and power. Urged on by fanatics in the North, they, at the same time, harassed and humiliated the former ruling classes.

The majority of white people, who had just seen the Negroes released from bondage, could not understand or tolerate the social revolution brought about by the freeing of the slaves. They could not see these poor blacks, ignorant and deluded, as their equals either socially or politically. The white South resented and resisted the attempts to enforce such political and social equality, although they resigned themselves to the enfranchisement of Negroes, and stood in line to vote with them at the polls.

Reconstruction programs were directed by radicals in Congress. Some radicals may have been idealistic in their aims but their hatred against the South was so great they endeavored to put into effect what might be called a Morgenthau Plan — a plan to ruin the South economically, politically, socially. Congress enacted force and punitive laws, and the working out of the details was left to adventurers and bureaucrats, who, in the name of liberty and democracy, and while backed by Federal troops, seemed to take sadistic pleasure in humiliating and riding rough shod over a defenseless people. Most of the new rulers of the South were not interested in the principles of good government or even in helping the former slaves. They were lining their own pocketbooks and wanted power. The South had reason to object to the Reconstruction laws, regulations and the methods of enforcement. Accordingly, they organized the Ku Klux Klan, leagues and secret societies of various kinds to protect and defend their rights.

---

*One of the most notorious of the turn-coat Southerners was James Hunnicutt of Virginia. Before the war he owned slaves in South Carolina, voted for secession and deserted from the Confederate Army. He was a preacher and later an editor of a religious paper. He preached hate and intolerance and became a radical leader of the Negroes and a power in Virginia. Claude Bowers tells about him in "The Tragic Era."

The radicals in Congress under Thaddeus Stevens, were not concerned with the long range effect of their narrow plan of retaliation and revenge. They did not try to help the South to recover by favorable legislation or economic aid. There was no Marshall Plan to assist the defeated and enfeebled South. The consequence was that it took the Southern people nearly fifty years to achieve an economic recovery that should have been started right after the war. Four years after the Franco-German war, the French had paid the four billion dollars amerced by the Germans. Today, nine years after the great World War II, Western Germany is flourishing and the people on their way to economic recovery. Likewise, Japan has been helped to restore its economy, thanks to the leniency and liberality of the victors. The South had no such aid when it laid down its arms. So it was that the Southern people for two generations could not forget or forgive their oppressors and the hardships forced upon them. It is only now that those unfortunate times are generally unremembered. While we still find a great many people, both North and South, "fighting the Civil War," Reconstruction days are not often the subject of discussion, and the hardships of the aftermath of the war seem to have been forgotten.

√ In telling the story of the Battle of Liberty Place in the period of Reconstruction I am emphasizing its importance, and will endeavor to show how the people of Louisiana suffered so many outrages that they were forced to take extreme measures. It is not my purpose to arouse animosities or bring back the hates of that dreadful era. I desire only to compile a record that will be complete in detail, and to interpret this phase of our local history. But above all I wish to honor those patriots who took part in one of the most glorious events in the history of New Orleans, and to preserve in compact form the record of their activity.

In the hurly-burly of those evil days, when carpetbaggers and scoundrels pillaged and defiled our fair land, there were many patriotic men and women who were willing to give their lives, if necessary, to regain their rights and to bring about honest elections and a just government for white people as well as colored. Some did die in the Battle of Canal Street on September 14, 1874, and the others who took part therein risked their lives. Not only in battle, for it was quite possible that, if defeated, they could have been sought out as revolutionists and traitors and hanged by Kellogg's gang.* In fact, four months later Gen. Phil Sheridan, Commandant of Federal troops at New Orleans,

---

*A. P. Field, Attorney-General for Gov. Kellogg, asserted in Washington that he would prosecute and hang for treason all engaged in armed resistance to Kellogg's government.

wired the Secretary of War that, if President Grant would issue a proclamation declaring White-League participants in the Liberty Place battle "banditti," and leave the matter to him, he would take care of things, hinting that a military commission would try them for murder.

This book attempts to give a detailed account of the Battle of September the Fourteenth, and, above all, to include the names of all those known to have been connected with the affair on the side of the White League. It is unfortunate that some records are missing and the names of many that deserve to be listed are among the unknown. And, of course, there were thousands not members of the military companies who were sympathetic with the movement. But a salute, likewise, to those unknown patriots, who by defying Kellogg and his crew, also took grave risks in attempting to restore liberty to their native land.

CHAPTER I

SOME LOUISIANA HISTORY AFTER THE WAR

The cause of the Battle of Liberty Place was the result of several years of the troubled Reconstruction period, the coerced adoption of the 14th Amendment, corrupt government, inefficiency, stealing of elections and the injustices of the carpetbag regime forced upon Louisiana by the Federal authorities, and more particularly the usurpation of the State government in 1873 by Kellogg and his "Custom House gang."

Louisiana politics of the time were complicated, and it is difficult to keep in mind the series of events that finally reached a climax in the Battle of Canal Street on September 14, 1874. At the time of the Canal Street Battle only nine years had elapsed since the close of the War Between the States. Yet in this short period momentous changes had occurred in the economic, social and political life of the people of Louisiana.

During the War the parts of the State of Louisiana occupied by the Federals were ruled by military government — George Shepley, 1862-64 and Michael Hahn, 1864-65. Federal-held Louisiana was the first Confederate territory subjected to reconstruction. It began in New Orleans in 1862 when Gen. Butler freed some slaves by encouraging them to leave their masters, and his enlisting some of them in Federal regiments. When Gen. Banks assumed command he modified this policy. He placed the hordes of freed or run-away Negroes under discipline and made them work. In August 1862 military Governor George Shepley took charge. He authorized an election for representatives to Congress. The vote was limited to citizens who had taken the oath of allegiance.

General Butler had partially emancipated the slaves and Lincoln's Emancipation Proclamation was issued in January 1863, but slavery was not outlawed in Louisiana until 1864 when a new constitution went into effect on July 23rd. This new constitution, abolished slavery but limited the suffrage to white males over 21, with the proviso that the suffrage could be extended to Negroes at the discretion of the legislature.

At this time there were two factions in the Republican Party which had sprung up to take control of Louisiana politics, radical and moderate Republicans who disagreed over Negro suffrage. In January 1864 in the election for that part of the State which was under Federal control,* Michael Hahn, who was a moderate Republican and opposed to giving suffrage to the Negroes, was elected governor over his radical opponent, Benjamin Flanders. President Lincoln favored the moderates, and conferred the power of the military governorship on Hahn on March 15, 1864. The constitution of 1864 under the leadership of Governor Hahn, because it did not give the right to vote to Negroes, displeased the radicals both in Washington and Louisiana. Although rejected by Congress, it served until a second and more radical constitution was adopted on March 11, 1868.†

In 1865 J. Madison Wells was elected governor. For a year or two there seemed to be hope of progress. President Johnson proclaimed amnesty in May 1865 for those former Confederates who had been leaders in secession. However, the radicals in Congress were in disagreement with President Johnson's efforts for moderate reconstruction. Thaddeus Stevens wanted to keep the property of the "Rebels" and criticized Johnson for restoring confiscated property to them.

On February 6, 1867, the Louisiana House of Representatives adopted a joint resolution in which the Legislature refused to ratify the proposed Fourteenth Amendment. Out of a House membership of 110 members, with ten being absent or not voting, 100 members voted unanimously against ratification and none in favor of it. Says Walter J. Suthon, Jr., in his brochure, "The Dubious Origin of the Fourteenth Amendment": "This was the last opportunity for a free and uncoerced expression of views on this amendment proposal by the duly elected representatives of the people of Louisiana."

On March 2, 1867, the Reconstruction Act was passed by the National Congress over President Johnson's veto. It contained harsh measures and provided severe punishment for ex-Confederates and recalcitrant whites. The South was then divided into five military districts, and the commanders of each district (in New Orleans, Gen. Sheridan) appointed the registration boards which were ordered to cause registrations to be made of all citizens 21 years of age or older. Registration was to be denied those who had participated in the "rebellion" or even to those whose right to vote was in doubt.

---

*The Confederate governor of the State was Henry W. Allen. Thus began the dual governorship which existed several times during the following thirteen years.

†Even Hahn's legislature was imbued with the idea of revenge. On October 12, 1864 a resolution was introduced into the Senate which ordered the institution of criminal proceedings against T. J. Semmes, Judah P. Benjamin, John Slidell, Henry M. Hyams, members of the Legislature who voted for secession and other Louisiana Confederates. This bill never became a law.

Half of the white citizens ordinarily entitled to vote were refused registration. Thus ex-Confederates were excluded from political activity.

All Negroes 21 or over were registered. As many of the new Negro voters were without birth certificates, or did not know their ages, they were given the benefit of the doubt, and undoubtedly thousands of those registered as qualified electors were under the age of twenty-one. In July 1867 the total registration in Louisiana under the new law was 127,639, of which 82,907 were colored and 44,732 white.

On March 6, 1867 General Philip Sheridan assumed command of the Fifth Military District (comprising Louisiana and Texas with headquarters at New Orleans) and the Louisiana radicals climbed into the saddle. On June 3rd General Sheridan removed the moderate Governor J. M. Wells from office and appointed the more radical Benjamin Flanders as governor. He also removed

"The First Vote" — From Harper's Weekly, Nov. 16, 1867.
Drawn by their famous artist, A. R. Waud.
— Collection of Leonard V. Huber

many other State officials as well as Municipal officials of New Orleans.

At that time the three or four short street-car lines of the city used cars drawn by little mules, with tinkling bells on their harness. Some of the cars were marked with a star and colored people were permitted to ride only in the "star" cars. General Sheridan refused to protect the street-car companies in this policy, and Negroes forced their way into the cars reserved for white people.

General Sheridan took other highhanded measures displeasing to Orleanians. He was extremely unpopular among the conservative people, and later bore a reputation second only to that of Gen. Ben Butler. We shall hear more of him later.

On September 27, and 28, 1867 elections were held to choose delegates for the Constitutional Convention. For the first time in the history of Louisiana, Negroes voted. Many white citizens did not vote hoping this would upset the plan of the Republican party, because it was necessary for the election to be effective that a majority of those registered vote. The total registration was 127,639, of which 82,907 were Negroes. The vote for the convention was 75,083 with 4,006 votes against it. There were 49 white delegates and 49 Negro delegates — only two of which were Democrats.

The constitution they wrote disfranchised nearly all the former Confederates, provided interracial schools, abolished segregation of all types, and scheduled an election on the basis of the revised suffrage. Embodying the principles of the 13th and 14th amendments, it was adopted on March 11 by a popular vote of 51,737 to 30,076. With the adoption of the constitution, Louisiana was readmitted to the Union on June 25, 1868. On July 9 the legislature ratified the 14th Amendment.*

---

*The legislative journals of that session 1868 reflect the presence and dominance of the military, all as provided for and contemplated by the Reconstruction Act.

The House Journal shows that on June 29, 1868, Colonel Batchelder opened the session by calling the roll and reading an extract from the order of General Grant. The Senate Journal for the same date shows the reading of instructions from General Grant to the Commanding Officer of the Fifth Military District emphasizing the supremacy of the power of the military over the provisional civilian government. It was under these auspices that the coerced ratification of the Fourteenth Amendment in Louisiana was accomplished.

Even under the puppet government, created in Louisiana pursuant to the Reconstruction Act, the ratification of the Fourteenth Amendment in Louisiana was not unanimous. In the Senate on July 9, 1868 the vote on ratification was 20 yeas and 11 nays. The record contains a protest by Senator Bacon against voting upon ratification "under duress" imposed by the Reconstruction Act, and an unavailing appeal by that legislator for an opportunity for a "free and unrestrained" vote.

— Walter J. Suthon, Jr., "The Dubious Origin
of the Fourteenth Amendment"

It must not be thought that all the people of the United States were in favor of Negro suffrage. In 1867 when Negro suffrage was being forced on Louisiana people, three states — Ohio, Kansas and Minnesota — voted against it. The vote was as follows:

	Against	For
Ohio	255,340	215,937
Kansas	16,114	7,591
Minnesota	28,759	5,114

However, not all the Louisiana leaders and ex-Confederates opposed extending the suffrage to Negroes. Duncan F. Kenner urged the people of the State to accept Negro suffrage. So did Gen. Beauregard and Gen. Longstreet, who had just arrived to live in New Orleans. Longstreet, in fact, joined the Republican Party. He said that we were a conquered people and the best thing to do was submit and work with the authorities, hoping thus to establish a constitutional government. In August 1867 he wrote General Lee for the approval of his (Longstreet's) position. General Lee refused to agree with him.

In the Republican Convention of 1868 to nominate candidates for state offices, there were two groups — the "Pure Radicals" as they called themselves and the more moderates. The "Pure Radicals" proposed Major Francis E. Dumas, Colored, for Governor, while the compromising faction wanted Henry C. Warmoth. Warmoth, 26 years old, won the nomination with 45 votes to Dumas' 43.

In "War, Politics and Reconstruction," Warmoth tells about the "Pure Radicals." Three San Domingo Negroes came to New Orleans and started a newspaper, the *New Orleans Tribune*. They organized the "Pure Radical" Party and urged Negroes to join and vote for Negroes. They told the freed slaves and former colored freedmen to assert themselves. They proposed to make Louisiana an African state and urged that the colored people follow the example of Haiti and Liberia. The *Tribune* attained quite some influence and from the close vote in the Convention it will be seen that they came near taking charge of the affairs of the State. The Negroes had been well organized by well meaning Northerners and "do-gooders."

Thomas J. Durant was the leader of the Republican Party in Louisiana after the War, and helped to organize the Negroes for his party. But he moved away from Louisiana after the riot on July 30, 1866 at the Mechanics Institute in which 48 persons were killed and many wounded. His residence was at the corner of Canal and University Place and he and his family were obliged to witness the massacre.

In the Spring and Summer of 1867 the Union League clubs of New York and Philadelphia sent organizers into the South to form Union or Loyal Leagues among the Negroes. The Union League Club of New York with John Jay presiding approved report of the chief organizer which showed that in Louisiana there were 94 clubs with 57,300 Negro members, as announced by the New Orleans *Republican* on November 17, 1867.

Negroes were also organized into Reconstruction Clubs, and Companies of "the Grand Army" — all in opposition to the white people of the State.

During this time the Freedman's Bureau had agents throughout the state, ostensibly to help the newly freed blacks, but actually to stir up trouble and cause dissension.

The election of 1868 inaugurated the sorriest decade in Louisiana's political history. First under Governor Henry Warmoth, then his successor P. B. S. Pinchback for a short time, and finally William Pitt Kellogg, the politics of the State were controlled by an ignorant electorate directed by unscrupulous Northern carpetbaggers and local turncoats. Tryanny, graft, waste, racial strife, injustice and crime prevailed. The bonded debt of the State rose from 10 million dollars in 1860 to 50 million dollars in 1876, although taxes had increased nearly 500% during the same period.

Governor Warmoth started some of the trouble by asking for Federal troops to assist him in maintaining order. There had been disturbances in the northern parishes of the State during the early months of his term. Secret organizations such as the Knights of the White Camellia — the forerunner of the White League — came into existence.

Henry Clay Warmoth, born in Illinois in 1842, served as a colonel in the U. S. Army, and was wounded in the fighting around Vicksburg. He was twenty-three years of age, when he opened a law office in New Orleans in 1865. Tall, handsome and with a pleasing personality, he soon had many clients whom he represented in Washington in pressing their war-time claims against the government, many of which were for losses of cotton, sugar or other commodities. His fees soon totaled large sums. Entering politics he was elected governor in 1868.

For several years, the name of Warmoth was a "hissing and a by-word" among Louisianians, but in 1872 he joined forces with the conservatives and Democrats to elect John McEnery governor. This later brought him recognition and acceptance among many of the best people. His book, *War, Politics* *and Reconstruction,* defends his course of action and makes interesting reading. He died in 1931.*

Elected as Lieutenant-Governor with Warmoth in 1868 was Oscar J. Dunn, a colored man and a former slave. Dunn was a plasterer by trade, and when young played the guitar and taught music. He died on November 22, 1871 of pneumonia at the age of 42. On the day of his funeral — the 23rd — the courts, including the Federal Court and the Louisiana State Supreme Court, closed as did the post office to allow the clerks to attend the services. Stores were closed and flags flew at half mast on public buildings.

Dunn was followed to his grave by the largest funeral procession ever seen in New Orleans up to that time. The pall-bearers were the Republican leaders: Casey, Packard, Kellogg, Warmoth, and so on. Two lodges of Free Masons (colored) led the procession, after which came Gen. Badger leading 580 Metropolitan Police; General Barber (colored) and with his staff leading the 2nd Louisiana Infantry colored troops, 500 strong; the 3rd Louisiana Infantry, 250 colored troops; followed by over 200 carriages of mourners. The procession moved from his house at 32 Canal Street, out to Claiborne to St. Louis Cemetery No. 2.

The *Republican* said it was an inspiring demonstration with 20,000 people taking part. The *Times* placed the number at 15,000 most of whom were colored. The *Picayune* reported that some white persons participated and that it was "a grand turn-out." All the papers wrote obituary editorials praising the deceased.

Governor Warmoth was a pallbearer and visited the house three times the day of the funeral. He had fallen out with Dunn, who had joined the opposition. In his book Warmoth writes much about the conniving that Dunn carried on with his enemies, but doesn't mention Dunn's death and his own apparent grief thereat.

Oscar James Dunn seems to have been a pretty decent sort but the biggest thing in his life was his leaving it.

Governor Warmoth had some difficulty controlling his legislature. Half white and half black with a Republican majority, it passed many laws that gave away valuable franchises, plundered the treasury, permitted graft, and enacted much legislation distasteful to the people of the State. In fairness to

*The writer as a youth often heard Gov. Warmoth denounced as a scoundrel and execrated by members of my family. Years later I met the old Governor, still tall and handsome and dignified, and found him to be pleasant and gentlemanly. His career in Louisiana politics may be best summed up in the words of David W. Pipes, an ex-Confederate soldier, and in more settled times a member of the Louisiana State Legislature: "The best of a bad lot."

Warmoth, it must be said that he vetoed many of these bad bills. For instance, James F. Casey, the Collector of the Port of New Orleans and the brother-in-law of President Grant, had the legislature, in order to "promote the interests of commerce," pass a bill giving the Louisiana Warehouse Company a monopoly "of the entire levee front from Common [sic — Toulouse?] to Poydras with authority to build sheds and tax all merchandise landed under them, and all steamboats and steamships that landed goods on the wharves." Further, the State was to guarantee the interest and principal of the bonds of the company to the extent of $1,500,000. Governor Warmoth vetoed the bill, but both houses passed it over his veto. However, the Governor refused to issue the bonds and there was no way to make him do it, so the scheme fell through. A congressional investigation later disclosed that Casey had locked up in his safe in the Custom House the sum of $18,000, contributed by stockholders to be paid $1,000 apiece to 18 senators for their votes. When the scheme failed the money was returned to the stockholders.*

Among the "bad" pieces of legislation enacted in 1868 with the aid and consent of Warmoth was the Metropolitan Police bill, placing the policing of New Orleans, Jefferson City and St. Bernard Parish, in the hands of this armed constabulary. The Metropolitan Police were controlled by a Commission of five members, and of the five, Gov. Warmoth appointed three Negroes and two whites. The Governor thus controlled the police instead of the authorities of the City of New Orleans. The Metropolitan police cost the State $800,000 per year.

Other instances of nefarious laws enacted by the Louisiana Legislature in Warmoth's term of office will be told about in another chapter.

In the election of Nov. 4, 1872, Governor Warmoth, who had become more conservative in the last year of his office and after many of his former allies had deserted him for the "custom-house gang," supported the moderate John McEnery for governor. McEnery and D. B. Penn as Lieutenant Governor had the backing of Democrats, Liberal Republicans and reformers against William Pitt Kellogg for governor and C. C. Antoine† for Lieutenant-Governor, the candidates of the radical Republicans.

---

*"War, Politics and Reconstruction" by Henry C. Warmoth.

†Caius Caesar Antoine, a Negro, the leader of the Black League, was "flamboyant, abysmally ignorant, diminutive" according to Bowers. In 1873 when he became Lieutenant-Governor and presiding officer of the State Senate, his common-law wife, Francoise, who weighed 214 pounds, made him marry her. The Legislature legitimatized their children by special act.

Antoine and other Negro politicians took over Pass Christian with its fine residences, Antoine becoming its social arbiter.

Antoine was a "dandy," and, according to Tinker, wore in public a top hat, frock coat, green gloves and a walking stick. On Sept. 16, 1874, after the Canal Street affair,

The McEnery ticket undoubtedly received the majority of votes in the election, but was thrown out by the Returning Board and Kellogg's ticket declared elected. The story of the conflicting returning boards is complicated and confusing. Warmoth's returning board first declared the McEnery ticket the winner. Lynch, one of his former members, refused to support Warmoth and organized another board. This last, without the possession of many of the ballots, returned the Kellogg ticket as the winner. There was a third board and it returned for McEnery. Judge Durell of the Federal Court issued an order at 2 o'clock in the morning instructing the U. S. Marshal to seize the State House and to prevent McEnery from taking office. He ordered that Kellogg and his candidates be installed in office and that the opposing candidates be excluded from the State House. All this was illegal and irregular but Marshal Packard knew President Grant would back him up with Federal troops as the attorney general of the United States had so informed him by telegraph. In the meantime Warmoth was impeached by the legislature in December 1872 for his manoeuvering of the returning boards, and P. B. S. Pinchback,* who was not legally elected lieutenant-governor, assumed the office of Governor until Kellogg could take over. In spite of the Lynch Board decision and the injunctions of Judge Durell, the McEnery faction set up a rump government in New Orleans. Several of the parishes recognized it as the true government.

There were then two rival governments in Louisiana as a result of the election of 1872, the Kellogg *de facto* and the McEnery *de jure*. Both of the governors were inaugurated on the same day — January 14, 1873. The Kellogg inauguration took place at the State House (the Mechanics Institute) where his legislature assembled. McEnery was inaugurated in Lafayette Square, where an immense crowd of citizens witnessed the ceremonies. The Odd

---

the New York Herald interviewed him in New York, the reporter prefacing his interview with: "Lieutenant-Governor C. C. Antoine of Louisiana, a young colored gentleman of elegant appearance and who is decidedly good looking —" But the New York World a month or so before was not so complimentary, it said he had "a head like a coconut — pure type of the Congo."

Among the colorful (no pun intended) personalities of the Reconstruction era in Louisiana was Pickney Benton Pinchback (1837-1921) mulatto, who was the son of a Mississippi planter and Eliza Stewart, an emancipated slave. Pinchback went to school in Cincinnati, Ohio, but he left to become a cabin boy and later a steward on a Mississippi River steamboat. Devol in his "Forty Years A Gambler on the Mississippi River," claims that he developed Pinchback into a "slicker," and helped him to succeed. During the War Pinchback raised a company of colored infantry and later a cavalry company. As Lieutenant-Governor of Louisiana he served as governor between December 9, 1872 and January 13, 1873 while impeachment charges were pending against Warmoth, and until Kellogg took office. In 1873 he was elected to the United States Senate, but denied the seat — contested for three years, he was presented by the Senate with $20,000 to cover his expenses. Pinchback went over to the conservatives and supported Nicholls in the election of 1876.

Fellows Hall was the McEnery State House, where his legislature assembled.

According to a statement of Lieutenant-Governor Penn, the Kellogg government was supported by whatever taxes it could collect. The McEnery government was supported by voluntary contributions, the officers of the government and members of the legislature serving without pay. McEnery spent much time in Washington trying to get the recognition of the Federal Government. Nothing came of his efforts.

The two governments continued to exist, waging publicity and newspaper battles all the while. On September 14, 1874 their rivalries reached a climax in the Battle of Canal Street. But Kellogg never gave up his *de facto* rule and ended his term in 1877.

CHAPTER II

CONDITIONS IN LOUISIANA
DURING RECONSTRUCTION

It is not the purpose of this book to tell the story of Reconstruction in Louisiana. This has been done in several works described in the bibliography. But in order to show how the people of the State were aroused and why they organized themselves to protect and resist inefficient and unjust government, leading to the Battle of September 14, 1874, it might be well to look at conditions in Louisiana during those terrible times.

This chapter records some of the observations of visitors, journalists and others, and the testimony of prominent persons who appeared before Congressional committees. Many of these statements seem fair and impartial, and, no doubt, paint an accurate picture of the Reconstruction era in Louisiana.

One of the best relations of the conditions in Louisiana during the decade after the War is that of Charles Nordhoff. He was a Republican and an abolitionist and a well-known journalist and writer of the time. James Gordon Bennett, publisher of the New York Herald, sent Nordhoff through the Southern States in 1875 with instructions to find out the truth and to report conditions as he found them. The result of Nordhoff's trip was a book, published in the Fall of 1875, THE COTTON STATES IN THE SPRING AND SUMMER OF 1875. The author visited all the Southern States and comments on the conditions and the affairs of each. He was in Louisiana in April, 1875 and writes at length of the situation there, after traveling all over the State and talking with and interviewing people of all classes and of varying political thought.

Nordhoff dedicated his book to President Grant, which dedication reads in part:

> The facts collected here seem to me likely to interest you, who, I sincerely believe, have failed to make the people of the Southern States contented, chiefly because in your exalted position, it was unfortunately difficult for you to know the real condition of those states, which has rapidly and continually changed from year to year of your administration. Had you been able to examine them for yourself in 1874-75, as you did in 1865, I can not doubt that your Southern policy would in very many particulars been different from what it had been.

Nordhoff came to Louisiana after the affair of Canal Street, after the November elections of 1874, and after the Congressional Committee's reports had been printed. But his statement of conditions and his analysis of them applies to the months and the years before September 1874, which conditions brought about that battle for liberty.

Nordhoff noted that in the election of Nov. 4, 1874 the parties divided on the color line. Only 5,000 whites out of 90,000 supported the Republican ticket according to Packard. Nordhoff comments: "Most [of the 5,000] are office holders, the greater part strangers in the State, many may be justly called adventurers."

From Nordhoff's Book

The following excerpts are from Nordhoff's book:

The inefficiency and corruption of the State government in all its parts—leaving lawlessness unpunished, countenancing the most monstrous and shameful frauds and continued thus for six disgraceful years, at last united all the whites in one party, whose aim is simply and only to oust the thieves. Opposed to them in 1874 stood those rulers with almost, but not quite the whole Negro population at their backs.

Meantime, so sore are the white people of the State over the too-long-continued misgovernment that they view every movement and every man with suspicion.

You cannot travel far in Louisiana without discovering that the politicans who, in the name of the Republican party, rule it and have done so for the last seven years, in all departments of its government, State and local, are vehemently and unanimously detested by the white people. I have been amazed to see how all white men, and many blacks to my knowledge—whether rich or poor; whether merchants, mechanics or professional men; whether American, French, Germans, Irish or Italian by birth; absolutely all except the office holders and their relatives—unite in this feeling of detestation of their rulers.

This small band of white men [about 5,000] have for more than 6 years monopolized all political power and preferment in the State. They have laid, collected and spent (and largely misspent) all the taxes, local as well as State; they have not only made all the laws, but they have arbitrarily changed them, and have miserably failed to enforce any which were for the peoples' good; they have openly and scandalously corrupted the colored men whom they have brought into political life; they have used unjust laws to perpetuate and extend their own power; and they have practised all the basest arts of ballot-stuffing, false registrations, and re-reporting, at election after election.

In the last election [1874] it was proved before a committee of Congress that the Republican leaders had in the City of New Orleans alone, made no less than 5200 false registrations. A few days ago I went down the river to attend court, in order to see the working of a Negro jury. The court had to adjourn for lack of a jury, and no panel had been drawn, because the names being taken from the registration lists of the parish, 36 out of 48 were found to be fictitious—and this in a country parish.

The Republican returning board was condemned as a transparent fraud by two Congressional committees, and has, as far as I know, no defender in Louisiana or in the country.

ROUT of the METROPOLITAINS, DEFAITE and METROPOLITAINS.
New Orleans September 14th 1874.

This illustration of the Battle of the Fourteenth, while crudely drawn, is probably the most authentic, although it limits the action to the fight around the Iron Building. The broad open space is not Canal Street, but Water Street or the river front. The scene is sketched by the artist as if he were on a steamboat at the wharf. Canal Street is at the right and a corner of the Iron Building can be seen with the Metropolitans massed around it. Captain

Vaudry's Company A and Captain Lord's Company B are marching up double-quick and Captain Glynn's men are already on the flank of the Metropolitans behind the freight and cotton bales. At the extreme upper left is Morgan's La. & Texas R.R. Depot. Compare this picture with the map (detail) on page 101.

— *Wood cut print from Leslies Weekly Journal.*

THE PORT OF NEW ORLEANS IN 1873

Note the bunches of bananas on the wharf in the foreground. As far as is known this is the first illustration of banana imports which began in 1865.

—From a print in possession of the Howard-Tilton Library

I know of one case in the last election where, the Conservative ticket being elected, the records of the election were carried by the supervisor from the parish to New Orleans and concealed in a house of prostitution, one of whose inmates was sent to drive a bargain with the Conservatives for their return.

I have myself seen colored members of the legislature—men who were slaves but ten years ago, and began life with nothing at that time—now driving magnificent horses, seated in stylish equipages, and wearing diamond breast pins.

New Orleans is one of the largest commercial ports in the U. S. It has a numerous body of intelligent and wealthy merchants, the equals of any of their class in New York, Philadelphia or Boston. The sugar planters of Louisiana, are, in fact, manufacturers; they have large sums invested in machinery, and their business requires much technical skill; and they are as a class, the equals in intelligence and character of Northern manufacturers. Now, all of these men, the cream of the population, with scarcely a single exception are united in opposition to the present rulers of Louisiana, whom they not only detest but dread.

Nordhoff thought that the governor of Louisiana was given too much power by the constitution of 1868. He had the authority to

— appoint and remove all officers concerned with registration and conduct of elections and counting of votes
— appoint and remove all tax collectors and assessors
— appoint constables, surveyors, and justices of the peace
— appoint the judiciary
— appoint and control the officers of the Metropolitan Police in New Orleans
— in addition he was the commander of the militia.

Continuing, Nordhoff writes:

A more thoroughly centralized government France did not have under either empire. Nor have these great powers been hesitatingly used.

Officers have been multiplied to an extraordinary degree, and at every new creation the governor had the appointment of a favorite. New parishes (counties) were formed by the division of old ones, and in every case the governor appointed all the officers. Judicial districts have been re-arranged and new ones formed, and the governor thereupon made his friends or allies judges. A trick became common by which officers elected refused to qualify, and thereupon the governor filled the artificial vacancies with men who could not have been elected. Finally, so careful have the leaders in this conspiracy been to maintain their influence and their creatures in the pettiest offices, that the members of the Legislature are usually members of the local school boards, and degrade the schools by making the teachers their political tools; and I have been in some petty villages of fifteen hundred or two thousand inhabitants, which have not for four or five years been allowed to put in office the town officers they elected; but after each election the result was disallowed, and the vacancies thus created were filled by the governor.

As an example of the way such matters were managed, Shreveport will answer, the better because it lies in a region where the whites have been accused of discontent with the Republican rule. Shreveport before reconstruction had a simple and economical city government. The mayor received a moderate salary, the Common Council were unsalaried. In 1871 the Republican Legislature imposed upon the place a new charter, which put it in charge of a mayor and four administrators, all salaries, all provided with clerks, and with office contingents. The governor was authorized to appoint these officers, and to fill all vacancies, until 1873, and they were authorized to issue bonds, and dispose of them "for the best interests of the city."

They seem to have issued not only bonds, but scrip, and this fell to forty cents on the dollar at last. In the spring of 1874 the administrators proposed to issue bonds to the amount of one hundred thousand dollars, to improve the streets. A tax-payers' association had been formed, and, having defeated this project, they offered the mayor to undertake the same work which had been proposed, and do it to his satisfaction, if they were allowed to raise money on tax receipts from citizens. Permission being given, they did the whole work for thirty-six thousand dollars. The police were demoralized by being paid in depreciated scrip; the tax-payers asked the mayor to discharge the police, and authorize an unsalaried citizens' patrol; and this, too, was done, and the city became at once orderly. In the fall of 1874 the Republicans were beaten, a Conservative city government was chosen, and the scrip stands to-day at ninety.

But this is not all. The new charter was passed in 1871. In 1873 the Legislature incorporated the Shreveport Savings-bank and Trust Company, and gave it for fifty years the "sole and exclusive right" to erect works to supply the city with water and gas, and to run a ferry across the river. Now, at that very time Shreveport had already a well-established gas company; a satisfactory ferry had long been in existence, and was a source of revenue to the city; and for waterworks there was no need. The company was to pay for all its privileges the petty sum of five hundred dollars a year. Now, then, among the incorporators named in the statute which gives these "exclusive rights," I find C. C. Antoine, then and still lieutenant-governor; William Harper, State senator; S. A. Hamilton, tax-collector; Frank T. Hatch, supervisor of registration; M. A. Walsh, the appointed mayor, and George L. Smith, member of Congress. The story is completed when I add that the incorporators were not merely endowed with "exclusive rights," but also allowed to transfer these to other persons unimpaired.

No ruler of a civilized community ever possessed greater powers than the governor of Louisiana under this constitution. It gives him actual and direct control of the whole of the election machinery, and of all the officers who handle the taxes, and, indirectly, he has had the appointment of almost all the local or parish officers of the State, as well as of the judiciary; for when a judge or other officer elected by the people did not serve the purposes of the corruptionists who controlled the State, if no other way to remove him offered, the Legislature was ready to create a new parish, or a new judicial district, or a new court, and thus enable its governor to put in a serviceable person. Here is an example: The constitution provides that all district judges shall be elected by the people. New Orleans has a strong Conservative majority, and elected Conservative judges; and, this being inconvenient to the rulers of the State, the Legislature of 1871 created a new tribunal, called the Eighth District Court, and authorized the governor to appoint a judge to hold until the next election. But, in 1872, Mr. Elmore, Conservative, was elected to preside over this court. Thereupon the Legislature, as soon as it met, abolished both this and the Seventh District Court, to both which Conservative judges had been chosen, created the "Superior District Court," authorized the governor to appoint its judge, to hold until 1876, and vested in this court, so organized, exclusive jurisdiction of all prerogative writs and the trial of all actions in which the title to any office— State, parish, or municipal—was involved. Another act of the same Legislature authorized the removal of cases where the office of judge was contested in any part of the State to this Superior District Court of New Orleans.

Again, the criminal jurisdiction in the parish of Orleans was formerly vested in the First District Court of that parish. In 1872, a Conservative, E. Abell, was elected judge of this court. Thereupon, in 1874, the Legislature deprived this court of almost all its important powers, and gave them a new tribunal, called the "Superior Criminal Court;" and this was specially vested with exclusive jurisdiction in all cases of violations of registration or election laws—and the governor was directed to appoint a judge to hold office until 1876. Now, remember that the Radicals, or Republicans, who thus created this court, were proved before the Congressional committee to have made five thousand two hundred false registrations in New Orleans alone in 1874. Of course, having their own court, no one was punished for this.

Again, by the charter of New Orleans, the police magistracy of the city was vested in certain "recorder's courts," whose officers were to be chosen by the "Administrators," or Common Council of the city. But the people elected in 1872 a Conservative board of administrators, and these chose Conservative recorders. Thereupon, Act No. 95 of 1873 was passed by the Legislature, which abolished the recorder's courts, created in their place metropolitan police-courts, and gave the governor authority to appoint the magistrates to preside in these courts.

In other parts of the State the same trick has been repeatedly played, of legislating an obnoxious—that is to say, an honest—judge out of office by creating a new district, thus giving the governor the appointment of one judge, or even several new judges. Take one instance as an example: In the parish of Natchitoches, in 1872, the grand jury indicted a parish officer for embezzlement. The parish judge, his personal friend, protected him by neglecting to draw a jury.

This was so common a trick that a law was finally passed which compelled the drawing of juries; but this law is evaded, for no jury was drawn in the parish in which I write this at this term of the court—people tell me because the parish judge was afraid that if a grand jury met it would indict him for a gross misapplication of trust funds.

However, in Natchitoches the case went before the district judge and a negro jury, who gave a verdict for forty thousand dollars. Thereupon, at the next session, the Legislature broke up the judicial district, and the governor appointed to be judge of the new district, which included Natchitoches parish, that parish judge who had corruptly protected the embezzler of public funds. The judge has since been driven out of the county—so he tells me; reputable citizens of the parish accuse him of being concerned in embezzling the school fund. The tax-collector, Boult, also driven from the parish, stands published as a defaulter in the last official State auditor's report, and acknowledged to me that he had, while tax-collector, been engaged in partnership with the Democratic member elect of Congress in buying up depreciated county warrants, which the county must redeem at par.

Both Myers and Boult continued, when I was in Louisiana, to hold office, and the condition of affairs in the parish may be gathered from the following details, which were confirmed to me by several citizens as existing in 1874: District Judge Myers was also treasurer of the school fund, and continues to be, though he has not been in the county since last July. Dr. Boult was tax-collector and member of the school board. His son, William Boult, was deputy-tax-collector and also deputy parish treasurer—two offices one of which ought to be a check on the other. A negro "police-jury"—a body which is the equivalent of our county supervisors—appointed an illiterate parish treasurer, who made this Boult his deputy. Another son, David Boult, was parish judge.

Nor is such a state of things uncommon. Before the Congressional committee appeared one Green, of Lincoln parish, and in answer to questions admitted that he was State senator, one of his sons tax-collector, another parish judge, and a third supervisor of registration. Of the members of the present Legislature some are parish judges, some tax-collectors, one is assistant secretary of state, and a considerable number are charged by their constituents with sharing the emoluments of office-holders whose appointments they have caused.

The complaint is universal that the officers charged with the execution of the laws are not only inefficient, but corrupt; that justice is not only denied, but openly sold; and in many cases the people have, after vain remonstrances, taken the law into their own hands.

"I have seen a district attorney, appointed by the governor, sell out a case for as little as ten dollars," declared a laboring man with whom I conversed, and the story was confirmed to me by several citizens of the parish whom I asked. One of the prominent citizens of the parish of Rapides said to me, "We have had neither protection nor justice for years. Matters became so bad that even the negroes got tired of bad government, and began to vote with us. We had no intimidation at the last election, because it was not necessary. But we would have intimidated if it had been required, for we could stand it no longer."

"When we drove out the parish judge and other rascals, our taxes had got up to seven and nine-tenths per cent. on a high valuation; and we concluded that we might as well stop there, and refuse to pay any more taxes," said the citizen of another parish.

Nor are even the highest judicial officers of the State untainted. In the North Louisiana Railroad case, the Supreme Court of the United States, in its decision delivered last winter, said:

> A property upon which had been expended nearly two million dollars, together with a large stock-subscription, a large grant of lands, and considerable movable property, was bought for fifty thousand dollars by the very persons who defeated a sale for a much larger price, and the purchase money was retained by themselves. * * * It is impossible to characterize this agreement as any thing else than a gross fraud. Its obvious purposes was to remove competition at the sale. It was a flagrant breach of trust on the part of Horne, and it was a fraud in Ludeling, with knowledge of the trust Horne had undertaken, to persuade him to violate his instructions and sacrifice the interests of his constituents, himself becoming a party to the violation. * * * *And it is further ordered, adjudged and decreed that the sale made by John T. Ludeling and his associates,* and the adjudication of the sheriff to them, together with the sheriff's deed to them, *be declared to be fraudulent and void, and be set* aside and canceled; and that a perpetual injunction issue commanding them and all the defendants to refrain from setting up or claiming any right, title, or interest under said sale or under said deed, etc.

Now, the John T. Ludeling here declared guilty of fraud and breach of trust is the present chief-justice of the Supreme Court of Louisiana, appointed by a Republican governor, and has been allowed by the Republican Legislature to retain his seat on the Supreme Bench of the State in the face of these terrible words of the United States Supreme Court. Public and political demoralization could hardly go farther than this.

Considering the character of the men with whom he acts, he was the right man in the right place; and it was but part of a general system when "Ludeling, Ch. J." decided, in 1870, in a case brought before his court, where it was attempted to upset an act of the Legislature on the ground that it had been procured by bribing the members, that "courts are not permitted to go behind an enrolled, duly authenticated and promulgated public statute, to inquire into the motives which may have influenced the members of the General Assembly in enacting it. Therefore, evidence tending to establish bribery and corruption against the members of the General Assembly, which, it is alleged, procured its passage, is not admissible."

Federal, State, and parish officers have banded together to maintain themselves in power, and have used the ignorant fears of the negroes to help them. They called to their aid every man unscrupulous enough to take part with them. By alarming the blacks by false registration, by arbitrary arrests and threats of arrests just before the elections, by cheating in the returning board, by tampering with the courts, by debauching the Legislature, by monopolizing offices, they have persistently prevented the honest people of the State from securing honest government. See here an example:

A young fellow, a white man, in the present Legislature, came to New Orleans from New York six years ago, so far an adventurer that his first occupation was to teach boys to travel on the velocipede. He was presently engaged as a subordinate clerk in the Legislature, and when that body adjourned he went to Mississippi, where, the Legislature of that State being still in session, he was also employed as a clerk. In the fall he returned to New Orleans, where Warmoth, then governor, made him supervisor of registration and election in an up-country parish where he had never been or lived. After the election he brought down the returns, which, by a coincidence not at all remarkable in this State, showed him to have received the unanimous Republican vote, and to be elected to the Legislature from the parish where he had managed the registration and election. Two years later (in 1872) he did not receive the Republican nomination; but, noways discouraged, he announced himself as an independent candidate. On his way to the parish, however, he was intrusted by the State committee with the Republican tickets for the parish voters, and it was discovered that his name and that of a Democrat had been mysteriously placed on these tickets. Thereupon the negroes threatened to lynch him, and he returned to New Orleans until just before the election. The returns showed his defeat; but the returning board seated him, regarding him as too useful a man to leave out. I am told that he found it necessary to call in the help of the last returning board also to seat him in the present Legislature.

Such cases were so far from rare that the Legislature of 1869 was made up almost entirely of supervisors of registration and colored men. Warmoth, the governor, selected as registrars a large number of men left in New Orleans after the war, and remaining there without regular employment. These were sent into the country parishes to register the voters; and they so impressed the negroes with their official power and dignity, that a majority of them were returned to the Legislature from parishes which they had never seen until they went there to superintend the election. Many negroes were dragged in as a matter of bargain; they had wit enough to demand a share of the honors. The Legislature so elected sat sixty days, at a cost to the State, for *per diem,* mileage, and contingents, of nine hundred thousand dollars. Each member is said to have received seven thousand dollars for the session; and it is related that a single committee of the House had eighty-seven clerks, who were paid ten dollars a day each.

A government so highly centralized as that of Louisiana can scarcely fail to be costly and corrupt. But it ought at least to secure peace and order.

I asked Gogernor Kellogg what was the real condition of the State in this respect, and he gave me a long and deplorable catalogue of disorders: parishes which refuse to pay taxes; others where the judges have been driven away; others where murders have been committed, and so on. Other Radical politicians spoke rather boastfully of these things, as a New York newsboy took pride in his sore toe. They related to me by the half-hour melancholy instances of crime and outrage—most of them dating back to 1866.

What they did not tell me was some such story as this, which, nevertheless, is true: In the parish of Plaquemine, which lies under the governor's nose, along the Lower Mississippi, below New Orleans, and which has had Republican rulers ever since 1868, thirty-three murders have been committed since 1868. Of these, thirty-one were of blacks by blacks, one of a white by a white; and one of a white man, a Northern man, a Republican and an office-holder, the tax-collector of the parish. This man was shot by a colored man for seducing his sister and turning the young girl adrift with her baby. Of these thirty-three murderers, not one has been hanged. Those who were apprehended mostly broke out of jail, and only last fall the Republican deputy-sheriff, who acted a jailer, was indicted for permitting three murderers and a defaulting tax-collector to escape out of his custody.

In other cases which I have on my notebooks, men sentenced to imprisonment for life for murder have been pardoned. No one, not even the governor, pretends that murder and lawlessness have been punished, though in many instances white citizens have helped the authorities to arrest white murderers. I am satisfied that since the year 1870, except in the Coushatta and Colfax affairs, most of the murders in Louisiana have been non-political in their origin, and a great proportion of them have been of negroes by negroes, mainly on account of jealousy in their relations with their women.

This does not lessen the degree of criminality. Nor does it take away from the duty of the rulers, possessing as these did, greater and more unlimited powers than the rulers of any civilized State in the world, to punish these crimes. The governor of Louisiana appoints, in effect, almost the whole judiciary and constabulary of the State; he has express authority to use the metropolitan police as a standing army in any part of the State, and to appoint an extraordinary constabulary force in any parish; his own judges superintend the selection of the juries, both grand and petit, and these are usually largely composed of colored men; he has also the militia; and, finally, he has the army of the United States ready to help him at his call. Is there any excuse for him if he permits lawlessness, murder, violence? When he and those who rule with him speak of murder and violence unrepressed, do they not fatally condemn themselves as incapable and unfit to rule the State? A United States army officer, an extreme Republican, after giving me an account of some murders of which he had heard, and which he believed to have happened, added, "But I must say that if the governor had been a man fit for his place, such things could not have happened. Let me be governor, and I would quickly, with the great power he has, put a stop to such things."

It can not be truthfully said that the State of Louisiana has been peaceful ever since the war. In the early days, between 1865 and 1868, there is no doubt that many barbarous and heart-rending murders and outrages were committed on the blacks. The white people, sore at their defeat in the war, unused to tolerate free negroes, fearful, to a degree that seems to a Northern man absurd, of combinations and conspiracies among the blacks to murder the whites and outrage their women, and rendered frantically furious by the sight of negroes assembled in political meetings, often at night, did, without doubt, commit atrocities of which I should be sorry to see any formal record made. Such crimes decreased from year to year, but I doubt if they entirely ceased until 1870. They happened oftenest in counties—of which Louisiana has a good many—where the negro population is as three, four, and in some cases even as nine, to one white; where a few white families, isolated from each other, are surrounded by a dense negro population; and where the dread of a rising to exterminate the whites is to this day the secret terror of every

Colored Rule in a Reconstructed(?) State.
(The members call each other thieves, liars, rascals and cowards)
COLUMBIA: "You are aping the lowest whites. If you disgrace your
race in this way you had better take back seats."
Cartoon drawn by Thos. Nast for Harper's Weekly, March 14, 1874.
— *Collection of Leonard V. Huber*

white man, the dread which makes him frantic and desperate when even a rumor
of conspiracy reaches his ears. I speak here that which I know.

Now, into such regions came white men, strangers, often fanatics, often knaves,
who gathered the freedmen together at barbecues and in camps, and told them of
their "rights." I was shown yesterday a colored man who still keeps in his house
the mule-halters he got in 1868, when a white man traveled through St. Mary's
Parish telling the blacks that "they had made the land what it was; had cleared it
and cultivated it; and they ought to own it; and the Government, which had set
them free, was going to give them each forty acres of land and a mule." The
blacks believed it. Many of them believe it still—just as there are planters

down here foolish enough to believe that the United States Government will pay them for their losses in the war.

All this irritated the whites, and aroused the fear of negro insurrection; and it led, in the remoter parts of the State, to many inexcusable acts of barbarity. Then came the reconstruction, in 1868, and the negro was made, not only a voter, but an office-holder.

It was, I believe, absolutely necessary to confer these rights upon him; he would never have been a free man without them. But it was a misfortune that demagogues and adventurers were his introducers to political life, and led him to regard not fitness, but color and numbers, as the reasonable claim to office. I have been opposed to slavery ever since I sat on my father's knee, and was taught by him that slavery was the greatest possible wrong; but when, in New Orleans last Wednesday, I for the first time saw negro legislators, I was unpleasantly startled— not because they were black, but because they were transparently ignorant and unfit. What, then, must have been the feelings of men who saw blacks, but lately their own slaves, and as ignorant as the mules they drove, preferred before them for office, set over them in authority, making laws for them—and making them very badly at that—openly plundering the State, bribed by rascally whites, and not merely enjoying, but, under the lead of white adventurers, shamefully abusing, place and power?

Even in 1874, in one of the northern parishes, the Republican candidates for sheriff and parish judge could not write. The negroes on many police-juries (supervisors of counties) are totally illiterate; yet they have complete power over the parish taxes, roads, bridges, and all county matters. Negro juries are called to sit upon intricate cases of commercial law and other matters which even intelligent men find it difficult to understand; and the black man himself has, it would seem, an instinctive appreciation of the absurdity of this, for it is notorious that a negro criminal always asks his counsel to get a white jury, if possible, to try him. Things which are commonplace here are unheard of with us. It was a matter of complaint to me the other day that in a certain county not a single colored man had been drawn on the grand jury this year. My instant and thoughtless reply was that I had never known a negro to be drawn on the grand jury in the county in which I live. But the cases are widely different; and it is absolutely necessary that the negro in the South shall take some share of the responsibilities of citizenship.

As for minor robberies, take this as an example: The parish of Plaquemine lies on the Mississippi, below New Orleans. It contains a large number of sugar-plantations; and, besides these, its people (mostly French creoles and colored men) cultivate rice and the orange. It is a charming, quaint country, and the small farmers, who mostly speak French better than English, are a quiet and simple-hearted people. In the year 1868, when reconstruction began, this parish had no debt, and six thousand dollars in cash in its treasury, which sum was turned over to the reconstructors. Among these was one who owned a small sugar-plantation in the parish, into which he had come as an officer during the war; he was elected to the State Senate, and, by a curious coincidence, the Legislature, of which he was a member, passed a law removing the parish seat from Point à la Hache, where it had been time out of mind, to a spot at Jesuit's Bend, farther up the river, and on this man's plantation. Of course, to get the county town removed to one's farm is not a bad speculation. Lawyers and many other people must live near the Courthouse, and they make a market for town lots. The records of the county were, in fact, removed; but the people made such a clamor that, after a struggle of a year, the project was given up. Presently this man became a bankrupt; but he is all right, for the governor has appointed him tax-collector of the parish, a place said to be worth ten thousand dollars a year.

A colored man from the island of Nassau also came in 1868. A white man, formerly in General Neal Dow's corps, which campaigned in this region, was another politician. He was made supervisor (member of the police-jury they call it here), and, soon after the reorganization, the parish authorities began to issue scrip in such abundance that in two or three years it fell to fifteen cents on the dollar. But it was always receivable at par for parish taxes. In 1872 the colored man above mentioned was State senator; another colored man was member of the Assembly, and another was sheriff. The Legislature passed a law authorizing these three, and two white citizens, to ascertain and report the outstanding debt of the parish, and to fund it. The three colored men are accused of issuing bonds illegally, and without consent of the whites, to the amount of $36,000 in exchange for scrip, much of which had been bought up by them and their friends at a great discount. On an investigation by citizens it was found that the seal of the court, which had to be affixed to these bonds by the parish clerk to make them valid, had not been affixed by him; but had been surreptitiously obtained and used by the three bond-issuers. The parish debt is now $93,000, and Judge Pardee, a Republican, but praised by everybody here as an honest and incorruptible man, has granted an injunction prohibiting the conversion of the remaining $57,000 of scrip into bonds. Finally, the last grand jury of the parish, composed of twelve colored men and four whites, indicted Butler for bribery and embezzling the school fund; Mahoney, for stealing the school fun; and Prescott, the parish judge, a white man, stranger in the parish, for subornation of perjury.

Now, then, the financial statement in Plaquemine parish stands thus: In 1868, no debt, and $6000 in the treasury; in 1875, a debt of $93,000. Meantime, in every year since 1868, taxes to the amount of from $20,000 to $25,000 have been levied and collected. And for all this large sum, amounting, taxes and debt, to cover $200,000 in six years, the parish has received neither roads, nor schools, nor levee repairs, nor public buildings. Before the War taxes never exceeded $7,000 a year.

Nordhoff says that in 1873 out of 272,334 children in the State only 57,433 were enrolled in schools. In one parish the treasurer of the school board used the funds for his private purposes and paid the teachers in script to the amount of $3,000.

In another parish $30,000 was spent and the schools were open less than a year. In two parishes the school treasurers absconded with large sums belonging to the school funds. In St. Martin Parish the treasurer defaulted the sum of $3,700. In St. James Parish the school board prudently burned the records when leaving office.

Continuing from Nordhoff:

The various petty monopolies and swindles to which State aid was so profusely given account for a small part of this huge debt and expenditure. Such extravagance as is mentioned by the auditor in his last report (1875), in the following words, accounts for more:

Thus the number of pages (in the Legislature), which by Act No. 11 of 1872 is limited to ten, at a compensation for each of $180, was increased more than sixty, and vouchers issued to them at from $150 to $180 each; nor was this practice confined to this particular class of employés, but was carried to other classes, such as enrolling and committee clerks, porters, etc.

He also, in the same report, complains that he has vainly tried to get the Legislature to adopt a new plan of assessing property for taxation which "would save the State $156,000 a year." In the auditor's report for the year 1871, complaint was made to the Legislature of the great cost of collecting the taxes. "In 1870," says this report, "the actual commissions paid on account of assessors was $181,975, and the amount paid to tax-collectors $215,411. In 1871 the commissions of tax-collectors amounted to $320,259, and that of assessors to $250,838."

Of course there were some heavy jobs, which helped to run up the debt. For instance, in the auditor's report for 1871, I find a statement that during the two previous years the State, under an arrangement with the firm of Jones & Hugee, lessees of the penitentiary, had issued $500 in State bonds for machinery for that institution. The lessees were to pay one-half their clear profits to the State. They paid nothing, and in 1870 transferred their contract to another set of men, the State agreeing thereafter to accept $5000 a year in lieu of all profits, with an increase of $1000 a year. Between 1869 and 1871, in two years, "the penitentiary had cost the State $796,000."

In 1868 the New Orleans, Mobile, and Chattanooga Railroad was chartered in Louisiana, and it was determined to connect Mobile and New Orleans with Houston, Texas. In 1869 the Legislature agreed to indorse the second-mortgage bonds of the road to the extent of $12,500 per mile, and to make the indorsement for every section of ten miles built. The company built seventy miles, and the State indorsed $875,000 of their second-mortgage bonds. The next Legislature agreed in addition to give the road a State subsidy of $3,000,000 of bonds, and of this they drew $750,000. The company now proposed to build a railroad from Vermilionville to Shreveport, and in 1871 the State agreed to take stock in this enterprise ($2,500,000), paying for it in bonds, and the whole of these bonds were delivered to the company when they had done one day's work on the road. They have never done any more.

That is to say, the company have built in all seventy miles of an uncompleted, and therefore, worthless road, and received from the State $4,250,000, or over $58,000 a mile, besides a grant of the use of a part of the New Orleans levee, valued at $1,000,000; and they have kept it all. Finally, it remains to be said that two different companies of Northern capitalists offered to build the Houston and New Orleans road without subsidy or State aid of any kind, but the Legislature would not give them a charter.

A great deal of money has been spent and squandered since the war on the reconstruction of the levees and their repair, and Democrats as well as Republicans have taken part in this jobbing, the greatest waste, however, being since 1868. Between 1868 and 1871, $4,750,000 of State bonds were issued for levee purposes, and still there are no levees worthy of the name. Most of the money was spent by a "State Board of Public Works," whose members were appointed by Governor Warmoth. In 1871 a different system was adopted, which is still in force, and under which a large part of the revenues of the State has been handed over for a long term of years to a private corporation, with privileges which enable it to misuse and squander them in a most shocking way.

By the act, this corporation, which was to furnish a million of dollars in capital stock, agreed to build and repair the levees of the State, and to be responsible in damages to the planters and farmers who should suffer loss by overflow or crevasse. In return for this, the Legislature gave it a million dollars down, before it began work, and the proceeds, annually, for a term of years, of a tax of four mills on the whole taxable property of Louisiana; and authorized it to charge, against this great fund, sixty cents per cubic yard for the work. But a great part of the levee work, when done by planters for themselves, has cost only from fifteen to eighteen cents per cubic yard, and thirty cents for the average of all kinds of work all over the State would be, experts tell me, a high rate. In fact, the first charge was so exorbitant that it has been reduced to fifty cents; and in 1874 the levee tax, which the company continues to receive, was reduced to three mills. But the company never had any money; the levees have not been kept in proper repair, and the losses from overflow have never been so great as since it went into operation; and, having no capital of its own, if it is sued for damages it must pay these out of the State fund; and thus, in fact, the tax-payers pay their own insurance. The company receives about $720,000 a year.

This was one of the most notorious jobs perpetrated by the Legislature, and attracted attention at the time because a great many members not only received bribes for its support—which was too common an occurrence to be noticed—but actually gave their receipts for the money paid them. The following letter, of which the original is before me, shows how openly legislative bribery was carried on under Warmoth's administration. The writer of it was then member of Assembly, is now State Senator, and member of the State School Board, and, I am sorry to say, is a negro:

House of Representatives, State of Louisiana,
New Orleans, February 25th, 1871

Gentlemen of the Finance Committee of Louisiana Levee Company:
SIRS,—Please pay to Hon. A. W. Faulkner the amount you may deem proper to pay on acount of Levee Bill, I being absent at the time under orders of the House. But would have voted for the bill had I been here. Mr. Faulkner is authorized to receive and receipt for me. Very respectfully, gentlemen,

Your obedient servant,
T. B. STAMPS.

Surely the brazenness of corruption could go no further than this—when a legislator claims a bribe on the score that he would have performed the corrupt service had he been in his place, and sends his friend not merely to receive, but to receipt for it.

The city of New Orleans is made to pay a very great part of the State tax, and has been besides, burdened in various ways by the Legislature, which has set apart a large part of its revenues for State or special purposes. It has now a debt of its own of about $22,000,000, and its tax-rate has been run up to three per cent. About $17,000,000 of its bonds are worth but thirty-five cents on the dollar in the market. Here is an example which tells the tale of wasteful mis-government: An estate, which could have been sold in 1867 for over $1,000,000, showed on its books, in 1872, this remarkable condition: After paying for insurance and usual repairs, the taxes levied that year on the property exceeded the entire rental by $540. In the next year, 1873, the receipts exceeded the taxes, repairs, and insurance by $900. Yet, in 1867, this property netted seven per cent. on over $1,000,000—that is to say, more than $70,000, after paying insurance, taxes, and repairs.

It is not the wealthy alone who complain. I have spoken with at least a dozen small property-owners in the city, and they all tell the same tale. In the country the small farmers complain that they are forced to pay the heavy taxes, while in the many cases their rich neighbors resist, and are allowed to refuse payment or to delay.

In the parish of St. Landry alone, as I think I have before stated, there were between November, 1871, and November, 1873, eight hundred and twenty-one sales of plantations and lands for taxes. Yet Louisiana is by nature one of the richest States in the Union, and New Orleans is one of the greatest commercial ports. Is it surprising that the whole white population of the State, except the office-holders and their relatives and intimates united, in 1874, in the endeavor to overthrow a party which has so abused its powers?

I spent some days looking through the acts of the Legislature of Louisiana since the first reconstruction Legislature, in 1868, and a more amusing and preposterous exhibition of wholesale legislative plundering it would be difficult to imagine. The bare titles of the acts whose sole and transparent purpose was plunder would fill half a dozen of these pages. I must content myself with a brief mention of but a few sample laws granting exclusive privileges, giving away the State's money, creating new offices, or adding to the taxes.

One of the earliest acts of the reconstructors—who are believed to have come into the State as the missionaries of great moral ideas—was the passage of a law giving the exclusive monopoly of selling lottery, policy, and "combination" tickets in the State to a company which calls itself the "Louisiana State Lottery Company."

Lest the profane should imagine that this monopoly was intended to promote the merely selfish advantage of the incorporators, it is distinctly stated in the charter, which forms part of the act, that the lottery company is a purely charitable and beneficient body, created for the unmixed benefit of the people of Louisiana. "The objects and purposes of this corporation are, first, the protection of the State against the great losses heretofore incurred by sending large amounts of money to other States and foreign countries for the purchase of lottery-tickets and other devices, thereby impoverishing our own people; second, to establish a solvent and reliable home institution for the sale of lottery, policy, and other tickets; third, to provide means to raise a fund for educational and charitable purposes for the citizens of Louisiana."

The monopoly is to last twenty-five years; it is made a criminal offense in any one unauthorized by the company to sell any kind of lottery-ticket anywhere in the State; the company is exempted from all taxes and license fees whatever—State, city, or parish; and for these monstrous privileges and exemptions it pays into the State treasury—for the educational fund—the petty sum of forty thousand dollars per annum!

The company is now composed almost entirely of a few men living in New York and New Jersey; on a million of capital they are believed to make not less than seven hundred and fifty thousand dollars clear profit every year; they have established policy-shops and petty gambling dens around the markets and other public places in New Orleans, which perpetually demoralize the laboring class, and particularly negro men and women, and over which the city government has no control; and they have agents and solicitors all over the State, tempting the poor and ignorant to gamble, providing for this end what they call a "combination game," which can be played even by the owner of a ten-cent piece.

In 1868 the Legislature chartered the Mississippi Valley Navigation Company of the South and West, and in 1870 an amendment to the charter gave the company $100,000 of State money, for which the State was to receive stock. The company got the money, but I can not hear that they are in business to-day, though they were authorized to "construct steamboats, warehouses, docks," etc. Another scheme was the Red River Navigation Company, which was authorized to receive $135,000 in State bonds.

The bayous or river estuaries of the State early became a fine field for swindling. For instance, the Legislature of 1870 passed an act incorporating a company to improve Bayou Bartholomew, in the northern part of the State, and granting State bonds to aid the enterprise. Within sixteen days after the passage of the act, State warrants to the amount of $118,000 had been issued to the company. The auditor at that time happened to be an honest man; he refused to recognize these warrents; suit was brought by the company, and the Supreme Court twice declared the proceedings fraudulent, Ludeling, chief-justice (whom the United States Supreme Court last year denounced for fraud in another matter), alone dissenting; and on a motion to remand the case for a rehearing, which Ludeling granted, Judge Wyly, dissenting, said, "Act 59, to improve the navigation of Bayou Bartholomew, never authorized a contract to exceed $40,000. I regard the contract for $118,000 for the work as a deliberate fraud upon the State. Not a single requirement for letting out and making the contract according to Act 59 seems to have been complied with."

Now, then, mark what follows. The claim was twice denied by the Supreme Court. The Legislature of 1874 created a board of audit, with power to settle outstanding liabilities; and this board, while I was in New Orleans, quietly allowed a large part of this claim.

A company whose main purpose appears to have been cattle-stealing was organized and chartered in 1874, under the title of "Society for the Prevention of Cruelty to Animals." The Legislature gave it sole and exclusive charge of all the pounds in New Orleans, with authority to seize and arrest animals of all kinds in the streets, and impound them, and charge the owners five dollars a day for their detention, and to sell them outright at the end of eight days. The summary arrest of goats in the outskirts of the city came near creating a mob of Irish women; and, to prevent cruelty to animals, the company at one time, I am told, began to arrest horses left standing in the streets while their riders were transacting business in the shops.

An act of the Legislature to improve Bayous Glaises and Rouge gave the incorporators sole and exclusive power to navigate these bayous with vessels of all kinds, exempted their capital stock from taxation of every kind, and allowed them to levy a toll on all vessels except their own, or which they allow to be used on these bayous. The improvements to be made were very slight.

In 1871 the Mississippi River Packet Company was incorporated by act of the Legislature. Among the incorporators were Antoine, now lieutenant-governor, then senator; Kelso, Monette, Pinchback, Ingraham, and Barber, all State senators, and Pollard, member of Assembly. The object of the company was to run steamboats on the Mississippi River. The State was pledged to subscribe $250,000 on the organization of the company; and, so far as I can see in the act, it was to enjoy no benefits or privileges whatever.

By an act authorizing a company to improve Bayous Portage and Yokeley, the State gave the company $100,000 by way of aid; and if the improvements should cost more than this sum, the company was empowered to lay a tax on all the lands benefited, to make up the deficiency, and to sell for taxes any such lands whose owners had not paid after sixty days' notice. No limit was set of cost, and the company was made its own tax-collector.

A company chartered to improve Loggy Bayou and Lake Bisteneau received $50,000 State aid, and the people say, pulled out about twenty stumps for the money. A company chartered to improve Bayou Terrebonne received the exclusive privilege to improve Bayous Boeuf and Crocodile, and was authorized to receive $80,000, a sum asserted to be preposterously beyond the value of the service.

The Mexican Gulf Canal Company drew $36,000 in bonds from the State in aid of its enterprise, then abandoned it and merged with another company for a different purpose; got control of the drainage fund; fell into the hands of one man; and he, in the name of the company, is now doing a necessary work of drainage at a cost a hundred per cent. higher than responsible citizens stand ready to do it for.

The Legislature even chartered a company and gave it the sole and exclusive right to clean privies in New Orleans, and to empty their contents into the Mississippi River; made it obligatory on citizens to have this service performed at fixed intervals; and established a scale of charges much higher than that at which the service had long been performed.

Even the purchase by the State of the St. Louis Hotel, to be used as a state-house, was a swindling transaction. Several members of the Legislature and others were chartered as the Louisiana National Building Association. They got from the owners of the St. Louis Hotel an agreement to sell that building at a set price, and, this done, made a lease of it to the State for nineteen years at $50,000 a year and entire exemption from taxation. They overshot their mark, and the outcry raised against this act of extortion compelled the annulling of the lease.

It is a singular fact that in the greater number of parishes the registration lists of 1874 show that the colored registered voters are more numerous, compared with the colored population, than the white registered, compared with the white population, taking the census of 1870 as a basis. For instance, in Plaquemine Parish the registry lists show one white name for every seven and one-fifth of the total white population; but one black name for every three and one-eighth of the total colored population.

In St. Charles the whites registered are on in three and a half, the blacks one in two and a half, of the respective population. In St. James, the white registry was one in four and a half, the black one in two and a half, of their population. In St. Landry, where it was pretended that there was intimidation, white and black both registered one in four and a half of their population. In Carroll, the whites registered five and one-third, and the blacks three and seven-tenths, of their population. In Terre Bonne, the registered voters stood—white, four and seven-eighths; blacks, three and two-thirds; and so on. In many parishes the proportions were reversed; but in the greater number the colored men registered a larger proportion to their population than the whites to theirs. This does not look much like intimidation.

Finally, the vote of 1874 was uncommonly full. "The whole number of votes registered was 167,604. Of these, 146,523 voted. This is a larger proportion of registered voters than usually vote in any of the Northern States." So say the Congressional committee.

Nordhoff's Conclusions

Nordhoff came to these general conclusions:

(1) There is not—any desire for a new war; any hostility to the union; any even remote wish to reenslave the blacks; any hope or expectation of repealing our constitutional amendment, or in any way curtailing the rights of the blacks as citizens.

(2) That the Southern whites should rejoice over their defeat, now is impossible. That their grandchildren will, I hope and believe. What we have a right to require is, that they shall accept the situation; and that they do. What they have a right to ask of us is that we shall give them a fair chance under the new order of things; and that we have so far greatly failed to do. What the Southern Republican too often requires is that the Southern Democrat should humiliate himself, and make penitent confession that slavery was a sin, that secession was wrong, and that the War was an inexcusable crime. Is it fair or just to demand this? Slavery is now seen, all over the South, to have been a huge economical blunder, and a proposition to re-establish it would not get 50,000 votes in the whole South.

In Louisiana the misconduct of Republican rulers drove out most of the white people who were property owners, taxpayers and persons of intelligence and honesty.

At first a considerable proportion of these were ranged on the Republicans side. Now - - - the Republican Party consists almost exclusively of the Negroes and Federal officeholders with . . . the Republican State and parish officers also.

Thus has been perpetuated the "color line" in politics—a great calamity to the Southern States. The Federal office holders are largely to blame for the continuance of this evil. The color line is maintained mostly by Republican politicians, but they are helped by a part of the Democratic politician who see their advantage in having the white vote massed on their side.

But public robbery was, after all, not the worst crime of the men who arose in the name of the Republican Party to govern these Southern States. The gravest offense of the "Republican" State governments was their total neglect of the first duty of rulers to maintain peace and execute justice. They did not enforce the laws; they corrupted the judiciary; they played unscrupulously upon the ignorant fears of the blacks and upon their new-born cupidity; they used remorselessly the vilest tools for the vilest purposes; they encouraged disorder, so that they might the more effectually appeal to the Federal power and the Northern people for help to maintain them in the places they so grossly and shamelessly abused.

The injury done to a community by the total failure of its rulers to maintain order, repress crimes, and execute justice, is more seriously felt in Louisiana than in any other of the States. - - - It is a wonder to me that society has not entirely gone to pieces in that State; and I became persuaded that its white population possesses uncommonly high qualities when I saw that, in spite of incredible misgovernment, which encouraged every vice and crime, - - - in spite of this, order and peace have been gradually restored and are now maintained, and this by the efforts of the people chiefly.

No thoughtful man can see Louisiana as I saw it last Spring without giving a high respect for its white people. - - - The attitude of the races there towards each other is essentially kindly, and only the continuous efforts of black and white demagogues of the basest kind keep them apart politically. The majority of the white people of the State are well disposed, anxious for an upright government, ready to help honest and wise rulers, if they could only get them, to maintain peace and order. I sincerely believe that whenever they are relieved of Federal oppression — and in their case it is the worst kind of oppression, they will set up a government essentially honest and just, and will deal fairly and justly with the colored citizens.

Testimony Before Congressional Committee

Among the witnesses who testified before the Congressional Committee investigating conditions in the South at the hearing in New Orleans in January 1875 was John C. Moncure of Shreveport. Mr. Moncure had been a candidate on the fusion ticket in November 1874 for the office of State Treasurer. In his testimony we find this comment on the activities of the Legislature:

Q. Yes: as to whether there were any plundering schemes, and what class of men were engaged in them at that time, and how they affiliated afterward?—A. Well, sir, there was a vast number of schemes in the sessions of 1871 and 1872 which certainly did not commend themselves to my judgment, and which I believe were plundering schemes. There were a vast number of schemes presented, and which were, some of them, not acted upon at all; but I recall to mind now one which I thought was a huge and monstrous scheme of plunder, which was called the State-house, as I understood at the time, was that it was supposed the constitutional limit the State for ten years of $500,000 a year for the purpose of building a State-house, making, of course, in all, $5,000,000. The reason why that plan was resorted to, instead of the direct plan of issuing bonds of the State in order to build the State-house, as I understood at the time, was that it was supposed the constitutional limit of the State debt had been reached, namely, $25,000,000, and that therefore any bonds issued would have been considered as unconstitutionally issued; and in order to avoid that difficulty this plan was resorted to to levy a tax of $500,000 a year for ten years, and I think there was a State-house commission probably included in the bill; that commission must have authority to issue certificates to persons with whom they might contract. We defeated that. I must do some of the republicans the justice to say that they joined with us and aided us in defeating it. It was defeated, not by direct vote. My opinion is if a direct vote had ever been taken upon it, it would have been passed; but we defeated it by a little parliamentary tactics, and the tactics we resorted to was this: the bill was referred to the committee of the whole house.

Well, then, I will say it was defeated by, I believe, the entire democratic vote of the house, of which I was a member, with the assistance of some republican votes; but it was a very long contest, and a very earnest one.

Mr. Moncure, when asked about bribery in the State Legislature, said that he had heard many rumors of such but did not know any facts to prove it. He said:

Indeed, I was very well satisfied that those influences were brought to bear upon members of the legislature; but the only thing that ever came under my immediate observation, or rather that came to me directly, was this single instance and single circumstance: When the bill for the construction of a State-house, or what was known as the State-house bill, was under consideration, a republican member came to me and said to me this: "Do you know that those lots around the place where the State-house is to be constructed are in the swamp?" I asked him, "What lots?" "O," says he, "those lots that belong to the members." I learned afterward that the lots around the place where this State-house was to be located had been distributed out among the members of the house who, I presume, supported the State-house bill.

Another witness at the New Orleans hearing was Mr. Louis S. Clarke from St. Mary's Parish. Mr. Clarke was from Ohio and had come to Louisiana in 1870. He voted the Republican ticket all of his life until the election of 1874. When asked by a Committeeman why he did not vote the Republican ticket then he said: "It is impossible for me to conceive how an honest man can be an intelligent man and vote the Republican ticket in Louisiana. That is my opinion." Mr. Clarke testified further:

Q. What is the condition in relation to the safety of life and property in your parish, and how has the administration of criminal law been conducted?—A. I consider property exceedingly insecure in Saint Mary's Parish. We lose largely in such things as cattle, hogs, chickens, garden-vegetables and such classes of property which are necessarily exposed. Complaints have been loud and continuous in that respect for a long while, and it seems to be impossible to correct the evil under our present government. I myself have a number of head of cattle which I am obliged to have watched all the time; I never allow them to go away from the stable, where they are kept at night, without a man to stay with them the entire day; I don't consider them safe otherwise; others who do not keep a man to watch them lose them regularly. It seems to be almost impossible in our country to hold property of that description.

Q. What is the rule as to punishing criminals?—A. It is rarely they are punished.

Q. Are your judicial prosecuting officers in that parish republicans or conservatives? —A. Republican, I believe, sir, entirely.

Q. Do you know anything about any murders that occurred in Saint Mary's Parish, whether for political or other causes?—A. I can remember within a circuit of about seven miles, where I live, of nine or ten murders in the late years that I have lived there, of negroes murdered by negroes. I can remember quite a number of similar instances in other portions of the parish that I have heard of, but I cannot place them. My impression is, and in fact I am sure, the number of negroes killed in our parish in the five years I have lived there will reach twenty-five; and if they will not reach more than forty, I am very much surprised. I am sure it will reach twenty-five, and I am sure I have heard of more than that.

A further witness before the Committee was Lieut.-Colonel Henry A. Morrow of the 13th Infantry, U.S.A. Col. Morrow had been sent into the parishes of Lincoln and Ouachita to investigate charges of misconduct and irregularities on the part of several officers and soldiers who assisted the deputy U. S. Marshal in making arrests there. He reported that the charges were justified and recommended that one officer be court-martialed. In his testimony he said:

Q. From your observation among the people generally, to what do you attribute the disturbed condition of this State?—A. That is a subject upon which I have thought very seriously, and I attribute the unsettled condition of the State of Louisiana, in the first place to a deep-seated opinion on the part of the people that they have been twice defrauded of their rights at elections; and, secondly, to a feeling that they have been imposed upon, if I may use that expression, by some of the processes of the law. There is also a feeling on the part of the people, which is more imaginary than real, in relation to the Negro. They do not regard the black man as exactly entitled to the position that he occupies. For instance, in the parish of Natchitoches, a jury of black men, as I was informed, not one of whom, or only one of whom, could write his name,* had sat in a case which involved $180,-000. That was regarded generally by both parties (for I talked with everybody) as something that was not right. I found the same thing elsewhere, that there was a feeling that the colored man had been placed in a position more important than his education or his virtues or his intelligence entitled him to.

* * * * *

Q. Have you heard complaints from the people on that score in regard to taxation and corruption in office?—A. O. it is a matter of universal complaint from one end of the State to the other, made all the time. On steamboats, on railroads, in hotels, in churches—everywhere—that is he one subject of conversation.

A. E. H. Wilmer, Bishop of Louisiana, appeared before the committee at New Orleans, on January 2, 1875. Part of his testimony follows:

Question. The committee would be glad, without administering the oath to

---

The census reports of 1870 show that of 87,000 colored voters 78,000 could not read nor write.

you, to receive any information that you might be supposed to give with reference to the general political condition of this section of the country—either political, social, or commercial condition.—Answer. Of the political condition of the State I am comparatively ignorant. I am not a politician. I have never voted, and do not concern myself much with political struggles. You speak of the business condition of the country. It is hardly necessary to add my testimony to what has been heard by the committee, that the state of depression and embarrassment in the country is almost without precedent, without any parallel in any civilized country. Our ruin is almost complete, our people are depressed are almost in desperation. Many of them who are able to afford it are preparing to leave the State; those who cannot afford to do so are doing the best that is in their power to struggle against the difficulties and trials that surround them. I am at a loss to enter into particulars unless I am asked a question under that head. I have nothing to say that you have not heard upon the subject.

Q. Perhaps, if you prefer to be questioned, I will state that it will be of interest to know, in your opinion, what are the main causes of this lamentable state of affairs which you have just called our attention to.—A. I can only attribute it to lost confidence, universal dissatisfaction, which has paralyzed the energies of the people, added to their very many losses by the failure of their crops, caused by the change in the system of labor. It is also due to the unsparing depredations to which they are exposed, and to their utter lack of power to bring the culprits, whoever they are, to justice. I think, even where the crops have failed, it would have been possible for our people to have sustained themselves by raising live-stock, poultry, vegetables, and everything of that kind, but there seems to be no encouragement for them. The universal sentiment is that they cannot raise anything because they cannot keep it; it is stolen from them. They are universally exposed to depredation, to a greater extent than you can imagine unless you visit the people and the country yourself; no statement of mine will enable you to comprehend it; so that, if the crop shall fail, they have no resources whatever, and they are reduced to the greatest possible extremity. It would affect you very much to hear the stories I could give you of the extreme poverty, destitution, and misery to which many people who were well off are reduced. But it would hardly be proper for me to do so. I would rather give you the causes, as you have suggested, and without any reference to the government. I think the want in the country is some manner of bringing those who defy all law, and who are brought before the courts of justice and depend upon the fact of their being able to get off, to adequate justice. There seems to be no particular disgrace attached to such persons, even if they are convicted and sent to the penitentiary; when they return, no taint attaches to their good name, but rather the contrary is the fact. I think I am speaking within bounds when I say that I know of no instance in which a person, known to be guilty of offenses, has lost anything in the esteem of his companions or friends by the act of thieving or violence.

Mr. Henry Ware of Iberville Parish, who owned the famous "Belle Grove" plantation in Iberville Parish after the War, testified before the Congressional committee that "for the last several years our officials have generally been colored men, or a very ignorant class of white men, and when they were not ignorant, they were foreigners, men brought there to fill appointments under Governor Warmoth." Testifying further, he said that G. B. Loud, Superintendent of Education, had 37 indictments brought against him for embezzlement.

DEFALCATIONS AND SHORTAGES

At the end of 1874 reports of the auditors of Public Accounts showed that the tax collectors of 18 parishes were at default, ten of them for amounts over $10,000. The largest was $20,548.

A list of defaults showed that Dave Young, President of the last radical State convention and a senator, was indicted for embezzlement of between $30,000 and $40,000 of school funds. Others indicted for the same offense were Murrell, radical ex-Senator; Mahoney and Butler of Plaquemine; Hunsaker of St. James ran off with $12,000 worth of school funds. The ex-Treasurer of the School Board of St. Tammany absconded wth $2,000. The recorder of Tangipahoa and one of his friends made away with a school fund and told the division superintendent that by order of the State authority, they had expended it for political purposes. In New Orleans the loss of school funds by mishandling and cheating and graft was enormous. In New Orleans the McDonogh Fund was diverted from the purpose for which it was directed and a large portion squandered and expended in unlawful business.

According to E. A. Burke, in his testimony before the Congressional Committee, there were more than 10,000 suits against delinquent tax-payers in 1874 and 8,000 in 1873 in the city of New Orleans.

REPORT OF CONGRESSIONAL COMMITTEE

Finally it is interesting to study the report of the sub-committee of the Congressional Committee headed by George F. Hoar, Chairman, which was adopted by the full committee and turned over to the House with the recommendation that it be printed.

The sub-committee members were Charles Foster, William Walter Phelps and Clarkson N. Potter and they signed their report on the Condition of the South on January 14, 1875. The report said in part:

> The general condition of affairs in the State of Louisiana seems to be as follows: The conviction has been general among the whites, since 1872, that the Kellogg Government was an usurpation. This conviction among them has been strengthened by the acts of the Kellogg legislature abolishing existing courts and judges, and substituting others presided over by judges appointed by Kellogg, having extraordinary and exclusive jurisdiction over political questions; by changes in the laws, centralizing in the governor every form of political control, including the supervision of the elections; by continuing the returning-board, with absolute power over the returns of elections; by the extraordinary provisions enacted for the trial of titles and claims to office; by the conversion of the police force, maintained at the expense of the city of New Orleans, into an armed brigade of State militia, subject to the command of the governor; by the creation in some places of monopolies in markets, gas-

making, water-works, and ferries, cleaning vaults and removing filth, and doing work as wharfingers; by the abolition of courts with elective judges, and the substitution of other courts with judges appointed by Kellogg, in evasion of the constitu- of the State; by enactments punishing criminally all persons who attempted to fill official positions unless returned by the returning-board; by unlimited appropriations for the payment of militia expenses and for the payment of legislative warrants, vouchers, and checks, issued during the years 1870 and 1872; by laws declaring that no persons in arrears for taxes after default published shall bring any suit in any court of the State or be allowed to be a witness in his own behalf—measures which, when coupled with the extraordinary burdens of taxation, have served to vest, in the language of Governor Kellogg's counsel, "a degree of power in the governor of a State scarcely exercised by any sovereign in the world."

With this conviction is a general want of confidence in the integrity of the existing State and local officials;—a want of confidence equally in their purposes, and in their *personnel*—which is accompanied by the paralyzation of business and destruction of values. The most hopeful witness produced by the Kellogg party, while he declared that business was in a sounder condition than ever before, because there was less credit, has since declared that "there was no prosperity." The securities of the State have fallen in two years from 70 or 80 to 25; of the city of New Orleans, from 80 or 90 to 30 or 40, while the fall in bank shares, railway shares, city and other corporate companies have, in a degree, corresponded. Throughout the rural districts of the State the negroes, reared in habits of reliance upon their masters for support, and in a community in which the members are always ready to divide the necessaries of life with each other, not regarding such action as very evil, and having immunity from punishment from the nature of the local officials, had come to filching and stealing fruit, vegetables, and poultry, so generally—as Bishop Wilmer stated without contradiction from any source—that the raising of these articles had to be entirely abandoned, to the great distress of the white people, while within the parishes, as well as in New Orleans, the taxation had been carried almost literally to the extent of confiscation. In New Orleans the assessors are paid a commission for the amount assessed, and houses and stores are to be had there for the taxes. In Natchitoches, the taxation reached about 8 per cent. of the assessed value on the property. In many parishes all the white republicans and all the office-holders belong to a single family. There are five of the Greens in office in Lincoln; there are seven of the Boults in office in Natchitoches. As the people saw taxation increase and prosperity diminish—as they grew poor, while officials grew rich—they became naturally sore. That they love their rulers cannot be pretended.

The Kellogg government claims to have reduced taxation. This has been effected in part by establishing a board to fund the debt of the State at 60 per cent. of its face-value. This measure aroused great hostility, not so much because of the reduction of its acknowledged debt, as because it gave to the funding-board, whose powers seem to be absolute and without review, discretionary authority to admit to be funded some six millions of debt alleged to be fraudulent. So that, under the guise of reducing the acknowledged debt, it gave opportunity to swell the fraudulent debt against the State. This nominal reduction of the State taxes has been accompanied by a provision that the parish taxes shall not exceed the State. But the parishes have, notwithstanding, created liabilities; judgments being recovered on these, the courts have directed taxes to be levied for their payment, and thus the actual taxes have been carried far beyond the authorized rates. Rings have been formed in parishes, composed of the parish officers, their relatives, and sometimes of co-operating democrats, who would buy up these obligations, put them in judgments, and cause them to be enforced, to the great distress of the neighborhood—a distress so general, that the sales of lands for taxes have become almost absolutely impossible.

The sub-committee finishes the report with the following sentence: "Your committee have not been able to agree upon any recommendation; but upon the situation in Louisiana as appeared before us, we are all agreed."

CHAPTER III

INCIDENTS OF RECONSTRUCTION

From official documents and reports of congressional investigations, from newspapers and other sources, much light is thrown on the chaotic conditions in Louisiana during Reconstruction Days.

Some incidents are mentioned here as they show the perturbed state of mind of the people of Louisiana which gradually led to the organization of the White League, the Battle of Liberty Place and the eventual overthrow of carpetbag rule.

In the Spring and Summer of 1865 Chief Justice Salmon P. Chase made a tour of the Southern States ostensibly for the purpose of learning about conditions, but, as many thought, to lay the groundwork for his nomination as Republican candidate for the presidency. He was accompanied by Whitelaw Reid, at that time a young journalist, who later became editor and owner of the New York Tribune. Afterwards Reid entered the diplomatic service and was minister to France, special ambassador to Queen Victoria's jubilee and in 1905 ambassador to Great Britain. He was on the commission that arranged the peace treaty between the United States and Spain.

At the end of his tour with the Chief Justice, Reid wrote AFTER THE WAR — A SOUTHERN TOUR, May 1865 to May 1, 1866, published in Cincinnati later that year. For Chief Justice Chase it was adulatory, but this adjective could not be applied to his opinions and comments about the Southern people. Here is what Reid said about New Orleans:

> A town where all their drains are above ground; where a cellar would be a cistern; where the river is as high as the roofs of the houses; and where, when you die, instead of burying you like a Christian, they tuck you away on a shelf, and plaster you in with lath and mortar—that's New Orleans.
>
> . . . . a town where half the inhabitants think of Paris as their home, and feel as much interest in the Tuilliers as the White House; that of the other half, the most were cotton factors or commercial men of some sort, with principles not infrequently on sale with their goods; that it is at once the most luxurious, the most unprincipled, the most extravagant, and, to many, the most fascinating city in the Union—the only place that before the war could support the opera through an entire winter; the only place where the theatres are open on Sunday evening; where gambling is not concealed, and keeping a mistress is not only in no sense discreditable, but even is made legal.

Among those who entertained Chief Justice Chase and Whitelaw Reid while in New Orleans was Thomas May. This young man came home from St. Petersburg, Russia and served in the Confederate Army. He later took the oath of loyalty and at the age of twenty-three was rewarded with a job in the U. S. Treasury Department at New Orleans. He owned "Maylawn" plantation, near the upper part of St. John the Baptist Parish, and freed his slaves before he was forced to do so. He claimed that his plantation was the first to operate with paid labor during and after the war and that he made a larger profit under the paid-labor system than under slavery.

In addition to the guests the luncheon was attended by Jacob Barker, Christian Roselius, Judge Whitaker, and Thomas J. Durant, orator and leader of the Radical Free-State party. Maj. Gen. Phil. Sheridan appeared, whom Reid describes as "a compact, little, big-chested, crop-headed, fiery-faced officer."

The Chief Justice and Reid had various experiences while in the city, and attended several "mixed" affairs. Reid describes one such event:

REVELRY IN PIERRE SOULÉ'S HOUSE*

In the evening we were taken to a fair held by the Catholic negroes—mostly of the old Louisiana free-negro stock. By one of the curious revenges of these avenging times, the fair was held in the elegant residence of no less a person than ex-Senator and ex-Minister Pierre Soulé. He who had so often demonstrated negro inferiority and the rightfulness of slavery was now an exile, seeking a precarious livelihood by the practice of the law in a foreign language, in the City of Mexico; while the inferior negroes were selling ice-cream from his tables and raffling fancy articles in his spacious parlors, for the benefit of the slave children's schools!

Nowhere else in the world could that scene have been witnessed. There were elegantly dressed ladies, beautiful with a beauty beside which that of the North is wax-work; with great, swimming, lustrous eyes, half-veiled behind long, pendent lashes, and arched with coal-black eyebrows; complexious no darker than those of the Spanish senoritas one admires in Havana, but transparent as that of the most beautiful Northern blonde, with the rich blood coming and going, under the olive skin, with every varying emotion; luxuriant flowing tresses, graceful figures, accomplished manners—perfect Georgian or Circassian beauties. Yet every one of these was "only a nigger." Many of them had been educated in Paris, and more than one Parisian wardrobe shimmered that evening under the radiance of Mr. Pierre Soulé's chandeliers. Some of them were wealthy; all were intelligent, and some conversed in the foreign tongue in which they addressed us, with a vivacity and grace not often surpassed in Washington ball-rooms. But they were only niggers. They might be presented to the Empress Eugenie; they might aspire to the loftiest connections in Europe; but they were not fit to appear in a white man's house in New Orleans, and the Chief Justice was eternally disgraced (according to the talk of the city next day), for having so forgotten dignity, and even decency, as to enter a parlor filled with niggers that were trying to play lady and gentleman!

---

*Pierre Soulé's residence was No. 396 Esplanade Ave.

These people were not always outcasts. Under the great Napoleon they were citizens of the French Empire. It was only when the flag of the free came to cover them that they was disfranchised; only when they were transferred to a republic that they lost their political rights. Hitherto they have held themselves aloof from the slaves, and particularly from the plantation negroes; have plumed themselves upon their French descent, and thus isolated from both races, have transferred to Paris an allegiance that was rejected at Washington.

"But now," as one of them very frankly said during the evening, "we see that our future is indissolubly bound up with that of the negro race in this country; and we have resolved to make common cause, and rise or fall with them. We have no rights which we can reckon safe while the same are denied to the field-hands on the sugar plantations."

Among the negro men present were several who, whether in complexion, clothes or conversation, would never have been suspected in any mixed company at the North of being other than intelligent and polished ornaments of the Anglo-Saxon race. Mingled with these were others of darker hues, ranging down to mulattoes, and even darker still; and among them were several negro officers whose behavior Generals Butler and Banks had highly praised. A group of beautiful ladies, apparently white, was suddenly invaded by a quaint old chocolate-colored dame, with high bandana wound about her head, subscription-book in hand, and in the most extraordinary squeaking tones, calling for the taking of shares in her raffle. She was the grandmother of two of the young ladies! Madame Mottier, a mulatto, or quadroon, in whose education I think Boston had some hand, seemed to be the inspiring divinity of the fair, to whom all looked for direction or advice. She is teacher in a colored school.

By and by Mr. Pierre Soulé's piano, under quadroon fingers, began a march, and mainly voices—albeit not from Rebel throats—swelled the chorus. And so we left them: negroes raffling fans and picture-frames and sets of jewelry in the Soulé parlors; negroes selling ice-cream in the Soulé dining-room; negroes at his piano; negroes in his library; negroes swarming amid his shrubbery; and yet as handsome, as elegantly dressed, and in many respects almost as brilliant a party as he himself ever gathered beneath his hospitable roof.

INTOLERANCE AND SOCIAL OSTRACISM

It was charged by many Republicans that the conservatives, or the old-time families, ostracized the Republicans and would not have anything to do with them socially. But witnesses before the congressional committee testified that this was true only to a certain extent. James Buckner said there was not much prejudice in the State against Northerners or Yankess as there was in the North against Southerners. His family owned a home in Brattleboro, Vermont, and went there in the summertime for years before the War. After the War the people there treated them so coolly that thy sold their place and never went back again.

But the ostracism that was practiced in Louisiana was not the kind experienced by Mr. Buckner in Vermont. The Louisiana people did not mix socially with undesirable "riff raff," scalawags and plunderers of the State's resources. Most of these were Republicans, but because a man was Republican it did not necessarily follow that he would be ostracized socially. In fact, there is plenty of testimony to prove otherwise. For instance, Mr. Louis S. Clarke was a Republican from Ohio who came to St. Mary Parish in 1870. He testified before the Congressional Committee:

> Q. Is it known among your neighbors generally that you are and have been a republican?—A. Yes, sir; I think it is generally known by everybody. I have always so stated.
>
> Q. Do you know of any ostracism of yourself, or anybody from the North, on account of their political opinions?—A. I have to state, sir, that I have never been better treated in the North than I have in this State, or more kindly; and that I have never known of a case where a northern man was treated unkindly in the South on account of politics.
>
> Q. From your general knowledge of the condition of affairs in this State, do you consider that a northern gentleman, or a man of standing and respectability coming here and being an open and avowed republican, would be affected in his social standing in any manner on that account?—A. No, sir; I am sure he would not.

With reference to ostracism, Judge James E. Trimble of Farmersville, Union Parish, testified before the committee as follows:

> Q. This objection you have made to this practice has grown out of no personal feeling in regard to it in any way?—A. I have no personal feeling with any man connected with it, nor have I any animosity against the republican party as a party, but I have against individuals. There are individuals in the republican party that I do not associate with and never have associated with.
>
> Q. Out of what does that grow?—A. Out of their personal misconduct or personal relations, which I regard to be disreputable and dishonorable.
>
> Q. Don't you think that class of men, when these facts are believed of them, lose social position everywhere?—A. I think so; not only in Louisiana, but in the Northern or Eastern States, and particularly in the State of Massachusetts, where I spent a number of years in college. I was educated in Massachusetts.
>
> Q. Is any other rule applied in that respect to it, except such feeling as grows out of a heated political canvass in regard to social positions; I mean any other rule than that which is applied elsewhere?—A. I think not; I make a distinction between social and political ostracism. There is some political feeling during a campaign. There is more or less felt on both sides, but I think as a rule there is no social ostracism growing out of the political opinions of men who are really worthy of any position in society.
>
> Q. This opposition you have, then, to officials in the republican party grows out of their character and conduct, does it?—A. Yes, sir.
>
> Q. And not out of any personal quarrel?—A. No, sir; I consider they have done a great injury to the republican party and the State.

Another witness before the committee was Mr. J. G. Hazard of New Orleans who was a cotton broker and who had been in the City about three years. His testimony was as follows:

> Q. What are your politics?—A. I have been a democrat from the time I was born until the present time.
>
> Q. Do you know the treatment that was received here by a gentleman who engaged here in politics, on the republican side, as far as social ostracism is con-

cerned?—A. I consider the reputation of that class of men that are connected with the politics of New Orleans, and of the men that are in politics in Louisiana, is such that they would not be received in any respectable society in the North and West.

Q. Do the republicans in this city as a mass, that are in official position and engage actively in politics, receive that kindness and social treatment that the people generally receive?—A. I cannot say; I should think not.

Q. You do not know whether they are ostracized or not?—A. There are so few of them here that I do not know. I never meet them in society. The democratic politicians as a mass are residents here, and of course are well known, and they constitute the better society of the city. The politicians of the republican party are mostly non-residents, and they are not in society for two reasons: one reason is that they are not known, and the other reason is that the character and general repute of them is such that they would not be received here.

Q. Do you think the fact of a gentleman coming here from the North and engaging in this city in politics would affect unfavorably his social standing?—A. Yes, sir; the way politicians have been carrying on here for the last eight or nine years.

Q. Well, do you think a republican gentleman coming here and engaging in politics on the republican side would be received in society?—A. If he was honest, probably he would be.

Q. What is your belief on the subject?—A. That is a question hard to answer.

Q. Would a gentleman coming here from the North to engage in politics with the democratic side be received in society here?—A. If he was not an honest man he would not. I believe that if the people had confidence in either republicans or democrats, that they were honest men, they would receive them very well.

Among the witnesses before the committee was Brigadier-General Francis T. Nicholls (who later became governor) who at that time was living in Assumption Parish next to his native Ascension Parish. Governor Nicholls lost an arm and a leg in the War and he was of the highest type of southern gentleman. He testified before the committee:

In regard to ostracism, we have several Republicans in our parish who occupy a good social position. Mr. Spizer Jones came down from Illinois, and bought a plantation there and he occupies a good social position. Another gentleman is Capt. August Bulon who was a captain in General Sheridan's cavalry. He is a Republican office-holder, and he is very highly thought of. What has been sometimes spoken of as ostracism is nothing more or less than an unwillingness on the part of our people to associate with a class of men whom they believe to be without personal character. That unfortunately has been the case to a considerable extent with Republican office-holders. They are men who, if they transferred their residences from Ascension [Parish] to Maine or Illinois, they never would be associated with by people of those states for the same reason that they are not associated with here.

Congressman S. S. Marshall from the select committee of the House, which was sent here to investigate conditions in the South, said in his comments about social ostracism which were included in the report of the committee:

> The exaggerated charges so often made against the southern people of intolerance and social ostracism an account of difference of opinion and action on political questions are not, in the opinion of the undersigned, sustained by the evidence taken by your committee. That the great body of the white people in Louisiana do not feel kindly toward, or recognize very cordially, the men who have fastened the Kellogg government upon them, and are engaged in its schemes of perpetuation and plunder, is unquestionably true. But this arises not from the fact that these men are republicans, but for the reason that the people honestly believe that they are no better than a gang of buccaneers, who for their own wicked purposes have used the name of republicanism to aid them in their schemes of fraud and plunder.
>
> Republicans, known to be such, and yet also known to be gentlemen of integrity and character, whether northern men or southern men, are well received, and have social recognition there to the same extent as in any other part of our country. Few, if any, of this class of men have any connection or sympathy with the Kellogg usurpation. Of this class of republicans a number were examined as witnesses before the committee, and of these were Judges Trimble and Beattie, of the district court, and Judge Howe, late judge of the supreme court of the state, some planters and merchants recently from the North, and others. All these stated without hesitation that in Louisiana, just as in other communities, a republican, Union soldier, or northern man, when known to be a gentleman of character, was well and cordially received, and that his social status did not in the slightest degree depend upon his political sentiments. Several witnesses, it is true, complained of having been maltreated and socially ostracized on account of their political sentiments, but in every case in which the matter was inquired into it was ascertained that this ostracism was the result of causes other than their political opinions.

Along with social slights and ostracism which certain Republicans endured at the hands of representative people of Louisiana, there was another form of ostracism practiced by Negroes. For instance, Mr. Moncure of Shreveport testified before the committee as follows:

> Q. Do you know whether there is any fear on the part of the colored people or solicitude of injury or ostracism on the part of their own race if they acted with the conservatives?—A. I heard very great complaints of it from some of the colored people themselves. I may state this in respect to that: There is a neighbor of mine, a colored man, who lives next door to me in the city of Shreveport, as respectable a man as I have ever known of any color, an excellent, good neighbor, a neighbor whom I would not exchange for any white man I know, scarcely, because he is quiet, kind, and accommodating. I saw him shortly before the election; he has never voted otherwise than with the democrats, because he is a property-holder and a taxpayer. I asked him if he did not intend to vote with us again this year. Says he, "I am compelled to decline to vote at all. I won't vote against you and I won't vote for those other people, but I cannot vote at all." Said I, "What is the matter?" "Well," says he, "if I do I cut myself off from my own race, from any own people, and from my own associates, and I am dependent upon them for my social intercourse; therefore I must abstain from voting." The name of that man is Isham Hill.

Mr. Louis S. Clarke of St. Mary Parish also testified:

Q. Do you know any instances of subsequent bad treatment of colored men on your ticket?—A. Yes, sir; the case of a Mr. Gordon occurs to me, a very intelligent and well-educated colored man, who worked with us from the start, as I believe from conscientious motives. He taught school in Pattersonville, and after the election his scholars were all withdrawn from the school at once, his school was entirely broken up, and he was in destitute circumstances, and has been ever since. He has been unable to collect any money for past dues from the negroes thereabouts.

Q. Was that colored man born there?—A. I think he was born in the North and educated there. He has always been a republican, and is yet, I think.

* * * * *

Q. Do you know if any portion of the colored people voted the conservative or compromise ticket in the late election?—A. A large number.

Q. Do you know anything of their treatment by republican colored people?—A. They have been in many cases ostracized on account of voting with us in the last election. I could give you a number of instances.

Q. Do you know of any instance of maltreatment?—A. Yes, sir. In one case, at a republican meeting in Franklin, a negro, who had been acting with the conservative party, asked some question of one of the republican speakers. I don't remember what the question was, but I know he asked it in a very respectful manner, which called the attention of the other negroes standing around, of whom there was a large crowd, and they immediately set upon, and I really think they would have killed him; perhaps not, but their actions indicated that they desired to kill him. He was protected by white men standing by, and the negroes finally desisted.

Q. Do you know any other instance?—A. Well, sir, there was a great deal of intimidation of this description just previous to the election. We were prevented, on one occasion, from holding a political meeting in the town of Brashear. A meeting had been appointed, and we took our speakers down there, two or three negro canvassers, who intended to speak on our side. They got information in the town that afternoon that they would be set upon by other negroes if we held the meeting, and they were apparently very much terrified. I was with the party myself that day, and I was determined that that meeting should be held in Brashear that night. I tried my very best to get the negroes to stay with me, but their information they said was so positive that they were afraid to stay in the town, and we did not hold the meeting there. We had only one other speaker besides these negroes, and we thought it useless to carry out our programme if they did not stay with us. On another occasion a negro who worked for me was in this same town, and was set upon and maltreated by some of the negroes at that place for his political sentiments. He had avowed himself as being on our side, or the conservative side.

CARPETBAGGERS

The New York Sun in its issue of September 7, 1874, inserts a vigorous article on the carpetbaggers now depredating on the property of the Southern people. The following paragraphs are gleaned from said article. (N. O. Picayune, Sept. 12, 1874):

Comfortably smoking his cigar at the sea-side capitol, far away from the post of duty and cares of the office, the President has fulminated one of his reckless orders, intended to strengthen the hands of the thieves, who during the last five years of Grantism, have spread ruin, desolation and outrage over the fairest portions of the Southern States.

He did not wait to hear the other side or to investigate the facts connected with the recent atrocities in Louisiana, Alabama and South Carolina, but proceeded entirely upon the one sided statements made by the Attorney-General, whose conduct upon another occasion when he played a similar part has rendered him utterly unworthy of any sympathy or respect.

It is notorious that Williams was crammed with false statements by Kellogg, Spencer, Patterson and other carpetbaggers, whose testimony would be questioned in a court of justice and whose whole career as unscrupulous knaves is surrounded with infamy. These corrupt adventurers are allowed to direct the policy of the Government affecting the property and rights of eight million of white citizens. They do it by using the Attorney General as an instrument of their vengeance and venality.

The information thus far obtained leads to the belief that there was organized in Louisiana by a few desperate carpetbaggers to incite Negroes to commit outrages upon the whites in one of the towns where their number would overpower resistance. The knowledge of this plot led to the summary treatment of the white ringleaders.

It is difficult for people at a distance, in the enjoyment of all the privileges of freemen to realize the actual situation of Southern society in the reconstructed states. Trampelled upon by alien adventurers, impoverished by war, their remaining substance stolen before their eyes, crushed by combinations of carpetbaggers and Negroes, and their wives and daughters insulted and outraged beyond all former experience, it is not surprising that these sporatic outbreaks should occur when new wrongs are menaced.

NEWSPAPERS IN NEW ORLEANS

The leading newspapers in New Orleans in 1874 were the *Picayune,* the conservative paper; the *Bulletin,* Democrat conservative; the *Republican* which was the official newspaper of the Republican Party and defender of its policies; and the *New Orleans Times* which was supposedly neutral. The *Times* was a good newspaper from a reportorial standpoint. The *Bee,* printed in French was conservative.

There was another paper called *LeCarillon.* This started publication in 1869 and discontinued in 1874. There were three radical papers, all owned by Negroes. *L'Union, Louisiana Tribune,* and *The Crusader.* The *Tribune* was owned and published by three San Domingo Negroes, who as has been told, organized and led the "Pure Radical" Party.

The *Picayune* and the *Bulletin* were generally together in the fight on the Carpetbaggers but at times they took a shot at each other. But the *Picayune* was particularly venomous against the *Times.* Here is what it said in its issue of July 2, 1874:

> The Times has invented a novel and ingenious method for getting at the facts in any case where doubt exists. When the Picayune, Tuesday morning charged the negro militia with certain evil and wicked purposes, the Times marched solemnly

Canal Street, looking West, at the time of the Battle of the 14th. Clay Statue is in the foreground with St. Charles Street at the left and Royal Street at the right. On the right is the Touro Building with Christ Church, where the Maison Blanche Building now stands, in the distance. (From Jewell's New Orleans, 1873)

—*Courtesy New Orleans Public Library*

around to Gen. Barber, the negro commander of that militia, and asked him if such things could be. Barber replying in the negative, the Times marched solemnly back and told the public to be tranquil—it was all right—Barber said so.

On the same system when Kinch Malone or any other of the cheerful fraternity are suspected of burglary in the future, we have only to go to him and ask as a man and brother, whether he is guilty.

The Times ought to patent this admirable plan. *Certes,* no one thought of it before.

However, the *New Orleans Times* was a pretty good paper and had some clever writers. In its issue of March 1, 1872 is a whimsical and humorous article about the last session of the Louisiana legislature for that Spring entitled, "Pegged Out." The Louisiana legislature adjourned *sine die* but the *Times* reports it as pronounced by one member of the legislature as *si-ne di-ne.*

Newspaper Editorials

Here are some examples of gatling-gun writing and violent editorial expression during Reconstruction days.

While we are willing, and always have been, to give the Negro everything he needs and should have to make him happy, free and contented, *we are not and never will be in favor of his ruling the State of Louisiana any longer and we swear by the Eternal Spirit that rules the universe we will battle against it to the day of our death if it costs us a prison or a gallows.* Let each white man make it his special duty to watch the pothouse scalawagers, as they have spotted skins and damn black hearts. Of course, these scoundrels have misrepresented everything they took occasion to describe in their infamous letters and dispatches. *Somebody ought to make these blackhearted villains angels at once,* for, from the present temper of the State, the quicker such monumental liars take unto themselves wings and fly away, the better.

—From the Shreveport Comet, October, 1874.

* * * * * *

Our dispatches this morning contain the gratifying intelligence that the infamous wretch DeKlyne is dead. Of all the low and dirty beasts that radicalism has imposed upon Louisiana, this scoundrel was the meanest and lowest.

Some squeamish people may think that now the fellow is dead he should not be abused. *We think differently;* such men are a disgrace *to humanity,* and, alive or dead, their infamy should be held up to the execration of the world, and the youth of the country taught to *loathe and despise* their memory.

—From the Shreveport Times, July 29, 1874.

* * * * * *

That they the colored people are, and have been, carrying on a relentless war upon the whites, is unfortunately too true. It is not, indeed, a war of arms, for in that they would not have the shadow of a chance, and they know it well, but it is a legislative war—a war of ruin and extermination through the army of sheriffs and their deputies.

And how has the white race met this war? We must answer, weakly, very weakly. They have shown no courage, no spirit of sacrifice, no public spirit whatever, in meeting the emergency. On the contrary, they have met this open, insolence defiance of these unscrupulous partisans with the most accommodating submissiveness. So far from breaking off relations with them as a public enemy, which they are in every true sense of the word, every planter, every employer, has run a race with his compeers as to which of them could employ the greatest number of negroes. They are kept fully occupied everywhere. By this means they are furnished with the ability to carry on that very war which they wage so relentlessly against their employers. The white man supplies them with food, clothing and money. They grow fat, strong, and insolent. They go to the polls and defiantly vote to ruin the very man who weakly and stupidly warms into life and strength the reptile which he knows is stinging him.

There is but one way now to manage the negro. He is, as a class, amenable to neither reason nor gratitude. He must be starved into the common perceptions of decency.

—From the Catholic Messenger, June 14, 1874.

*   *   *   *   *

The vigilance committee of Saint Martin's last week ordered Judge Kreider and son to leave the country, and they went to New Orleans, leaving the balance of the family behind on their plantation. We are told that the charge against them was that they had been caught drilling negroes. We have known the Messrs. Kreider for years, and can scarcely believe that they could be guilty of such conduct. However, we think the committee must have had good grounds for action, and hope to see some effort made to vindicate their course, if they were right. If wrong (and vigilance committees do sometimes make mistakes,) we hope to see these citizens allowed to return to their home. Yet we believe more justice has been done in Attakapas by these organizations during the past two years than by all the courts of Louisiana. But when a negro is murdered, the act is viewed in a different light, and the best logic of its editor is invoked to justify the deed. For example, read the following from the same issue:

That most quiet and orderly community, the Ile Piquant settlement, have found it necessary to organize themselves into a vigilance committee to protect themselves from the outrages and pillages of a few bad men in their midst, whom the law has failed to bring to punishment. The Ile Piquant committee number 125 of the best citizens of this parish, and for weeks past they have constantly had a portion of their number on patrol duty.

On Wednesday night, the 19th instant, a notoriously bad colored man, named Jacques Boutte, alias Jack Jacobs, was caught in the act of stealing and killing a calf of beef belonging to Zeon Olivier, Jr., a most respectable colored citizen of the vicinity. He was assisted by a colored boy of good family, but as it was presumed the latter did not know the animal did not belong to Jacques, he was allowed to go home, while the principal in the crime was taken into custody.

On last Thursday evening, in the presence of perhaps 200 citizens, the thief was tried before a jury of citizens, while one acted as prosecuting attorney and another defended the prisoner. It was fully proven by witnesses that he not only had committed this theft, but had for years been a professional cattle-thief; and in consequence the jury decided that the best way to get rid of this villain, that lived by preying upon honest people, was to hang him.

—The Sugar Bowl, Aug., 1874.

*   *   *   *   *

From the *Sugar Bowl* (New Iberia)

Five Hundred Dollars Reward—The undersigned having learned that unknown persons are circulating the *report that he has received in his shop and shaved and cut the hair of colored people,* offers the reward to any one who can prove that it has ever been done by him or his employees, with his knowledge or consent.

Laurent Bazus

REPORT OF COMMITTEE OF 200 CITIZENS

An interesting pamphlet printed in 1873 shows that the leading citizens of New Orleans continued in their efforts to obtain relief from Federal authorities. This pamphlet was entitled

Report of the Committee of
Two Hundred Citizens
Appointed At a Meeting
of the
Resident Population of New Orleans
on the
12th December, 1872
(Picayune Steam Press, 66 Camp Street—1873)

The committee went to Washington and appealed to the President and the Senate Rules Committee. Their statement in the pamphlet concludes:

We recommend that all of the people of this State be organized to accomplish reform in our State administration, and to promote economy, retrenchment, and official responsibility.

We recommend the preservation of a temperate, moderate and sedate deportaged, assisted, and that which is needed for their improvement, guidance and progress be assured; and that this be a standing principle of act and counsel in the dealings toward them.

We recommend the preservation of a temperate, moderate and sedate department on the part of our people, so that we may show to the world that the inherent force and strength of our population is equal to the occasion of maintaining ourselves in the presence of an ignominious government, imposed by usurpation, violence and fraud, according to the report of a committee [U S Senate Committee] over whom we had no influence or control, and in which we had no representation.

Thos. A. Adams, Chairman
John A. Campbell
J. N. Lea
J. A. D. Rozier
Alexander Brother
I. H. Stauffer

N. O. March 22, 1873

NEGROES ON CONSERVATIVE SIDE

Quite a number of the colored people were conservative in their attitude and were not aligned with the Republicans. For instance, the testimony of William Alexander, colored, of 537 St. Charles Street, New Orleans, before the Congressional Committee testified that there were five conservative colored clubs in New Orleans. He voted with the Conservative Party and helped to organize the Conservative Club with 750 volunteer members. These men were not forced to join, but organized for the purpose of getting jobs as well as taking part in politics for better government. He stated that the Republicans tried to intimidate his organization, that they shot at the members at various times and beat them up. He stated that he himself was shot at three or four times, and with ten other men was forced to stay indoors at Brown's Hall for ten days while Negro Republicans waited outside to kill them if they came out. There was bitter feeling between the colored Republicans and the colored Conservatives. Alexander testified that he first voted in 1864. Here is an excerpt from his testimony:

Q: How old does a colored man have to be before he votes?

A: I didn't see them pay any attention to any particular age at all. They just called a man up and let him show in his ticket. They didn't care what age he was.

Witness said he couldn't read writing — read printing slightly — couldn't read his own name. He said he was born in 1859 which would have made him 5 years old in 1864. It probably was 1849. Even then he would have voted when 15 years old.

Sundry Items

It was charged that the white people and the Negroes could not get along together and there was considerable bitterness between them. John Young, a lawyer of Houma, Louisiana, testified before the congressional committee that he was a native of Ohio and had come to Louisiana in 1844. He said: "I have not exchanged a cross word with a colored man since the surrender, and I never had but one who treated me with the least impertinence and he was a soldier and he was stationed there during the War."

* * * * *

Testimony before one congressional committee about Negroes on juries stated that Negroes preferred to be tried by an all white jury because they had a better chance of justice. This is very much the attitude of the private in the U. S. Army today who under recent regulations is permitted to be tried by men of his own rank, rather than by courtmartial by officers only. Nearly all prefer to have officers.

* * * * *

Governor Warmoth addressed the bankers on bribery, saying: "I told how these much abused members of the Legislature are at all events as good as the people they represent. Why, damn it, everybody is demoralizing down here.

Corruption is the fashion." Warmoth claimed that the bankers tried to bribe him with $50,000.

*   *   *   *   *

The chairman of another congressional committee stated that several witnesses testified that persons who bore arms in the War are not the persons who have anything to do now with exciting public feeling or creating disturbances — that the Confederate soldiers were generally quiet and peaceable in their purposes and conduct.

General Thomas testified, "As I stated before I have never met a soldier that has not accepted the situation. They are peacemakers always, I think and if they have participated in any disturbance, it is greatly against their volition, in my opinion."

CHAPTER IV

FORMATION OF THE WHITE LEAGUE

Although there were several White Leagues in Louisiana, the New Orleans organization was "the" White League and was an active group from 1874 to 1877.

But the idea of the White League emanated in the country. There was a White Man's Club or Caucasian Club organized on May 22, 1867 in the Parish of St. Mary by Judge Alcibiade deBlanc. This was a forerunner of the several White Leagues which came into existence six or seven years later.

As far as can be learned, there was no Ku Klux Klan in Louisiana, but similar organizations or clubs known as the "Knights of the White Camellia" were organized in a few of the parishes. Several parishes later organized White Leagues, but from the testimony before the Congressional Committee studying conditions in the South these leagues were not as numerous as some have thought. General Nicholls testified before the Congressional Committee that there was no White League in Ascension Parish, and that in that parish there was no group organized for the purpose of intimidating anybody.

Mr. F. S. Goode, an attorney of Terrebonne Parish, testified:

> We had a White League. It was called a White League, but our White Leaguers, so called, were nothing more nor less than political clubs. They held their meetings in churches and school houses, and frequently under the trees. I made frequent speeches at those clubs, which were invariably listened to by colored men, who had as good an opportunity of seeing what was going on at those meetings as anyone else had * * *.

Governor Kellogg said in his testimony before the Congressional Committee, "I suppose it is unnecessary to state that there were many White League clubs throughout this city and State."

And from General Fred Ogden's testimony before the same committee it would appear that there were other leagues but that he knew little about them and was rather vague about the extent of the organization and its membership. Excerpts from his testimony read:

> Q. Are you the chief officer of the State—does this organization extend to all the parishes of the State?—A. There are organizations in parishes throughout the State over which I have no control.
>
> Q. Is there a general head?—A. There never has been any appointed for the State.
>
> Q. Does the organization contemplate a general head?—A. Not that I know of.

HEROES AND MARTYRS — September 14, 1874

1. Gov. John McEnery — 2. Lt. Gov. D. B. Penn — 3. Hon. R. H. Marr — 4. Hon. E. J .Ellis — 5. Gen. F. N. Ogden — 6. Dr. Cornelius Beard — 7. Col. W. J. Behan (In Memoriam) — 8. E. A. Toledano — 9. Fred Mohrman — 10. W. C. Robbins — 11. Charles Brulard — 12. S. B. Newman — 13. John Graval — 14. Alb. M. Gautier — 15. R. G. Lindsey — 16. J. K. Gourdain — 17. A. Bozonier — 18. Maj. W. A. Wells — 19. J. M. West.

(From a composite photograph made by Lilenthal of New Orleans. Courtesy Howard-Tilton Library)

CHARLES J. LEEDS, MAYOR OF
NEW ORLEANS, 1874-76

The Leeds Foundry, at the corner of Delord and Constance Streets, made the piece of artillery that Capt. Glynn's Company attempted to use in the battle but which couldn't be fired. The company was lucky it didn't explode. The captain of Section D of the Crescent City White League was Archibald Mitchell, superintendent of the Leeds Foundry. This business contributed m o r e members to the League than any other in the City. The headquarters of Sec. D were at the Foundry, and in the building were hidden guns imported for the Leaguers before the fray. Charles J. Leeds is listed in one roster as a private in Sec. D, Capt. Mitchell's company. The picture is from a portrait in the Louisiana State Museum and is reproduced with its permission. It is probably a portrait of Leeds when a younger man. Leeds' activity in W h i t e League a f f a i r s brought about his election as mayor. (Photo by Frank H. Allen)

CAPT. GEORGE H. LORD

CAPT. W. T. VAUDRY (above)
CAPT. JOHN GLYNN, JR. (below)

CAPT. D. M. KILPATRICK (above)
(Afterwards U. S. Sub-treasurer)

CAPT. H. DUDLEY COLEMAN (below)
(Afterwards Member 51st Congress)

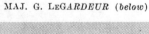

CAPT. FRANK McGLOIN (above
(Afterwards Judge of Appeal Cour

MAJ. G. LeGARDEUR (below)

Q. Do you know anything about the number of this organization throughout the State?—A. Nothing officially. I have an idea that it extends to some extent in almost all the parishes of the State; but I have no official data.

Q. You think there are similar leagues in all the parishes of the State?—A. I have heard that there are leagues in all the other parishes of the State. But I am perfectly free to say to you that I do not know anything about the extent of the leagues in those parishes.

Q. Is there, to your knowledge, any connection by which the leagues might be united?—A. I think they might be united if I gave the order.

Q. They would then obey voluntarily?—A. Yes, sir; they would then obey voluntarily.

Q. I want to see if there is any center by which they would be compelled to come together?—A. No, sir.

Q. Then the larger organization is here, of which you are chief?—A. Yes, sir. I know that there are organizations of the White League in other parishes, but I have no control over them. But I believe that if I was to call upon them for assistance that it would be rendered to me.

Q. There is no representative of the parish leagues whom you could order?—A. No, sir.

Q. So that your testimony would be that there are merely other organizations in these parishes of kindred purposes to yours?—A. Yes, sir.

Q. Was this league in the city of New Orleans organized first, or were those in the parishes organized prior thereto?—A. It is my impression that the White League organization existed in one of the parishes in the northern part of the State before it existed here. But I know nothing at all of its origin, or platform, or purposes, or anything of that kind.

The White Leagues seemed to be especially strong in southwest Louisiana. There were organizations in St. Landry, St. Martin, St. Mary, Lafayette and New Iberia. In Opelousas a notice in the *Courier* dated June 27, 1874 reads:

Opelousas, June 27, 1874

A public meeting of the white citizens of Saint Landry will be held at Opelousas, July 4, 1874, to discuss the principles of the White League and the issues it presents to the country.

The ladies are specially invited to attend.

Speeches will be made in both French and English.

A grand barbecue will be given on the occasion, to which the white citizens of Saint Landry and adjoining parishes are cordially invited.

A notice calling the people to a meeting to organize the White League in New Iberia appeared in the *Louisiana Sugar Bowl,* the official journal of the White League on July 19, 1874. It said:

Doubtless this will be the grandest meeting ever held in the place.

TO THE WHITE PEOPLE OF THE PARISH OF IBERIA, LOUISIANA.

Fellow-citizens: The time is near when the voting population of our State and parish will again be called to the polls to select certain of their State and parochial officers. Love of liberty, honor, and honesty, a proper respect for ourselves, families, and friends, and the hope of retrieving the fortunes of our State and people, physically and morally, demand, in tones that no true man can disregard, that our sloth and indifference be cast aside—that we be up and doing. The experience of past years has demonstrated that those who now hold the government are incompetent to rule; that their administration can but result in oppression and desolation: that from their rule can come but corruption, demoralization, and degradation in every department of life. Look about you, and what do you behold? Alas! naught save desolated, abandoned, and uncultivated fields, a disheartened, discouraged, and disgraced people; the State bankrupt in fortune and in name. Can you bear it longer, that negro ignorance, solidified in opposition to white intelligence, and led by carpet-bag and scalawag impudence and villainy, shall continue to hold the State, your fortunes, and your honor by the throat, while they perpetrate upon you indignities and crimes unparalleled? Will you permit this without an effort to drive back the robbers? For years the negroes have been organized in the interest of their own race; for years they have persistently presented the issue to the white people; for years they have rejected every offer of conciliation and united effort in favor of good government. You know the fact. You cannot have been blind to it. What shall you do? We answer: *Organize the White League!* Our sister parishes of Saint Landry, LaFayette, St. Martin, Saint Mary, and others, have done so, and their white population is being enthusiastically and rapidly marshaled into a compact mass, to do battle at the polls for intelligence and good government. Shall the people of Iberia remain behind? No! else they will betray the mandate intrusted to them by nature. No! else their white superiority will be but the accumulation of their weakness and disgrace. No! Organize the White League in your midst.

Fellow-citizens, the White League has in view no violation of law, State or Federal. It does not propose to interfere with the rights of any one. It does, however, propose to meet at the polls the issue presented by the negro population. It does propose, by compact and legal action on the part of the whites, to force the government of the State from the hands of that villainy and ignorance which are ruining and disgracing both whites and blacks. It does propose to snatch the prey from political speculators and thieves, and to make carpet-baggers and scalawags and ignorance powerless for evil by driving from our legislative halls and the people's offices those who have no interest in the State save that of plundering her and her people. It does propose to restore the State to the hands of intelligence and to good government, so that its affairs may be administered for the honor, the benefit, and happiness of all. To do this our white population must be united. The negroes, under their apostate leaders, encouraged by your moral weakness in the past, are a unit. Will the whites permit dissension to rule among them? If so, shame on them! Then retire all other questions into the background; sink into oblivion all past causes of complaint and jealousy. Let each and all remember that they are whites; that they have a sacred duty to perform; that the cause of their race, of good and intelligent government, is theirs, and they will reap a glorious success.

Fellow-citizens! It is your oppressed and beloved Louisiana that appeals to your heart and good sense for aid; for prompt, positive, and united action. You will not, you cannot refuse her. To these ends we recommend that a grand meeting be held at New Iberia, on Saturday, July 25, 1874, which every person, without regard to past party affiliations, is invited to attend.

The same paper reported the meeting of the Central Committee.

CENTRAL COMMITTEE MEETING.

MEETING OF THE PARISH CENTRAL COMMITTEE OF THE WHITE LEAGUE, FOR THE PARISH OF IBERIA.

New Iberia, *August* 12, 1874.

The first regular meeting of the White League central committee was held this day, the following members present, viz: Messrs. H. Patout, Charles Clerc, R. S. Perry, Viel Darby, F. Duperier, John N. Webster, president White League Club No. 1, First ward; H. B. Bayard, president Club No. 2, First ward; E. Montague, sr., vice-president of New Iberia Club No. 1; B. D. Dauterieve, president of Fausse Pointe Club; J. A. Decuir, president of DeBlanc Club; Jules Babin, vice-president of Coteau Club.

The committee was duly organized by the election of Hypolite Patout as president, Veil Darby as vice-president, and R. S. Perry, secretary.

On motion, and after due discussion, the following resolutions were adopted:

1st. *Be it resolved,* that the officers of each club be required to cause to be prepared lists of all persons of their respective sections of the parish, qualified by age and residence to be voters, making separate lists of the whites and blacks, and noting on each such as may, from any cause whatever, be unable to reach the places for registration and voting; also such as may be disqualified by any cause, and noting especially the names of foreigners, speaking particularly whether or not naturalized; and to make due return of said lists to this central committee; and, further, that said officers cause committees from their respective clubs to be appointed for these purposes.

2d. *Resolved,* That the president of this committee appoint a committee of attorneys, whose business it shall be to aid and assist before the courts in obtaining and completing the naturalization-papers of all foreigners entitled to the same.

3d. *Resolved,* That the secretary of each club shall be required to report to the central committee the proceedings of each meeting of his club, and to make such special reports as said committee may from time to time call for.

4th. *Resolved,* That each club be requested to insert the following article in the constitution, to wit: While every member is expected to vote for the regular nominee of the White League for office, each binds himself not to vote, under any circumstances, for the competitor or opponent of such regular nominee.

5th *Resolved,* That for the purpose of making nominations for the different offices, a convention, to be composed of delegates from each club shall be convened by the central committee at New Iberia, at such time and on such basis of representation as said committee may hereafter determine.

6th. *Resolved,* That we urge upon the officers and members of the clubs to be firm and united, to present constantly an unbroken front to our potential enemies, and at the same time to be circumspect, just, and law-abiding; and especially that the officers of clubs impress upon the members the necessity of being calm, peaceful, and orderly.

7th. *Resolved,* That we recommend to the members of the White League to rebuke and discourage the ambition and chicanery of office-seekers, and by so doing vindicate the right of voters to choose their own candidates for office.

The president then appointed Messrs. W. F. Schwing, C. O. Delahoussaye, U. S. Haas, and Julius Robertson, on committee on naturalization-papers.

On motion, the committee then adjourned, to meet again at 10 a. m. on the 22d instant.

H. PATOUT,
President.

R. S. Perry, *Secretary.*

Dr. George J. Colgin, a practicing physician of New Iberia, testified before the committee with reference to the White League and its policy:

> The resolutions and call read set forth, in my opinion, the real motives and wishes of the White League. It became at once a powerful party, drawing into its ranks the great majority of the white people. The leaders of the organization have to this day shown themselves moderate, liberal-minded, fair men, denouncing all violence, and advocating nothing but peaceable measures in all emergencies. In Iberia Parish, of which alone I speak, they control the people, keep them orderly and fair in their behavior, and in consequence of this there was no violence or intimidation practiced toward republicans, black or white, within my knowledge, on account of their politics.
>
> As a practicing physician, with many patients among the colored people in my parish, I had many opportunities to converse with them, and did often avail myself of the opportunity, and in no instance did a colored man ever complain to me that the white people tried to intimidate him, and thereby try to prevent his registering or voting according to his own choice. During the canvass the colored people had frequent meetings in different parts of the parish in clubs and mass-meetings, where speeches were made by both white and colored republicans, without restraint.
>
> Almost the entire white male adult population joined the league; about fifty in the western part of the parish did not join the league, but formed a democratic club, calling in the Moncure Club. There were also some fifty in town of New Iberia who did not join the league, but voted with it. This unanimity of the whites caused the colored people, who had always been closely and thoroughly organized, generally meeting at night in their hall, (Grant's Academy,) not more than three hundred yards from my house, to reflect seriously upon the situation.
>
> The White League clubs in Iberia Parish numbered over one thousand members. There was not a single office-seeker. The candidates were chosen, nominated, about ten days before the election, and the nominees were known as liberal-minded, honest, and competent men.
>
> The republican committee had publicly nominated but three—a judge, a sheriff, and a representative. These not giving satisfaction, democratic clubs were formed in two wards of the parish by the colored men, the members of both voting the White League ticket.

Dr. Alfred Duperier, a native of New Iberia and a practicing physician, stated to the Committee: "I am not aware of any act of intimidation practiced in my parish by the White League organization; do not belong to the same; have openly disapproved of the same."

Louis S. Clarke in his testimony said of the League:

> Q. Is there any White League existing in your parish?—A. Yes, sir.
>
> Q. State what sort of an organization that is.—A. We always held our meetings with open doors and open windows, without an exception. It was just like any political organization; the organization of Saint Mary's Parish did not differ in any respect that I know of from any political one in the North. The name I always regarded as an unfortunate one. I was at the North when the organization was formed in Saint Mary's Parish, and before I joined I found by inquiring that there was nothing secret in the organization in Saint Mary's Parish; that it was simply a political party; and I considered it my duty to join it when I found that out.

Q. Were colored men of the opposite side present at these meetings, and did they hear what was going on?—A. On several occasions; there was nothing to keep them from being present.

Q. Is there any armed organization in your parish?—A. No, sir, none whatever.

News of the League's activity in St. Martin Parish was relayed to the New Orleans Republican in this dispatch:

WARLIKE ACADIA.

The latest intelligence from Saint Martin indicates that the White Leaguers are placing themselves on a war footing. It is stated that an iron gun with a four-inch bore has been undergoing repairs at Lutzenberger's foundry. Men have also been employed in raising from Bayou Teche two brass Napoleon field-pieces which were thrown overboard at a period during the war, and formerly belonged to Fuller's battery. These guns were in comparatively good order, and have already been mounted. Solid shot are being cast at the foundry above named. Six barrels of powder and several cases containing fixed ammunition have been received from the White League ordnance department in this city. The commissariat furnished by the Government during the overflow still holds out, and the fiery orator of the Attakapas, Colonel Alciabiades DeBlanc, is traveling through the country stirring his followers up to deeds of desperate valor. All of these preparations are being made to receive the Metropolitan army of invasion. Intelligence of the intended early occupation of that section by Federal troops had not reached there at last accounts.

* * * * *

Among interesting testimony in the hearing before the Congressional Committee was that of J. H. Gageby, U. S. Army, talking about the White League in St. Martinville, he was asked the question: "What is the designation of a U. S. officer or a northern man among those people? Is it a Union man or a Yankee?" He answered: "They generally call them Yankees; that is what they call me."

The Crescent City White League

In New Orleans, the White League, as such, came into existence on July 2, 1874. The New Orleans White League was organized or formed by the same gentlemen who had organized the Crescent City Democratic Club in 1868. This was a secret society composed of members of the Chalmette Club, a social club which later merged with the Boston Club in 1873. It is interesting to note that the reason this club was kept secret was that it conducted a Carnival ball and parade, namely, the Twelfth Night Revelers. But the patriotic members of this social club felt that they owed their services to the State as well, and so became active in politics. Among its original organizers in 1868 were Gen. Fred Ogden and F. R. Southmayd.

On July 1, 1874, the members of the Crescent City Democratic Club came out in the open and changed the name of the club to Crescent City White League.* The *Picayune* of July 2 published the charter of the new organization and its platform in full. The names of the officers were as follows:

President:	F. N. Ogden
1st Vice-Pres.:	W. J. Behan
2nd Vice-Pres.:	W. I. Hodgson
Corres.-Sec.:	Donaldson Jenkins
Recording-Sec.:	Theodore Shute
Treasurer:	W. A. Bell
Marshal:	W. T. Vaudry
1st Asst. Marshal:	John Payne
2nd Asst. Marshal:	Harrison Watts

Among the other members were:

Col. J. B. Walton
Benj. R. Forman
F. C. Zacharie
Archibald Mitchell
J. D. Hill
C. L. Walker

The platform which won the approval of the conservative press is too long to be included here, but one paragraph reads: ". . . . and while we declare it is our purpose and fixed determination not to interfere in any manner with the legal rights of the colored race, or of any other race, we are determined to maintain our own legal rights by all the means that may become necessary for that purpose, and to preserve them at all hazards."

General Fred N. Ogden in his testimony before the Congressional Committee furnished a copy of the Constitution of the Crescent City White League.

Constitution

We, the undersigned, citizens of Louisiana and of the city of New Orleans, adhering to the platform of principles of the Crescent City White League, due hereby, for the furtherance of the objects of that league, unite ourselves to form a club under the following constitution and by-laws:

ART. I. This club shall be called 'The Crescent City White League' of New Orleans.

---

*James Buckner, a member of the committee that proposed the adoption of a constitution and the change of name, testified before the Congressional Committee that the White League was so named to offset the Black League.

ART. II. The object of this club is to assist in restoring an honest and intelligent government to the State of Louisiana; to drive incompetent and corrupt men from office; and by a union with all other good citizens, the better to maintain and defend the constitution of the United States and of the State, with all laws made in pursuance thereof; and to maintain and protect and enforce our rights, and the rights of all citizens thereunder.

ART. III. The officers of this club shall be a president, two vice-presidents, a corresponding and a recording secretary, a treasurer, a marshal, and two assistant marshals; which officers shall be elected by a majority of the club, and who, after their election, shall serve until the club shall dissolve, or they shall resign, or for cause shall be removed from their position, in which cases the club shall elect members to fill the vacancy. Besides these officers there shall be such officers appointed by the president as the necessities of the club for its more efficient organization may demand, who shall serve in the position to which they shall be assigned by the president, and in which they shall be respected by the club.

ART. IV. This constitution may be amended only at a meeting which shall be advertised three times for that purpose, when a two-thirds majority of the members present shall be sufficient to adopt any amendments which may be offered.

FRED N. OGDEN, Chairman
F. R. SOUTHMAYD,
JAS. BUCKNER,
JNO. N. PAYNE,
SAM'L. FLOWER,
Committee.

General Ogden's testimony before the Committee concerning the White League throws much light on its method of operation, its purposes and its activities. The following excerpts are pertinent:

Q. What was the necessity of your organization? What did it grow out of?—A. It grew out of the situation of affairs which existed here. We had, under this usurpation, a military brigade of police, backed by a negro militia, in which our citizens were in terror all the time. We did not know how far they would extend their outrages upon us. Men were arrested without any form of law. Police were sent into the country for the purpose of executing the orders of this colored government, and the negroes, from information I received from all quarters, were drilling and arming in the back part of the town, and there was a feeling of dread and apprehension on the part of our people.

Q. As regards life and property?—A. Yes, sir.

Q. What do you mean by the metropolitan brigade?—A. I mean the police in this city.

Q. Are they armed?—A. Yes, sir; with the most approved munitions of war.

Q. Were they out on the 14th of September?—A. Yes, sir; and I have seen them turn out before that.

Q. Did they drill with arms?—A. It was generally understood that they drilled with arms. They were organized as a part of the militia of the State.

Q. You spoke of negro militia; is that the general militia of the State.—A. Yes, sir. They hold commissions from Governor Kellogg.

Q. Were they all black, or did white men belong to it?—A. It was my impression that it was all black.

Q. That was the necessity to which you refer?—A. Yes, sir.

Q. Had there been any such organization as a Black League before your White League was organized?—A. I have heard that there was such an organization, but I do not know.

Q. When was this league organized?—A. On the 1st of July, 1874, we organized as a club.

Q. Is it secret in its character?—A. Not at all; there is the constitution under which we have acted; and there is no oath nor obligation in it beyond an oath that they should observe the constitution and platform of the club, and also yield obedience to the orders of the officers.

Q. Why was it called originally the "White Man's Club?"—A. Simply because we thought that the white people in our State were the only ones that could be depended upon in the condition of affairs that then existed in the State.

Q. Did you contemplate the holding of offices simply by white men?—A. No. sir; the political machinery of the State we had nothing at all to do with. Our constitution says that we will defend the rights of all classes of people.

Q. How large is the organization in the city and in the State?—A. I have no official data of the numerical force in the State; but in the city of New Orleans I think, sir, that our roll will call from 2,500 to 2,800 men. [This was in January, 1875].

Q. How are these 2,500 men divided; in companies and regiments, or battalions?—A. I am free to say that since the action of the 14th of September, in order to get them all under command for our defensive purposes, I have organized so far two regiments of infantry and one regiment of artillery, but those terms have not yet been applied to them.

Q. Are those regiments all officered?—A. Yes, sir; they are officered.

Q. By what authority officered?—A. Simply by this authority, that we had to protect ourselves.

Q. It was an organized force when the affair of the 14th of September took place?—A. Yes, sir; partially organized.

Q. By signing this constitution which you have put in evidence; how soon after this organization commenced, on the 1st of July, did it assume a military character?—A. It assumed a military character immediately upon its organization; military to this extent, that on its organization officers were appointed and their orders were obeyed.

Q. Did it at that time, or does it now, possess an armory or armories?—A. No, sir.

Q. No arms belong to the organization, but belong to the individuals of which it is composed?—A. Yes, sir; in regard to the organization of the present White League, I will say that there is another club of which I was president also, and they purchased guns for themselves and their companions, and they furnished one of the companies of the league.

Q. Are the guns kept by the individuals in their own houses?—A. They are kept by individuals.

Q. Are the meetings of the organization regular in time?—A. The different companies, as I see by the papers, have regular meetings, but so far as the Crescent

City Club, the mother club of all of them, is concerned, we have had very irregular meetings since the 14th of September.

Q. Then I understand that besides the White League organization in this city there are a number of smaller clubs of the same name and character?—A. I do not think that I could call them clubs. I would designate them as companies; that is their title.

Q. Does your estimate of 2,500 or 2,800 membership include all these other companies or clubs?—A. Yes, sir.

Q. So that the whole number of members included in any of these organizations which go under the name of the White League Club, and of which you are commander, number only about 2,800?—A. About that.

Q. Are there any rules or orders issued by you, or from the head of the organization, with reference to military drill?—A. No, sir, not by me. They have been drilled by the officers of the companies. On the contrary, I have sometimes issued orders to officers prohibiting drills.

Q. Each company with reference to its drill acts upon its own responsibility?—A. Yes, sir.

Q. Where did these drills take place?—A. In different places in the city and on the street.

* * * * *

Q. Do you know whether in your organization there are any republicans?—A. I can say this: I do not know whether the gentleman is a republican or not—he served with us on the 14th of September—but his name is Lieutenant Robbins*. He was in the Federal Army. I had only become acquainted with him a few days before the 14th of September.

* * * * *

Q. I understand this organization of yours is purely voluntary; any man can leave it if he chooses?—A. Yes, sir.

Q. And any man can come into it that you choose to take in?—A. Yes, sir.

On July 2, 1874 the *Picayune* printed an account of the meeting of independent clubs, which were later to become part of or affiliated with one organization known as the White League. The article gives the list of clubs with their delegates.

According to notice, the gentlemen of the Executive Committee of the Independent Clubs assembled last evening at their rooms, No. 46 Magazine street. Mr. Hinman, their chairman, explained that the meeting was called for members of the Executive Committee and of the Committee on Credentials only to hear the report of the latter before submitting it to the delegates in general council.

The chairman of the Committee on Credentials then submitted the following report:

New Orleans, July 1, 1874.

Hon. M. Hinman, Chairman, Executive Committee Independent Clubs, and Gentlemen of the Convention:

We, the undersigned, Committee on Credentials, appointed at the last meeting of your honorable body, would respectfully report the following clubs represented and delegates to be admitted:

**Could this have been Major W. C. Robins who was killed on the 14th; who came from Philadelphia and had been an officer in the U. S. Army during the war?*

Crescent City Club of '72—F. Holyland, J. O. Nixon, Jr., James O. Walker, Delegates.

Minute Men of '68-'72—M. Hinman, President, John Calder, R. W. Galespie, John F. Tannehill, Delegates.

Gratz Brown Guards, Second Ward—Harry Wilde, President, John Rareshide, Robert Montgomery, R. Martin, Delegates.

Wingfield Rangers—James Wingfield, President, Thad. Waterman, Delegate.

Crescent Mounted Club—Sam'l. Henderson, President, W. A. Wells, Emile O'Brien, Delegates.

Fifth Ward Independent Club—F. Romain, President, L. Querouze, Delegate.

Pendleton Guards—Jno. Glynn, President, E. A. Ducros, Delegate.

Central Hancock Club—J. Pinckney Smith, President.

Constitution Club—Dr. Mercier, President, Charles Delahoussie, N. E. Bailey, Delegates.

Third Ward Liberal Club—Jno. Conners, President, M. Custe, M. Franley, Delegates.

Fulton Street White Club—M. W. Hanlin, Delegate.

Seventh Ward Skimmer Club—James Soloman, Delegate.

Eighth Ward Wide Awaken—Wm. Swan, President, A. D. Bernoudy, Delegate.

Frank Blair Guards, '68—Dan Smith, Vice President.

Ninth Ward Independent Club—E. H. Brown, President, Gus Laget, D. Morgan, Delegates.

Second Ward Liberal Club—C. L. Van Houten, Delegate.

Swan Cadets—W. L. Bowden, President, A. R. Moulair, S. C. Pellayor, Delegates.

Booth Guards, Third Ward—Pete McDermott, President.

First Ward Reform Club—M. H. Marks, Delegate.

Seymour Cadets—J. J. Litton, President.

Jonas Legion—P. J. Sullivan, President, John P. Canna, J. R. Sutton, Alex. McConnell, Jr., Delegates.

Walker Guards—Phil Munch, President, J. V. Guillotte, Delegate.

Frank Blair Guards '72—Dudley Selph.

Eighth Ward Reform Club—E. Desdunes.

Seymour Videttes—Jos. Zingle.

McCloskey Guards—W. J. Kelley.

Seymour Legion—H. G. Morgan, President, Henry Renshaw, Delegate.

Infantes D'McEnery—Gabriel Pratz, Delegate.

Fifth Ward Workingmen's Democratic Club—Alf. Bellanger, President.

Tenth Ward Independent Liberal Club—L. L. Lavis, C. O'Donnell, Harry T. Hays.

Sixth Ward Liberal Club—A. A. Kerr, President.

Seymour Southrons—M. McNamara, Henry Taylor, Delegates.

Tenth Ward New Club—Henry Meyers, President.

Twelfth Ward Reform Club—H. E. Shropshire.

Wiltz Guards—Wm. Stevenson, President.

Second Ward Democratic Club—Chas. H. Schneck, President, J. S. Hodgins, M. Killnde, M. Seay, Delegates.

Third Ward Independent Club—J. C. R. Selig, Charles Byrnes.

Fossil Guards—R. L. Bruce.

Respectfully,

HARRY WILDE, *Chairman*

THAD'S. WATTERMAN, E. QUEYROUZE, *Committee.*

Another organization, military in nature, which became affiliated with the White League and fought on the 14th of September, was the First Louisiana Regiment, known as "Louisiana's Own." It was organized by Colonel John G. Angell, a former Confederate soldier, according to John W. Kendall in his "History of New Orleans." The First Louisiana was a secret anti-radical organization with a military background, and in the beginning was called the YMCA — Young Men's Cooperative Association. Each member possessed a double barrelled shot gun firing buck shot or ball. The regiment was supposed to be a part of the McEnery militia but no commissions were ever issued. Most of the members were ex-Confederate soldiers, and the companies drilled in cotton presses and various halls.

Other companies and clubs such as those listed above were organized. Some were known as "Protector League" companies.

Governor Kellogg in his testimony before the Congressional Committee said: "Thus the campaign went on, clubs were being formed,* especially in the city under the auspices of the White League, numbering in some instances, one hundred, one hundred and fifty, and more, composed in a large part of the young and middle-aged men, who were clerks in stores, artisans, mechanics, workmen and so forth."

In another place in his testimony, however, Governor Kellogg asserted that the leading people of the city were members of the White League. He said: "There was one called the Crescent City White League Club, that I have referred to specifically; that was one club, and a club composed of some of the best men in the city, unexceptional in their private relation except that they were outside the law."

Edward A. Burke (Dept. of City Improvements of the City of New Orleans), a Republican who did not belong to the White League, said in his testimony:

> I subsequently ascertained that it was a protective union of white men, not based upon hostility to the blacks, but found to preserve the State from disorder. The race issue sought to be raised in this campaign was in my opinion, superinduced by the fact that the rule of the colored race and white adventurer over the Southern States had plunged those states under $400,000,000 of debt for while they received no material benefit—The treatment of the colored men on Sept. 14th by the White League—satisfied me that they bear no hostility to the colored man; that they are true and loyal citizens—organized for no purpose of hostility toward the National Government.

---

*Gov. Warmoth in "War, Politics and Reconstruction" says that there was an organization in New Orleans called "The Innocents," comprised mostly of Italians, and with the same purpose as the White League companies.

The river front at the foot of Canal Street in 1873. (From Jewell's New Orleans)
— Courtesy New Orleans Public Library

The question often asked was: "Where did the White League get its arms?" The question was partly answered by the information conveyed in a newspaper article. The *Pittsburgh Telegraph* interviewed a dealer in military supplies in Pittsburgh with this result:

White-League Arms and Their Use

Learning that arms in considerable quantities were being shipped South from the Great Western Gun Works in this city, a Telegraph reporter called at that establishment this morning for further information. Mr. J. H. Johnston, the proprietor, said he had been getting orders for about six weeks past. The trouble seemed to have commenced down there about the middle of August. The arms, mostly muskets, were sent principally to the States of South Carolina, Alabama, and Mississippi. In small towns they generally ordered from fifty to seventy-five guns to a lot. They seemed to be organizing in companies. The guns are some that Mr. Johnston bought up shortly after the war very cheaply, and is selling them at very low rates. Most of them are furnished with bayonets; generally with those long, villainous-looking blades known as the saber-bayonets.

In ordering them through the mail, asked the reporter, is it ever intimated what is the object in ordering such large quantities? No, replied Mr. Johnston, except in one letter, in which the writer said they expected some trouble down there, and they were going to prepare for it. My impressions are, however, that they fear an uprising of the blacks.

Do they order many small-arms? asked the reporter. Mr. Johnston. Most of the orders are confined to muskets. However, occasionally they want a few navy revolvers.

Reporter. Do you send ammunition South also? Mr. Johnston. Yes; and it's very evident they mean business for they generally order cartridges for the muskets. I recently received an offer for 15,000 rounds of cartridges.

Mr. Johnston stated that occasionally he received orders for a better class of arms than the common muskets. As, for instance, he recently filled an order for seventy-five breech-loading rifles.

It occurred to the reporter that perhaps the authorities might interfere with the traffic, and as much was intimated to Mr. Johnston. To this he answered that there was no martial law in force, and he didn't see how the authorities were to interfere. The guns were his and he thought he had a perfect right to sell them. He had sold, in all, from 800 to 1,000 muskets, and he expected to sell all he had on hand. He now has orders for several hundred guns, and additional orders are coming in.

White League Finances

The method of financing the White League is not known exactly, nor have I been able to locate a financial statement of any of the organizations. James Buckner, one of the incorporators of the Crescent City White League, testified before a Congressional Committee that the league was sustained by voluntary subscriptions. He stated that between five and six thousand dollars was raised in New Orleans to buy arms and ammunition. A Belgian rifle cost

$2.50 and most of the men bought their own. Undoubtedly some were aided by the League. And some of the rifles and guns cost more than $2.50.

CONGRESSIONAL REPORTS ON THE WHITE LEAGUE

Comment on the White League from the report of George F. Hoar from the Select Committee on the Condition of the South on behalf of the Special Committee: Charles Foster, William Walter Phelps, and Clarkson N. Potter (Jan. 14, 1875, Report No. 101, 43rd Congress, 2nd Session.):

> In this connection we refer to the White League, mentioned in the message of the President. In the last campaign of Louisiana the opposition was composed of various elements, democrats, reformers, dissatisfied republicans, liberal republicans, old whigs; and in order to induce the co-operation of all, some of whom refused to unite with an organization called democratic, they took the name of "the people's party;" called in some localities "the conservative party;" in others, "The white man's party;" in others, "the White League;" and had ordinary political clubs under these names throughout the rural districts, which were ordinary political clubs and nothing more; neither secret, nor armed, nor otherwise different from usual political organizations. These must not, however, be confounded from similarity of name with the White League of the city of New Orleans.
>
> That league is an organization composed of different clubs, numbering in all between 2,500 and 2,800; the members of which have provided arms for themselves, and with or without arms engage in military drill. They have no uniforms, and the arms are the property of the individuals, not of the organization. They comprise a large number of reputable citizens and property-holders in the city of New Orleans. Their purpose they declare to be simply protective; a necessity occasioned by the existence of leagues among the blacks; by the hostility with which the Kellogg government arrayed the black against the white race; and by the want of security to peaceable citizens and their families, which existed for those reasons, and because, also, of the peculiar formation of the police brigade.
>
> On the other hand, the republicans assert that this is an armed body of volunteers, existing for the purpose of intimidating the blacks and overthrowing the Kellogg government. That it had any considerable relations outside the city of New Orleans, or that it was intended in any way to interfere with the rights of the colored citizens, did not appear; nor, on the other hand, did it appear that there was any extensive secret league among the blacks of any kind.
>
> That the White League would readily co-operate in any feasible scheme for overthrowing the Kellogg government, your committee do not doubt. So will substantially all the white citizens of Louisiana. Such organizations may be dangerous, and are very rarely to be justified.

On March 3, 1875 Congressman S. S. Marshall in his report on Conditions in the South, after his Committee had taken its testimony, made this comment:

> Unless all the rules by which evidence is to be judged and weighed are to be disregarded and ignored, it seems to me that it is very clearly established that the organization in New Orleans known as the White League is not a political organization or formed for political purposes, but that it originated out of the necessities arising from the utter inefficiency of the metropolitan police, paid by the city, it is true, but under the command of the governor. It was proven that crime and lawlessness were rampant; that robberies and burglaries were of almost daily occur-

rence; that citizens, and even ladies of the highest position and respectability, were assaulted and robbed on the most public streets in broad daylight; and that, finally, the very best class of the citizens—merchants, bankers, professional men, and others—organized under the name of the White League for protective purposes.

It will thus be seen that two different Congressional Committees condoned, so to speak, the White League and justified its existence. It could hardly be otherwise with honest men, because as Americans these Congressmen realized that the liberties which our common ancestors had fought for were being denied peaceful and law-abiding citizens, and that the people of Louisiana were ruled by a tyrannical, inefficient and grafting government which had gained power by theft of ballots or the crookedness of a "returning board," and continued in power by the aid of the Federal Government and the presence of Federal troops.

In their hearts these congressmen sympathized with the red-blooded Southerners who had enough spunk to resist injustice and tyranny and were willing to risk their lives and property in this resistance.

The Best People Backed the White League

The best citizens of the State joined in the movement to oust the Kellogg government. When they lost the election of 1872 by fraud — it was generally conceded that the McEnery ticket, a fusion ticket representing the Democrats, conservatives and some Republicans, had won the election — the better class people began to seek ways and means to redeem the State from bondage. The result was the organization of clubs and leagues to promote the interest of good government and to obtain justice at the polls even at the risk of life and limb.*

In New Orleans the best people led the White League movement. The members of the social clubs were most active. "For, as I have before intimated, a plan of it is laid and concerted (as all other matters of importance are) in a club." So wrote Joseph Addison over two hundred years ago. From the Chalmette Club, many of whose members were the founders of Twelfth Night, famous carnival organization, came the first incorporators of the White League. Many members of the Boston and Pickwick Clubs joined the White League. The call to arms and the strategy of the Battle of Liberty Place were planned by a committee which met at the Boston Club.

Of course, hundreds of White Leaguers were not members of social clubs but they were all decent and self-respecting citizens, and any descendant of a member of the White League of 1874 may well be proud of his ancestry. In

---

In 1872 Hugh McCloskey and Archibald Mitchell attempted the organization of a military force at a mass meeting held at the Iron Building.
— Times-Democrat

fact, the membership of the League while including many from the more humble walks of life, actually was a most representative one. I have already quoted Gov. Kellogg who said the Crescent City White League was "composed of some of the best men in the city, unexceptional in their private relation. . ." And the Congressional Committee of Jan. 14, 1875 which said: "They comprise a large number of reputable citizens and property holders in the City of New Orleans." Congressman Marshall, a month and a half later, reported: ". . . . finally, the very best class of the citizens — merchants, bankers, professional men, and others — organized under the name of the White League for protective purposes."

General Badger testified:

> Q. What is the character of the men composing the White League?
>
> A. Most of them are gentlemen of good standing, and men of property; others, I believe, are not.

The rolls of the White League and its military and "protector" companies who were on duty on September the 14th, 1874 contain the names of New Orleans' best. In the course of time it will become an Honor Roll upon which those of generations remote from now will be proud to find their names listed.

CHAPTER V

BACKGROUND FOR BATTLE

In the Spring and Summer of 1874, the people of Louisiana were becoming more restless under the tyrannous and illegal government of William Pitt Kellogg. In New Orleans there was considerable disorder and the colored population was getting out of hand.

James Lewis (colored), the Administrator of Improvements for the City of New Orleans, testified before the congressional committee: "It was generally customary, however, that when the colored militia turned out for the soda water fountains and ice-cream saloons to close their doors." White women were on occasion insulted and crime was rampant. Negro Republicans beat up and mistreated the Negro Conservatives. An air of tension prevailed.

The *New Orleans Bulletin* on September 5, 1874 reported:

> There was a turbulent time about the Third Ward Polling Place on Poydras near Liberty. Gangs of riotous Negroes, incited by ex-coroner Pat Creagh and ex-Special Officer, Billy Welsh, committed the most flagrant outrages against the white people in the neighborhood.

Mr. J. M. West was assaulted and beaten by a crowd of Negroes and arrested for carrying concealed weapons.

The *Bulletin* continued:

> The intelligence that the government has ordered U. S. troops to Louisiana has been accepted by the carpetbaggers and Negroes as a license to commit all sorts of outrages, and the effect upon the Negro population was almost instantaneous. From being comparatively polite and decent, they became excessively arrogant and insulting.

On June 30, 1874 the city was alarmed by the appearance of the following article in the *Picayune* of that date:

> A BLACK LEAGUE—WHAT ITS MEMBERS PROPOSE TO DEMAND—THE FOURTH OF JULY APPOINTED—A GRAND COUP FOR CIVIL RIGHTS.
> Information reached us yesterday of a determination on the part of the colored people now in our city to seize the occasion of the coming Fourth of July for a grand *coup* on the white people to enforce their "civil rights," if need be, at the point of the bayonet; certainly, in so far as drinking-saloons, soda-water and refreshment stands are concerned, and, as far as possible, otherwise. The details of the undertaking appear to be about as follows:
> On that day there was to have been, and, in as far as is known, will yet take place, a grand parade of the colored militia, who have all been furnished with the finest kind of arms and ammunition by the State government. They have been also in the past furnished with ball-cartridges, or at least had them at their armories in easy reach.

THE BATTLE OF LIBERTY PLACE

On this day in question, it was decided by the members who had joined the league, and who are nearly all members of the militia, to have their ammunition-boxes filled with *ball-cartridges* and their guns loaded for instant use. On their march, and wherever they desired, they were to enter all saloons, soda-water stands, and other places of public resort, and demand eatables and drinkables, and, if refused, they were to take them and break everything in the establishment. If resisted, they were to at once fire and kill the proprietor and as many white men as possible, and then, supported by the other colored people who would rally to their support, and, as was expressed, take it for themselves, kill all the men and *keep all the women.*

This scheme may at first appear wild and not worthy of belief, but it was stated to members, and by them believed, that they would be supported by the authorities, and even after they had killed a lot of white men nothing would be done to them and they would easily escape punishment. To the ignorant negroes, the plunder which they could gather during this sack of our city would be sufficient reward, besides the satisfaction of killing off the white men, to induce them to embark in anything, and the leaders firmly believed they would be supported.

The plans of these outrageous communes had, our informant states, so far proceeded, and meetings had been held, one particularly among the colored people in the Second ward, when a prominent white radical addressed them, when some inkling reached one of the commanders-in-chief, and it was ascertained all the balls and cartridges were at once secured and removed where the negroes could not get them. Nothing daunted by this, however, the members were instructed by their leaders to go to the different gun-shops throughout the city and purchase powder, ball, and as many cartridges as possible, without exciting alarm. This, it is stated, has been done, and not a negro on that occasion but will have, where they can easily be obtained, twelve cartridges with cap and ball.

Still further information having reached the powers that be, it appears the metropolitan-police brigade, the only protection the citizens have, will not parade that day, but be placed on guard at the different station-houses throughout the city, to at once quell any disorder. This may throw a damper on the negroes; but it is said that their feelings have been wrought up to such a pitch, not only by their own speakers, but by certain white orators, that they claim they are bound to have what they call *their rights anyhow,* and if they do not get them, they will take them at all hazards.

In this respect it has been stated, unofficially of course, that it would be better to have the proprietors of saloons along the line of march of the colored vandals to close their places as the procession went by.

This, indeed, it is stated, will be the only course by which riot and bloodshed can be spared, and the proprietors are therefore cautioned.

In the face of all this, the question very naturally arises, will the white people of this city quietly submit to these threatened outrages? When it is publicly stated that every white man should be killed, and every negro have a white wife, certain it is that it is time to be up and prepared for the worst. Not that any one should seek or counsel collision; it is only suggested that on that day every white man in the city be prepared.

On July 1st the *Picayune* ran another article:

THE BLACK LEAGUE—EXCITEMENT OVER THE PICAYUNE'S DISCLOSURES—THE TIMES INTERVIEWS GENERAL BARBER FOR INFORMATION—A RESUMÉ OF THE SITUATION AND A SURVEY OF THE PROBABILITIES.

When we gave publicity yesterday morning to an exposé of the designs harbored by an organization known as the Black League, we fully understood that it would produce great excitement; that it would elicit indignant denials from all interested quarters; that it would be received with doubt by the quiet and conservative element of the community.

We were prepared for all this and have not been disappointed.

We understood also, that such a publication should not be made except on the most satisfactory evidence and after the gravest consideration. We went further—and we will say here in public, as we did in private yesterday, had not other circumstances pointed to such designs on the part of the blacks; had not their conduct during the past few months been irrisistibly suggestive of a resolute purpose to possess the State; had not each day's developments both here and in the country indicated the approach of some grave crisis, no amount of proof as to this special matter would have induced us to publish such an article as that of yesterday morning. But all these conditions existed. For weeks past the air has been thick with signs of coming conflict. Everybody has spoken of it; everybody has counseled preparations; and yet, when the Picayune calls attention to one specific case and offers one specific illustration of the necessity of being on guard, there is a vast amount of surprise, and pooh-poohing, and virtuous reproach.

Let us take, for instance, the comments of the evening papers:

We all know pretty well what line the Times is on; statistics, foreign policy, abstract philosophizing—anything but local interests. If the Times didn't follow its established routine of looking after "cheap transportation," "the grain-trade," "cotton-spinning," &c., at stated intervals; if it didn't watch the intrigues of Russia in Afghanistan and keep a severe eye on the encroachments of the Hague in Cambodia—if it didn't do these things, or something equally majestic and far-seeing, why, then it *might* have to take some notice of home affairs, and that, you know, would be awkward, very awkward, indeed.

The Times wants the current to flow placidly and smoothly along—no matter if it be down hill; smoothness is the prime requirement. Consequently the Times, having been notified that something violent and uncomfortable had been spoken of, and that the public was agitated, employed an able-bodied young man to compose a sedative.

One must be struck with the profound and ingenious manner in which this sedative was composed. Assuming that an act of violence were in contemplation by the negro militia and that inquiry were set on foot, who are the parties who, first and loudest, would deny and contradict the proposition?

A. E. Barber, brigadier-general of colored militia; James Longstreet, commander of State militia; the adjutant-general; the superintendent of police.

Every intelligent citizen of New Orleans knows, without being told, why these parties would deny the rumor, and the public can therefore appreciate the striking capability displayed by the Times in interviewing them and none others as to the reported plot of the Black League. Governor Kellogg being absent the Times was not able to add his testimony to that of General Barber, the adjutant-general, and the chief of police; but it must be seen that, with the material on hand, the Times has succeeded in hitting on the very men who, above all others, would not if they could, and could not if they would, give full and honest testimony in the case.

With which valuable and reliable support the Times comes gravely forward and says: Nonsense, gentlemen; there's nothing in all this. We refer you to our distinguished friend, General Barber, who, being a colored man and a militia officer, ought to know all about it. It is all bosh. Let's get back to our affairs in Europe,

Asia, and Africa. And we presume everybody—that is, everybody who believes in the Times—will do so.

As for the Bulletin, it has so repeatedly striven to produce the same excitement which our article of yesterday produced; it has so constantly pointed out the existence and danger and the necessity of preparation; and, finally, it so evidently believes that a plot, similar if not identical with the one described by us, has been formed—it is, in short, so entirely of our way of thinking as regards the white man's question, that we omit any reference to criticisms which evidently spring from a small malice it has not the magnanimity to forego, even in such a crisis as the present.

A REVIEW OF THE SITUATION.

But let us look at the state of affairs on its own merits. There are some people in New Orleans who don't feel like accepting the statements which General Barber sees fit to make through the columns of the Times, and perhaps such people might like to consider the probabilities from a more satisfactory standpoint.

Ever since the spring meeting of the Jockey Club, when this same General Barber presented himself for admission to the grand stand—which admission was very naturally refused—we know there has been a regular avalanche of civil suits for damages against saloons, theatres, and other places of public resort. Pinchback, Joseph, Barber, and a dozen others have made issues and brought them to trial, nearly always with a verdict of some sort in their favor.

This is only one phase of the movement, yet it bears the look of a deliberate and organized scheme.

Another and much graver one has been manifest in the shipment of

ARMS TO THE PARISHES.

When the prosecuting witnesses in the Grant-parish case returned home after the trial, it was known that they took at least seventy stand of arms, with bayonets and fixed ammunition. The spirit in which they left here cropped out on the occasion of a difficulty between the captain of the steamboat and some party just as the bell was ringing to put off, when the notorious Ward, leader of the Grant-parish riot, stepped up to the captain's adversary and said, in the hearing of several gentlemen: "Shoot the damned white hound!" "We'll see you through."

Since that time, how often have we heard of other shipments of arms to the country. How often have we heard from our friends and correspondents in the country of the negroes being armed and organized?

Why is it that in every parish, while the word 'democrat' avails nothing to rouse men from their apathy, the summons of the 'White League' acts like magic everywhere?

Do these facts mean nothing? Do they prove that the entire white population of Louisiana feels uneasy and apprehensive, or are they mere fancies of the disordered mind which no one should trouble himself to notice?

HERE IN THE CITY.

And how is it here? We assume that not even General Barber will undertake to deny that the demeanor of a certain class of negroes has been for some months past significantly insolent and overbearing. Even among the thieves and ruffians we have noticed an access of daring and intolerable outrage. Within a few weeks there have been several assaults by negroes upon white ladies—some in broad daylight, and in the most thickly populated portions of the city.

Have we not observed in the cars, on the streets, at the saloons and places of public resort, a growing persistency of assertion, and a manifestation of resolve, which could only spring from settled and well-defined purpose?

AMONG THE ORGANIZED BODIES.

Scarcely a man who pays any attention to political affairs but has heard, in such shape as to convince him, of the tone taken in the negro clubs. It has been well known for some time that there was a movement among the negroes to secure practically all the nominations for their race; and those who have become acquainted with the nature of the proceedings had at club-rooms know that the temper toward the whites has been one of increasing animosity.

ON DECORATION DAY.

The conduct of the negro militia on decoration day is quite fresh in everybody's memory. They then did, on the spur of the moment, what we yesterday asserted they had arranged to do deliberately and comprehensively on the 4th. They entered a saloon in large numbers and, with boisterous and threatening deportment, essayed to realize those 'civil rights' which seem to form their dearest aspiration. A pistol-shot, an accidental blow, would then have been sufficient to bring on the crisis which we apprehend, and which yesterday morning we endeavored to avert.

Is there anything monstrous or even improbable in supposing that the negroes, having been foiled in that attempt, will seek to renew it on the first convenient opportunity—the more particularly as General Barber and their other leaders continue to assure them, by example as well as precept, that the privileges in question are rightfully and inalienably theirs?

Is there anything foolish, considering all these facts—knowing that the negroes are thoroughly organized on political as well as military basis; that they are drilling nightly in different parts of town; that, above all, their bearing is becoming more and more aggressive as the campaign thickens—is there anything foolish, we ask, in supposing that the time has come for us to take measures of protection?

THE LESSON OF THE AFFAIR.

The case seems very plain. If the plot referred to in yesterday's Picayune had actual existence, our disclosures will serve to thwart it; if there never was such a plot, our article will only have the effect of promoting on the part of the whites an organization which all must admit to be imminently necessary. It matters little whether the issue be made on the 4th or later, at a soda fountain or the polls; no one who has intelligently watched the events of the past few months can doubt that the issue is among the most probable of things, and that our only safety—the best preventive, or, failing that, the surest cure—is effectual preparation.

The public will, of course, decide for itself in this matter. We have given them the material for an opinion, and they may agree with us that there is wisdom in vigilance, or they may accept those assurances of General Barber with which the Times appeals to their respect and confidence. We have our own idea, which is that the negro has ruled and robbed and menaced us quite long enough.

And in the *Picayune* of July 4th, appeared the following article on the same subject:

The Republican Alliance: its constitution, oath, by-laws, grips, signs, passwords and signals.—Full particulars of the secret negro organizations as existing in the parishes.—An intercepted document.

The formation of White Leagues everywhere among the parishes makes it interesting to know what style of organization exists in opposition, among the negroes. The Leagues have been quite frank in avowing their purpose to be the restoration of the white man to power and supremacy; accident enables us to be equally explicit touching the purposes of the Republican Alliance.

The Custom House at New Orleans in 1873. The site was at one time on the levee and Fort St. Louis was built on it. In two hundred years the Mississippi River receded nearly four blocks to the East by building up an extensive batture. The cornerstone of the Custom House was laid in 1849 with Henry Clay as orator of the occasion. It was years before the building was completed. In fact, it was never completed according to the original plan, as the upper floor was never finished. In 1862 General Butler used the Decatur Street side as his office. The United States Post Office was here until 1915. This view from Jewell's New Orleans agrees with the sketch of the same building in the scene of the Battle of the 14th of September which appeared in Frank Leslie's Illustrated Weekly of October 3, 1874.

— *Courtesy New Orleans Public Library*

Most people understand that these parish organizations of the negroes are arranged in New Orleans by a central council, fashioned after one model, and so adjusted that the entire negro force of the State is fused into a single body, manipulated through secret channels and utilized accordingly as necessity and expediency may demand.

The superficial reader may incline to wonder why an organization with such pure and patriotic aims should bind its members to secrecy and provide for their use such an elaborate system of signs, signals, pass-words, &c.

But readers who study more closely—who evolve the significance of the announced platform and the possibilities which may be made to spring from the oath—such readers will be able to harmonize the seeming discrepancies without any trouble. Let it be remembered that this document is intended for the governance of people who are ignorant, credulous, prejudiced, and irresponsible; who understand none of its high-sounding phrases or patriotic declarations; who only know that they are sworn to secrecy and obedience, and that at certain given signals they must assemble for whatever purpose their leaders may have in view. Let these things be borne in mind, we say, and the full relevancy of the 'Republican Alliance,' in all its menace and meaning, grows curiously clear.

CONSTITUTION.

ARTICLE I. This association shall be known as the Republican Alliance, and shall have for its object the protection of life and property and the best interests of the republican alliance.

ARTICLE II. All republicans becoming members of this association shall subscribe the following

OATH.

"I do solemnly swear that I will not deprive any person or persons on account of race, color, or previous condition, of any right, privilege, or immunity now enjoyed by any other class of persons. That I will not reveal but conceal all the political workings of this association from those not members thereof, and will not expose any sign, grip, or password used to distinguish a brother member. That I will not support the nomination or election of any person not a member of this order to any office of trust, profit, patronage, or representation in the parish or State governments until there should be no member of the alliance in nomination therefor, and that if I am elected or appointed to any office under the parish, State, or United States governments, I will not give patronage to any but worthy members of the republican party, giving the preference to competent members of this order. I do further swear to assist, protect, and defend, to the utmost extent of my ability, any brother member of this order in danger or distress; that I will support the Constitution and laws of the United States and of this State, and of this council and of the grand councils of the order, and that I take this oath without mental reservation or purpose of evasion whatsoever. So help me God!"

SIGNS AND PASSWORDS

HAILING-SIGN, DAY.

With the thumb in right vest-pocket, rap three times with forefinger on pocket; answer in same manner use left hand, first and second fingers.

HAILING-SIGN, MOUNTED.

Raise the hat with the right hand, seizing it at the back of the head; answer in same manner.

SIGN BY SOUND.

Three raps—pause—one rap. Answer. Three raps—pause—two raps.

PASSWORD.

Lost, oh found.

RALLYING-SIGN.

The hailing-sign in use, with the words: Will you have the truth? Answer. Hear, hear.

DANGER-SIGNAL.

By night, with voice, Ho! ho! Answer. Hey! hey!

IN CORRESPONDENCE.

Draw a light line diagonally downward from left to right, across the first capital A in the letter.

GRIP.

With the thumb make a short pressure over the person's thumb. Answer by pressing the thumb over the forefinger between the first and second joints.

A true copy.

Attest:

(SEAL)

D. J. M. A. JEWETT,
Superior Grand Secretary.

These articles in the *Picayune* greatly excited the conservative citizens of New Orleans and hastened the formation of the White League.

The leaders of the McEnery *de jure* government became very active. Governor Penn, who was acting governor in the early part of September 1874, tells in a statement he made about the affairs of the White League many years later, that he and others had perfected a plan to kidnap Governor Kellogg and some of his associates and take them out to sea. Governor Penn's plan was to place members of the White League in strategic locations at or near the Statehouse — at that time the old St. Louis Hotel on Royal Street — and at a signal they were to rush into the building, seize the state officers and take them out to sea or to a foreign shore. All to be done without bloodshed. While they were gone the duly elected officials in the McEnery government would take charge, and would become the *de facto* government as well as *de jure*. Penn was enthusiastic for the plan and so were many others. But McEnery would not agree to this scheme, so no attempt was made to put it into effect. It will be seen that Governor McEnery was something of an appeaser, and his idea was that to get control of the government to which he was entitled he must placate the powers in Washington. In fact, he spent much of his time in Washington trying to get recognition. Governor Penn as acting governor was always reluctant to start any trouble and hoped to avoid riots and the shedding of blood.

Seizure of Arms

Now there occurred a series of incidents which helped to bring on the Battle of the 14th. Arms were being brought into New Orleans and Governor

Kellogg with General Badger* of the Metropolitan Police endeavored to stop the flow of these arms. General Badger testified before the congressional committee:

> Arms came here in great numbers for the purpose of arming the White Leagues. Some had obtained their arms by the 1st of September, some had not; but they were constantly arriving. I learned from some of the gun-dealers that they had received large orders for arms from that organization, and in one or more instances I notified them that the authorities would probably not permit them to be distributed, and, in at least one case, a quantity of five hundred that had been ordered, the order was countermanded, and they were not sent here, to my knowledge. They may have been sent here after the 14th of September, after I was wounded.

On Tuesday, Sept. 8, 1874, about 3:30 P. M., Special Officer Pecora, accompanied by Ruiz, seized, at the corner of Camp and Canal Streets, a furniture wagon said to have been loaded with guns. Their authority for this action was a warrant sworn to by Special Officer Smith to the effect that said guns were intended for a riotous purpose, and to be used in the commission of a breach of the peace.

The cases contained guns and ammunition. The guns, 72 in number, reached New Orleans from New York by steamer in the regular course of commerce and were delivered to Mr. Olivier's store on Canal Street, and subsequently bought by Armand Guyol, Leon Fremaux and others. It was while being delivered to the purchasers that the arms were seized by the police, taken to the Central Station and afterwards turned over to Mr. Curtis, the property clerk.

Guyol and Fremaux then appealed to Judge W. T. Houston, First Justice of the Peace for the Parish of Orleans, of the Sixth District Court, who issued a writ of sequestration for 48 guns† with bayonets to be sequestered from A. Pacora, Supt. A. S. Badger and R. Curtis, property clerk. Pecora filed a reply that he had been instructed by Judge McArthur, of the First Metropolitan Police Court, not to turn these arms over to the sheriff but that they must be held to be used as evidence in the case against Guyol and Fremaux. This promoted a conflict between Judges Houston and McArthur with legal complications.

---

*Gen. A. S. Badger, Supt. of the Metropolitan Police in New Orleans, was born in Boston, Massachusetts. He came to New Orleans in 1862 when the city was occupied by the Federal forces as a colonel in the U. S. Army. He settled in Louisiana and married here.

†Armand Guyol's claim was for 24 muskets with bayonets, known as Prussian muskets, and 1,000 cartridges containing a charge of powder and a conical leaden ball —all of the value of $92.00. (Armand Guyol was of a prominent Louisiana family and related to Miss Louise Guyol, well-known writer of the present day. Miss Guyol assisted Ben Ames Williams in the research for material used in his novel of Reconstruction, "The Unconquered.")

Judge Houston hailed Badger, Curtis, Judge McArthur and W. R. Whitaker of counsel into his court and tried them for contempt. On Sept. the 10th before a filled courtroom Judge Houston found them all guilty and sentenced them to imprisonment for 24 hours in the Parish prison. Constables took the men to the prison in cabs. Before having been there an hour pardons arrived signed by the Governor and all were released.

On the same day Armand Guyol, Jr. and Leon J. Fremaux were arraigned before Judge A. H. McArthur (of the First Municipal Court of the City of New Orleans) upon charges made by James L. Smith that they with other persons unknown to him were conspiring to commit the crime of assault and battery upon L. D. Larrieu and other registration officers, and upon Octave Roy and other officers of the Metropolitan Police force; that they had in their possession a large number of stands of arms and a large quantity of ammunition for the purpose of arming various and numerous persons to affiant unknown belonging to a secret and unlawful organization known as the "White League" and so on.

The case was postponed until Sept. 16th, but, of course, never came to trial because the White Leaguers had upset the regular procedure of affairs.

On Thursday evening, the 10th of September, the steamship *City of Dallas* of New York tied up at the wharf near the French Market and prepared the discharge of cargo the same night as usual, but the Customs Officer found on board six cases for A. Olivier labeled "hardware," which did not appear on the manifest. The customs officials refused to deliver the arms to Mr. Olivier. Next day he went to see General Badger of the Metropolitan Police who had taken charge of the six cases of arms. Mr. Olivier told Badger that he had imported the arms as part of his business to sell to his customers. Badger informed him that he would have to return the arms to New York or he would lose them all. Mr. Olivier then agreed to re-ship them to New York.

From the Picayune of Sept. 11, 1874

MORE ARMS SEIZED.

———

THE DETECTIVES TAKE THREE MORE BOXES OF ARMS FROM OLIVIER'S GUN STORE, SEVENTY-TWO MUSKETS.

———

MR. OLIVIER ARRESTED AND TAKEN UP TO THE SIXTH PRECINCT STATION.

———

POLICE JUDGE MILLER ISSUES THE WRIT OF ARREST AND THE SEARCH WARRANT FROM METROPOLITAN HEADQUARTERS.

Yesterday, [Sept. 10th] about the hour of 12, passengers and business men who were on Canal street, between Camp and Magazine streets, noticed that a considerable number of men, who were evidently not loafing, had assembled in different parts of the locality designated. Some of these men were recognized as metropolitan police in citizens' clothes, by those who chanced to know their faces; and others that were there happened to be widely known as members of the detective corps of this city. It was for a while currently reported that they were suspiciously watching a well known hardware store on that part of Canal street, and no active demonstration on the part of these men was expected to-day. But at a little after three o'clock an active demonstration took place; at that time several of the detectives entered Olivier's Gun Store, and presented him with a search warrant and a writ of arrest. No resistance to these proceedings was made on the part of the proprietor of the store. The boxes of Prussian rifles were not concealed; but, on the contrary, in as conspicuous a position as any of the articles in the place.

The detectives immediately took possession of the boxes, which were properly marked as to their contents and the name of the consignees. These were taken down stairs, placed upon a vehicle, and without any hindrance on the part of the bystanders were driven round to police headquarters, where they found a berth beside those which were captured on Tuesday evening.

In an incredibly short space of time between forty and fifty metropolitan police had assembled in close proximity to the gun store in question, in order to back the detectives in effecting their search warrant and writ of arrest, by force if necessary.

This writ of arrest and warrant was issued yesterday [Sept. 10th] at midday by Police Judge Miller, of the Fourth Municipal Police Court. The place where it was issued and delivered was at police headquarters on Carondelet street. It is covered by the same case under which the seizure of the first lot was accomplished, the affidavit being made by the same party, and the writ executed by the same men, with one or two in addition to their former number.

When the writ of arrest was served on Mr. Olivier he made no resistance, but surrendered himself, and was taken up to the Sixth Precinct Station, on Rousseau, near Jackson street.

The affidavit sworn to and the charge made against Mr. Olivier are substantially the same as those of Messrs. Guyol and Fremaux, and this gentleman will probably be a defendant in the same trial.

The Metropolitan Guard, who were present or near the gun store at the time of the seizure, marched in a solid body up to police headquarters with the arms as a sort of armed escort for safe conduct. No demonstration was made by the people to intercept the arms on their way to their new destination; nor at the time was there likely to be any, as the streets are usually comparatively deserted at that hour, as was the case yesterday, and nobody seemed cognizant of the fact that any arms were seized, excepting some fifty or sixty citizens who happened to be on Canal street at the time.

An hour later the news of this additional outrage had circulated pretty freely, and a crowd of several hundred persons assembled on Canal street, between Camp and Magazine, who in an angry and excited manner, but with bated breath, talked over the new phase of events that has turned up in the last three days.

The burden of their discourse was, now that the Municipal Police Judges have taken unto themselves the authority to order the invasion of the private rights and property of the people, what was the next step to be expected.

Mr. Olivier was arraigned before Judge Miller, under the charges mentioned, in the Fourth Municipal Court, and released on bond to appear before Judge Mc-

Arthur on next Wednesday, with Capt. Fremaux and Mr. Guyol.

The *New Orleans Times* of Sept. 13th, 1874:

REPORTED DISTRIBUTION OF ARMS IN THE SECOND WARD

Rumor—the veracity of which we will not vouchsafe—hath it that a large number of guns was distributed last evening to the residents of the Second Ward.

Nine boxes, each containing twenty-four guns, similar to those seized at Messrs. Olivier & Co.'s store—so the story goes—were brought in on the Jackson Railroad yesterday evening, and concealed in the neighborhood of the depot. Last evening they were conveyed to a point near Leeds' Foundry, where a body of men was awaiting their arrival. Immediately on the arrival of the guns they were issued to those in waiting, the recipients taking the weapons to their respective homes.

In corroboration of this statement, at a quarter to 10 o'clock last night John McMullen was arrested on Gasquet street, between Roman and Prieur streets, by Officers Cartwright and Lewis, and conveyed to the First Precinct Station, charged with carrying one of the guns.

The gentleman, who says he is a United States Deputy Constable, had one of the muskets in his possession when arrested, and upon bringing him to the station, a revolver was found on his person, and after an interview between Gen. Badger and the officers, a charge of carrying concealed weapons was entered against him, and he was released on parole to appear when notified.

The *Bulletin* of the 13th commented on this incident as follows:

Last evening, Saturday, as a gentleman was passing out Gasquet Street with his musket on his shoulder, two of the mounted police rushed upon him and demanded his surrender. Overpowered, he had to comply, and was led to the Central Station a prisoner. It is left to Louisiana to be the only State where a man cannot walk the streets openly bearing arms. It is evident Badger intends to seize every white man's gun and pistol while the negroes openly parade theirs. How long will this thing last?

Another account says that Mr. McMullen was an "old gentleman" returning from a hunting trip and that he was arrested by three Negro policemen on horseback. The White League faction contended that his right to bear arms as guaranteed by the Constitution was infringed upon.

There is no doubt that the members of the White League companies were buying arms, importing most of them from the North. But the White Leaguers claimed that they had a perfect right to purchase and own guns and arms; that it was a right guaranteed under the Constitution. The seizure of guns by the Metropolitan Police incensed the people of New Orleans, and was denounced as illegal, unjustified and the act of a dictatorship.

GOV. KELLOGG'S TESTIMONY

Governor Kellogg, in his testimony before the Congressional Committee a few months later, had this to say about the importation of arms by the White League and his belief about its being illegal:

It became evident that arms were being brought here in large quantities; I had information from New York and Baltimore, especially the latter, stating that large shipments of arms were being made by both rail and steamboat, notably one invoice of 26 cases of arms and a large quantity of ammunition. A portion of these arms were sent through Mr. Olliver, [Olivier—Kellogg misspells his name all through the testimony and mispronounced it] a merchant on Canal Street. The local authorities constantly called my attention to it, and, while I regretted the apparently increasing necessity of action, I felt constrained at last to consent to legal proceedings being initiated, looking to the seizure of those arms where they were clearly consigned to clubs.

The first seizure of arms made under legal process was when they were being taken to the Fifth ward club upon a dray. (If it was not that club, it was some other club in the lower portion of the city.) There can be no question, and I need not dwell upon it, that the arms were brought here, consigned, in large quantities, both by rail and steamship, for the avowed express purpose of arming the White League, which had, in addition to this platform I have submitted, printed in the Picayune on the 2d of July, pledged themselves—and I will furnish the committee in this connection with a copy of their pledge—to array themselves against the constituted authorities of the State government.

Thus it was that on the 12th and 13th of September we were confronted with this condition of things. Here were clubs organized already and being increased and augmented, largely armed, and being drilled openly and in defiance of law, as we assumed—drilling in club-rooms, drilling in vacant lots, and drilling in the public streets. Thus it was, just before the *émeute,* as it is popularly termed, on the 14th of September, we were confronted with the fact, that was indisputable, that large quantities of arms were coming here, shipped by both rail and steam ships from Baltimore and other cities, purchased for the avowed and express purpose of arming what was called the White League clubs, and among others was a considerable invoice that had come down on the Mississippi.

Mr. Olliver, the hardware merchant I referred to a short time since, had received the invoice that he had sent to the club, and in transit it was seized. Several smaller invoices had been taken from his store, and he was fully advised that such would be the case. A day or two afterwards Mr. Olliver called and consigned over voluntarily to the police an invoice of the arms upon the Mississippi. It was done without any opposition on the part of Mr. Olliver, and it was done after some hesitation on the part of the local authorities to invade the premises of a private citizen. The arms on the Mississippi, I desire to state, were for a certain club in the city, and my information is such that I do not care to state even the source of the information or the name of the club unless I am especially required to do it, as it was given to me in confidence by one of the members. I stated to this gentleman that I would be glad if I could consistently let these arms go off from the ship, but that I did not think that I could do so; that the bringing of arms, evidently in large quantities, was so formidable, so systematic, and so concerted, and promised so disastrous results to the peaceable community—not only to the peace of the community here but throughout the State and other States, as I had information from other States that they were pursuing the same course in regard to the color line—that I did not see how I could consistently interfere with the action of the police in endeavoring to stop these arms.

So the 14th of September came, and I think, as it is asserted by our friends of the opposition, that the real intent was to go down and take the arms from the Mississippi* for the benefit of this club or the club entitled to them. We were aware

---

*To obtain the arms which came out on the steamship Mississippi was an objective point with both parties. The police, we hear, were the first to appear and de-

of that fact a night or two before. A large quantity had escaped the vigilance of the detective and came in by the Jackson road. The car was switched off on a side track and run to Wiltz's foundry, and some twenty-five cases taken out of the car, the arms taken from the cases, and the men being there, they were distributed to them. I received notice of that within an hour, and an officer arrived there just as the men were taking the last arms. It was very nicely done.

We had known that they were going down to the steamer to take those arms, and the police were in readiness and it is not likely that a large force of police would have been called in requisition, were it not that the day before that a very inflammatory proclamation, or call, rather, signed by quite a number of the business men and firms in town, was published in the local papers, calling upon the people to meet that day in front of the Clay statue, accompanied with the assertion that they intended to be free.

There was in the body of this call a reiteration of some of their grievances, saying that arms belonging to private individuals had been seized, thus denying to the people the constitutional right to bear arms. This same statement had been industriously and assiduously published and repeated in the different papers of the State in those parishes where this thing was fomenting very actively, and it was stated that the Constitution gave the right to a citizen to bear arms. And that clause of the Constitution was constantly quoted as if it was the whole text bearing upon the question of bearing arms, ignoring the language of the clause, "that a well regulated militia being necessary to the security of a free State, the right of the people to keep and bear arms shall not be infringed;" but omitting the first part of the clause, they simply asserted that the Constitution provided that the right of a citizen to bear arms should not be infringed. So, every man, unless he had the Constitution, or was like some of our friends, members of Congress, pretty well acquainted with the provisions of the Constitution, he took it for granted that he had the constitutional privilege to go on the streets or in the cars with his arms, while expressing the purpose at the same time to overthrow the constituted authority of the State and inaugurate revolution, and to meet in broad daylight at the Clay statue for the purpose of co-operating with another organization whose platform avowedly announced its intention of overthrowing the constituted authority of the State. This produced the collision.

The assemblage at the Clay statue passed resolutions calling upon the governor to abdicate, and appointed a committee to request him to do so. The governor told them he could not recognize or receive communications from an armed assemblage in defiance of law. It is unnecessary to go into details of what followed. I never saw the committee. The meeting was addressed by the speakers. Some of them made use of very excitable and inflammatory language; telling them, in substance, after the report of the committee, that they must go home and get their arms and come back. Before the announcement that they should go home and get their arms, a large assemblage of the people appeared. It appears that they immediately left the meeting and commenced barricading at certain points, and developing that degree of discipline and strength that showed the whole thing so far as the armed appearance was concerned, it was a concerted movement.

---

mand the delivery of the arms, and were refused. After that General Ogden, commanding the citizens' troops, applied for them, but the master of the ship declined to surrender them to any except the particular individuals to whom they were consigned. As to the number of these arms, reliable information could not be obtained. Some asserted the number to be ten thousand, and others alleged that the number was seven hundred. Up to this writing neither party had been able to obtain possession of them.
— New Orleans Times, Sept. 15, 1874

I recur again to what I stated, that the primary movement was, to take the arms from the Mississippi. After they had been directed to go to their homes and places of rendezvous and meet, then it was the local authorities, having already taken precautions in consequence of certain information which we had, growing out of the difficulty and of the declared intent the night before, moved up under direction of General Longstreet from Jackson Square, their place of rendezvous near the arsenal, to Canal street.

The Arrival of The Mississippi

The Steamer *Mississippi* reached New Orleans from New York on Saturday evening, September the 12th. She carried a consignment of rifles and ammunition to be delivered eventually to the White League or its members. Governor Kellogg had advance information about this shipment of arms, and issued an order that the arms be seized. As the *Mississippi* had arrived Saturday night and Sunday was a holiday she would begin discharging her cargo Monday morning.

Affairs were now approaching a crisis and the White League would have to act, or lose the large shipment of arms, and perhaps lose "face" with its followers and the public.

Accordingly on Saturday night a secret meeting of the leaders of the White League and Angell's militia was held at the suggestion of Acting-Governor Penn. These leaders were reluctant to take any radical action that might lead to bloodshed unless they felt that the public stood behind them. Gov. Penn said in his recollections written years later:

> A meeting of prominent leaders connected with the McEnery government was called, I stated that I was unwilling to engage in any movement of that character which would only bring disaster; but if a public meeting were called at the Clay Statue* and the citizens of New Orleans showed a spirit of determination to overthrow the Kellogg government, that I, as the acting governor of the State would call out the militia and drive Kellogg's forces from the city. As a result of these deliberations, the meeting was called to assemble at Clay Statue at 12 o'clock on the 14th of Sept. 1874.

Accordingly the following announcement appeared in the newspapers of Sunday, the 13th. The papers commented on it likewise in news and editorial columns.

CITIZENS OF NEW ORLEANS!

> For nearly two years you have been the silent but indignant sufferers of outrage after outrage—heaped upon you by an usurping government.
>
> One by one your dearest rights have been trampled upon, until, at last, in the supreme height of insolence, this mockery of a Republican Government has dared even to deny you that right so solemnly guaranteed by the very constitution of the

---

The Clay statue erected in 1858 was in the middle of Canal Street, between St. Charles and Royal Streets. The site of several famous mass meetings, it was at the foot of this statue that in 1861 Dr. Samuel Choppin aroused the people and secured enlistments for the Confederate Army. He led the crowd in singing La Marseillaise.

CITIZENS' MASS MEETING IN CANAL STREET, AROUND THE CLAY MONUMENT

This is the caption under the illustration which was published in the October 3, 1874 issue of Frank Leslie's Illustrated Newspaper. Note that the artist, Aaron P. Thompson, made this sketch from the viewpoint of the Crescent Billiard Hall, as we see Henry Clay facing the River, and Moody, the Shirt Man, was located on the corner of Canal and Royal.

— *Courtesy Howard-Tilton Library*

GUIDON OF BATTERY "C" CARRIED INTO BATTLE ON SEPTEMBER THE FOURTEENTH

A treasured relic of the battle of the 14th of September is this beautiful silk guidon in the possession of Mr. J. J. Meunier of New Orleans who inherited it from his father, Jules F. Meunier, a member of Battery "C", Captain Glynn's Company.

Note the powder stains at the left. At the top of the frame which encloses it is the original staff which was shot in two by a bullet. The break can be seen in the photograph.

The guidon is about 24 inches by 36 inches. The cannon are gold on a background of red silk.

(Photograph by Frank Allen through the courtesy of Mr. Meunier)

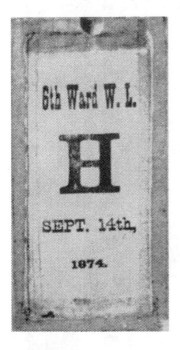

(*At Left*) The badge reproduced here was worn by White Leaguers in a parade celebrating the victory of the Fourteenth, probably on November 7, 1874 after the election, or at a meeting or parade in the Spring of 1875. This badge — a piece of white ribbon imprinted — is in the La. State Museum.

There was no official badge of the White League. George W. Cable in a story in The Century Magazine for August 1889 tells of White Leaguers ordering the closing of a "mixed" school after "flashing" their badges. F. R. Southmayd, then living in Chicago wrote The Century (Nov. 1889) that the Leaguers had no official badge and wore none. Cable replied that "it was common to wear a small button-hole bow of narrow black velvet ribbon with a dotting of white silk on both edges — a badge of the League." It may have been un-official, wrote Cable, or worn only by some companies.

Medal (actual size) presented members of the White League who participated in the affair of the Fourteenth. This bronze medal with the silk ribbon in perfect condition is in possession of Mr. J. J. Meunier of New Orleans and was given to his father, Jules F. Meunier.

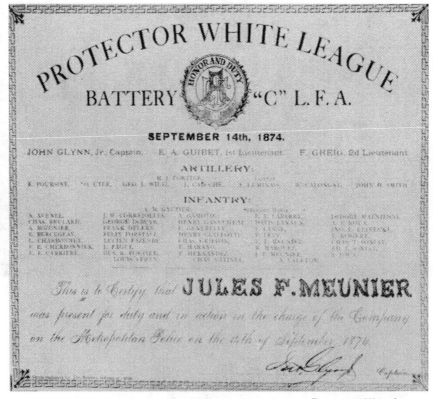

Certificate presented to members of his company — Battery "C" — by Captain John G. Glynn, Jr. Now in possession of J. J. Meunier of New Orleans, son of Jules F. Meunier. (Reduced in size, slightly under one-half)

United States, which in Article Two of the Amendments declares that "the right of the people to keep and bear arms shall not be infringed."

In that same sacred instrument, to whose inviolate perpetuity our fathers pledged "their lives, their fortunes and their sacred honor," it was also declared that even Congress shall make no law abridging "the right of the people peaceably to assemble and petition the Government for a redress of grievances." It now remains for us to ascertain whether this right any longer remains to us.

We, therefore, call upon you on MONDAY MORNING, the 14th day of September, 1874, to close your places of business, without a single exception, and at 11 o'clock, A. M., to assemble at the CLAY STATUE, on Canal street, and in tones, loud enough to be heard throughout the length and breadth of the land, DECLARE THAT YOU ARE, OF RIGHT OUGHT TO BE, AND MEAN TO BE FREE.

(Signed)

M. MUSSON
SAM. BELL
HENRY RENSHAW
JNO. I. ADAMS & CO.
SCHMIDT & ZEIGLER
HARRISON WATTS
W. H. CHAFFE,
CHAS. CHAFFE
J. J. GIDIERE
H. S. ADDISON
J. M. FRANKENBUSH
W. W. EDWARDS
MILLER & DIEHLMAN
SAM FLOWER
NEMMAN & KENT
BEHAN, THORN & CO.
M. HILLARD
B. F. GLOVER
JOHN W. PARSONS
J. B. CAMORS & CO.
N. HINMAN
J. B. SINNOTT
S. H. BOYD
W. W. JOHNSON
J. B. LEVERT
E. B. BRIGGS

JNO. M. PARKER
O. HUARD
PERRY NUGENT
WM. SANCHEZ
M. GILLIS
E. F. DELBONDIO
KEEP & RAYMOND
JULIUS VAIRIN
ROBERT HARE
W. J. HARE
J. J. WARREN
EMILE J. O'BRIEN
S. B. NEWMAN, JR.
JAS. R. BALFOUR
PAUL E. MORTIMER
LEEDS GREENLEAF
J. M. VANDERGRIFF & BRO.
S. K. RUSS
HOLT, MURRAY & CO.
PAUL SANAGER
WOODS, SLAYBACK & CO.
EUG. SONIAT
LOUIS BUSH
WM. A. BELL
JNO. N. PAYNE
HENRY DENEGRE

A Mass Meeting Called

In addition to the newspaper publicity, notices were posted on the sides of buildings and poles. Long strips of paper with date and time of meeting printed on them were pasted on the curbing at street corners in many parts of the city.

In the meantime, officers of the various Protector Companies of the White League and Angell's militia regiment were alerted and instructed to have their companies assembled, armed and ready for action at their various posts by eight o'clock Monday morning. They were to await instructions from Acting-

Governor Penn and the commander of the day, General Fred Ogden, who at that moment had not yet been placed in command.

The members of the White League and Angell's militia companies were not supposed to attend the meeting at the Clay Statue on Canal Street. The orator, who told the crowd of some five or six thousand who had assembled that noon on Canal Street, to go home and get your guns and return here, was speaking rhetorically or with his tongue in his cheek. Such a disorganized mob would have been scattered by one volley from the guns of the Metropolitan Police. The organized groups who were to take part in the fighting were already armed and at their posts of duty.*

The meeting at Clay Statue was a sounding board to determine the feeling of the citizenry, while it gave opportunity for a committee to make demands upon Gov. Kellogg to abdicate and perhaps secure control of the government of the State without further ado.

But there was behind the scenes a group of able, determined leaders who had a definite plan of action, backed up by a well-disciplined organization of patriotic and public-spirited men. Kellogg and his minions overlooked this fact, and thought the White League an assembly of loosely organized groups that would dissolve with the first salvo of grape-shot. In this they were sadly mistaken.

In fact there was some doubt in the minds of the Kellogg crowd that the White League would actually do any fighting. From the *Times*:

> The Hon. Edward Booth, of this city, was interviewed by a Times representative, and in response to an inquiry. Mr. Booth stated that he did not believe there would be any more public meetings for the purpose of deliberating upon action, but that he opined the object of the people was to create such a condition of affairs as would necessitate, as a last resort, military government in this city.

A PLAN OF BATTLE

As a consequence General Longstreet and his staff had no plan of battle. The general probably thought that all he had to do was to march the Metropolitan Police toward any group or armed body of men who would disperse after a few volleys. Gen. Badger, the commander of the Metropolitans, had twenty or thirty detectives, some of whom were members of White League

---

Early on Monday morning the lower part of the third district began to show indications of an armed gathering, in the appearance of numerous squads of men in twos and threes, and later on pickets were posted at almost every street-corner, while at appointed rendezvous the forces were in the receipt of continued accessions until noon, when at various points were concentrated bodies of citizens armed with rifles and shot-guns, but resting thereon as if awaiting further orders.
— N. O. Times, Sept. 15, 1874

companies, circulating around, and from their reports he thought there might be some trouble, but he was not worried over the outcome.

On the other hand the White Leaguers had a plan. They did not disclose it to many beforehand. The *New Orleans Times* of Sept. 23 carried an article based on an interview with Governor Penn, a former military officer, which showed that he and General Ogden were excellent strategists. The article said:

On Friday before the movement was made, the plan of operations was adopted in this city by Lieutenant Governor Penn and Gen. Frederick Ogden. It was determined upon that in the event of the demand for Gov. Kellogg's resignation being denied as it was supposed it would be that then the effort should be made to obtain possession of all the de facto State officials, together with their offices, records, etc.

In the event of that refusal it was agreed that the forces under Gen. Ogden should not assume the initiative, but should maintain a strictly defensive attitude, to which end a line of defense was drawn on Julia street, the right flank resting on the river front and extending to the New Basin, whereupon would be its extreme left. In the rear was the artillery and reserve at Tivoli Circle. This position was admirable in its control of the approaches from several streets, and from the numerous outlets made an excellent and very strong place of concentration in the event of it being necessary to fall back upon that station. The line on Julia street had an admirable constructed breastwork on each street, running parallel to the flanks of the line.

These Defences were composed of the upturned iron street crossings, protected by guards, wagons, mattresses, generally four to five feet in height. The advance of skirmishing parties in a narrow street against these obstructions, exposed to the concentrated fire of sharpshooters, shielded by the breastwork, would have been practically useless, and the employment of artillery would have been equally valueless, because the same concentrated antagonistic fire would have been made under cover of the artillery that the defence could have run up from Tivoli Circle and placed in position.

It was supposed that Major General Longstreet, with the command of metropolitans and such portions of the brigade of colored soldiers as would accompany him must of necessity assume the initiative, and leaving the State House denuded of all defense, march in search of the armed opposition. It was not supposed this attack would be made on the levee; but rather that it would commence by attempting to penetrate the line of defense which would have exposed the attacking force to flank movements that would have caused the assailants to have been surrounded, and would have left the State House entirely within the power of the defensive victorious party.

Governor Penn informed a TIMES representative that the plan of which the foregoing is a skeleton had been agreed upon without any subsequent modification. The movement was confined strictly to this city and there was no understanding of any sort between those who were in it at New Orleans and those in the country. There were between twelve and fifteen hundred men in it belonging to the State militia, and it was assumed that aid would be given by a force of citizens, numbering from one thousand to fifteen hundred men additional. In the event of the capture of the Kellogg officials, it was not proposed that any one of them should be molested, except that they were to be retained as prisoners until their promise was given that each one of them would leave the State. Governor Penn, in a conversation with the writer on this subject, was very positive in disclaiming the idea that any injury would have been offered to any of the State officials in the event of the latter being taken, and said that he well knew, from the excellent discipline of the force under his control, that no attempt would have been made by them to have maltreated the prisoners, who, on the contrary, would have had their lives defended by his command.

It had been alleged in the public prints that a number of gentlemen had counseled to effect the movement. Gov. Penn in allusion to this said that he had assumed all the responsibility of the movement from its inception, and any subsequent division of the burdens by any person voluntarily coming forward to its aid was at variance with the original programme, which was, that he alone was to assume the initiative and maintain whatever responsibility might result therefrom.

Gov. Penn reiterated his statement heretofore published in the TIMES, that he had never for one moment contemplated any interference whatever with the representatives or the property of the General Government, against which no hostile demonstrations of any kind was ever proposed or entertained.

The meeting satisfied the leaders of the White League that the people of New Orleans were behind them.

Judge Alexander Walker said of the Canal Street gathering: "I have never seen a more representative meeting in New Orleans. All classes were there, — bankers, merchants, doctors, lawyers, workmen, laborers, clerks and journeymen, were all together, and all of one mind, that Kellogg must go."

Gov. Penn in his reminiscences years later said: "The mass meeting took place at 12 o'clock. An immense crowd assembled. I left the Boston Club [The Boston Club at that time was on Carondelet Street where the City Branch of the Whitney Bank now is] a little before 12 o'clock and walked through that vast crowd .... I went to military headquarters on Camp Street to meet Ogden and Angell and the officers assembled there."

Penn's headquarters were at the meeting room of the Howard Association* on the second floor of 58 Camp Street, just below Poydras. When Governor Penn arrived at headquarters, the first decision to be made was the selection of the commander-in-chief. As there were two armed bodies, one commanded by Gen. Fred Ogden and the First Louisiana Regiment commanded by Col. Angell, Gen. Ogden requested that the Governor decide who was to be in supreme command. According to Kendall the question was settled without friction when Col. Angell declared at once that he was ready to serve under Gen. Ogden, obey his orders, and cooperate with him in every way. Gov. Penn thereupon issued General Order No. 1, appointing Ogden as Provisional General of the Louisiana Militia and investing him with full command. Gen. Ogden's promotion then advanced Col. W. J. Behan to the command of the White League.

*The Howard Association was a relief organization that aided yellow fever victims. It was active in all epidemics and did great work in the scourge of 1878.

In addition to General Order No. 1, Gov. Penn issued a proclamation to the people of Louisiana and another to the colored people of the State of Louisiana, both of which follow:

A Proclamation to the People of Louisiana

For two years you have borne with patience and fortitude a great wrong. Through fraud and violence the Government of your choice has been overthrown and its power usurped. Protest after protest, appeal after appeal to the President of the United States and to Congress have failed to give you the relief you had a right under the constitution to demand.

The wrong has not been repaired. On the contrary, through the instrumentality of partisan judges, you are debarred from all legal remedy. Day by day taxation has been increasing, with costs and penalties amounting to confiscation of your property; your substance squandered; your credit ruined, resulting in failure and bankruptcy of your most valued institutions. The right of suffrage is virtually taken from you by the enactment of skillfully devised registration and election laws.

The judicial branch of your Government has been stricken down by the conversion of the legal posse comitatus of the sheriff to the use of the usurper, for the purpose of defeating the decrees of the courts; his defiance of law leading him to use this very force for the arrest of the sheriff himself, while engaged in the execution of the process of the court.

To these calamities may be added a corrupt and vicious Legislature concocting laws, in violation of the constitution, for the purpose of guarding and perpetuating their usurped authority—a metropolitan police paid by the city, under the control of the usurper, quartered upon you to overawe and keep you in subjection.

Every public right has been denied you; and, as if to goad you to desperation, private arms are seized and individuals arrested. To such extremities are you driven that manhood revolts at further submission.

Constrained from a sense of duty, as the legally elected Lieutenant Governor of the State, (acting Governor in the absence of Gov. McEnery), I do hereby issue this my proclamation, calling upon the militia of the State, embracing all persons between the ages of eighteen and forty-five year, without regard to color or previous condition, to arm and assemble under their respective officers, for the purpose of driving the usurpers from power.

Given under my hand and seal the 14th day of September, 1874.

D. B. PENN, Lieutenant Governor.

EXEC. DEP'T., STATE OF LOUISIANA,

New Orleans, September 14, 1874.

(General Order No. 1.)

1. Gen. Frederick N. Ogden is hereby appointed Provisional General of the Louisiana State Militia, and will at once assume command and organize the militia into companies, regiments and battalions.

2. Gen. Ogden will report the names of his staff, regimental and company officers to this department forthwith, to be commissioned.

By command of

D. B. PENN,

Lieutenant Governor, Acting Governor and Commander-in-Chief of Louisiana State Militia.

NEW ORLEANS, Sept. 14, 1874.

To the Colored People of the State of Louisiana:

In the grand movement now on foot against the enormities of the rule of Kellogg's usurpation, rest assured that no harm is meant towards you, your property or your rights.

Pursue your usual avocations, and you will not be molested.

We war against thieves, plunderers and spoliators of the State, who are involving your race and ours in common ruin.

The rights of the colored, as well as of the white races, we are determined to uphold and defend.

D. B. PENN,

Lieutenant Governor, Acting Governor and Commander-in Chief
of Louisiana State Militia.

The *Picayune's* description of the meeting:

MASS MEETING

THE ASSEMBLAGE AT CLAY STATUE

At about half-past 11 o'clock Mr. R. H. Marr and other gentlemen of the Committee of Seventy, called together the people around the Crescent Billiard Saloon.*

Some five thousand men quickly assembled and M. Musson was unanimously called to the chair, which he took.

Vice Presidents—Sam. Bell, H. Renshaw, J. I. Adams, Perry Nugent, Sam. Flower, S. H. Boyd, M. Gillis, Robert Hare, Jules Vairin, Louis Bush, J. J. Gidiere, J. K. Russ, J. J. Warren, Jules Tuyes, J. M. Seixas, J. B. Woods. Secretaries— W. J. Buddendorf, A. Kearns, H. C. Thomas and L. A. Harris.

Mr. Marr then read an address to the people of Louisiana, showing the right the people had to bear arms. He then read a series of resolutions, as follows:

Whereas, at a general election held in Louisiana on the 4th day of November, 1872, Jno McEnery was elected Governor by a majority of nearly ten thousand over his opponent, William Pitt Kellogg, and D. B. Penn, Lieutenant Governor, by a majority of fifteen thousand over his opponent, C. C. Antoine,

And whereas, by fraud and violence, these defeated candidates seized the Executive chair,

And whereas, from time to time by other irregular, fraudulent and violent acts, in the face of the report of the committee of the United States Senate, appointed to investigate the affairs of Louisiana, "That the existing government of the State is a usurpation, the result of violent abuse of judicial functions, and sustained simply by force," W. P. Kellogg has continued himself in power, to the great wrong and outrage of the people of the State of Louisiana, and to the imminent danger of republican institutions throughout the entire country.

And whereas, with a view to controlling and determining the results of the approaching election, to be held in Louisiana in November next, he has, under an act known as the "registration act," and passed for the purpose of defeating the popular will, secured to himself and his partisans the power of denying registration to *bona fide* citizens, whose applications before the courts for a mandamus to compel the assistant supervisors to enroll and register them has been refused, the registration law punish the courts if they dare to take cognizance of such appeals.

The second floor of this building is now occupied by the Pickwick Club.

Mass Meeting of Citizens before the Crescent Hall, corner of Canal and St. Charles Streets, as pictured by the New York Daily Graphic, Sept. 23, 1874. Note the St. Charles Hotel at the left.

And whereas, by false and infamous representations of the motives of our people, he has received the promise of aid from the Federal army, placed at the orders of the Attorney General of the United States, and subject to the calls of United States supervisors, for the purpose of overawing our State and controlling the election.

And whereas, in the language of the call for this meeting, "one of our dearest rights have been trampled upon," until at last, in the supreme height of its insolence, this mockery of a republican government has even dared to deny that right so solemnly guaranteed by the constitution of the United States, which declares "that the right of the people to bear arms shall never be infringed."

Be it resolved, That we reaffirm solemnly the resolutions adopted by the white people of Louisiana, in convention assembled at Baton Rouge, on August 24, 1874:

That the white people of Louisiana have no right to deprive the colored people of their rights.

That W. P. Kellogg is a mere usurper, and we denounce him as such.

That his government is arbitrary, unjust and oppressive, and can only maintain itself through Federal interference; that the election and registration laws under which this election is being conducted, were intended to perpetuate the usurpation by depriving the people, and especially all naturalized citizens, of an opportunity to register and vote.

Therefore, in the name of the citizens of New Orleans, in mass meeting assembled, and of the people of the State of Louisiana, whose franchise has been wrested from them by fraud and violence, and all of whose rights and liberties have been outraged and trampled upon—

We demand of WM. PITT KELLOGG HIS IMMEDIATE ABDICATION.

Resolved, That a committee of five be immediately appointed by the Chairman to wait upon W. P. Kellogg, to demand of him an immediate answer, and to report the result of such interview to this meeting.

Mr. Marr continued to speak. The committee would wait on Kellogg, would go without arms, open or concealed, and would immediately report to the meeting Gov. Kellogg's answer to the demand of the people. Mr. Marr asked the meeting not to adjourn until the committee reported Kellogg's answer.

The following gentlemen were then named as the committee: R. H. Marr, Jules Tuyes, J. M. Seixas, J. B. Woods and Samuel Choppin.

At about 1 o'clock, the committee sent to Kellogg returned in carriages amid a series of cheers that never were heard in all history, until the very air rang with shouts.

Mr. Marr appeared at once on the gallery and made the report of the committee. The committee had called at Kellogg's office, but found him not there.

Henry C. Dibble, who reported himself as being on Kellogg's staff, received them, and they laid the demand of the people before him. Dibble demanded a few moments consideration, retired and then returned with a communication nominally from Kellogg, but with no signature thereto.

This communication recited that Kellogg had learned that large bodies of armed white men were congregated in various portions of the city, at the same call as the mass meeting, and who were summoned to enforce the demand of the people; that he could only regard this as a menace, and a menace to which he could not yield; but if the people would meet peaceably in mass meeting, he (Kellogg) was perfectly willing to listen to their petitions.

The committee replied to Dibble that it was false, that there were no armed men on Canal street, and that no men had been called to enforce the demand of the people, and that if Kellogg resigned he would not be at all hurt.

Mr. Marr then left it to the people to decide what they should do, whether they should endure this any longer, or rise and drive out the usurper.

Cries of "Hang Kellogg," "We'll fight," "Call out the troops."

Dr. Beard then came forward, and with glowing words called on the people to defend their rights, to come armed to hold the city against Kellogg and all his hirelings, to make the whole city an armed camp, and never to leave it until the last of Kellog's gang left the city. Their wives, their brothers, would bring them food and cheer them in their fight.

The crowd received this with another round of cheers, and called for immediate action and for leaders.

Mr. Marr then addressed the people, telling them to go home and get their arms and report at Canal street at half past 2. At that time they would find leaders and an organized body there, who would properly draft and arrange all military matters and furnish guns; and that then the action to be taken by the people could be determined on.

In the greatest earnestness, enthusiasm and excitement the crowd broke up in couples and groups.

MONDAY, THE FOURTEENTH

The *New Orleans Times* in its relation of the events of the morning of the 14th reported:

At an early hour, say 9 o'clock, members of the various leagues and other politican organizations were on the move. Small detachments or squads were in various parts of the city and appeared to be going to their respective places of rendezvous.

RENDEZVOUS OF WHITE LEAGUERS.
Sept. 14, 1874. (From Harper's Weekly, Oct. 10, 1874)

At ten o'clock it was reported that a strong force, said to be a White-League guard, was stationed at the junction of Chartres and Esplanade streets. The particular object in guarding that point and preventing persons from passing at that point could not be learned.

The guard at the Junction of Chartres and Esplanade streets was widely estimated at eight hundred men, but the number probably did not exceed 250 or 300. They are under arms and maintain all the discipline of well-drilled troops.

A like collection of forces was reported in various portions of the city.

A report was announced at Clay's statue, as early as ten o'clock, that a large force of the White-Leagues under arms had assembled at Eagle Hall.* A portion was quartered in Coliseum Place, and many more were assembled in and around the hall.

It was apparent that, so far as the people in the streets were concerned, there was no absolute knowledge as to what would happen, or what would be the character of the meeting. Some said "A fight;" some said the purpose was to guarantee the safe landing of arms from a steamship just in port from New York, but a majority thought the action would not be warlike. A meeting, resolutions, speeches, and a strong protest would be made, and then all would be quiet again.

The absence from Canal street of well-known leaders was remarked, and that was regarded as the most ominous indication of the morning.

*Eagle Hall — the headquarters of the White League — was two-story brick building on Prytania Street between Urania Street on the South leading to Coliseum Place and Felicity Street on the North running towards the River. It had a gallery overlooking the sidewalk. Afterwards for many years it was occupied by Ballejo's Grocery Store, noted for fine groceries and remembered by many Orleanians of today. The building somewhat altered is still there.

In the southern portions of the city, after ten Sunday night, were traversed by little bands of men, numbering from four to ten in each squad. These parties were so numerous as to suggest the possibility of their members having returned from meetings, although no public gathering is known to have taken place.

The southern and western portions of the city gatherings of men commenced about nine o'clock Monday, but it would be impossible to state from the conversational tone pervading the various groups whether these assemblages were prompted by any other motive than the indulgence of speculation as to the meeting to-day.

About nine o'clock a. m. Monday, a very considerable body of men gathered about various localities in the Fifth ward. Some of them exhibited revolvers, pistols, knives, and those with whom the Times representative entered into conversation stated they "had guns which they would use when needed."

The tone of these groups was rather of uncertainty as to their intention than the indication of fixed purpose in any fixed direction. Those who did indulge in sanguinary threats were youths mostly under or having only recently attained their majority.

Canal street was thronged with male pedestrians all morning, and, about ten o'clock, a number of stores on the western end of Canal street were closed.

As the hour of noon approached, the stores on Canal street, and on the cross streets for several squares on either side of Canal, were rapidly closed, and by 1 o'clock all business was suspended. In the meantime the number of people steadily increased in all the main thoroughfares.

In addition to the barricade of Poydras and Camp streets, numerous other crossings in the Third ward were similarly defended, Commercial alley and Saint Charles being blockaded by a street-car forcibly taken from the Saint Charles street track.

These barricades and the stationing of pickets were precautionary measures against attacks by the metropolitans, and not to the interference of peaceably-disposed wayfarers, who were permitted to come and go without hinderance. This plan is an adaptation of the system adopted by the Parisians in the various revolutions inaugurated.

At 2 p. m., upwards of four hundred men were resting on their arms under the awnings on Poydras and Magazine streets, awaiting the commands of their officers.

Numerous other bodies were drifting around, some armed and others not, preserving strict military discipline throughout.

At two o'clock of the afternoon of the 14th, according to the testimony of General Badger before the Congressional Committee, a body of armed men took possession of the City Hall. The telegraph office was seized and communications with police stations interrupted. The *New Orleans Times* reported the seizure as follows:

Early in the afternoon a detachment of citizen soldiery, under the immediate command of Captain Frank McGloin, arrived in front of the city-hall, where the mayor and administrators, with the exception of Mr. Fitzenreiter, were then in executive session, presided over by Mayor Wiltz. Capt. Frank McGloin entered the hall, and, asking for the mayor, told him that he (McGloin) demanded the immediate surrender to him of the city-hall. Mayor Wiltz replied that he was a native of New Orleans, and that he well knew that he (Wiltz) was no coward, but that he would not surrender possession of the hall to any one. The mayor then asked the authority whereon this demand to surrender was based, while the captain, answering that he did so by order of Lieutenant-Governor Penn, added that he supposed he would have to resort to force, and accordingly ordered a sergeant and ten men into the building.

An overt act had been committed and Longstreet and Badger decided to act. Longstreet ordered Badger to advance to Canal Street with his force of Metropolitan Police. In a short time the battle was on!

Citizens erecting a barricade of street-cars and bill-boards on Canal Street. (From Frank Leslie's Illustrated Newspaper, Oct. 3, 1874)
— *Courtesy Howard-Tilton Library*

CHAPTER VI

THE BATTLE OF CANAL STREET

Immediately after the meeting at the Clay Statue, it became evident that serious matters were at hand.

The result of the meeting and the fact that various members of the White League, armed with every variety of weapon, were taking positions in all parts of the City, was reported to Gen. Badger who at that time with nearly all of his force of Metropolitan Police was at the police station at Jackson Square, on the ground floor of the Cabildo. Gen. Badger had a Gatling gun and a few small brass Howitzers. Several police captains were in charge of their commands, all well armed and apparently in good spirits.

The headquarters of Gen. Ogden, Commander-in-Chief of the League with his staff, was at Kurscheedt & Bienvenu's store at 114 Camp Street.

By three o'clock in the afternoon, the White Leaguers had disposed their forces in accordance with good military tactics — armed and prepared for action. Their lines were laid along Poydras Street, running from St. Charles to the river. Barricades were placed at every street running parallel to St. Charles. On Camp Street a barricade of barrels and logs was erected. At St. Charles Street horse cars were overturned and the pavements were pulled up forming a sort of ditch or ravine.

Gen. Longstreet, Adjutant General of Kellogg's militia, and Gen. A. S. Badger, Supt. of the Metropolitan Police, were in command of the Kellogg forces. At the State House, the old St. Louis Hotel, on St. Louis Street, between Royal and Chartres Streets, there were 400 colored militia. All the doors and windows in this building were locked, bolted and barricaded. There was a gathering here of idle Negroes, many of them with political affiliations.

At the Cabildo in the Third Precinct Police Station on the lower floor, and the Supreme Court rooms in the upper floor of this building, were several hundred Metropolitan Police, amply provided with guns and ammunition. Orleans Alley ("Pirate's Alley") and St. Ann's Alley (Cabildo Alley) were shut off from all traffic including pedestrians, and guarded by the police. In Orleans Alley there were some 30 Uhlans (cavalry) with their horses tied to the Cathedral fence and in Jackson Square was the artillery.

Headquarters of Gen. Ogden at Kurscheedt & Bienvenu's Store at 114 Camp St. (N. Y. Daily Graphic, Sept. 23, 1874)

From St. Louis Street downtown all the stores on Royal Street were closed, as well as stores in the other parts of the City, and a continuous crowd kept pouring into Canal Street.

After the departure of the committee that demanded his resignation, Kellogg took refuge in the Customhouse. Gen. Longstreet tried to get instructions from the Governor on what to do. The Governor told the General he had things in charge and he, the General, was to handle the situation.*

In the basement of the Customhouse were 150 Federal troops. Several hundred Negroes were likewise congregated there.

Gen. Longstreet, in arranging the "plan of battle" for the engagement which was likely to ensue, ordered Badger to base his force on the Customhouse, so that his artillery could enfilade South Peters, Tchoupitoulas and the

---

*There was no intention, so far as I was concerned, to provoke any collision but, it seems to me I can well leave with General Longstreet, in command of the militia of the State, and General Badger, in command of the metropolitan police, discreet and experienced officers, to their judgment and discretion what course to pursue. I gave no specific order. I told Judge Dibble, who was acting on my staff, I having left the State-house, I think, about 10 or 11 o'clock, to state to General Longstreet that he, commanding General Badger, as he did, must use his own judgment in regard to the disposition of the local force. Suffice to say that the forces were moved up near the custom-house. It is disputed who fired the first shot, and I think it is immaterial. There was a collision; 11 or 12 men were killed on the side of the local authorities, and I am told those wounded at that time and who subsequently died, numbered very nearly as many again; fifty on the part of the police and militia were wounded, and I am unable to say how many of the opposition — making a grand total of killed and wounded of 90. The State-house was taken possession of; and the rest is a matter of history.

— Gov. Kellogg's testimony before the
Congressional Committee

The St. Louis Hotel became the State House in 1874 when the Louisiana Legislature authorized the purchase of the building. The original St. Louis Hotel was completed in 1838 at a cost of $1,500,000. It burned in 1841 and was rebuilt immediately at a cost of $1,000,000— one of the world's finest hotels, with statuary and mural decorations by great artists. Closed in 1862 when the city was captured, it re-opened in 1866, but soon closed again. When it became the State House the sec- ond story was floored over to be used as the House of Representatives. Much damage was done to the rooms and appointments by the legislators, their friends and the general public. On the 14th of September several thousand persons were cooped up in the building, and in the spring of 1877 some 800 of Packard's followers lived there for two months in a state of siege without garbage disposal and with little care for the property. In 1884 after the capital was moved to Baton Rouge, the building was sold and opened as the Hotel Royal. This failed after a while, and re-opened in 1903. This venture did not succeed. The building stood until 1915 when it was torn down, not because of safety requirements, but because the owner would not spend the money to rat-proof it. The illustration is from Jewell's New Orleans, 1873, but the drawing probably shows the building as it stood before the War.
—*Courtesy New Orleans Public Library*

streets where the enemy seemed strongest. Badger suggested that in this arrangement his left flank would be exposed to danger and that the troops should be posted nearer to the river. Longstreet resented this suggestion. He gave a written order that his plan would be carried out.*

At about three o'clock Badger sent about 150 men up Chartres Street to be stationed in front of the State House.

At four o'clock 500 Metropolitan Police with six pieces of light artillery under Generals Longstreet and Badger advanced up Chartres and Decatur Streets and stationed themselves around the Customhouse where Kellogg himself had taken refuge. Ten men under Sergeant Taylor were sent up to Canal Street to disperse the crowds of people, but when the squad reached Camp, a shot was fired at them whereupon the sergeant and his men fled ingloriously.

The forces of the White Leaguers were in formation all the way from St. Charles Street to the river. A few minutes after four, the Metropolitans opened fire with one Gatling gun and two 12-pounder Napoleon guns. A short fight ensued. Detachments of the White Leaguers, under Col. Behan and Captain Glynn, went up on the levee and hiding behind cotton bales and freight attacked the Metropolitan Police on their flank. The Metropolitans scattered and ran back towards the Customhouse. Badger was shot from his horse and his men, thrown into disorder, left him and fled. Capt. McCann of the Metropolitans surrendered to the White Leaguers. Other Metropolitans threw down their guns, pulled off their hats and coats and ran. Some jumped into the river. The citizens' forces captured two Napoleon guns and one Gatling with ammunition, and 75 to 100 Winchester rifles. General Badger was wounded four times while endeavoring to rally his stampeding forces. His life was saved by a White Leaguer.

The fight lasted only about fifteen minutes. The Metropolitans retreated to Jackson Square. General Ogden had his horse killed under him and he fell to the ground but got up unhurt. There was some little sniping by the Metropolitans from the Customhouse and buildings on Canal Street. The United States soldiers in the Customhouse took no part in the action.

The losses of the White League were 16 killed and 45 wounded, and of the Metropolitan Police, 11 killed and 60 wounded. It is believed that more of the Metropolitan police and their allies were killed than is shown by the record. Some of those killed were bystanders who took no part in the action.

---

*Eleven years later in a newspaper interview, Gen. Badger blamed Longstreet for the wrong disposition of his troops with consequent quick defeat. Longstreet a few days later replied that he did not give such an order to Badger. The statements of these two generals are given in another place.

Various estimates of the strength of the opposing forces have been made, most of them exaggerated. Some have said that the White League "army" numbered from 6,000 to 8,000 men. Actually the total enrollment of the White League companies and the companies of Angell's regiment of militia, "Louisiana's Own," numbered about 1800.* Of these only three or four hundred took part in the fighting. But all the others were on duty and held their posts during the day and many during the night.

Of the Kellogg forces the Metropolitans numbered about 550 with 400 colored militia in the Statehouse, and according to Col. Richardson there were three regiments of Negro militia garrisoned in the old Parish Prison on Tulane Avenue.

The next day the White Leaguers captured the Statehouse and the police headquarters in the morning. The Battle of Canal Street was over but the triumph was shortlived as later events proved.

New Orleans Times' account of the fight, September 14, 1874.

THE CONFLICT—BATTLE ON THE LEVEE BETWEEN THE WHITE-LEAGUERS AND THE METROPOLITANS—THE LEAGUERS ROUT THE POLICEMEN, CAPTURE THREE GUNS, KILL TWENTY OF THEM AND WOUND MANY OTHERS—SEVEN WHITE-LEAGUERS KILLED—A SHARP ENGAGEMENT OF CANAL STREET NEAR THE LEVEE— THE METROPOLITANS DRIVEN OFF—THEY TAKE REFUGE IN THE CUSTOMHOUSE

At 1.30 the streets leading to the general rendezvous of the White Leaguers were peopled with squads of armed men, in bodies of forty and fifty, marching to the appointed meeting-places, preparatory to reporting at Clay statue.

At 1.35 a body of one hundred and sixty men, armed with Winchester rifles and muskets, under command of Colonel Lagardere [LeGardeur], marched up Camp street from Canal, attended by a very numerous concourse of curious people.

AT 3 P. M.—THE RENDEZVOUS ON POYDRAS STREET.

At 3 o'clock the concentration of citizen forces on Poydras street, in the neighborhood of Camp, amounted to perhaps six hundred men, and their command was assumed by Col. F. N. Ogden.

The forces were supplied with five brass field-pieces, which had been cast at two of our city foundries, and until 4 o'clock no active measures were taken beyond the sending out of pickets at each corner as far as Canal street on the north, the levee on the east, and Baronne street on the west, the main body resting on their arms awaiting further developments.

At the same time a barricade was thrown up on Camp street, at its intersection with Poydras, the material therefor being furnished by old lumber, dry-goods boxes, &c., which were brought from wherever they could be found.

The Picayune in its account of the events of the 14th reported that at 10 p. m., 600 or 700 White Leaguers were permitted to go home, leaving about 1,000 armed men on duty all night.

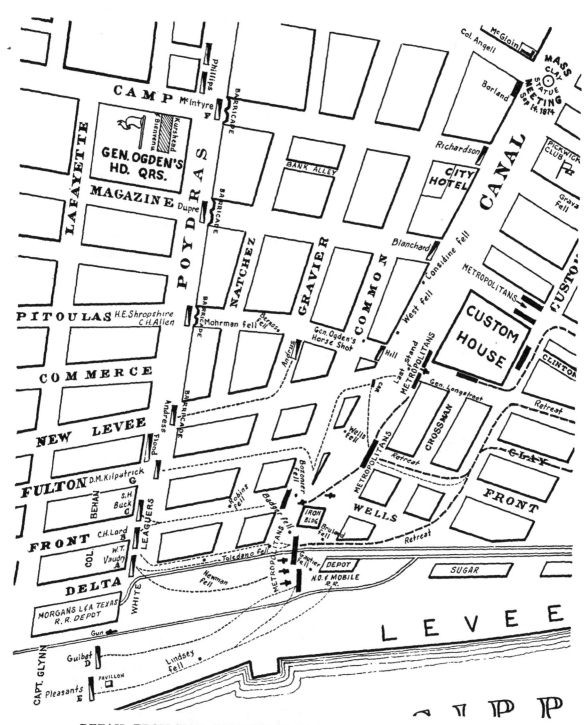

DETAIL FROM MAP, "BATTLE OF NEW ORLEANS FOR FREEDOM"

September 14, 1874

The complete map, somewhat reduced and without the printed description of the battle, is printed elsewhere in the book. The section of the map shown here gives the disposition of most of the units engaged, and plots the course of the battle. The action began on the river front and the heaviest fighting took place there, with the Metropolitans making their last stand in front of the Custom House. From there they retreated to the Arsenal at the Cabildo on the Corner of Chartres and St. Peter. The spots where most of the martyrs fell are marked. Gourdain was killed on Chartres near Conti.

This detail does not show the movement of Capts. Tennison and Phillips, who as a feint, took their companies from the Corner of St. Charles and Poydras to Carondelet across Canal and down Bourbon, turning at Bienville where they attacked the Metropolitans in the rear at Chartres and Bienville as they retreated.

In addition to this, the iron bridges at the street corners were taken up, and it looked altogether as if the intention was to remain intrenched until attacked.

At 3.45 p. m. a commotion on Canal street, at the Camp-street crossing, turned out to indicate that the metropolitans were on the march up Chartres street, attended by eight pieces of artillery, and commanded by Generals Longstreet and Badger. Reaching Canal street they drove the citizen pickets, who retreated up Camp street to Poydras.

The metropolitans turned down Canal street to a point before the custom-house, where they halted.

At a quarter to four o'clock the police under command of Generals Badger, James Longstreet and staff, arrived at the head of Canal street where, without delay, they were placed in line of battle.

One company of police was stationed on the levee side of the iron building, guarding the rear. On the upper side of the building another company was assigned. A line of police then extended across Canal street, near Old Levee street. Two brass twelve pounders and a mitrailleuse were then placed facing the woods, while a detachment of men blockaded the pavement on either side of the guns. A six-pounder was then placed in a position commanding the upper portion of Old Levee street. Squads of men patrolling the crossings of the streets, and the mounted police out as skirmishers, describes the position of the 600 metropolitans as they appeared before the fight, being so arranged as to form a square in the center of which were the officers.

At this time the White-Leaguers, about fifteen hundred strong, were on Poydras, awaiting the signal to call them to the fray.

At four o'clock about three hundred White-Leaguers, under command of General Ogden, marched out on the levee and down toward Canal street, being in a measure protected by the freight.

In the meanwhile the metropolitan scouts had reported the move and in an almost incredible time the position of the guns and men was shifted facing the levee.

With unflinching courage the White-Leaguers continued their march, notwithstanding the action of the police was plainly visible. On they went, until directly opposite the head of Canal street, where a halt was ordered.

Almost instantly the metropolitans opened fire with the Winchester rifles, which was instantaneously responded to by the White-Leaguers.

The deadly mitrailleuse of the police was then brought to bear and one round fired, echoed by the twelve-pounders belching forth their missiles of destruction, one of the balls striking a lot of hay, setting it on fire, which broke forth in a sheet of flame and volumes of smoke, increasing the danger of the White-Leaguers.

Nothing daunted by this new adversary, the White-Leaguers maintained a steady fire, telling with fearful effect in the metropolitan ranks. After the first few rounds the police cast discipline to the winds, and some fled with fear, while others stood their ground. Several policemen, in particular, placed themselves on the lower side of the office in the Chattanooga Railroad station, where, screened from the bullets and buckshot of the White-Leaguers, they kept up a running fire.

The order to charge the battery was then given to the White-Leaguers, and with a victorious shout they advanced upon the foe, who turned and fled pursued by their adversaries, who ever and anon would deliver a ball with telling effect at the retreating foe.

In the charge General F. N. Ogden's horse was shot and instantly killed, but nowise deterred by this accident, the general led on his men on foot.

The guns were then taken possession of and in a short time the battle-field was deserted, all engaged in following the defeated metropolitans.

The police sought refuge in the custom-house, which was opened on their approach, where they assumed positions in the topmost portion, and continued their fire at the White-Leaguers, who returned ball for ball.

On the battle-ground lay about ten policemen, some dead and others dying, killed and wounded at the first fire, and only one White-Leaguer, who was evidently killed in the charge, as he lay about midway between the levee and the iron building.

In and around the station were four more dead metropolitans, while on the front streets six more had yielded up their lives.

THE POOR PEELERS—THEY WERE SADLY DEMORALIZED

It appears that only about fifty metropolitans succeeded in getting in the custom-house, while the balance ran to the Third-precinct station, where they remained.

Last evening, after the fight, as about fifty of them were hurrying to the station, they were met by a squad of White-Leaguers. Immediately upon seeing them the metropolitans at once said that they wanted to go home, and surrendered their guns and pistols; some of them even taking off their coats to conciliate their captors.

THE SITUATION AT 6 P. M.

At 6 p. m. th situation was in *statu quo* on the upper side of Canal street. All firing had ceased, and the league were engaged in erecting barricades. In some instances the barricades were made of a rude jumble of boxes and planks, while in others the granite was torn up and placed in an upright position, making a very effective barricade. The men were resting on their arms or burnishing them up for after-use. Pickets were placed on the sidewalks to prevent people not belonging to the league from congregating and blocking up the passage. Barricades were erected on nearly all the street-corners from Canal street to Julia, between Saint Charles and the levee.

MIDNIGHT.

At midnight the situation was unchanged. Twenty-one hundred additional arms were distributed to the leaguers, who maintained a strict watch over their barricades. Sentinels were thrown out at every corner as far as the south side of Canal street, and passengers not belonging to the league were challenged. The barricades were by this time entirely built, and the companies were congregated in the neighborhood of Poydras street.

(From the *New Orleans Bulletin-Supplement,* Sept. 22, 1874)

The Revolution. The Events of Liberty Week. The Fight—The Victory—The Spoils—Incidents

The week which has just ended will be a memorable one in the history, not of our State only, but also of the entire American Union. For the first time since a drunken and corrupt judge, backed by the arbitrary power of the *thing* who disgraces the office formerly dignified by Washington, Jefferson and Madison, has succeeded in fastening upon our necks the galling yoke of the knaves and plunderers who have so long tried the patient endurance of our people, an opportunity was furnished by the oppressors themselves to teach them a lesson they cannot soon forget.

After robbing us of our substance for two long and weary years, Kellogg and his gang had become so thoroughly satisfied that they were "masters of the situation," and that Louisianians had no rights which they were bound to respect; that their insolent and outrageous violation of every private right, consumating as it did in the armed robbery in broad open daylight of arms belonging to the citizens of the State, and the proclaimed intention of the boasting cowards who formed the chief reliance of the usurpers to ride rough-shod over us, aroused the spirit of resistance of our fellow citizens and led to the meeting of Monday, the 14th inst.; the call upon Kellogg to vacate an office he had no earthly right to hold, the attack of his hirelings upon the people and their swift and disgraceful repulse and flight after a few shots had been fired, and their Gatling and Napoleon guns upon which they placed such confidence, had been wrested from their cowardly hands by a handful of gallant and half-armed citizens.

A brief summary of the events of the week will not be inappropriate and this we shall now endeavor to give in as few words as possible, our main object being to place every occurrence in its true light, and to give every one concerned his due meed of censure or of praise, nothing extenuating, or setting ought in malice.

On Monday morning, Sept. 14th, it was evident to even the most casual observer that something of more than ordinary importance was about to take place. The faces of citizens indicated a spirit of determination and here and there bitter expressions of denunciation of the usurper could be heard at the street corners. At about 9 o'clock the different meeting rooms of the various clubs, and the headquarters of the militia of Gov. Penn began to put on a show of battle. Squads of men, armed with whatever weapon that could be obtained, hurried through the various streets to report for duty.

At the Custom-House were some 150 soldiers companies D and E, 16th Infantry, from Baton Rouge. These were stationed in the dungeons, the warehouses on the basement floor of the old granite building.

On the outside were gathered several hundred Negroes who evidently thought that building a house of refuge in case of danger.

The State-House was filled with Negroes under arms, together with a large body of metropolitans, who posted their guards on the galleries.

The Third Precinct Station was heavily fortified.

A heavy body of police were quartered in the arsenal and Supreme Court room, thoroughly prepared to repel any advancing column. Hand grenades had been carried to the upper floors, and square blocks of paving were placed ready at hand to be thrown on any attacking party. The different police stations, with the exception of that on Carondelet street, were thronged with men awaiting telegraphic orders to move.

The 1st Regiment Louisiana militia, under command of Col. John G. Angell were assembled at the headquarters of the different companies.

The situation at the time showed that thorough preparation had been made for any emergency; and from the readiness with which any call would be answered, it was evident there had been an able brain at work planning the operations and the possessor was Gen. Fred. N. Ogden.

The Meeting. Pursuant to call, the citizens who had not yet attached themselves to the different organizations assembled at the Clay Statue to the number of five thousand. On all sides could be heard expressions of intense hatred of the Kellogg Government, and vows to end it should a chance present itself.

The meeting was opened at 11:30 A. M. by Mr. Marr and resolutions read, one of which contained a provision demanding the immediate abdication of Kellogg.

A committee of five unarmed and unattended were appointed to call upon Kellogg with this message from the meeting. After an absence of half an hour, the committee returned, driven hurriedly up Royal street between a throng of thousands, who filled with street and sidewalks, awaiting with expectation the report. In a few minutes the report was read from the gallery of the Crescent Saloon, and when it was known with what indignity the representatives of the people had been received, shouts for a fight rent the air.

Dr. Beard stepped forward and advised all to retire to their homes and arm themselves. This was received with vociferous yells and the gathering immediately hurried away to prepare for the struggle. It was now evident a fight would take place. Couriers hurried to the headquarters of the several commands opposed to Kellogg and marching orders were given.

The excitement was increasing every moment. Men who had no rifles or shotguns carried their pistols, and every man prepared as best he could for the coming battle.

At 12:30 bodies of armed men marching with military precision were seen in all parts of the city, hastening to Poydras street, which had made the first line of defense.

Companies A, B, C, D, E, and G, of the Crescent City White League, marched down from Eagle hall, and took up their position at the head of Poydras street, right resting on the river. Col. Angell's command assembled on Poydras street, between Magazine and Camp, two companies occupying the office of the *Morning Star* newspaper.

At Jackson Square Station. At Jackson Square almost the entire force of the metropolitans were assembled at 12:30 o'clock. Guards were stationed at all points leading into the police building inside, and the force at the station was crowded to excess by metropolitans. The armory, which was in the hands of Capt. Gray, was occupied by the artillery. Eight guns were there ready for service, and as the attack was expected on the steamer Mississippi for the guns there concealed, the police mounted guard.

Two o'clock in the Afternoon. The rapid concentration of the Penn troops along the line of Poydras street was almost completed by this hour. From the river to Baronne street every thoroughfare was closely guarded.

Orders were soon given to build barricades, and with a will the men went to work. On the levee bales of freight, barrels and boxes were brought into requisition, and a hasty fortification was thrown up. At the corner of Camp and Poydras streets barricades were formed of barrels filled with earth, timber, and the iron plates of the crossings. At the corner of St. Charles and Poydras streets cars were run off the track and placed across the street to obstruct an advance.

At the corner of Poydras and Carondelet streets the iron plates were also removed and placed in an upright position, flanked by boxes and such other material as could be found. Down St. Charles street the streets running at right angles were blockaded with street cars, as far as Canal street. Another line of defense was soon afterwards erected on Julia street, at the intersection of those thoroughfares running parallel to the river.

At four o'clock the stir on Canal street showed that there was something in the wind. The crowd swayed this way and that everyone being on the *qui vive* for what was to come. In a few minutes the metropolitans, under the command of Gens. Longsteet and Badger, moved up Chartres street, the pickets of the citizens retiring without firing. The police turned out Canal street, and with their artillery, halted in front of the Custom House.

Citizens skirmishing with the police. (N. Y. Daily Graphic, Sept. 23, 1874)

Preparing for the Battle. The police then moved down the river at the head of Canal street—one company taking position on the river side of the iron building, another company on the opposite. Two Napoleons and a Gatlin gun were then wheeled into position pointing out Canal street with a reserve of police infantry in the rear. Another heavy gun was put in place, bearing upon the levee, backed by a mountain howitzer.

About this time, eight mounted *peelers* trotted back on Canal street until they reached Clay Statue, when they wheeled and went towards the river, amidst the jeers from the crowd lining either sidewalk. At 4:10 Gen. Ogden, with about 200 of the citizens' army, took up a line of march down the levee, close to the river at times, under the cover of the piles of freight. In a moment the police battery was wheeled so as to bear upon the front of the advancing foe.

At this moment the metropolitans opened fire on the crowd on Canal street with one of their pieces. This was the signal for the citizens' party. In an instant the sharp crack of the Winchesters, the deadly "bang" of the Remingtons, of Company E, on the right, and the death-dealing shotgun was heard.

The citizens wasted but a few shots. Keeping up a steady fire, the effect was soon evidenced by the demoralization in the Radical ranks. Many of the police turned tail and fled, taking refuge wherever it could be found. Several dropped, shot dead. Colonel Behan at this moment called on his boys, consisting of Sections A, B, D, E and G, to charge, AND WITH a YELL they rushed for the artillery.

It was but the work of a moment. The desperation of the men had been aroused, and it was with the greatest difficulty that they could be kept from overrunning discretion and going too far. They were more than brave. Badger's artillery was gobbled up in a minute, and several who were first on the pieces waived their hats, signals of their success.

The police then fled precipitately. Rushing down Crossman street and Canal for the Custom-House, for shelter they gave up the fight and left the field to their victorious enemy. Distributed on the battle field were lying the bodies of the usurper's guards. Near the guns in the space of forty feet eight were stretched out lifeless. As soon as their defeat was sure those who had taken refuge in the Custom-House opened fire from the windows, Mr. Casey on the contrary notwithstanding. Dibble was seen to fire from a window and several state that he killed a man. Longstreet retreated like a cur with his legion, and it was only by a miracle that he escaped with his life.

After the Battle. The white men, now satisfied with the rout of the enemy, took up their original positions, with heavy outposts and videttes. Both parties rested on their arms during the night, and except a reconnaissance in force up Chartres street, which was driven back, everything was *in statu quo*. Early Tuesday morning orders were given to prepare for a movement down to the State-House. Col. Angell's battalion was in line at the corner of St. Charles street and Canal streets, and at 8 o'clock marched down quick-step to the State-House which was surrendered.

After garrisoning the building the command double-quicked to the Third Precinct Station, and as the back bone of the enemy had been broken, it surrendered to Col. Angell. This virtually ended the war. Every piece of artillery had been taken; the arsenal, with the arms accumulated by Kellogg to keep the people down, captured; and the stations surrendered. The victory had been won and the day was ours. We give below the reports of several companies and their action during the engagement.

CRESCENT CITY WHITE LEAGUE

SECTION A

Section A, Capt. Vaudry, commanding, assembled at Eagle Hall at 9 o'clock, and on the reception of orders moved down to the head of Poydras street, on the extreme right of the White League Line; remained there until advance was made, when they marched down the levee until they were engaged. The captain had great difficulty in keeping his men back, so great was their desire to charge.

When the charge was made, assisted Section E, engaging the enemy whenever seen. After the victory marched to Tivoli Circle, where all prisoners were placed in their charge. Among those who were conspicuous in their endeavors to relieve the boys from the annoyances of bivouac were: Misses Meta Huger, Mary Cuggy, Alicia Bardy, Eleanor Cuggy, and Mrs. Bardy and Mrs. Crawcour.

SECTION B

Capt. Geo. H. Lord, commanding; J. O. Nixon, Jr., Lieutenant; Jno Mahoney, Orderly Sergeant; 40 rank and file—Met at Eagle Hall, 10 o'clock, Monday; at 2 P. M. started down with Crescent City White League. Reaching Poydras street, took position on the left of Company A on right of division. When police opened fire, companies C, A, and B were ordered to advance and fire down the Levee, and to charge the battery. Charged past Conery's corner and took the battery. After expending all ammunition, reformed in original position. None killed or wounded, except two volunteers—one in the head and the other in the arm and the side. Remained on Poydras street until Tuesday 12 M., when they were ordered to the steamship Mississippi, to take arms from her. Escorted the arms up to the Central Station. From there fell in for parade and were dismissed at the starting point.

SECTION C

The following is the position and operations of Section C, of the Crescent City White League, commanded by Capt. S. H. Buck, assisted by the late Major

Robbins, which occupied the position of the line on Poydras street at the intersection of Fulton street.

This section advanced at a charge simultaneously with the advance on the levee. One of the section, Mr. Savage, was shot before its line moved, and Major Robbins by the time they had advanced half way to Canal street, where they drove the metropolitans from the howitzer gun planted at the corner of Canal and Fulton, where Mr. Wells was shot, who, however, was not of the section.

The section started with sixty-five men, and lost six of their number, Major Robbins, then Assistant Marshal, and Messrs. Savage, Maes, Robinson, Pollock and Potts.

Section C, when the first advance was made on the levee, were so eager to participate, it was impossible to restrain them. Capt. Buck, after vainly endeavoring to keep his men back in position, and finding it useless, took the lead, and they advanced down Fulton street at a charge bayonet under a heavy fire from the enemy.

So soon as the the police saw this advance on what was their right flank, they abandoned the Napoleon and fled, section C sending after them a volley. All this command behaved with the utmost gallantry and Capt. Buck must be congratulated on his soldierly company.

SECTION D

Archibald Mitchell, Commanding; W. McBride, First Lieutenant, J. O'Donahue, Second Lieutenant, C. Green, Third Lieutenant, and 102 men in file.

This section were placed in position at the corner of Julia and Camp streets, at 3 o'clock on Monday evening, retaining position until 4 o'clock on Tuesday morning, protecting the second line of defense. On Tuesday morning moved down to the corner of St. Charles and Canal streets, to act as a reserve in case of resistance at the State-House and Third Precinct Station.

SECTION E

Section E, Commanded by Reuben Pleasants, were probably the best armed and disciplined company engaged in the fight. Capt. Pleasants had taken great pain with the drilling and organization of his men, and when the test came this was evidenced by the soldierly manner in which every man acted.

When an advance down the levee was ordered Capt. Pleasants fired his by fours down the right until they came to the high piles of grain, too high to fire over. Capt. Pleasants then ordered his men in two ranks, and they meandered through the corn and oats until they reached the foot of Gravier street, every man eager to get a shot at the enemy.

In a few minutes Badger raised his hat as a signal to open firing, and the Gatling gun commenced its grinding damaging the steamboat Selma and sending its missiles over the heads of Section E. Capt. Pleasants still retained the fire of his men until the first feeding hopper of the Gatling gun had been exhausted. Then it was that Section E with their Remington breech-loaders opened with deadly effect. At the first volley seven of the police gunners fell killed or mortally wounded.

Capt. John Glynn's company of the artillery then coming up charged in open ground and Section E advanced in line. The police by their heavy fire had been driven from the guns and it was the work of a moment to rout the enemy. Section E wasted no ammunition, every shot went to its mark and every one that missed the police artillery men struck the reserve, which was foolishly placed immediately in line in the rear.

The honors heaped upon this section are more than deserved. The intrepidity of the men, the coolness and strategic skill of their commander, Capt. Pleasants, deserve the highest encomiums. They fought like veterans, and the name of Section E, like Capt. Jno. Glynn's company, will be household words with our people.

Section G

Under command of Capt. D. M. Kilpatrick, Section G went into action with 35 men and 2 officers. This company was composed of the youngest men in the action, most of them being between the ages of 18 and 25 years. They advanced steadily under their captain, striking the enemy on their right flank. It was just at this moment that Gen. Ogden rode up and ordered them forward more rapidly, which they obeyed with a yell and at a double quick; seeing which, Gen. Ogden left them, going to the left of the line, but had gone but a short distance when his horse was killed under him.

They continued driving the enemy in behind and finally from, the iron building, head of Canal street, as well as from the Chattanooga Railroad shed. Here Lieut. Fred Parmele surrendered. Private Bailey throwing his arms around P.'s neck, assisted Captain K. in saving him from the then infuriated boys. The Captain ordered Bailey and another man to take him, Parmele, to the rear. Parmele afterwards signed a parole to never again take up arms against Louisiana. Meantime those of the metropolitans who had succeeded in getting off the field rallied under Flanagan, and took positions under cover of the U. S. Custom-House, on Peters street, near Canal where they had placed the only piece of artillery they had saved, and which they were using to enfilade Capts. Pleasant's and Vaudry's commands, who were then attempting to take off the captured artillery.

Some fifty or sixty Metropolitans were in support. Seeing and realizing the position should the enemy succeed in massing here, the company was immediately ordered to close up and drive them off. As they advanced they were met with a terrible volley from an unseen enemy behind the windows and on the roof of the United States Custom-House. Several of the boys were wounded here, and they were forced back to Common street, where they were immediately rallied, and under cover of a deserted street car on Canal street, they held their position, driving all except two men from the gun, and wounding in the legs and lower part of the body upwards of twenty of the support.

The enemy broke and retired in disorder. An advance was again ordered this time across Canal to the head of Crossman street, on the flank of the enemy. They again fell back. The company closed up on them to Customhouse, where Longstreet and Flanagan vainly attempted a rally; a few shots, however, were only necessary, when they broke and ran towards Jackson Square in great disorder. Here the company was withdrawn, and their attention was given to Gen. Badger, he being cared for by and under the immediate instructions of Capt. K.—his noble action in this affair is too well known by the entire community to need comment here. The boys of this command, one and all, deserve great credit for their gallantry while in action.

Washington White League

The Washington White League received orders to assemble at their headquarters at 9 o'clock A. M. Monday morning, September 14, 1874, and at the appointed time every man was at his post.

We waited until 1:30 P. M., when we received orders from Gen. Ogden to report to him at the corner of Camp and Poydras streets.

GENERAL BATTLE BETWEEN THE METROPOLITAN POLICE AND CITIZENS AT THE FOOT OF CANAL STREET

(N. Y. Daily Graphic, Sept. 23, 1874 from sketches of A. Zenneck of New Orleans)

Zenneck was in the Battle — private in Co. B, 1st La. Inf. Note the "Iron Building" in the center of the picture with the Custom House at the left and Christ Church far out on Canal Street to the West. The "Iron Building" was the depot and reservoir of an independent waterworks company which suspended operations at the beginning of the War Between the States. It was afterwards called the "Free Market" because on August 16, 1861 it was opened for the distribution of food and supplies to indigent families of Confederate soldiers. Planters and merchants furnished food and vegetables, one merchant sending two hogsheads of sugar and ten brls. of molasses on the opening day. This iron structure was in the middle of Canal Street, southeast of the Custom House, about where the Liberty Monument now stands.

At about 3, of 3:30, we received orders to go down town, as near the Custom-House as possible, and charge upon any metropolitan police that might have assembled there. When we reached the corner of Chartres and Custom-House, we were saluted with a volley from a body of metropolitans who had congregated at the rear of the Custom-House, which had no effect whatsoever upon our men, who immediately returned the fire, when a sharp conflict took place, during which we lost one man killed and three wounded. After fighting about twenty-five minutes, the Washingtons rested in good order and returned to their camp at the corner of Poydras and Camp streets.

We have received from a reliable source that Judge Dibble was firing upon us, from a window in the United States Custom House, and also that Capt. Lawler, the metropolitan, was very severely wounded in this battle. Our officers are: A. B. Phillips, Captain; E. N. Bardon, First Lieutenant; Geo. Berwin, Second Lieutenant; C. Gehlbach, Second Lieutenant Jr.

Angell's Battalion [Regiment]

Battery A, commanded by Capt. Jno. Glynn, was on the right of the line, at the head of Poydras street when the charge was made, they, together with section E, of the Crescent City White League dashed to the front, sections A, B, and C advancing on the extreme right flank and exposed to galling fire. Battery B suffered heavily as they charged as infantry. The following tribute to their courage and dash will be read with interest.

New Orleans, Sept. 2(?), 1874.

Editor New Orleans Bulletin:

In your account of the charge made of the metropolitan artillery by the citizen soldiery, at the foot of Canal street, on the evening of the 14th, which appeared in your Sunday's edition, you unintentionally overlook the fact that among those who were conspicuous for their heroism and courage on that day, and the first to reach the deserted guns of the flying metropolitans were the gallant members of Capt. John Glynn's company.

The other companies (including my own) who were present and participated in the capture were those of Capts. Pleasants and Lord, who have received merited eulogies from press and public.

Feeling assured, Mr. Editor, as an old fellow-soldier, you will award to the brave boys of Capt. Glynn's company their just measure of praise.

I remain, very truly yours,

W. T. VAUDRY,

Capt. Com'g Co. A, C. C. W. L.

Capt. Glynn's Command

We give below the action of Capt. Glynn's command on the memorable 14th of September, which was crowded out of our supplement this morning:

In accordance with instructions. Protector White League assembled at their headquarters Monday morning at 10 o'clock. Shortly afterwards orders were received from Gen. Ogden by Capt. Glynn to move his men to Leed's Foundry, and await orders. This company was armed with breech loading shot guns, fifteen of them being reserved as cannoneers.

Thence the command moved down to the corner of Camp and Julia, at which point Capt. Buckner, staff officer, communicated orders for Capt. Glynn's command to take position on the levee at the foot of Poydras street to the right of Col. Behan's command, Section E, under command of Capt. Pleasants, with Lieut. Guybet, of Glynn's Battery, on the right. By the shortest route, Capt. Glynn moved down to the foot of Poydras street where they found the police in position at the foot of Canal street, their line extending from the iron building to the Mobile passenger depot.

The estimated force of the police in position was about 250. Capt. Glynn's company, in coming into position, was exposed to full view of the police whilst passing the open space. As soon as the line was established, with Section E on the right, the police changed the point of their guns and brought to bear four Napoleons and a Gatling gun. In a few minutes the police opened fire with their artillery and infantry, which was immediately answered by Glynn's command.

The effect of their first fire was marked, and the police wavered, noticing which, Capt. Glynn ordered his men to advance and fire under cover of the freight, the left being unprotected. In a moment there was a break in the enemy's ranks, and by the time the column had advanced a hundred yards the police were in full flight, with exception of those who had charge of the Gatling gun, which kept its fire up for considerable time.

In a few moments Glynn's command charged and occupied the position originally held by the police, quite a number of them taking cover behind the Mobile passenger depot, these kept up a running fire and killed Gautier and Brulard at short range. Shots were also received by the command, at this point, from the Custom-House. Part of Capt. Pleasant's and Lieut. Grubets' men having crossed Canal street, in front of the depot, succeeded in driving the hidden police from the depot; after their rout, Capt. Glynn ordered the captured guns to the rear. His command then, at orders, entrenched themselves in their original position for the night, and thus remained until ordered out for review.

ANGELL'S REGIMENT

Company A, of Col. Angell's regiment, Capt. Borland in command, formed at 10 o'clock Monday morning, on Natchez street, opposite Bank Place. When the uptown commands moved down, Company A was marched rapidly to the corner of St. Charles and Canal, and thrown across St. Charles street. After remaining in this position for some time, and ascertaining that the metropolitans were moving up from the Third Precinct Station, the company was ordered to occupy the second and third stories of the building immediately across St. Charles street from Crescent Hall. Capt. McGloin, (company B, same regiment), arriving at the same time, took possession of the Crescent Billiard Hall.

We thus held the corners, and made it almost an impossibility for the enemy either to advance out Canal or come up Royal. At this time the metropolitans were forming at the head of Canal street, near the iron building. A reconnoitering party of about six or eight mounted metropolitans were now seen moving slowly out Canal street, with arms ready. As not a shot had been fired at this time, and the officers were determined not to be tempted into any act of aggression, strict orders were at once given to the men to fire under no circumstances without an explicit order should be given.

The mounted men passed slowly by in short range, and absolutely jeered at our men, and although they were trembling with eagerness (being mostly young and ardent boys) not a shot was fired. The metropolitans rode slowly by to about the middle of the Touro Row, and they returned slowly back to their command at head of Canal street. As soon as they had joined the main body fire was opened on the men on the levee and action began. It is our impression that these men were sent up Canal street for the sole purpose of drawing our fire, in order that we might be called the aggressors. The ruse failed—our men suppressed all desire to fire, and were immovable.

The company occupied the same point during Monday night, keeping pickets out down as far as Customhouse and Bienville streets, and along Canal. It was a member of this company who first entered Jackson Square Station, at about 2 o'clock A. M. From him it was learned that the men there were much demoralized, and through this scout negotiations were started looking toward a surrender of this place. These negotiations were kept up until seven o'clock Tuesday morning. During the night frequent skirmishes occurred betwen the pickets, and the scouts from Companies A and B, acting together, captured twenty metropolitans altogether. These men were throughly armed and were *uniformed out and out as United States soldiers.*

At 7 o'clock Tuesday morning, according to previous arrangement, Sergt. Bahncke came up and had a conference with the officers of companies A and B. After some conversation, nothing being arrived at, he was escorted out of our lines by one of the officers of Company A, who accompanied him into the Third Precinct Station. There he found the men generally demoralized, but divided on the question of surrender. This officer at once returned and advised Col. Angell to move at once in force, and demand a surrender, assuring the Colonel that the temper of the men was such that they would be compelled to surrender.

The State-House at this time was filled with armed negro militia and metropolitans. Col. Angell, with companies, A, B, and E, moved directly down Royal street, company A in advance, and on arriving at the State-House, a white flag was displayed. Company A immediately took possession, and companies B and E and proceeded down to the Third Precinct. During the short interval between passage of the officer of company A up Chartres street from Jackson Square, and the arrival of company A at the State-House, the negro militia had disappeared, and only a few white metropolitans remained to make the surrender.

On Monday Capt. McGloin's company, B, of Col. Angell's command, received orders to move 20 men with side arms to occupy the City Hall. This was accomplished by Capt. McGloin, and twenty minutes afterwards Lieut. Clem Walker followed with 40 men with long weapons and side arms, and guards were immediately stationed at the Hall and vicinity and the Police telegraph taken possession of, in order to break up the enemy's communications. At about a quarter to three o'clock, Capt. McGloin moved his company down to Canal street, and occupied the corner building known as the Crescent City Billiard Hall, which the whole-souled and patriotic proprietor, Mr. Hitchcock, immediately placed at their disposal.

The company had now been increased to 120 men, and a select detail of riflemen, under Lieut. Charlie Boarman, were posted on the roof of the building. All the corners on the upper side of Canal street, for two or three blocks each way, were thus occupied by Col. Angell, so as to give the Metropolitan Brigade a warm reception as their line should advance up Canal street, as was their evident intention. This arrangement was maintained up to 8 A. M. the next morning. During the night scouting parties were sent down into the Second District, and Mr. Bailey succeeded in bringing in a couple of metropolitans as prisoners from their picket line.

It being reported that the Kellogg forces at the Arsenal and Jackson Square were much demoralized, Lieut. Walker took down a detachment to test the situation.

At about 3 o'clock, the detachment proceeded as far as the corner of St. Peter and Royal streets, when a picket of three police were surprised and two of them captured, one of them escaping. On the next corner above the detachment marched upon a picket of ten of Kellogg's militia, and the scouting party, numbering six men, approaching them in the dark, being mistaken for Kellogg scouts, took them by surprise, and being much frightened, they were readily taken prisoners.

Lieut. Walker having sent the prisoners up under escort, taking from Capt. Mc-Gloin, who had come down with a strong detail for support, an extra man as a courier, concluded to go down to Jackson Square and interview the commander. Capt. Bahncke met him as the picket escorted him in, and finding Capt. Lawler inside, wounded and too much under the influence of opiates to treat with, made demand of Capt. Bahncke for the surrender of the arsenal and police station at Jackson Square. He found the metropolitans and colored troops, of which latter there were some 300, reported as posted in the upper stories, rather sick of the situation, and not relishing the prospect of the breakfast entertainment which Walker assured them they could look for in the morning, though a few spoke of fighting it out.

Capt. Bahncke said that he could not surrender the place without an order from Kellogg, and asked time to report to Kellogg, and return again. Lieut. Walker said that he could have until 6 o'clock, but Bahncke said he could not return until 7, and having the assurance that the attack should not be made until that hour, he saw Lieut. Walker out of the lines, just before daybreak. At 7 o'clock Bahncke met Walker and stated that both Kellogg and Gen. Longstreet had told him to reply that the Arsenal and Jackson Square must be held at all hazards.

This was immediately reported to Gen. Ogden, and preparations for the advance were immediately made. As the line was put in motion, the four hundred colored militia, under Gen. Badger, in the State-House, commenced leaving in hot haste, and a short while after the arsenal and Jackson Square were in the hands of Col. Angell's battalion.

Company C of Col. Angell's battalion, D. A. Blanchard, captain and L. L. Lincoln, E. A. Kirk and F. Selle, lieutenants, were the advance picket on Common street between Camp and Levee, but, having no muskets, were placed on duty at the State-House immediately after its surrender, the men being armed with revolvers. There they remained on duty for thirty-six hours. During the night of Tuesday, an attack being anticipated, they were supplied with muskets and reinforced by three companies.

Company E, Angell's Battalion, on Monday Morning, were the first to take up position on Poydras street. They were under the command of Lieut. Frank Richardson and numbered thirty-five men. At half-past two they were detailed as videts on the front, and during the engagement were at the corner of Magazine and Gravier streets, a portion of the command being still on outpost duty.

After the engagement they remained all night on the extreme right on picket duty and at half past 1 o'clock in the morning, repulsed a reconnaissance in force of the enemy. Tuesday morning they formed with the rest of Col. Angell's Battalion, marched down to the State-House and Third Precinct Station. This company, Wednesday night, was detained to guard the last mentioned place.

In other editions of the *Bulletin* several companies that had been omitted from previous reports of participants were mentioned and information about their activities given. Here is a letter about Captain Augustin's company:

New Orleans, Sept. 22, 1874.

To the Editor of the N. O. *Bulletin*:

Sir—I fail to find mention in your "Events of the War" of the Louisiana Rifles, commanded by Capt. Augustin. This company was composed with but a few exceptions, of members of the old Dreux Battalion. In our rank and file were such men as Dr. T. S. Kennedy, Hon. B. F. Jonas, Administrator Chas Frizenreiter, Capt. Lyons, of Ball, Lyons & Co., Dr. Cullen, etc. We were stationed on the right of Capt. Mitchell's command, corner Julia and St. Charles; our company numbering 80 men, were divided into patrols of 20 each, commanded alternately by Lieutenants Wm. Woelper, (Secretary to Gov. McEnery), Addison and Renaud. The purpose of this patrol was to prevent the assembling of Negroes and prevent scouting parties from leaving the enemy's lines. It did duty from New Basin to Esplanade street, frequently exchanging shots with the enemy's pickets. By placing this on record you will oblige

A PRIVATE IN THE RIFLES.

On Sept. 24 the *Bulletin* printed this:

SECTION F. Owing to the fact that we did not receive any report from Section F, of the Crescent City White League, their action during the late revolution was omitted. This company, commanded by that sterling officer, Capt. Thos. McIntyre, assisted by Lieut. Hyatt and Sergeant Warren Holmes, marched down from Eagle Hall and took position at the corner of Camp and Poydras streets, which they held until 2 o'clock Tuesday. The rank and file of this command did their whole duty and deserve honorable mention.

And on the 25th:

Capt. O. M. Tennison, of the Seventh Ward White League, informs us that on the memorable 14th of September, he, in command of one half of the active members of the Seventh Ward White League, and a detachment of the St. John White League, Capt. Vautier, joined the command of Capt. A. B. Phillips, of the Washington White League, cooperated with him and took part in the skirmish, at the corner of Customhouse and Chartres streets. Not knowing that the movement was intended only as a feint, Capt. Tennison retained his command, and a portion of Capt. Phillips's company, on Chartres street, after the head of the column had moved off, but deeming his force too small, he shortly afterwards moved off and joined Capt. Phillips again on Poydras street.

From the New Orleans *Daily Picayune,* September 15, 1874:

W<small>AR</small>

T<small>HE</small> U<small>PRISING OF THE</small> C<small>ITIZENS</small>

B<small>ATTLE AT THE</small> H<small>EAD OF</small> C<small>ANAL</small> S<small>TREET</small>

B<small>ADGER</small> M<small>ORTALLY</small> W<small>OUNDED</small>

E<small>LEVEN</small> M<small>ETROPOLITANS</small> K<small>ILLED AND</small> M<small>ANY</small> W<small>OUNDED</small>

T<small>HE</small> M<small>ETROPOLITAN</small> A<small>RTILLERY</small> C<small>APTURED, AND</small> T<small>HEIR</small> F<small>ORCES</small> D<small>ISPERSED</small>

R<small>ESIGNATIONS AND</small> S<small>URRENDERS</small> A<small>MONG THE</small> P<small>OLICE</small> F<small>ORCE</small>

T<small>HE</small> C<small>ITY IN</small> P<small>OSSESSION OF THE</small> C<small>ITIZENS</small>

BARRICADES

At about three o'clock, the citizens were pretty well organized all over Poydras street, along which their lines were laid out. Barricades were at once begun at all the streets running parallel to the river. Some of these were of very good construction. At Camp street, a barricade of barrels and logs was erected, at St. Charles street a triple barricade of horse cars was erected, strengthened by pulling up the pavement of a gutter and thus leaving a formidable ditch across the street.

At Magazine street another formidable barricade was erected.

TCHOUPITOULAS STREET

Tchoupitoulas was the only street open, and this was found a serious inconvenience, as the metropolitans kept up a constant fire down the street, and rendered crossing a dangerous affair, and the construction of any line of defense almost impossible. Five citizens were wounded in crossing, though slightly; one man was killed or rather mortally wounded; being a stranger his name was unknown.

THE POLICE LINE

At about 4 o'clock the metropolitans were stationed on Canal street, one wing with about 200 men and one gun were stationed on the north side of the Custom-House, commanding Tchoupitoulas street. The other division, about 250 strong and commanded by Gen. A. S. Badger in person, with four guns, occupied the south side of the Custom-House.

THE POLICE ADVANCE

At a quarter past 4, Badger, with his men and guns, marched forward on the Levee. The other body of police prepared to support him, but being fired on when near Common street, they returned to their old quarters near the Custom-House. The Badger army kept on until they had almost reached Gravier street, and ensconced themselves behind some bales of hay.

THE FIGHT

Suddenly a volley, or rather a dozen volleys, were fired on them, some from the buildings, some from the street, and Companies A, B, and E of the Crescent City White League, headed by Gen. Ogden and Capts. Buck, Gallagher and W. B. Pleasants, charged upon the metropolitans in the most gallant and noble manner. They received the fire of the metropolitans without flinching and kept straight on in their charge. Seeing this, the metropolitans wavered, scattered and rushed off toward the Custom-House. A volley of the citizens brought down eighteen men at the first fire, all of them seriously injured, those slightly wounded making off. Among the fallen was Badger, who was vainly endeavoring to rally his men. Badger was mortally wounded, being shot through the arm, leg and side. It is said that he fired on his own men when he saw them running, and that it was by his hand that Corporal McManus fell.

When the citizens came up he surrendered and begged for a mattress. This and other comforts were provided him.

THE PURSUIT

The pursuit of metropolitans was kept up almost to the very doors of the Custom-House. About forty fell on the field, some of them being only slightly injured. Eleven, however, were killed, and four, among them a mulatto, (the only negro hurt), were mortally wounded. About a dozen others were severely wounded. The remainder were only slightly hurt. The metropolitans were perfectly panic stricken. About fifty of them ran up into the Custom-House, where all the Radical

(*Left*) GEN. BADGER IN FRONT OF THE GEM SALOON

This was on Jan. 10, 1872 when, under orders from Gov. Warmoth, he marched the Metropolitan Police to the Gem saloon to demand the surrender of the Carter Legislature which had its headquarters there.

The Gem saloon at 127 Royal Street was founded in 1851 and for seventy years was popular and well known for its drinks and good food. It was the gathering place for organizations, political meetings and stag parties. The Mistick Krewe of Comus was organized at the Gem. Old timers remember the restaurant which specialized in sea foods and which kept the floor covered with sand. (The picture is from Scribner's Magazine of May, 1895 — courtesy of Leonard V. Huber)

(*Right*) MASS MEETING AT CLAY STATUE ON SEPTEMBER 14, 1874

This scene is somewhat different from others illustrating the same event. One shows the address being made from the Crescent City Billiard Hall, at the left here, another from across the street, corner Royal and Canal. The picture is anachronistic because the buildings shown were not there in 1874. For instance on the corner of Carondelet and Canal is the old Pickwick Club, easily recognizable, which was not built until 1884. The artist, Corwin K. Linson, drew on his imagination when he made this illustration for Scribner's Magazine, issue of May, 1895. (Courtesy Leonard V. Huber)

The front of the Washington Artillery Hall in St. Charles Street between Girod and Julia — 1894. (*From Washington Artillery Annual of 1894*)

Today at Alexandria, La., awaiting repairs and final "resurrection" — *Courtesy Thos. Harrison, Historian Military Dept., State of La.*

CANNON CAPTURED ON SEPTEMBER 14TH BY THE WHITE LEAGUERS

The two howitzers, named by their captors, *Resurrection* and *Redemption*, were taken from the Metropolitan Police on the 14th and were kept concealed until 1877, although cash rewards were offered by Gov. Kellogg for knowledge of their whereabouts. Thomas Harrison, Military Historian, Office of the Adjutant General, Jackson Barracks, has furnished the following extract from the Minute Book No. 1 of the Washington Artillery, 1875-1879, Report of Col. W. M. Owen, July 20, 1878, Pg. 323: "After the installation of the Nicholls' Government, two 12-pounder bronze howitzers that had been taken from the Metropolitan Police on the 14th of Sep-

tember, 1874 and put away in a safe place, were resurrected, mounted and placed in the arsenal, thus adding to the armament."

When the Washington Artillery became a unit of the U. S. Army and its effects distributed, its flags, trophies and war mementoes were placed in a room in the Louisiana State Museum. There the two cannon were on display until some time in 1954 when they were removed to Alexandria, La., to be repaired. The only wheelwright available who can fix a wooden wheel is eighty years old and the guns must wait on his time and convenience.

HOTEL ROYAL — OLD ST. LOUIS HOTEL As it looked in 1894. The hotel originally had 237 rooms and could accommodate 700 persons at one time. There were 30 bath rooms. Much of the space was taken up with the lobby, numerous dining rooms, a ball room and smaller meeting rooms. There is still standing at 507-509-511-513-515-517 Chartres Street a building which was connected with and used by the hotel but which was not part of the original structure.

White citizens tearing off the uniforms of disguised "Metropolitans," as pictured in Frank Leslie's Illustrated Newspaper of Oct. 3, 1874.

— *Courtesy Howard-Tilton Library*

chiefs were assembled, and refused to leave there. Some ran up Canal street and were shot, and the remainder escaped and dispersed in all directions. Some, however, organized and escaped.

Longstreet's Division marched up with a reinforcement during the fight, but apparently changed his mind, and with the accessions from such of the metropolitans as escaped Badger's fate, retreated to Jackson Square, leaving behind to the citizens one Gatling, two 12-pound Napoleon guns and one howitzer.

The news of this victory, diffused all along the line, encouraged the citizens, and about 6 o'clock they marched down and appeared on Canal street, but there were no *peelers* there; they had retreated and were ensconced in the arsenal at Jackson Square, dispirited and frightened, and kept together solely by Longstreet, who plead with them to stay and fight.

Police Headquarters

Their sole cannon appeared to be a 12-pound Napoleon, pointing down St. Anne street, over which Longstreet personally presided.

There appeared to be little if any desire on the part of the metropolitans to fight. They wanted to go home, and hardly knew what to do. Their only hope, they honestly confessed, was the United States troops, and they peered forward, ever, like sister Annie, looking for them.

The Police Desert and Surrender

At about half-past 6 a body of *peelers,* from thirty to forty in number marched down the street. The citizens prepared to charge on them, when the *peelers* called for a conference, and said they had had enough fighting and wanted to go home. They surrendered willingly to their guns and pistols, which were distributed among the citizens. Most of them took off their hats and coats to avoid recognition and dispersed for home. The citizens to whom the *peelers* surrendered were an unattached troupe from the Sixth Ward, about fifteen in number.

Farther down town were several parties of citizens, but they had very little skirmishing to do, and no one, citizen or metropolitan, was known to be killed.

The Fight Elsewhere

Along the remainder of the line there was not much fighting. During the big fight on the Levee, about twenty boys charged down Tchoupitoulas street, ran off a large quantity of metropolitans and captured a caisson, amid a perfect torrent of balls, three of them falling in the charge, and brought the caisson within lines at St. Charles street.

At Tchoupitoulas street several men were injured, one, a laboring man, being shot through the breast, and supposed to be mortally wounded.

On Magazine street, a car driver whilst driving his car was fired into by the metropolitans and killed, his brains being scattered all over the car.

Down Town

Down town there was no regular fighting, but skirmishing was kept up all the day long. A body of citizens on the corner of Royal and Conti were fired on half a dozen times by the metropolitans, who advanced on them. One man, whilst crossing Royal street, was killed by the police; one policeman was also slain there.

Canal Street

On Canal street there was generally quiet, large bodies of unarmed citizens congregated to look on, and there was very little fighting. The police from the Custom-House kept up a fire on the citizens on the street, killing two inoffensive lookers-on. Two metropolitans, who were flying from the battle-field on the Levee, were dashing up Canal street, when they were fired upon by the crowd and both killed. Several citizens were wounded on Canal street from the Custom-House fire, but not seriously.

The Citizens Victorious

At about 7 o'clock the citizens were in complete possession of the city, save the St. Louis Hotel, occupied by about a dozen *peelers* and a gang of negroes, and the Third Precinct Station, occupied by the remnant of the metropolitan brigade, now only about two hundred in number, and rapidly decreasing by desertions and resignations. Among the resignations we may mention that of Capt. McCann.

The City Hall, the telegraph offices, the streets were all held by the citizens, and with Lieut. Gov. Penn, acting as Governor.

Gov. Penn's Remonstrance to the Custom-House

Acting Gov. Penn, hearing that the citizens had been fired on from the Custom-House, issued an order to Gen. Ogden to communicate with the Collector of Customs, or whoever held the command at the Custom-House, and to inform him that the citizens had been fired at from the Custom-House by certain persons lodged therein, and to demand from him that this be prohibited.

The shots fired were by the defeated policeman who took refuge in the Custom-House, and who kept up a constant fire therefrom. Mr. Fred Mohrman, clerk of the Administration of Commerce, was killed whilst peaceably walking on Tchoupitoulas street. Mr. J. M. West, an old newspaper man, was also killed by this volley whilst he was standing on the neutral ground taking notes.

Gen. Badger's wound is serious, but not necessarily fatal. If he dies it will be from loss of blood and not from the wounds. He will certainly lose his leg.

During the entire fight no Negro was killed. One metropolitan, a mulatto, was wounded at the foot of Canal street.

Surrenders

Twenty-five policemen, who were stationed in a building on Decatur street, were cut off at the rout of Badger's forces. They were visited by half a dozen citizens and promptly surrendered to them their arms and retired from service. A force of about a dozen men, at the Central Police Station, likewise surrendered when called on to do so. The station was then taken possession of and guarded by citizens.

THE SITUATION AT MIDNIGHT

At 12 o'clock the city, after the terrible events of the day, had assumed some sort of quiet. The citizens held supreme control of the city. Their men, however, were stationed only above Canal street. There the streets were perfectly guarded. Sentinels were stationed along Common street, who prevented any persons from passing within the line. At Poydras street the barricades were held by a large body of armed men, who patrolled the streets in the neighborhood. Gravier, Exchange Alley, Common and all the streets running from the river were also barricaded at their junction with St. Charles street, with horse cars.

At the store of Kursheedt & Bienvenu, the headquarters of the Citizens' party was established. Communications poured in there the night through, and it required quite a number of clerks and a large staff to carry on the business.

Ammunition and food were here distributed; every half hour or so a captain or sergeant might be seen reporting the state of his squad or detachment; indeed this was the centre point of all action. Gen. F. N. Ogden presided, with a number of subordinate officers.

The citizens' troops were stationed from the levee out to Rampart street. Their back lines extended as far as Julia street; beyond this straggling bodies of men might be seen, ready to do duty if called on, but apparently not on service.

About 10 o'clock six or seven hundred men were granted leave of absence to return home, with the understanding that they were to report to-morrow. This left about a thousand men under arms during the entire night within the limits of Julia, Rampart, Common and the levee.

WHITE LEAGUERS GUARDING A LEVEE.
September 14, 1874. (Harper's
Weekly, Oct. 10, 1874)

THE REPUBLICAN'S ACCOUNT OF THE BATTLE

The *New Orleans Republican,* according to Henry W. Robinson's article in the Louisiana Historical Quarterly of October, 1924, was a good newspaper both in its news and editorial columns. He writes: "That the paper should have been published at all, and its reporters permitted to move freely among the White League to gather the many details told in its account, shows how perfect was the discipline of the White League and the good order it preserved." Omitting the description of the mass meeting in the morning, the *Republican* describes the fight as follows:

This condition of things was reported to General Badger at that time at the Jackson square station, with nearly all his force. He had a Gatling gun and three small brass howitzers for canister. The several police captains had charge of their commands, all apparently well armed and the men in good spirits.

Meantime, the various companies of the White League, armed with every variety of weapon, appeared in the streets, taking position in various portions of the city. Fully 3000 armed men were in their ranks. The corner of Poydras and St. Charles streets was selected by General Ogden, the Grand Commander of the League, with his staff, from which point the movements of the organization were directed. About four o'clock a barricade of lumber, boxes, iron plates from the street crossings, etc., was thrown up across Camp street.

A few minutes before four o'clock General Badger issued an order for his command to march. They started up near the levee and met with no opposition until near the head of Canal street. Arrived on the levee, —the artillery—three brass pieces and two Gatling guns—were deployed, and the infantry properly detailed to support them. No organized enemy appeared to oppose them. They were on open ground, near the iron building, but almost instantly a dropping fire from behind hay and cotton bales commenced on them. Loose and lively moving crowds of citizens were on Canal, Common, Gravier and the cross streets, and on hearing each shot they rushed one way or the other.

The police took their exposed position surrounded by apparently 600 men behind the bales of cotton and hay. Their attention was directed somewhat up the levee, where the greater strength of the enemy seemed to be, and sitting on his horse, General Badger raised his hat and gave the order to fire. At the first discharge every loose citizen sought cover, and there was a tremendous stampede ensued for the side streets. The excitement spread to Camp street, and men knew not which way to turn. Many called, "It's a false alarm; it is only done to keep carriages and cars away," but the fight of the day was going on with unparalleled vindictiveness. At the first discharge of the cannon every cotton and hay bale seemed to blaze with fire. Only heads and arms were presented as targets for the Winchester's of the police. Badger sat his horse, encouraging his men, and seemed to have a charmed life, for several men dropped every second. Not a man flinched while he had support, but the fire of their almost unseen enemy swept them away like wheat before the reaper.

A fifth of the force lay on the levee dead or so wounded as to be unable to move. Not enough men were left unhurt to support the artillery, and standing at the guns were not one-half enough to work them. Unable to see hardly a foe fall, but the crack and blaze coming unceasingly from the bulwarks before them, a fire from roofs and windows behind and above them commencing and a man falling at each report, the majority who could walk sought the iron building, carrying their

"Sharpshooters Behind Cotton Bales" as captioned by Frank Leslie's Illustrated Newspaper, Oct. 3, 1874.
— *Courtesy Howard-Tilton Library*

wounded. All but the commands of Rey and Joseph, which were somewhat out of the line of the main fight were demoralized. Every man in sight was blackened with powder and stained with his own blood. Sergeant John McCann, a most conspicuous target, stood discharging his Winchester till the last shot was gone, and then, unarmed, received a disabling wound in the leg. Badger still sat his horse, cheering his men, and Captain Gray, with every man of the artillery killed or wounded, was loading a piece without assistance as coolly as he would have inspected it in the armory.

The contest lasted not more than ten minutes, and then the police were driven back from their charge. The fire from roofs and windows and vantage places redoubled, and of those who reached the Customhouse only two were without a mark.

As the last of his men melted away General Badger still sitting conspicuously on his horse was made the target of a hundred Belgian rifles and was seen to fall as Gray drove home a charge in his gun. Private Simons, slightly hit, called for one man to go and help him take him away, but the fire was unremitting. Nearly all were disabled and there was no one to help. A retreat was made by the main body to the Customhouse and in the hands of the enemy were left two Gatling and one twelve pound gun.

The rest of the force retreated to Jackson Square station with all the guns, picketed the streets and prepared for further resistance.

When shots were heard in the neighborhood of the Customhouse, the Leagues in reserve on Poydras street barricaded Tchoupitoulas, Magazine, Camp and Carondelet streets crossings. Bridges were torn up and horse cars were taken from the tracks and used to build the barricades.

By this time nearly every place of business was closed, and the central portion of our city in a state of fiery excitement. Non-combatants were seldom disturbed, and they generally passed to and fro as they pleased. Curiosity led many men into dangerous positions, especially on Canal street, where several unarmed men were wounded and killed.

General Ogden, commanding the White League, had his horse shot under him, and he barely escaped serious injury.

Owing to the general confusion the reporter found it almost a matter of impossibility to make a correct list of the killed and wounded.

General A. S. Badger, beloved of all his command and the object of universal admiration for his cool self-reliance and unflinching courage, fell pierced with three musket shot, though the one in the leg is the only serious one, being a bad fracture of the bone below the knee.

After the fight was over the dead and wounded were removed to the Customhouse, where Drs. Ames and Schumaker attended to the wants of those who needed their services.

14TH SEPTEMBER. OFFICIAL REPORT OF GEN. FRED. N. OGDEN

Headquar's La. State Militia, New Orleans, Sept. 17. Col. E. J. Ellis, A. A. G.

Colonel—I have the honor to report, that on Monday, Sept. 14, at 1 P. M., upon the uprising of the citizens en masse, and immediately on receipt of commission from Lieut. Gov. Penn, Acting Governor during the temporary absence of Gov. McEnery, appointing me Major General commanding the State Militia, and in pursuance with his orders to assemble my troops, I at once proceeded to form a defensive line of battle on Poydras street—my right resting on the levee, my left on Carondelet street—with the intention of throwing the city into a military camp, for the purpose of thoroughly organizing the State forces.

With commendable alacrity the following commands reported at my headquarters on Camp, near Poydras street, viz:

Crescent City White League, Col. W. J. Behan commanding, composed of

Section A, Capt. W. T. Vaudry.

B, George H. Lord.
C, S. H. Buck.
D, Archibald Mitchell.
E, R. B. Pleasants.
F, Thomas McIntyre.
G, D. M. Kilpatrick.

The Eleventh Ward White League, Capt. F. M. Andress.
The Tenth Ward White League, Capt. Edward Flood.
The Sixth District White League, Capt. C. H. Allen.
The Sixth Ward White League, Capt. O. M. Tennison.
The Washington White League, Capt. A. B. Phillips.

The St. John White League, Capt. Charles Vautier.

The Second Ward White League, Capt. R. Stewart Dennee.

The Third Ward White League, Capt. J. R. S. Selleck.

Major Legardeur, with Capt. A. Roman's company (the remainder of his battalion being present unarmed.)

Col. John G. Angell, commanding 1st Louisiana Infantry, composed of the following companies:

Company A, Capt. Borland.

Company B, Capt. F. McGloin.

Company C, Capt. Blanchard.

Company E, Lieut. F. A. Richardson.

Together with two (2) companies of artillery, under Capt. John Glynn, Jr., Acting Chief of Artillery, and Capt. H. D. Coleman.

As before stated, my line of defense was formed on Poydras street, at 3 P. M., the right, under command of Col. W. J. Behan, consisting of companies A, B, C, E and G, Crescent City White League, and commands of Capts. Flood, Andress, Allen and Shropshire, supported by one twelve-pounder gun, extended from the Levee to Tchoupitoulas street.

The centre, composed of the commands of Capts. Dupre, McIntyre and Phillips, extended from Tchoupitoulas to Camp street; the left, with the commands of Capts. Roman, Tennison and Vautier, from Camp to Carondelet street.

Col. John Angell was ordered by me to take position on St. Charles street, above Poydras, to guard against attack from the Central Police Station, on Carondelet street.

Major J. D. Hill, of the above battalion, with Company E, Lieut. Richardson commanding, was directed to place himself on the corner of Camp and Common streets, to check any advance of the enemy by way of Chartres and Camp streeets.

Capt. H. D. Coleman's company of artillery, supported by Section D, Crescent City White League, under command of that trusty leader, Capt. Archibald Mitchell, together with Capt. Dennee's Section, were stationed at the corner of Camp and Julia streets, and the Louisiana Rifle Club, together with the unattached forces, under command of Major John Augustin, at the corner of Carondelet and Julia streets, with pickets on the extreme left and right, formed my reserve force and second line of defense.

While strengthening my lines and arranging my troops more perfectly, the enemy, consisting of about 500 metropolitan police, with six pieces of artillery, under Gens. Longstreet and Badger, moved by way of Chartres, Peters and Decatur streets, taking position on Canal street, about the United States Custom-House and in front of the Iron Building and Mobile Railroad Passenger Depot, leaving a reserve of the First Louisiana Brigade to guard the State-House and Arsenal at Jackson Square.

At 4:15 P. M., Brig. Gen. Badger, with about 300 metropolitans, armed with the most improved weapons, one Gatling gun, and two (2) twelve-pounder Napoleon guns, opened fire upon my extreme right, which was promptly responded to by that gallant, experienced and vigilant officer, Col. W. J. Behan, whose celerity and brilliancy of movement is deserving of the highest praise.

Capt. Pleasants, Section E, C. C. W. L., whose command was armed with improved weapons and amply supplied with ammunition, gained the enemy's flank and poured a deadly fire into their ranks, which caused them to waver.

Capt. John Glynn, Jr., finding his piece of artillery useless, acted with the promptness and dash of a trained soldier, and ordered Lieut. E. A. Guibet to charge, which he did with gallantry, in conjunction with Company A, Capt. Vaudry, and B, Capt. Lord, down the open levee and street, driving back the enemy and capturing his guns.

At the same time Company C, Capt. Buck, Company G, Capt. Kilpatrick, and commands of Capt. Allen, Shropshire, Andress and Flood, charged down Front, Peters and Tchoupitoulas streets, forcing the enemy completely from his position. To this result Major J. D. Hill contributed by a timely withdrawal of his command from the position assigned him, and aided materially in driving the metropolitans from their last stand.

In the meantime Capt. A. B. Phillips was ordered to make a flank movement on the enemy's right, in which he was assisted by Capt. Tennison's command and a position of the St. John White League. He met and dispersed a body of them at the corner of Chartres and Customhouse streets, losing two (2) killed and three (3) wounded, and then returned to his former position, in the centre of my line.

After removing the captured guns I resumed my original position, with the intention of preparing for an advance early the next day upon the enemy's stronghold below Canal street; but so complete, in my opinion, was the demoralization of the enemy from the action of Monday, evidence of which I had received during the night from citizens and soldiers active in our cause, corroborated by the surrender to my command of large bodies of metropolitans, that the capture of these strongholds seemed but a question of time. To press this capture, Col. Angell, supported by Capt. Coleman's artillery, was ordered to move forward early in the morning of these points, leaving his position occupied by the commands of Capts. Mitchell and McIntyre.

By 10 o'clock A. M., Col. Angell was in the possession of all the enemy's important points below Canal street, having received material assistance in this movement from Capt. Macheca.

Information of this result was immediately transmitted to your headquarters. The judgment displayed by Col. Angell, together with the gallantry of his officers and men in effecting these captures, merit the highest commendation.

I take pleasure in mentioning the prompt obedience to all orders and the heroic devotion to duty shown by officers and men throughout my entire command.

From the nature of the action it was not possible for all my forces to have been engaged; but I do not hesitate to state that had the necessity arisen, all would have acted equally well.

My thanks are especially due to the efficiency and meritorious conduct, before and during the action, of my staff, consisting of Messrs. T. Lee Shute, James Buckner, F. R. Southmayd, John N. Payne, Sam. Flower, Wm. A. Bell, Walter Hare, Dr. J. D. Bruns, J. B. Walton and Fred. Holyland; to the gentleman who volunteered as aids, Messrs. Moore, Greenleaf, Pierce Hardie, Buddendorff and Tobin; also to Major E. A. Burke and Capt. W. B. Krumbhaar, of your staff, for assistance in their respective departments.

E. C. Kelly for valuable information furnished; to Messrs. Kurscheedt & Bienvenue, for kind services during Monday night and Tuesday. To Messrs. Geo. Williams and W. Robinson for efficient courier service. To Col. Robt. Wood, for valuable aid in procuring arms. To Capt. W. H. Morgan, for procuring ammunition for captured artillery. To Mr. J. H. Smith, for use of horses for artillery. To Messrs. D. Prieur White, Ed. Ferrigan and Vinet, for their kind personal services.

The enemy's loss must have been very heavy, from the number of dead and wounded left by them on the field. Their chief, Gen. A. S. Badger, fell into our hands, severely wounded. My command suffered in the charge of the 14th a loss of twelve killed and thirteen wounded (several have died since), among them some of our most respected and prominent young citizens. Thus was the life-blood of our best people poured out upon the altar of their country.

Sorrow fills the heart while relating that in the nineteeth century—an age of boasted civilization—and in the American Union, whose corner stone is freedom, there can be found injustice so great as to require a sacrifice so dear. In the signal victory of the 14th of September, we must acknowledge with profound gratitude the hand of a kind and merciful God.

The opportunity afforded through the mistaken strategy of a sagacious military leader, by which we were enabled to strike a blow for freedom, which, in decisiveness of character, has scarcely a parallel in history, can surely be ascribed to no human power.

To that God who gave us the victory we commit with confidence and hope the spirits of our immortal dead; and strong in the consciousness of right, record anew our holy purpose that *Louisiana shall be free.*

I have the honor, Colonel, to subscribe myself, very respectfully,

> FRED N. OGDEN,
> Major General Commanding.
>
> T. LEE SHUTE, Col. and A. A. G.

LONGSTREET'S REPORT

We have been favored by General Longstreet with the following official memorandum of military movements on Monday last. An official report of the battle will not be made until General Badger has sufficiently recovered to attend to its compilation:

The State forces were posted: Metropolitan Brigade, about five hundred men (artillery and infantry) at Jackson Square; First Brigade, four hundred and seventy-five infantry, at the State House. The plan was to hold these positions until the insurgents came out and attacked at Jackson Square, as we had learned that they had arranged to do so.

A plan was also arranged for active operation with the State troops, in case it became necessary or important that such operation should be ordered.

This plan was to move the troops from Jackson Square up the levee, including the main artillery force, with the lesser column from same position up Peters street, in echelon with the main column, the force at the State House remaining stationary, as pivot of operations and echelon to two moving colums.

Troops remained in position according to original plan until 3 p. m., when from information received it was supposed that the insurgents had changed their plan, and were assembling at Clay statue on Canal street. The Governor then ordered the State forces to move out in accordance with the plan for active operations.

Arriving at Canal street, the leading column, composed of two companies of infantry and one of artillery, deployed. The mounted force, eight men, were then ordered forward to the Clay statue to warn non-combatants to clear the street. The commander of the Metropolitan brigade was then to ride forward, read the riot act and order the insurgents to disperse. The cavalry men, however, reported that there was no organized force on Canal street. The officer in charge of these men on his return reported one of his men wounded by some straggler on Canal street. In a very few moments after the insurgents were reported to be moving from Lafayette Square to the levee through Poydras and other streets.

The position of the main force of Metropolitans was changed, making the line of battle at a right angle to line of levee. When this new line was established the insurgents were seen advancing, apparently to attack, covered and protected by a slowly moving freight train on the railroad track.

It soon became evident that the attack was at hand, when the Metropolitan artillery opened with its Gatling gun and two Napoleons. The insurgents still advancing, returned fire with infantry, their artillery seeming to be in disorder or confusion.

Under the fire of the insurgents, Captain McCann, commanding one of the companies of Metropolitans, gave a false alarm and drew his company from its position, and he soon went over to the enemy. This movement, together with the accurate fire of sharpshooters from windows and roof tops in all directions had a very demoralizing influence upon the other infantry company, which fell back under the severe fire and left the artillery exposed and unprotected.

General Badger, commanding the Metropolitans, dismounted and assisted in serving his guns. He soon fell, however, very severely (and it was feared mortally) wounded. The Metropolitans then retired in some confusion through Tchoupitoulas street as far as the Customhouse street front of the Customhouse building, many of them entering the building. Those who did not enter the building retreated to Jackson Square.

During the night application was made for a supply of ammunition for troops at the State House and Jackson Square, the State ammunition having been exhausted, except about eight rounds per man at the State House and probably thirty at Jackson Square. The United States could not supply this ammunition, and none could be had from other sources. Under such circumstances it was thought better not to hold the State House Tuesday, as there was not ammunition enough to resist more than one assault, that the surrender which must of necessity speedily follow would not justify further loss of life.

The want of ammunition and military supplies in State arsenals was due to the Attorney General of the State, who had enjoined the militia appropriation to twenty thousand dollars, made by the Legislature at its last session.

GEN. BADGER'S ACCOUNT OF THE BATTLE OF THE 14TH

Gen. A. S. Badger, in his appearance before the Congressional Committee about five months later, in his testimony gave this account of the affair of the 14th:

Q. I want you to come down now to September 14, and briefly state the circumstances of that uprising. A. On the Saturday night previous, I believe it was the 12th, at or about 12 o'clock, a large quantity of arms was deposited at Leeds's foundry, or the immediate vicinity, on Saint Joseph street, from a freight-car on the Jackson Railroad. That evening, White League companies went there, some of them having arms. I presume they went there for the protection of others, perhaps, but many of the companies went there unarmed, and these arms were distributed to them and they marched and scattered about the city and created considerable excitement. A mass-meeting was called on that day or the next, just about that time, to assemble at Clay's statue, Canal street, at 12 meridian. On the 14th of September it was feared by the authorities that trouble would accrue out of this mass-meeting. The mass-meeting assembled and speeches were delivered. And finally the meeting was adjourned, and the people assembled were advised and directed by the speakers to go to their homes, get their arms and re-assemble at 2 o'clock. I think that was the time designated.

The White-Leaguers on that day were assembled at their various places of rendezvous; companies were assembled at their various meeting-rooms or armories, as they might be called early in the morning from 6 to 10 o'clock, and were held under arms awaiting orders. Immediately after the meeting dispersed, in pursuance of a direction to disperse and get their arms, the White League companies assembled on Poydras street and vicinity, and at about 3:30 o'clock in the afternoon I received an order from General Longstreet to move my brigade (consisting of two battalions of infantry, a battery, and escort of cavalry) to the vicinity of the custom-house, leaving one battalion about half way between the State-house and the custom-house. I obeyed the order and moved the battery and the first battalion on Canal street opposite the custom-house and in pursuance to the law I called out to the crowd— of course many did not hear me, because there was considerable excitement at the time—for peaceably-disposed citizens to disperse. I sent Sergeant Taylor with a squad of cavalry down on each side of Canal street to direct peaceably-disposed citizens to disperse. That squad was fired upon and one man struck in the arm. When Sergeant Taylor returned he notified me of the fact of his being fired upon and pointed the man out to me, and I could see the white lining of his jacket torn out where the bullet had evidently passed through.

I then had information that the organized companies of the White League were moving out Poydras street and down the levee. I communicated that fact to General Longstreet, and he immediately ordered me to change my front to meet the movement of the White League. I ordered the battery on the levee on the head of Canal street, and after the battery went into position I saw an armed detachment moving down the levee behind the freight. Fearing that that company would move down so as to completely command my position and my detachment, and from the fact that the detachment of cavalry had already been fired upon, I directed Captain Grey to fire with the Gatling gun only. He fired at this approaching armed body with the Gatling gun, and then we were opened upon by a large body of White-Leaguers who were behind the freight, who had already reached there without my knowledge.

I did not know they were there. They instantly replied to the Gatling gun. A Gatling gun fires only one ball at a time, and is not supposed to do a great deal of execution, like a Napoleon gun. The whole battery opened, and my battalion opened then. After the White-Leaguers replied to a Gatling gun and the cannoneers were all shot down, killed or wounded; four of them, I believe, only escaped out of the battery.

Q. Your battery was in an exposed place?—A. It was in a very exposed place; the White-Leaguers were behind freight; the freight was cotton-bales, or a large quantity of it was cotton-bales.

Q. So the freight made a very effectual barricade for them?—A. Very.

Q. And the mischief would be done to you in your exposed condition rather than to them behind the freight?—A. O, yes; they were almost completely sheltered, while we were completely exposed. We also received a fire from the buildings in the vicinity. About that time I was badly wounded, and of course did not know much more about the fight. My left arm was broken, my right leg was broken, I was shot in the right hand and through the body. I received four wounds. I would like to state here, however, that the members of the White League took me up and treated me very kindly indeed; they took me to the hospital, and did everything that was within their power to give me comfort and assistance.

Q. Did some of them want to kill you?—A. Well, I have heard so, but I did not hear any person make any such threat, or did not see any effort made, except when being carried to the hospital by my White-League friends there were some loafers in the rear; they were not near the fight I can assure you; down at the corner of Dauphine street or Bourbon street they cried out once, "Kill him," "Kill him," when they learned it was me, but that did not amount to much; they were kept away by my friends.

Q. How many were killed on the 14th of September?—A. On the part of the Kellogg forces, or in my brigade, some twelve or fourteen were killed or have since died, or perhaps fifteen, and some sixty or seventy wounded; on the White League side I presume some twenty-five were killed, and perhaps some seventy-five or eighty wounded. It is a matter well known how many were killed on each side; I don't remember the numbers now, but those numbers are approximate.

Q. The White League was successful on the 14th. were they?—A. They were.

GEN. BADGER'S STATEMENT YEARS LATER

On July 21, 1885, Gen. A. S. Badger, who was then Collector of the Port of New Orleans, gave an interview to the *Times-Democrat* in which he gave some other details of the Battle of Canal Street on the 14th of September in 1874.

Gen. Badger stated that the State's forces, commanded by Gen. James Longstreet, consisted of two brigades, one composed of colored men under Gen. Barber stationed at the Statehouse (the old St. Louis Hotel) and the other consisting of 350 men* under his, Badger's, command.

Gen. Badger stated that he was called to headquarters of Gen. Longstreet and shown a diagram of the streets around the Customhouse and was told to take a position on Canal Street, opposite the Customhouse and covering Peters Street. He suggested to Longstreet that the levee would be the best position as the enemy would probably move down the levee to take possession of the arms from the *Mississippi*. He also told Longstreet that the meeting at Clay statue did not amount to anything, but the force to be watched was the White League which were resting on their arms at the armories. Longstreet said that if it were necessary the levee could be occupied later in the day. Badger received an order to take up a position as indicated on the map in use that morning, as from information received the White Leaguers would not move down the levee. "I had hardly taken my position when I saw the enemy marching down the levee."

---

*The number usually given in other reports is 500 men, and Badger himself in testifying before the Congressional Committee said there were 500 men in the Metropolitan Police force and 100 supernumaries.

Continuing, the interview,

"The enemy opened fire. I replied with enfilading fire of Gatlin gun." Couriers reported to him that a large force was massed at the head of Poydras St. He sent word to Longstreet who was in charge of a force in echelon at corner of Chartres and Customhouse Sts., asking him to come to his aid. Longstreet ordered him to move out and take possession of the levee. Badger tried but before Longstreet's reinforcements came "the battle went against us."

"Barber's brigade, which was composed almost entirely of colored men, were in the State House, and were not utilized, and as I had heard, were badly frightened."

Gen. Badger said that he was not shot from his horse but his horse was shot from under him. He was wounded four times. "When my men saw me fall they left the field in quite a hurry."

He thought that if his men had taken a position on the levee the result would have been different.

In the *Picayune* of July 29, 1885, Gen. Longstreet at Macon, Georgia, gave out a "release," saying that he did not order Badger to move out to Canal St., but the acting Secretary of State ordered him to do so. After finding that Badger had gone to Canal Street, Longstreet rode out to see him and pointed out that his position was faulty and that he should move his forces nearer the levee. But the Leaguers were already there. He says both sides opened fire simultaneously, and the fight seemed to last five minutes when Badger's men came streaming back. He attempted to rally them, but couldn't.

Col. Frank Richardson's Account

An interesting account of the battle is that of Col. Frank L. Richardson, which was printed in the Louisiana Historical Quarterly in October 1920, Vol. III, No. 3 under the title of "Recollections of Sept. 14, 1874." Richardson took an active part. Military companies were formed several months prior to the event and held secret meetings and procured arms. He wrote:

> My company was part of a battalion, known as Louisiana's Own, Col. John G. Angell, Commander. The meeting place was my law office then 54 Camp St., upstairs. Col. J. D. Hill was second in command, Dawson Blanchard, Frank McGloin, A. Mitchell, F. L. Lincoln and Euclid Borland were captains of the companies of the battalion.
>
> At the same time the *White League* had been organized by Gen. Fred N. Ogden and held its meetings at Eagle Hall on Prytania, corners of Urania and Felicity Streets. They were well supplied with Springfield rifles and a good supply of cartridges and well drilled. Wm. J. Behan, George Lord, Wm. Vaudry, Rufus

Pleasant, Dudley Coleman, Archie Mitchell, McIntyre and Sam Buck were the principal officers.

There were other companies, unattached, organized to participate in the movement. These were commanded by Captains Glynn, Guibet, Macheca, Phillips and Stewart. Few of the companies had a complete supply of ammunition and arms. In my company there was no uniformity of arms and not more than four or five rounds of cartridges to each man, these were made from buck shot, some in my office at 54 Camp St., and others at private houses in the city.

The day had been fixed for making the attack on Monday the 14th, as a consignment of arms, which was on board the Southern Pacific Steamer, *Mississippi,* was expected to arrive at the Bienville Street steamship landing that day. It had been determined to take them by force, if any attempt should be made by the Metropolitan Police to seize them and prevent the guns reaching the commands which were expecting them. Orders were issued for all members of the White League and Angell's Battalion to meet Monday morning at their respective headquarters.

At my law office on Monday morning the members of my company assembled. They were: B. R. Forman, Capt.; myself, Frank L. Richardson, 1st Lieut.; John Overton, 2nd Lieut.; Octo Ogden, 3rd Lieut.; and the sergeants were Dan Colcock and Doctors Pratt and Miles and Judge Henry Renshaw. Among those in the ranks were Edward Douglas White, now Chief Justice of the United States.

Most of the soldiers in my own company as well as the others were Confederate soldiers and did not require much instruction. The command of the company soon fell to me, as our captain stated that on account of his wife's illness he could not remain. On orders from the Colonel the battalion was ordered to deploy out from Magazine to Baronne Streets, along Common and to rally at the head of Poydras St. later in case of firing being heard on the levee. At 12 o'clock in the day a call was made for the citizens to assemble on Canal Street around Clay's monument, which at that time was at the corner of St. Charles and Canal Streets. Then Judge Marr, Dr. Beard, and Dr. Bruns and other speakers told of the tyrannical government under the Radical Kellogg regime and called upon them to take up arms in resistance. But in fact only those who were then assembled at their respective headquarters were expected to take parts.

Col. Richardson said that the radical forces numbered about 3,000, mostly Negroes, under Gens. J. Longstreet, Baldy and Badger. They thought the White League was a small force assembled on Common from Magazine to Baronne, "A mere mob who responded to the public call." Gen. Ogden had planned to march out Poydras to the Levee front and proceed to the ship at foot of Conti to obtain the consignment of arms.

At about two o'clock, I was ordered to the corner of Poydras and Camp with my company. Shortly after we had reached that position on that corner, Gen. Ogden came down from his station at Eagle Hall. He had about 300 men in file of fours and they marched out Poydras toward the river at a double quick step. They were well armed with Springfield rifles and with a good supply of ammunition and moved with the swing of old soldiers.

No orders having been received by me, the old rule in war times being, in the absence of orders, go where the firing is heaviest, I moved a double quick time with my company as far as Tchoupitoulas St. and out towards Canal. In a few minutes the firing began, Coleman's battery fired from the foot of Poydras with a cannon that had been overhauled at Leed's foundry and Gen. Badger fired his cannon from the foot of Canal, near the old Free Market Bldg., and then the White Leaguers under Rufus Pleasant moved out on the river front, among the freight lying there and fired up Canal, and two other companies under Behan and Lord charged across the open space on the levee front, towards Badger's Command, while my own company fired at the enemy drawn up facing Canal Street, on the lower end of the Custom House from Tchoupitoulas St. At a point where the Liberty Monument now stands, Gen. Badger fell, badly wounded, and many of his men were killed. The rest retreated—the enemy who ventured out of the Custom House on the riverside also broke and ran into the building.

Some firing was done from the windows of the Custom House. Gen. Longstreet seeing that his Negro troops would not stand fire retreated to the rear of the Custom House and was last seen galloping on his horse down town.

Few are now living of those that participated in what, though a small effort, yet resulted in redeeming the entire South and causing the country and Congress to become democratic, for the first time after the War Between the States.

PROCLAMATIONS

Late that afternoon Acting-Governor Penn issued General Order No. 2 and a proclamation offering amnesty to members of the Metropolitan Police who would lay down their arms. Both of these documents are reproduced here.

> Headq'rs. Executive Department of La.
> New Orleans, Sept. 14, 1874.

(General Orders No. 2.)

1. The Lieutenant Governor and Commander-in-Chief congratulates the troops in the field and the citizens of Louisiana that so far victory has been with the brave men who have bared their breasts for their country's liberty and honor.

2. He appeals to all able-bodied men of the city and State to repair at once to the ranks, bringing with them whatever arms and munitions of war they may possess.

3. He appeals to the women and non-combatants to forward to Major E. A. Burke, A. C. S., whatever food, blankets and clothing they may be able to contribute.

4. The Lieutenant Governor announces with unfeigned sorrow the loss of several gallant and noble citizens, killed and wounded in the conflict with the hireling hordes of Kellogg. These brave heroes and noble patriots have yielded their lives in a cause that is just and holy. Their comrades will avenge their loss, and their grateful state will embalm their memories.

The loss of our enemies in the engagements that have occurred can not be accurately stated. Our troops have captured three 12-pound Napoleon guns, one Gatling, a considerable number of small arms, besides some prisoners.

General Badger is believed to have been mortally wounded. A number of the enemy have been killed and wounded.

The Lieutenant Governor and Commander-in-Chief promises full protection to any and all men who, misguided, may have been induced to join the ranks of the usurper, and now may leave his service.

By command of Lieut. Gov. D. B. Penn.

E. JOHN ELLIS, A. A. A. G.

* * * * *

PROCLAMATION.

Whereas, it is probable that men identified with the interests of this community by life-long residence, and by adoption have been influenced to continue their connection with the metropolitan police force of this parish, and to array themselves antagonistically against their fellow-citizens, be it therefore known that I, D. B. Penn, Lieutenant and Acting Governor of the State of Louisiana, do hereby issue this, my proclamation, offering life and liberty to all members of the metropolitan police force who will lay down their arms and assist no longer in the perpetuation of W. P. Kellogg and the murder of their fellow citizens.

By command of Lieut. Gov. Penn, Commander-in-Chief.

E. JOHN ELLIS, A. A. A. General.

CHAPTER VII

THE DAY AFTER

After the defeat and dispersion of the Metropolitans on Canal Street on the late afternoon of Monday there remained two bodies or units of Kellogg's forces still intact or possibly three. The defeated 2nd Battalion of the Police retreated to the 3rd Precinct Station at the Cabildo; the battalion of Negro militia were still at the State House on Royal Street; and regiments of Negro militia were presumably at the old Criminal Courts building on Tulane Avenue. This last contingent is not mentioned in the press reports of the events of the 15th as a force to be overcome. It is possible that they had already joined the militia at the State House or disbanded. The *Times-Democrat* in its account of the Battle of Liberty Place, published on Sept. 14, 1909, states that there were three regiments of Negro militia on Tulane Avenue that morning.

As soon as the brigade of Metropolitans, or what was left of it, had disintegrated and retreated, the military leaders of the League had to decide whether to go in pursuit immediately or to move more slowly. It was not so much the police that mattered, but to reach the small group which remained, the Leaguers would have to pass or by-pass the State House on Royal Street where the Negro militia was stationed. This body of soldiers was said to have numbered 3,000, but Gen. Badger in his testimony before the Congressional Committee stated that it numbered 450 men. Perhaps some of the men from the Tulane Avenue post arrived later.

In any event to attack and capture this well-armed force inside a building with thick walls was a rash and dangerous enterprise. But this did not deter the victorious Leaguers. Gov. Penn had difficulty in holding them in restraint. Some of his advisers wanted him to attack the State House (formerly the St. Louis Hotel). The governor thought it would be a useless sacrifice of life.

He thought he had a better plan which proved successful. He tells about this in reminiscences of some years later. He sent emissaries to scatter his proclamation (given on another page) among the Negroes in the State House — soldiers and civilians — and "to inform them that if by daylight I found them in the building, I would proceed to attack them and would not be responsible for the consequences. . . . . . The result was that that night they left it, like rats from a sinking ship, going out in every conceivable outlet, and even down the posts of the verandas. Before daylight not one remained in the building."

All the night of the 14th detachments of the White League bivouacked in the streets in various parts of the city. Patrols made the rounds, and pickets were stationed at street corners. Street cars did not run that night, all except the Baronne Street line, having stopped at four o'clock. The *Republican* adds that there was no performance at the Academy of Music.

No one was molested and there were no disturbances. Only two men were arrested for drunkenness. But late wayfarers had to give a good account of themselves before being permitted to travel.

That portion of the city from Canal to Poydras and from Baronne to the river was in a state of military defense and the street corners were still barricaded. There were about fifteen street cars overturned and blocking the corners around Common, St. Charles, and nearby streets.

At about one o'clock Tuesday morning several squads of Metropolitan advance guards felt their way up Royal, Chartres and Decatur Streets as far as Canal. When the White League officer in command found this out he ordered a squad to advance and charge the "Mets," upon which most of them threw down their arms and fled while those who were unable to flee fast enough were captured and taken as prisoners to the White League guard house. In the meantime hundreds of others deserted their stations at the State House and the Jackson Square police station, and went home.

To press the capture of the State House and the 3rd Precinct Station Col. Angell's companies of La. Militia were ordered forward that night.

Capt. Borland's Company was stationed opposite Merriam's Billiard Saloon on Monday night. About two o'clock A.M., a deserter from the Metropolitan's at Jackson Square came in and said that the troops were ready to surrender. The Captain, fearing a trap, sent one of his men, N. E. Bailey, Jr., with the deserter whom he had disarmed, to the Police Station in the Cabildo. Mr. Bailey walked right in and learned that while many of the men were willing and anxious to surrender, the officers would not agree to it.

Mr. Bailey then went back to his command while the deserter was allowed to interview some of the Metropolitan pickets. More than twenty of them gave up and were taken to headquarters, Mr. Bailey himself capturing twelve men. The *Bulletin* says that all these captured black and white Metropolitans had on the uniform of United States soldiers but confessed to the "cheat."

THE SURRENDER OF THE STATE HOUSE TO THE WHITE LEAGUE

(From Frank Leslie's Illustrated Newspaper of Oct. 3, 1874)
This view seems to be from Chartres Street. The old St. Louis Hotel
was a long rather narrow building facing what is now the Civil District Court Building. The main entrance was on St. Louis Street
with entrances also on Royal and Chartres Streets.

— *Courtesy Howard-Tilton Library*

About this time, between four and five o'clock in the morning, Lieut. Clem Walker of Captain McGloin's Company, was patrolling near the pickets at the Jackson Square precinct. He walked boldly up to the station and said he had come to treat for a surrender. He was brought inside the arsenal and met Sgt. Bahnke who was in command, while Capt. Lawler, dangerously wounded and almost in a stupor from narcotics, mumbled that he would not surrender. Sgt. Bahnke reported that he had 100 Metropolitans stationed downstairs and 300 upstairs and that he would not surrender unless he was ordered to do so by Gov. Kellogg. He promised to see the governor to get his orders and asked for another meeting at seven o'clock.

When seven o'clock came Sgt. Bahnke reported that Kellogg had ordered him to hold the arsenal (the Third Precinct Police Station) at all hazards. The White Leaguers then began to prepare to march on the building. At this evidence of aggression the Metropolitan Police threw up their hands in a token of surrender, reversed their cannon and fled in all directions. Twelve Metropolitans and 3,000 stands of arms were captured.

One Negro was found dead in the Station, killed by an explosion sometime earlier; some of the police said it was done intentionally. No shots were fired by the White Leaguers but a few police accidentally fired their guns wounding one White Leaguer in the leg.

Just before the capture of the Jackson Square Police Station, the Statehouse was taken. The old St. Louis Hotel was crammed full of armed Negroes and Metropolitans, who presented a formidable appearance on the galleries. Lt. Newman came by, moving down Royal Street with two companies. As soon as they approached the Statehouse, a white flag was waved and the White Leaguers took immediate possession. They found that the whole building had been deserted except for a few white Metropolitan police. The "vast hosts," according to the *Bulletin* had scattered to the four winds, leaving everything behind — arms, uniforms and ammunition, enough for a division. Capt. McGloin's company then marched down and took possession of the Jackson Square Station.

By 10 o'clock Tuesday morning Col. Angell was in possession of all important points below Canal Street. Besides his own companies — Capt. Borland, Co. A; Capt. McGloin, Co. B; Capt. Blanchard, Co. C; Lieut. Richardson, Co. E — he was ably assisted by Capt. Macheca.

It was not until ten o'clock Tuesday morning until Sgt. Van Kirk who is hereafter to be known as the "last of the Metropolitans," was captured amidst wildest excitement. He was escorted by the White Leaguers and marched through Lafayette Square under a strong guard to headquarters, at Kursheedt and Bienvenu's store on Camp Street. As Van Kirk was recognized by some, quite a crowd followed, shouting and jeering at him. So many people gathered outside of headquarters on the pavement and in the square that Gen. Fred Ogden appeared on the gallery. He requested the people not to give way to their feelings and make no further demonstration. "There must be peace and order in the city." At this advice the crowd ceased and dispersed quietly. The war was now over and the last man captured.

Spunky Capt. Lawler

An interesting story about Captain Lawler of the Metropolitans is related by the *Republican*.

After the debacle at Canal Street, the Second Battalion, or what was left of it, retreated to the Third Precinct Station at the Cabildo. Capt. Lawler was in command. Wounded he went to the Statehouse where Dr. Newman dressed his wounds. He was resting when he learned at nine o'clock that affairs at the Third Precinct were in bad shape. The men were becoming demoralized and order was fast becoming disorder. Capt. Lawler then went to the Cabildo and, arriving with his shirt stained with blood and in intense pain, soon changed conditions. The other officers had gone to the Customhouse for aid — so they left word — and did not return. Capt. Lawler then had a force of about 125 men with two cannon and plenty of ammunition. After midnight when the White League began to extend its pickets below Canal Street, it occurred to Capt. Lawler that there might be some men in the Customhouse who would be of more service at Jackson Square. With ten men he started to the Customhouse to get reinforcements. After a little skirmish he reached the Canal Street entrance of the Customhouse, but found only forty men who were willing to take any more chances on fighting. With his fifty men he then marched back to the station and after disposing his men to the best advantage, and attempting to get some rest, he stretched himself out on a sofa. At five o'clock he awoke and found that conditions had changed for the worse. With the exception of the new recruiting officer, Sgt. Bahnke, and not more than ten others, every man of his force had deserted. Not a member of the Metropolitan brigade remained.

Capt. Lawler remarked, "Well, we will do what we can with what we've got." Later thirty more men came in and soon the building was fired upon. Capt. Lawler, trusting that the League did not know how great the desertions had been, and hoping that more help might come, made a show of force in which two of his men were killed. He was almost alone when word was brought to him that the Statehouse would soon surrender. At half past eight he was told that it had surrendered, and he was advised to do the same and that Col. Angell would come to see him. Unwilling to expose his weakness, Capt. Lawler cleared the squares around him with a few scattering shots and consented to meet Col. Angell "half way."

In the meantime, cannon from Leed's Foundry had been brought down Bourbon Street, accompanied by some 2,000 men. This is the way the story is told by the *Republican,* but it is doubtful whether there was any such number as 2,000 of White Leaguers. Continuing the *Republican* said:

> The disabled, deserted, defeated, but still defiant Lawler gave up his sword. He had five men and two guns to surrender.
>
> With the instinct of a soldier he sought the Customhouse, and made his final report to his superiors. Then he started for home. Friends gathered round and begged him to stay where he was safe, or at least take off his uniform. No, he would go, and undisguised. Crossing his arms over his wound he wearily went up Canal Street.
>
> At the corner of Royal street a company of White Leaguers, flushed with triumph, passed him. To the mortifications this last, best and bravest of the captains of the Metropolitan Brigade, was added the pang of seeing many of the most trusted of those who promised fidelity to him the night before marching with shotguns on their shoulders as gleeful as the rest. Here Maurice Hart, Esq., and a few of his friends surrounded him and generously insisted that he should not be permitted to go through the streets unprotected; and they escorted him home.
>
> Late in the day, an incident occurred which revived his spirits. Colonel Angell, accompanied by two other gentlemen, called at his room, and with a few pleasant words, returned him his sword. "I am glad," said he, "to get that sword back again."

People Out on the Streets

On Tuesday morning the mood of the people of the city was one of excitement and enthusiasm. Newspapers with accounts of the fight of the previous day were bought as fast as they came from the presses.

The streets generally were full of people. Large numbers of persons visited the scene of Monday's battle, and there was a continual stir around the entrance of the Customhouse. At the corner of Magazine and Canal Streets there were many bullet holes and marks of a shower of bullets, some of which indicated that they had been fired from the Customhouse.

Others visited the Third Precinct Station which showed the results of some sharp fighting there. On the banquette of St. Peter Street, near the corner of Chartres, were large pools of blood, some coagulated into lumps, which indicated loss of life and the wounding of others.

The *Bulletin* remarked:

> New Orleans will scarcely ever witness again in this century such scenes as marked the day yesterday, and made it memorable forever in the hearts of the people. It was a day that it were worth a lifetime to see, and the joy of the people fairly irradiated their countenances as they walked in peaceful throngs about the city. There was nothing like rowdyism or blustering evinced by any one; the bar houses were closed as well as most of the places of business, and everybody seemed content to express in quiet fashion his satisfaction at the glorious result of the effort of the people to relieve themselves of a despotism which had become unbearable.

The city soon assumed its usual summer quiet. Ladies appeared on Canal Street, the barricades were pulled down and the horse cars commenced running again. According to the *Picayune,* "Negroes also came out, apparently in a very satisfied mood, and did not give the least indication of either fear or disgust."

About noon of the 15th the following announcement appeared in the several daily papers, and was posted on the walls throughout the city:

> The citizens of New Orleans are invited to assemble this day, at 2 o'clock p. m., at the residence of his Excellency, Lieut. Governor Penn, at No. 236 St. Charles street, to conduct him to the State House.
>
>
>
> R. H. MARR
> SAM'L. CHOPPIN
> JULES TUYES
> J. M. SEIXAS
>
>

REPORT OF GEN. OGDEN TO GOV. PENN

Gen. Ogden, commanding forces in the field, addressed Tuesday morning the following report to Gov. Penn:

HEADQUARTERS STATE MILITIA.

New Orleans, Sept. 15, 1874.

Lieut. Gov. D. B. Penn, Acting Governor State of Louisiana:

Sir: I have the honor to report that I am in entire possession of the city. All the points heretofore occupied by the enemy are under my charge, to wit: the State House arsenal and all police stations.

I await your further orders.

F. N. OGDEN,
Gen. Commanding Forces in the Field.

T. Lee Shute, Adjutant.

Immediately upon the reception of the above report, Gov. Penn issued the following order:

HEADQUARTERS EXEC. DEP'T. OF LA.

Sept. 15, 1874.

F. N. Ogden, Major General Commanding State Troops:

General: In the name of the now free people of Louisiana, I return to you, on behalf of our enfranchised State, my solemn and heartfelt thanks. To your skill and gallantry and the glorious spirit and courage of the citizen soldiery of New Orleans, we owe to-day our new born *liberty.*

I shall communicate my orders to you at the earliest moment.

By command of

D. B. Penn,

Lieutenant and Acting Governor

and Commander-in-Chief.

J. Dickson Bruns, A.A.G.

The Mayor issued the following proclamation:

MAYORALTY OF NEW ORLEANS, Sept. 15, 1874.

CITIZENS OF NEW ORLEANS:

It becomes my duty to congratulate you upon the restoration of the duly elected and rightful State authorities.

After enduring for nearly two years the control of usurpers, their acts of tyranny have at length called for resistance. This was instantaneous, universal, and entirely successful, not a single usurping official being now in the exercise of his functions within the limits of this city.

The employment of force became a necessity. We deplore the resulting loss of life, while we honor the memory of the noble men who fell in defense of the rights dear to all who deserve to be free.

Upon this signal and most honorable recovery of your political and civil rights let me advise you extreme moderation. Resume your avocations as soon as dismissed from organized ranks. Use the utmost forbearance towards those who hold political opinions adverse to yours. Interfere with no peaceful assemblage of your fellow-citizens of any race or color.

Use all your influence to preserve the peace and to maintain the supremacy of the law. Prove to the world that you can be as forbearing to those who have usurped and abused authority as you were patient and long-suffering under their tyranny. Seek no revenge for past injuries, but leave your fallen enemies to the tortures of their own consciences and to the lasting infamy which their acts have won for them.

LOUIS A. WILTZ, Mayor.

The New Orleans Cotton Exchange posted on its boards Tuesday morning a notice that it would close that afternoon. The notice read:

"This Exchange will be closed at 1 o'clock P. M., as a mark of sympathy with the movement to establish the legitimate government of Louisiana."

The *Picayune* commented that this was one proof that the overthrow of Kellogg was not the work of a clique, but of the entire people of the State. It cited the fact that the Exchange was composed of the entire cotton trade of the city, a trade of $100,000,000 in extent, and that the membership embraced the most intelligent and wealthy citizens of New Orleans.

This point is further borne out in reading the list of prominent business men, bankers and heads of insurance companies who signed the following telegram sent to President Grant on the morning of the 15th:

TELEGRAM TO PRES. GRANT

To U. S. Grant, President of the United States, Washington, D. C.:

The Kellogg Government is completely deposed. Perfect confidence restored. We feel that we are free once more and, hank God for the calmness and courage of our citizens. Not a single case of lawlessness. The colored population and all other citizens perfectly secure in their lives and property.

A load of degradation and oppression lifted from our people, and we are now hopeful and encouraged for the future. Business men greatly encouraged. As loyal citizens of the United States we confidently rely upon you for the recognition and guarantee of the State under McEnery and Penn, who have the confidence of all good and true men of Louisiana.

Sam'l. H. Kennedy, President State National Bank.
Thos. A. Adams, President Crescent Mutual Insurance Company.
Wm. S. Pike, Pike, Brother & Co., bankers.
Isaac N. Marks.
Moore, Janney & Hyams.
Jas. I. Day, President Sun Mutual Insurance Company.
Edw'd C. Palmer, President Louisiana Savings Bank.
George Jonas, President Canal Bank.
Patrick Irwin, President Hibernia National Bank.
Wm. C. Black.
Chas. B. Singleton.
John Henderson, President Hibernia Insurance Company.
H. S. Buckner.
Louis Schneider, President Germania National Bank.
L. B. Cain.
Hy. Peychaud, President Hope Insurance Company.
J. W. Hincks, Secretary New Orleans Insurance Company.
P. Fourchy, President Merchants' Mutual Insurance Company and Mutual
    National Bank.
Am. Fortier, President Bank of America.
Hoffman, Marks & Co.
Thos. Layton, President Southern Bank.
Isaacson, Seixas & Co.
M. Musson, President New Orleans Insurance Association.
S. H. Kennedy & Co.
and many others.

The work of installing another set of officials under the new regime pro-gressed rapidly. Thomas Boylan was appointed Chief of Police. Mr. Graham, the State Auditor, took possession of his office and began putting it into work-ing trim. Lusher, as State Superintendent of Public Education took charge of his office, as did Attorney-General H. N. Ogden.

CITIZEN-SOLDIERS IN REVIEW

After the State House had been occupied and the Third Precinct Station taken over, the citizen soldiers marched to the head of Canal Street. There the entire command formed in line preparatory to marching in review before General Ogden to be later dismissed and permitted to go to their homes.

About 12:30 or 1 o'clock the companies in military array moved out Canal Street to Camp and up that street to Eagle Hall where they broke ranks and were dismissed. The *Times* said there were 2,200 or 2,300 men, but the *Republican's* estimate of 1,500 is probably more nearly correct. They carried with them the trophies of their late victory consisting of three guns captured and several flags, and, of course, their own guns and small arms used in the fight. The *Picayune* in its account said:

> They marched along Canal street, not uniformed, indeed, but with the old true swing they learned twelve years ago, and with the gallant tread of men who are patriots and warriors. As they passed the Custom-House, where the United States troops were quartered, and saluted the national presence, loud, thrilling cheers rang out and caps were waved from every window on the Canal street *facade* of that vast edifice. The soldiers inside recognized the soldiers who filled the great thoroughfare beneath and paid sincere, spontaneous tribute to their courage and their dignity.
>
> It was a gratifying spectacle, full of meaning to all who witnessed it.

The *Republican* reported the incident in this way:

> Colonel Behan a little before three o'clock [one o'clock] assembled most of the armed men, say 1500, and marched them through some of our principal streets. They had all the captured artillery and arms, presenting a very warlike appearance, minus uniforms, except one mounted man who wore a fanciful Confederate jacket. They bore the flags and guidons of the old State militia, which had been taken from the St. Peter street armory in the morning. This march, it seems was the last display before dismissing a majority of the men to their homes for a rest. The artillery and most of the arms were deposited in the first precinct stationhouse.

As the citizen-soldiers marched up Camp Street they went by "headquarters," just below Poydras where General Ogden reviewed them. As each company marched by the men cheered him lustily. Here is the *Bulletin's* account:

> It was an inspiring sight to witness these gentlemen go by with a step as firm and a bearing as martial as though they had been trained soldiers, and it was more than exhiliarating, it was simply glorious, to hear the spontaneous and hearty cheers to their gallant leader, to whose unflinching courage, admirable executive qualities and indomitable perseverance we are mainly indebted for our rescue from the usurpation of Kellogg. It was a well deserved tribute to as gallant and meritorious a gentleman and soldier as ever drew a sword in a holy cause.
>
> The greatest enthusiasm was evinced by the immense concourse of people that lined the banquettes when the captured guns and flags went by, and there were many jokes over the various articles, such as epaulettes, etc., etc., which had been

captured from the metropolitans and were sported by the soldiers. Some of the boys, who had evidently not had a square meal for twenty-four hours, had loaves of bread stuck up on their bayonets, which they drew upon occasionally as hunger pinched them.

Inauguration of Gov. Penn

As a result of the notices asking people to assemble at the residence of Lieut.-Governor Penn at 2 o'clock, several thousand people gathered at 236 St. Charles Street, waiting to congratulate him. The Governor soon arrived and reviewed a large number of prominent people, leading citizens, merchants, professional men, including Mr. Marr, Dr. Choppin, Gen. Fred Ogden, and Judge H. N. Ogden.

It will be remembered that Governor McEnery was not in the city so that it became necessary to install Lieut.-Gov. Penn as acting governor. Accordingly the ceremony of inaugurating another governor in place of Kellogg took place that afternoon. Here is the *Picayune's* description of that event:

After receiving quite a number of citizens, Gov. Penn mounted his carriage with Mr. Marr and others, and drove down St. Charles street at the head of a procession of citizens, numbering not less than three or four thousands.

The street on both sides was filled with ladies and gentlemen, the former waving their handkerchiefs, the latter shouting until they were hoarse. Slowly the procession moved down to Canal, and thence to the State-House, the street being so filled with people that it was almost impossible to move. Along the route there could not have been less than twenty or thirty thousand persons.

At the State-House there was great confusion, owing to the immensity of the crowd. Part dashed up the stairs, that cracked and threatened to fall at this over-

Mr. R. H. Marr addressing the White Citizens at the St. Charles Hotel. (From **Frank Leslie's Illustrated Newspaper**, Oct. 3, 1874)

weight; a thousand or more found refuge in the Chamber of Representatives, and the rest rushed out on the gallery. In the street there was assembled about ten thousand people, extending from Bourbon to Chartres, and from Conti to Toulouse.

Gov. Penn was, of course, called on first, and read a short speech. He recited the despotism the people had suffered, and congratulated them that this was now ended. Peace and order were established.

Gov. Penn called on the people to assemble in the various churches at 1 o'clock, this morning, to offer thanks to God for the great mercies he had shown, and to beseech Him for a continuance for his protection.

E. John Ellis made a very short address. He congratulated the citizens over their victory and referred in eulogistic terms to Gov. Penn, who had been the head and front of this movement, and to Gen. Fred Ogden, the gallant gentleman and high-toned, chivalrous soldier, who, no politician, no office seeker, led the citizens to a victory that resulted in their regaining their liberty. Mr. Ellis ended in counseling peace and order, praying that no act of oppression or intolerance would dim the lustre of victory.

R. H. Marr, glowing with enthusiasm, was then called forth. Mr. Marr counseled moderation and quiet. There must be no disturbances; the citizens owed this to themselves to vindicate their movement by their order. But especially to the Negro must they be just and lenient. If the people of Louisiana, white and colored, united, the State would once more see peace, prosperity and happiness.

Gen. Fred. Ogden was called on to speak, but excused himself on the ground that he was not a speaker.

The entire time consumed in these speeches barely amounted to half an hour. Gov. Penn then retired to the Executive chamber, and held a consultation with leading citizens.

The crowd, however, did not leave the State-House for an hour or more after breaking up, but enjoyed themselves in cheering Penn, McEnery and others.

The *Bulletin* reported the inaugural procession in part:

We have witnessed many processions in this city in our time; have seen the enthusiastic throngs that sent our boys off to the army during the late war, but there never was before such a grand and truly sublime spectacle as was presented by the immense concourse of people who acted as a volunteer escort to place D. B. Penn, Lieutenant Governor, in the office to which he had been elected by a vast majority, but which he had been illegally and violently prevented from occupying by Kellogg and his armed janissaries, backed up by the United States troops.

No pen can depict the wild and overmastering excitement of the overjoyed people, no words can give any idea of the tumultuous shouts and cheers that greeted the Lieutenant Governor as he moved slowly forward, and we will not attempt to give even a faint idea of the enthusiasm of the ladies, God bless them! They waved hands, handkerchiefs and flags in token of their joyous approbation, and Gov. Penn was kept busy answering their salutations and the bows from the gentlemen who pressed forward to see him.

We saw aged men with tears of joy in their eyes rush up to the carriage, and seizing the Governor's hand say, "God bless you!" "Thank God for this."

It was a grand triumphal march of people redeemed from thraldom, and it makes one's heart throb faster and the blood tingle pleasantly through the veins to think of it all.

Pres. Grant Hears Kellogg's Appeal

In the meantime Gov. Kellogg kept the wires to Washington hot with his appeals for help. President Grant acted immediately and on the morning of the 15th issued a proclamation in which he stated "it has been satisfactorily represented to me that turbulent and disorderly persons have combined with force and arms to overthrow the Government of the State of Louisiana," and that by law if the Legislature were not in session by application of the Governor, he could use the military and naval forces of the United States to put down the insurrection, he therefore commanded "said turbulent and disorderly persons to disperse and retire peaceably to their respective abodes within five days from this date."

Ironically news of this proclamation reached New Orleans about the time that the citizen-soldiery were making their triumphal march through the streets on their way to break ranks and go home.

Gov. Penn Wires the New York Papers

Gov. Penn, alert to the importance of the proper publicity, sent the following telegram to the *New York Herald* which was published in the issue of the 16th:

> The North can form no idea of the robbery and spoliation to which we have been subjected. My movement was necessitated by the attitude of the people. They demanded it. I am now in full possession of the government of the State. The colored people are satisfied and contented. A strong brigade of colored troops fully organized and armed and in the service of the usurpation refused to fire a shot in his defence. The most perfect peace and good order prevail. We are thoroughly loyal to the Federal Government, and in the operations of the past two days there have been no excesses or violations of law. This government is the only one now in existence in Louisiana.

At the request of the *New York Times,* Governor Penn telegraphed that paper a statement which appeared on the 17th. The statement read as follows:

> The revolution and overthrow of the Kellogg Government was not a party or political movement, but one of the people to get rid of a government which was universally believed by the people to be a usurpation; and the officers administering the same corrupt, dishonest, and incapable, who had already inflicted vast mischief, and were continuing to plunder the people as if bent on their ruin and universal confiscation. Kellogg's promises of reform and repeal of oppressive legislation and of war against the plunderers were never kept. Even his funding scheme was one of corrupt jobbery, and the bonds of the State had fallen to twenty cents on the dollar. The people were reduced to absolute despair. If Kellogg ever intended, he was incapable of achieving any reform. His administration held out a bleak prospect of impoverishment and constant turmoil. His own party had grown de-

fiant of him. His attempt to defeat the renomination of Debuclet, a most respected colored man, had brought on him the bitter hostility and opposition of the colored people. The race acquiesce in and are even relieved by the change. They only need guarantees, which Penn and his friends can give, of the protection of all their political rights, and a faithful execution of all the reconstruction amendments and acts of Congress. There will be no violence under such an administration.

The attempt to continue Kellogg in power by Federal arms will require an army of 5000 men in nearly every parish. The Kellogg local officers are superceded. The registration is proceeding under new registrars, well known and respected citizens.

There never was so thorough and complete a revolution achieved with so few excesses. The people armed because a fully armed and disciplined military was employed to crush them.

The fighting and loss of life resulted from an advance, in hostile array, of the Metropolitans, who opened fire with artillery up the streets. This was done by order of Longstreet. Kellogg repudiated it. The killing of the citizens produced the conflict which followed. Since the cessation of fighting peace and order have prevailed everywhere.

Union soldiers have numerously participated with the citizens in the resistance to a Government which has only been supported by the State officials and jobbers.

The Federal authority has throughout been treated with the greatest respect. Federal soldiers are greeted with cheers, and received and entertained with kindness and hospitality.

CHAPTER VIII

INCIDENTS OF THE CANAL STREET AFFAIR

In the excitement of the Battle of Canal Street and the temporary overthrow of the Kellogg Government, many incidents occurred which are interesting and which throw light on the uprising. They are the footnotes of history.

From the newspapers of the day, from the reports of participants and their families, and from tradition are obtained many of the items which follow.

Episodes of the Battle

One reason for the defeat of the Metropolitans was the lack of protection on their left flank. This was later a matter of dissension between Generals Longstreet and Badger. They allowed the White Leaguers to occupy the levee, where hiding behind cotton bales and freight, the enemy could shoot down the unprotected police.

However, this flanking movement by Gen. Ogden was not a matter of chance. From the *Times-Democrat* of Sept. 14, 1909, we learn some of the details:

> Company C proceeded down the levee. An L & N train pulled slowly along across Canal St. by prearrangement and the company marched under its protection. At a signal the freight train began moving rapidly and disclosed to the astonished Metropolitans the company on their flank. Gen. Badger commanded, "Commence firing"! and the Leaguers started firing too.
>
> Gen. Ogden's horse was shot from under him and he pitched forward on the banquette of Tchoupitoulas St. knocking him insensible. Gen. Behan took command.
>
> The police as they fled discarded coats, ammunition, everything which hampered speed. They ran into Custom House, down the streets, etc.

Said the *Bulletin*:

> The flight was most disgraceful, the men throwing down their guns, pulling off their hats and coats, and some of them actually jumping into the river to avoid the deadly missiles which by that time were decidedly numerous. In the fight the citizens captured two Napoleon guns and one Gatling gun, with ammunition, besides some 75 or 100 stand of Winchester rifles.

The police deserted their artillery. For years afterward the State government posted a reward of $500 for the return of the two guns and other arms.* When the incident was forgotten, one day the guns were brought out from the secret hiding place and placed in the Washington Artillery Armory. These guns are now in the State Museum at the Cabildo.

Three regiments of Negro militia were garrisoned in the old Parish Prison on Tulane Ave. and were to march down along the New Basin Canal and attack the Leaguers from the rear. To prevent this, Leaguers under Capt. Peck kept a position at Tivoli Circle (Lee Circle). The Negro militia never came.

The article in the *Times-Democrat* continues:

> One of the most astonishing things about the whole battle was the behavior of the crowd. Cheering thousands watched the conflict from every vantage point. They crowded every window, doorway, and balcony which offered a view of the scene, and they filled the street at the very edge of the line of fighters. No one apparently even thought of danger, but gazed on the battle as if it were a panorama arranged for some great holiday.

> The newsboys were recklessness personified. They darted in and out between the lines of men and in front of the very guns. When the police fled the newsboys were close behind them, themselves picking up the Winchesters which the frightened constabulatory were throwing aside.

> In the river were excursion boats which had promised to convey the crowds to the rowing regatta [at Carrollton.] They were filled to their loading capacity, with men, women and children, who crowded the decks which gave a full view of the conflict, and many of the bullets of the police which missed the White Leaguers struck the boats. One shot from a piece or artillery went through the boilers of one boat.

NEGROES ON THE FOURTEENTH

The *Picayune* pointed out that during the uprising and the battle of the 14th as well as the activities of the White League the next day, no colored

---

Stolen State arms — Proclamation of reward.

STATE OF LOUISIANA, EXECUTIVE DEPARTMENT,

New Orleans, October 31, 1874.

The following-described arms, the property of the State of Louisiana, have been taken from the custody of the legally-constituted authorities of the State and are retained in the possession of unauthorized persons: Two mountain-howitzers, caliber 4.62, model of 1861, weight 220 pounds, marked T. H. R. on the face.

Three hundred and one Winchester rifles, made for bayonet-attachment, numbers ranging between 31,120 and 34,163, marked L. S. M. on butt-plates.

Six hundred and twenty-four Springfield breech-loading rifles, model of 1870, caliber .50, marked L. N. G. on butt-plates.

Ninety-three Spencer carbines, caliber .50, marked L. N. G.

Notice is hereby given that the State of Louisiana will pay a reward of $50 each for the recovery of the two howitzers, and $100 additional for such evidence as shall lead to the conviction of the person or persons illegally retaining possession of them; also a reward of $10 for the recovery of each of the above-described rifles and carbines, and $25 additional for such evidence as shall lead to the conviction of any person illegally retaining possession of any of the said weapons.

Given under my hand, and the seal of the State hereunto attached, this thirty-first day of October, in the year of our Lord eighteen hundred and seventy-four, and of the Independence of the United States the ninety-ninth.

WILLIAM P. KELLOGG

S. N. Packard, United States Marshal at New Orleans in 1874

Originally from Massachusetts he came to Louisiana after the War and became active in politics. Said the *Graphic*: "He is the chief of the so-called 'Custom House Ring.' He is the person who executed the famous Durell midnight order by which the McEnery government was ousted from the State House." Packard later ran against Nicholls for the governorship and claimed the election. The White League in the Spring of 1877 kept him and his government bottled up in the State House, the old St. Louis Hotel, until Hayes became President and recognized Nicholls as Governor of Louisiana. (This picture is from a sketch in the N. Y. Daily Graphic of Sept. 25, 1874 which was made from a photograph by Washburn of New Orleans.)

C. C. Antoine, Lieutenant-Governor of Louisiana

On another page will be found a short article about him. (This picture is from a sketch in the N. Y. Daily Graphic of Sept. 25th, 1874 made from a photograph by Petty and Quinn of New Orleans)

Judge Henry C. Dibble

Judge Henry C. Dibble was an officer of volunteers during the War. Coming to Louisiana he entered politics and became a Warmoth adherent. In 1874 he was Judge of the Eighth District Court of Louisiana and a colonel on Gov. Kellogg's military staff. The *Graphic* said: "Report has it that his legal experience is of the slimmest possible character." (From a sketch in the N. Y. Daily Graphic made from a photograph by Washburn of New Orleans)

A Carpet Bag

Photograph of a carpet bag — about one third actual size — at the Louisiana State Museum. Many of the adventurers and spoilsmen who came South after the War wrapped up their meagre belongings in a piece of carpet, sewed a handle to the bundle, and sallied forth to gain fame or infamy and certainly fortune. (*Courtesy of the Museum — photo by Frank H. Allen*) private citizen was killed, maltreated or even insulted. This is an impressive fact, as a few colored men used incendiary language and seemed to want to provoke trouble.

The only lawful officer of the State who was allowed to keep his office after the deposition of Gov. Kellogg was a colored man, the State Treasurer. His renomination had been bitterly opposed by Gov. Kellogg on the avowed grounds of his color. When the State House was occupied by the "insurgents," Dubuclet, the Negro state treasurer, with his deputies continued to carry on the affairs of his office without intrusion or interruption. On the second day of the new regime a sentinel at the State House, not knowing Dubuclet and that he was the treasurer, refused him admission, whereupon Dubuclet went home. As soon as Governor Penn heard of the incident he ordered one of his aides to go to Dubuclet's residence in his, the Governor's carriage, and apologize to Mr. Dubuclet for the unintentional rudeness of the sentinel.

During the troubles of Monday and Tuesday the colored people pursued their vocations and came and went as freely as the most important or influential white men, according to the *Picayune*.

According to Tinker, on the day of the 14th "not a Negro could be seen." But this generality probably applied to the section of the city patrolled by the White League — from Canal to Tivoli Circle (now Lee Circle) and from Carondelet to the River. At that time not many Negroes lived in that area. Undoubtedly the servants went about unmolested as did others of peaceful intent.

The *Times* in its issue of the 16th had this to say about Negroes on the day of the battle, under the head of "The Freedmen":

> The impression had freely prevailed on Monday that no Negroes appeared on the streets, in fear of molestation at the hands of the League. This was erroneous, the Negroes freely circulating through the city, except at the time of the fighting, when they concluded, in common with many other, that it was safest to retire. They seemed to understand that no injury was intended them by the League, and accordingly appeared, save the more prominent colored officeholders.

The Horse Cars

Some fifteen cars were turned over and used as barricades around Common and St. Charles and nearby streets. As the tracks for this type of car were more simple than those of today, and the streets were paved with cobblestones — further uptown not paved at all — it was easier to put the tracks in condition again. Here's what the *Picayune* said in its issue of the 17th:

> The return of the horse cars to their various depots bear evidence to the order, the good behavior and decency observed even in the midst of the fight. On Camp,

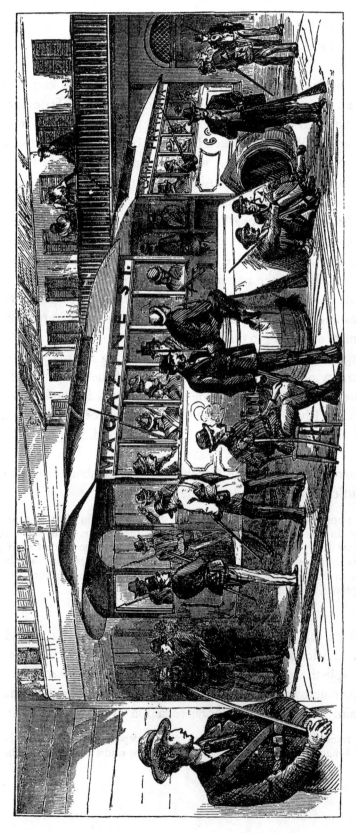

A STREET BARRICADE, GUARDED BY WHITE LEAGUERS
September 14, 1874. (Harper's Weekly, Oct. 10, 1874)
—Courtesy Leonard V. Huber

St. Charles and various other streets the cars were stopped during the fight and placed across the street, forming efficient barricades. On Tuesday morning, when order was re-established, the cars were again put on the track and were soon running. No damage had been done them, and the money boxes, although with no one to guard them and public and free to all, were found perfectly intact, not one forced or opened. The money, which amounted to a large sum, was taken out by the receivers and turned over to the various companies. And all this in the mid of tumult and confusion, when larceny was but too easy.

This testimony to the honesty of Orleanians attracted attention in other cities. Maybe we were not so honest but the White League patrols were efficient and prevented pillage and theft. In any event the following from the *New York Commercial Advertiser,* a Republican newspaper, issue of September 25, said:

> New Orleans papers announce the curious fact that the fare boxes in the various street cars used as barricades on the 14th inst., though containing in the aggregate a large sum of money, were found to be undisturbed when the cars returned to the stations. That thing couldn't have happened in New York.

The Valiant General Barber, Commander of the Negro Militia

There are two stories in vogue about the behavior of Brig.-Gen. Barber, Commander of the 2nd Battalion of Louisiana State Militia, an all-Negro outfit stationed at the old St. Louis Hotel on Royal Street. The first version appeared in the *Bulletin* of September 26th, only twelve days after the event, and is more likely to be the truer account. It reads:

> It is said of Brig. Gen. Barber, of the African Brigade of State Militia, that, immediately on evacuating the State House, he rushed wildly for the nearest livery stable, and, stripping himself of his uniform, went actively to work grooming the horses and washing the buggies in the stable. This he considered the safest way of eluding the White Leaguers, whom, he feared, might make of his valuable person some other use than that of a "black board" for the Straight University. Suffice it to say the disguise was complete and successful, and the hero of the fight resigned his situation on the installation of Kellogg, and resumed his military office, but sans epaulettes and sans *chappeau de bras.* When will he appear again in command of that brigade?

A more popular account is that given by Governor Penn in a newspaper interview, giving his reminiscences of the 14th of September, published years later. Gov. Penn related that Gen. Barber had sought refuge in an undertaker's shop nearby; that he put on his full-dress uniform and laid himself out in a coffin as if prepared for burial. In this manner he escaped discovery.

GENERAL LONGSTREET.
(Harper's Weekly, Oct. 10, 1874)

GENERAL JAMES LONGSTREET

Gen. Longstreet was a strange figure during the period of Reconstruction. Born in South Carolina in 1821, he was graduated from West Point in 1842. After serving in the Mexican War, where he was severely wounded, and receiving two brevets for gallantry, he had earned the rank of major by 1861. When South Carolina seceded, Longstreet resigned and became a Brigadier General in the Confederate Army. His record is well known. He was criticized for his part at the Battle of Gettysburg, and many blamed him for the Confederate failure. This seemed to set heavily upon Gen. Longstreet and when the war was over, he joined the Republican Party to accept a Federal office at New Orleans.

After the affair of the 14th, the newspapers had much to say about Longstreet. From the *Bulletin*:

> We saw Gen. Longstreet riding on Canal street, Monday afternoon, ordering citizens to "disperse and go home," that he intended to "rake the streets with cannister." Such says the World (N. Y.) has not been done in this free country since the Boston massacre, when Major Pitcairn at the head of the King's troops marched upon the citizens on King street, and exclaimed: "Disperse ye Rebels!" In Pitcairn's case it was in dispute *who fired the first shot,* in the present case there is no room for doubt. The Gatling gun opened the fire upon the citizens. It was Longstreet's aggressive nature that induced him to make the attack. He wanted blood

from this community and he got it, but the fortune of war did not this time favor him, he was thrashed, badly thrashed and fled with a wound across his body to the protecting wall of the United States Custom-House, where he knew the citizens would not follow him.

The *Republican* in its issue of Sept. 27, 1874 published a reprint of an article in the Chicago *Inter-Ocean* written by its special correspondent in New Orleans in which he wrote:

I referred to General Longstreet just now. As everybody knows, he is thoroughly reconstructed; he has been a federal officer, surveyor of the port, and has been as active as any in this war of races, commanding the colored men against his old comrades of the rebellion. For this he receives, perhaps, the most intense hatred of any, and I myself have heard men say that they "would shoot Longstreet on sight." The papers have demanded his life, and they call him "a recreant traitor," "the betrayer of the dearest interests of the South," and all that sort of thing.

While Penn and Kellogg and Longstreet and Casey were talking just before that conference of the factions that lasted most all of yesterday, Penn spoke of the quiet of the city, and Kellogg asked if he thought his (Kellogg's) life would be safe if he went into the street.

"I think so," said Penn.

"Would you dare," said Kellogg, "walk down to the State House with me on one arm and Longstreet on the other?"

"Well, I don't know," hesitated Penn. "It would be risky business if Longstreet was along."

So the old General has to keep pretty close. Did you ever see him? A tall, portly, dignified gentleman of the old school, who wears ruffled shirts, and a fob chain dangling on his nankeen trousers. Grayish sandy side whiskers, and a head that is just bald enough to add to his dignity. A deep set, small blue eye, with bush eyebrows, and deep wrinkles running across from temple to temple, that look as if they had been cut there by a sculptor's hand. This is Longstreet.

"A fine old country gentleman,
  One of the good old kind."

I was talking with him last night, while that long-winded conference was in session. He sat in one chair, with his feet in another, his wrist bands and collar unbuttoned, waving a great fan across an arc of about four feet, that measured his "breadth of beam," with the radius of his lower vest button, and I asked him—

"General, these people seem to be pretty savage on you, down there, don't they?"

"I don't know!" he replied, indifferently. "Maybe they do."

"Why, yes, they call you a recreant and a traitor, and they say you've betrayed the interests of the South."

"There exists a difference of opinion," he replied, "as to what the interests of the South are. I think they are one thing, they think they are another. That's the way we happened to get separated."

This is the *Bulletin's* comments about Longstreet in article headed, "Too Thin":

Longstreet says the fight was not continued Tuesday morning, because he was "short of ammunition." This is a little too weak. The citizens who first entered the Jackson Square Police Station found a room filled with boxes of cartridges, to which they helped themselves. He also tries to make a scapegoat of poor old Attorney General Field for withholding the appropriation of $20,000 made by the Legislature, for want of which he hadn't ammunition. Fudge! He knows, as well as we do, that he and his force were whipped, thrashed, routed, infantry and artillery, by 160 men—men, too, mostly who fought under him in the war in Virginia— men whose bravery and soldierly qualities made his reputation.

Go and hide your head, poor, defeated, Longstreet. A man we once loved and admired—we have followed you in forty battles. You were to us all that was great and brave, but now you have shed the blood of our best young men. You thought the appearance of your battery of Napoleons and Gatling gun would put to flight the "mob." You little reckoned on the sudden crushing defeat that was to come in such short time.

In its issue of the 15th of September describing the fight of the day before, the *Bulletin* made this comment:

> Gen. Longstreet was seen for a few moments, but judiciously made himself scarce, disappearing in a most unaccountable and ungallant manner, when he heard the well known yell of his old troops, many of whom were in the citizen soldiery that had so unexpectedly to him shown up to confront the Hessian soldiery of which he had demeaned himself so far as to take command. It is to be regretted that he did not show up more prominently instead of sending his lieutenant Badger where the balls were thickest.
>
> The men who fought under him in Virginia from Bull Run to Gettysburg would have been pleased to have seen more of him.

An oldtimer, Mr. Poupart, who lived down on Royal Street and when he died was the oldest stock broker on the New Orleans Stock Exchange, says that when Gen. Longstreet heard the rebel yell, he remarked: "I have heard that yell before." And he rode into the Customhouse.

In December 1874, two months after the engagement of Canal Street, Gen. Longstreet resigned as Adjutant General. He was appointed Levee Commissioner for another year. In 1875 he moved to Gainesville, Georgia, and was Minister to Turkey for a term. During the rest of his life he held numerous Government jobs.

The bitterness against Gen. Longstreet has healed. But even today when he is mentioned there are those who blame him not only for "failing" General Lee but for his inglorious part in Reconstruction.

Ben Ames Williams, writer and a grand nephew of Longstreet, in the last book he wrote, "The Unconquered," shows the general in a more favorable light in that he believed him to be sincere.

General Longstreet died January 2, 1904.

GENERAL BADGER.
(Harper's Weekly, Oct. 10, 1874)

The Wounding of General Badger

General Algernon S. Badger, the commander of the Metropolitans, was severely wounded during the melee and at the time it was not thought that he could live. According to his own statement before the Congressional Committee several months later, he was shot four times; his left arm was broken, his right leg broken, he was wounded in the right hand and then shot through the body. This last wound laid him low, as he later stated, he was shot from his horse and his horse was not shot from under him.

All this while he was bravely trying to rally his men and force them to fight. He is said to have shot one of his men while running away. General Badger lived up to the tradition and conduct of a U. S. Army officer.

As he lay on the ground, the firing now over, a crowd gathered, some of the members of which wanted to kill the general.* These would-be assassins,

*A CARD.
Editor New Orleans Bulletin:
In the New Orleans Republican *of Sept. 22, is a statement that I attempted to kill Gen. Badger while he lay wounded on the battle field on Monday, Sept. 14, 1874, and that an eye-witness, who was with the White League, can testify to the same. The author is evidently some mean, low-spirited creature, whom it would be flattery to call a coward, and the statement is an untruth. I did not war on wounded men last Monday week, and instead of attempting to kill Gen. Badger, I volunteered my services to the gentlemen attending his removal, as several of them will testify. Therefore, I pronounce the statement in the* Republican *as utterly false and malicious.*
JOHN DONOVAN

let it be said, were not members of the White League. Capt. Kilpatrick came up, and with a revolver in one hand and a sword in the other, stood with one foot on each side of the general's prostrate body and threatened to kill the first man who attempted to touch him. This account is given in the *Times-Democrat* in its issue of 14th of September 1909, 25 years later.

The *New Orleans Times* of Sept. 15, 1874 in its account of the Battle of the 14th ran this paragraph:

THE SHOOTING OF GENERAL BADGER.

General Badger was shot in the arm, leg, and right side, and while lying there he was approached by a man with fixed bayonet, who seemed bent on killing him. General Badger saw his motion and said, "I'm going fast enough; it's no use to kill me." A bystander, one of the league, then interfered and saved his life. He was afterward kindly cared for by the White Leaguers, and conveyed to the Charity Hospital.

One tradition is that Gen. Badger was a Mason as was Capt. Kilpatrick. The general gave the Masonic sign which brought the captain to his rescue.

On another page we find that Capt. Joseph Macheca claims that he was the one that rescued Gen. Badger. History, however, has discounted Capt. Macheca's claim and gives credit to Capt. Kilpatrick for rescue of the doughty general.

General Badger was taken to the Charity Hospital and attended by some of the best surgeons in the city. The newspapers gave daily reports of his progress. Eventually he recovered but had his leg amputated. He says in his testimony: "I would like to state here, however, that the members of the White League took me up and treated me very kindly indeed; thy took me to the hospital, and did everything that was within their power to give me comfort and assistance." General Badger testified that while prostrate he heard no threats to kill him, but that on the way to the hospital at the corner of Bourbon or Dauphine he heard shouts of "Kill him! Kill him!" coming apparently from "loafers" following the White Leaguers who were taking him to the hospital. "But that did not amount to much. They were kept away by my friends."

It is interesting to note that on the morning of the 14th, Gov. Penn met General Badger on a street car and spoke to him. Gov. Penn in his recollections of the event said: "When I left my home on that morning and got into a St. Charles Avenue car to go to the Boston Club to meet the members of the committee, I met General Badger in the car, and we exchanged salutations. I joined the committee and Badger kept on I presume to go to the Statehouse."

Gen. A. S. Badger was born in Boston and came to New Orleans in 1862 when it was occupied by Federal troops. He was a colonel in the U. S. Army and remained here until the end of the war. He married a New Orleans girl. After his gallant action on the 14th he became rather popular in the city in spite of his most unpopular affiliations.

CAPTAIN MACHECA OVERLOOKED

It seems that in the newspaper accounts of the Battle of the 14th, Captain Macheca was not mentioned for his accomplishments. He claimed credit not only for saving Gen. Badger's life, but for capturing the arsenal and State House and also for helping take possession of the celebrated consignment of arms that came on the *Mississippi*.

The accounts of the affair do not say that Capt. Macheca performed any of these exploits, except that Gen. Ogden in his official report credits Capt. Macheca with being of great assistance to Col. Angell.

Actually the arms from the *Mississippi* were taken from the steamer by Capt. Lord's company about noon Tuesday the next day, and carried to the Central Police Station.

Here is a statement which Capt. Macheca published in the *Bulletin* of September the 17th:

A CARD FROM CAPT. MACHECA.

Having seen advertised in the daily papers of the 15th inst. that Capt. Kilpatrick received the credit of capturing Gen. Badger, I will state that I was the first one to pick him up, when two or three more came up 3 or 5 minutes afterwards. Capt. Kilpatrick came while I was in the act of carrying him into our lines, but being badly wounded, it was impossible to carry him on a mattress, then I and several others suggested to place him on a plank. The plank being too short, we took one of the doors of the Chattanooga Railroad depot. He was then placed on it, and myself and ten or twelve others, with Capt. Kilpatrick, carried him to the Charity Hospital.

On the 16th inst. the papers also stated that Col. Angell captured the Arsenal and Station-House, he himself having credit for same. I will state that the surrender of the Arsenal and Station-House, with about 3000 stands of arms, 2 guns, about 300 colored troops, and about 75 whites, I and my company of Italians were in possession of the whole, fully 15 minutes before any officer made their appearance.

The first officer that came was Col. Angell, to whom everything was turned over by me; he then ordered my company to take possession of the arms and ammunition on the steamship Mississippi. According to orders I went with my company and made demand of the arms and ammunition, which was refused by the discharging clerk and captain, saying that said arms was private property, that they would not deliver them unless under protest; I told the captain that I would give him a receipt for them; he then made a protest against my company for taking the arms. I was then ordered by Capt. McGloin, who arrived immediately after, to place guards to watch the freight of the steamship Mississippi and New Orleans.

Col. J. Leeds then came with a company to take charge of the arms which were consigned to him. He then told me to report with my command at headquarters. Gen. Badger is still alive and can testify to the above; also Sergeant Banker who, at the time had charge of the Arsenal and Station-House.

Respectfully yours,

JOE P. MACHECA, Captain McEnery Guards.

Under the heading HONORS, the *Picayune* of Sept. 27, 1874 wrote: "We may be delivering Capt. Fagan up to martyrdom by publishing this note, but it seems due him to run the risk":

> *Dear Town Talk*—In the *Bulletin's* account of the occurrences of last week I am pained to find no mention of a gentleman who participated largely in the affair, and is entitled to as much glory and as many laurels as any one connected with it.
>
> I allude to Capt. Wm. Fagan* of the firm of Wilson & Fagan, Front street, whose retiring modesty has no doubt caused his being overlooked.
>
> It was when the firing was hottest, that disdaining the shelter of the freight piles, he stood exposed on the top of one of them, and by word and gesticulation inspired his men with heroic daring, and then led them on to victory.
>
> Hoping that you will publish this as an act of justice to a brave man, I remain yours, respectfully,   JUSTICE.

PROMINENT DOCTORS OF NEW ORLEANS SERVED WITH THE WHITE LEAGUERS

In checking the occupations of the participants of the Battle of September 14, 1874, the number of physicians who enrolled in the various companies on that date is astonishing. The following physicians and surgeons were members of the various companies:

Walter Bailey	Samuel Logan
H. Bayon	W. R. Mandeville
H. Bezou	A. B. Miles
John M. Cullen	Geo. K. Pratt
Henry D'Aquin	E. Seghers
James B. Davis	Howard Smith
L. G. Durr	Warren Stone, Jr.
Thos. H. Kennedy	C. H. Tebault
Otto Kratz	Jno. A. Thurber (Dentist)
A. Landry	L. A. Thurber

In addition to the physicians listed, these leaders were physicians:

Warren Brickell	J. Dickson Bruns
Cornelius Beard	Samuel Choppin

---

*In rosters he is listed as 1st Lt., Sec. E, CCWL.

It is interesting to note that Col. John G. Angel was a dentist. He is listed in the directory as Dr. John G. Angel who lived at 152 Julia Street.

In addition to Doctors Samuel Choppin, Charles Beard, and J. Dickson Bruns, leaders and orators of the occasion, others famous in their day gave their time and services to the cause. Some were even privates in the companies engaged in fighting, but were "promoted" from the ranks to work in the medical corps.

The *Picayune* of the 18th had this to say:

> While great honor is paid the companies of Gov. Penn's militia that were in the fight by the citizens of New Orleans, the efficient work of the military medical corps, under the command of Dr. Brickell, should receive its just dues of public approbation; of these, Doctors Warren Stone and Wm. R. Mandeville, surgeons, have shown untiring zeal and unremitting attention in the treatment of our wounded men, and the wounded metropolitans who were made prisoners, ever since the eventful evening of Monday. Under their hands some of the men who were most dangerously wounded are now doing extremely well, considering the nature of their injuries, while others, severely wounded, are rapidly recovering. Dr. J. T. Scott has also been prominent in rendering able and assiduous attention, and to his fine skill and delicate offices are due much relief from pain.

And on the 22nd the *Picayune* printed a letter from a grateful "citizen-soldier":

> In thanking our medical friends for the valuable services rendered by them during the engagement on Monday last, and since, we ought not to omit in our list the able ambulance corps, formed under the direction of Prof. Sam Logan, and having amongst its members Prof. Bemiss, Dr. Howard Smith, Dr. Pratt, of Carrollton, Dr. Norman, and others. Mr. Finlay's drug store, on Camp street, was their headquarters. Some of these gentlemen performed their duty on the battle ground, under the heaviest part of the fire, in a most praise-worthy manner.
>
> As a citizen-soldier, representing many others, we sincerely thank them. I am, Mr. Editor, yours truly,
>
> A CITIZEN-SOLDIER.

Years later, in its issue of September 15th, 1891, the then *Times-Democrat* included in its history of the Battle of the 14th a paragraph about the medical corps as follows:

> The engagement on the 14th of September was unexpected and was wholly unprepared for. No medical staff had at that hour been organized. Between 7 and 8 p. m. on that day Drs. C. H. Tebault, Samuel Logan and Howard Smith, who were serving in the capacity of privates in the company commanded by Archibald Mitchell, were called upon by Dr. Samuel Chopin, medical director on acting Gov. D. P. Penn's staff, and were promoted to other duties, as it was believed the principal and decisive battle would come off the next day.
>
> Dr. C. H. Tebault was appointed on the acting governor's staff, in connection with the late Dr. Warren Brickell, as medical purveyor of the post. Dr. Samuel Logan was placed in charge of the ambulance corps and the old Touro Infirmary was made the general hospital, where the wounded were to be cared for. By 10 a. m.

the medical staff reported everything in readiness for the very busy and decisive day whose first hour was ushered in with the reports of medical staff of readiness for the supposed dangerous work ahead. The patriotic druggists of the city contributed freely in the shape of chloroform, bandages, styptics, sponges, opium, etc.

The Demand for Newspapers

Just as today, in times of excitement the people want to read all they can about affairs, so it has always been. The *Picayune* of Sept. 16th said:

> During the last two days our power press has been as busy as the citizens in the barricades. For almost every shot fired, a paper has been published to encourage and cheer the people. The news traveled slowly during the fight; there was but little communication, and even after it was all over, truth and falsehood, rumor and fact, were so mingled that is was impossible for any one to know what was going on. The papers had to be depended on, and immense work it required of the press to supply the popular demand for the latest news "from the front."
>
> From 9 o'clock yesterday morning until 3 p. m., the press never stopped working, and yet this immense supply barely diffused the news of our victory throughout the city. People back of town and at Carrollton could not get the news because the papers were sold before the boys got out of sight of the office.

The Surrender of Captain McCann of the Metropolitans

The *Bulletin* of September 15th in its account of the engagement of the day before tells of the surrender of Captain McCann, who had been in command of the 3rd Precinct Station, in these words:

> It gives us pleasure to record that that gallant gentleman, Capt. Wm. McCann, surrendered himself to the forces of Gen. Ogden. Capt. McCann says he surrendered because Gen. Badger, being almost killed, he would follow no other man on the metropolitan police, and that he would fight no longer for the police, but for his family alone.

However, the *Picayune* didn't think so much of the Captain and in its issue of the 16th expressed itself as follows:

> The *Bulletin,* in speaking of the surrender of Gen. McCann, of the police force, takes occasion to allude to him as "that gallant gentleman." In full accord with the *Bulletin* so far as regards the present action of our people, we beg respectfully to dissent from any such commendations of Capt. McCann. The species of gallantry displayed by that person is not among our articles of admiration. It does not appear that he contemplated a surrender until the defeat of the metropolitans was assured, and we can see nothing worthy of praise in his prompt desertion of a cause —evil though it may have been—only when that cause was assured of disaster. Whatever sympathy we have goes to Badger, Lawler, McManus—brutal bully as he was—and the others who suffered by death or grievous injury. Captain McCann strikes us merely as a hireling who was quite willing to serve our oppressors so long as it seemed safe, and equally ready to turn upon them when it became prudent. He is entitled to our forbearance and protection, but we find no place for him in our esteem, and see nothing in his career to evoke compliment or eulogium.

AID TO WOUNDED MAN REFUSED

Under the caption, COWARDLY ACTION, the *Bulletin* of the 17th reported:

> During the fight on Monday, Frank Owens, private watchman of the Sugar Shed Company, a one-legged man was standing near the corner of Conti and Front streets, watching the progress of the battle, when he received a ball in his remaining leg and fell to the ground. Several persons near him picked him up and carried him to the Brokers' Exchange Coffee-house situated at the corner of Conti and Front streets, of which S. Prats is proprietor.
>
> This place was closed, but after some rapping the men with Owens succeeded in rousing the people inside sufficiently to have one door opened. They asked permission to put the wounded man inside out of the way of further harm; but, it is said, this permission was refused, and the door was slammed to and locked. The action of the parties in the house, as a matter of course, excited considerable indignation, and was generally pronounced cruel and cowardly.
>
> Owens was carried elsewhere and attended to.

The next day the same paper printed an announcement under, A CARD:

> I, the undersigned, proprietor of the Brokers' Exchange, do effectually deny of having refused any assistance to the said FRANK OWENS TARPAULIN MENDER, wounded on Monday evening, September 14, while standing at the corner of the sugar-shed "D," foot of Bienville street, when carried to my place. To the contrary; I have offered and given all that was at my disposal, and having no convenient place for a man in his condition, and no way of getting any medical attendance, I could not accept him in thinking it better for his friends to carry him where he could get proper attendance.
>
> L. PRATS.

"OUTSIDERS" HELPED

Several ex-Federal Army soldiers fought with the White Leaguers. Among them were William C. Robbins, a former major in the U. S. Army, who was killed in the action. There were quite a number of newcomers to New Orleans who participated, some of whom had been "Yankees." Even visitors joined in the fray. From the *Picayune* of the 16th:

> We have the pleasure of meeting Mr. W. I. L. Holland, editor of the Holly Springs (Miss.) *Reporter*. This gentleman, who arrived here the day before yesterday, with the object of transmitting to his valuable journal correct information as to the action of our people against its usurper, Kellogg, did not hesitate in shouldering a musket on behalf of the noble cause of a down-trodden people. He joined one of the citizens' military companies and rendered efficient service. Mr. Holland is a gentleman of intelligence and patriotism, and we commend him to the kind hospitalities of our citizens. He is stopping at the City Hotel.

THE TROOPS THAT CAME TOO LATE

Governor Kellogg was taking no chances. He knew that the White Leaguers were going to make a move of some kind on or about the 14th, and, although he had a trained force of Metropolitan Police with artillery as well about 3,000 Negro militiamen, all at his command, he telegraphed General Grant to send more soldiers to protect him. (There was already one company of Federal troops in the Custom House during the fight, but they took no part in the action.) President Grant ordered the 3rd Regiment U. S. Infantry under Gen. John R. Brooke then at Brookhaven, Mississippi, to move to New Orleans without delay. Had Gen. Brooke been able to comply punctually with the order, he would have arrived in time to prevent the fighting or to take part in it. Then there would have been no fight or a bloody encounter in which the poorly-armed citizen soldiers would have probably come out second best.

But the White League's "intelligence" knew about the proposed movement of regular troops, and the staff set about to delay and postpone the arrival of the soldiers. On the staff of Gov. Penn and General Ogden was Major E. A. Burke (he was not a member of the White League, but volunteered to help and was placed in charge of the commissary department). According to W. O. Hart in his account of the battle of the 14th, Major Burke was connected with the New Orleans, Jackson and Great Northern R.R. and had been a telegraph operator.

> On Sunday afternoon he personally telegraphed the engineer on the locomotive that was to pull the train with Brooke's troops, and instructed him to delay the train and when it had been halted to report the fact.
>
> On Monday afternoon a message reached Penn's headquarters that trouble had developed in the driving gear of the locomotive at a way station where repairs could not be made. The engineer had loosened a pin in a shaft. It was many hours before another locomotive could reach the train, and the Third Infantry did not reach New Orleans until Kellogg's forces had been defeated and dispersed.

The *Times* reported the arrival of the troops:

> The four companies of the Third Regiment, which arrived here from Holly Springs Monday, were stationed inside of the Customhouse. All the entrances to the building were guarded, and even approach thereat is impossible. At the head of the iron stairs at the main entrance was placed a guard of soldiers in close line round, ready with their guns pointed at the door. This precaution was taken as they anticipated an attack.
>
> Many wounded police were taken from the Customhouse under guard, and not a few dead. It is understood that all the higher officers of the Kellogg government are in the building, and food and clothes are being carried in there.

THE WHITE LEAGUERS LACKED ARMS

The Kellogg propagandists continued to harp on the immense quantities of arms that were being brought into New Orleans to be used for riots and revolution. Actually the amount of arms and the ammunition for use in them was limited. The *Times* reprinted an article in the N. Y. *Tribune* of September 22nd under the caption, THE CANARD ABOUT GUN PURCHASES IN NEW YORK, which read in part: "With reference to the recent rumors of a large shipment of arms to the South: a careful inquiry among the agents of manufacturing companies and large dealers shows that in the main such reports have been unfounded."

The White League companies and Col. Angell's companies were ill equipped and poorly armed. The men used old army rifles, muzzle-loaders and pistols.* Some few cases of new or usable second-hand rifles had been brought into the city as we know, but there were not enough to arm 2,000 men. Consequently those who could get hold of a gun of some sort were lucky. Just how many of those who were on duty that day carried a good gun we do not know. We know that some did not.

Walter J. Stauffer tells of his father's (W. R. Stauffer) participation. He was only twenty years old and the only gun he could get hold of was an old muzzle-loading rifle. After spending the morning with the other White Leaguers at Eagle Hall his company moved down to Poydras Street, and took up a position on the extreme right, that is to say next to the levee. Young Stauffer's company was "A," commanded originally by Captain Harrison Watts but on this day by Capt. W. T. Vaudry. This company was in the heat of the action, and it was with difficulty that the Captain could restrain his men and hold them in line when ordered to charge. Stauffer's muzzle loader didn't work very well. He took his stick pin out of his cravat — think of going into battle with a tie and stick pin, in formal dress, so to speak! — and attempted to clean the little nipple which held the cap that fired the powder. He never did get his gun to shoot. But he moved forward just the same. Another Leaguer next to him had a Winchester rifle, and placing it on Stauffer's shoulder, fired at a "Met." The concussion deafened young Stauffer so that he could hardly hear for nearly a year. A compatriot nearby in the act of firing was hit in the shoulder just as he said, "Watch me get that fellow!" (Today he would have employed a stronger epithet!) Many other Leaguers "brought their own" — guns and ammunition — and the quality of the firearms was often not of the best and the quantity of ammunition limited.

A good gun was a treasure. Besides the Kellogg crowd were seizing rifles and guns wherever they could find them. This led many persons to hide firearms in unlikely places. Stamps Farrar used to tell that his grandmother, Mrs.

---

*Writes one member of the White League: "More than half the men in our companies had no other than small pistols."

I. D. Stamps, owned a Playel piano* and that for several days two or three guns were hidden in the top of the piano.

NEWSPAPER AMENITIES

Gov. Penn placed a guard at Longstreet's house, at the office of the *Republican*, the official newspaper of Kellogg's government, and at different gun stores.

In its issue of the 15th that newspaper published the following ACK-NOWLEDGEMENT:

> The REPUBLICAN takes pleasure in acknowledging courteous and kind attentions during the heat of the excitement yesterday from Messrs. Overton and Payne, of General Ogden's staff; Thad Waterman, Esq., representing Mr. Penn, and Messrs. Byerly, Simpson and Moise, of the Bulletin. Messages were received from Messrs. Penn and Ogden, through their respective aides, after the White League party had obtained full possession of the streets, assuring ample protection to the office in case any violent demonstrations were made thereon.

And the *Picayune,* not to be outdone in chivalrous expression, said on the 16th:

> The *Republican* pays our soldiers several compliments on their discipline, bravery, and courtesy, and especially in the case of their chivalrous and humane interference in behalf of Gen. Badger, when wounded and a prisoner.
>
> The *Republican* has been an open enemy—unscrupulous in its mode of warfare, we have thought, at times, but it knows how to be frank and grateful, we perceive.

THE METROPOLITAN POLICE

The Louisiana State Legislature on October 20, 1868 passed a bill taking the policing power of the City of New Orleans away from the mayor of the city and placing it in the hands of the Governor of the State. This was a measure of Gov. Warmoth to increase his power, and authorized the organization of the Metropolitan Police Force under the direction of a board of five police commissioners for New Orleans, Jefferson City and the Parish of St. Bernard. Governor Warmoth appointed three Negroes and two white men on the board.

Gen. J. B. Steedman, a general in the Union Army from Ohio, was the first chief of police. The City Council of New Orleans protested the proceedings, "in view of the illegality of the metropolitan police bill and the utter incapacity of the police under it to maintain order." The Council organized another police force, and the mayor directed Thomas E. Adams, the former chief of Police to resume his duties. The matter got into the courts, and Steedman was recognized as the legitimate head of the police. The court decision

---

Walter Stauffer says that ever afterwards the only tune that could be played on the piano was "Dixie"!

was backed up by General Rousseau in command of the Federal troops in New Orleans.

The Metropolitan Police numbered about 500 with 100 supernumeraries and 20 or 30 plain clothes men or detectives. In 1874 most of the latter were busy mixing in with the White Leaguers. General Badger testified before a Congressional Committee that 400 men would have been enough to police the city, preserve order and protect property.

General Badger admitted that the public looked upon the Metropolitan Police as a paid soldiery of the State used for the purpose of oppression and as a militia. The police spent so much of their time in guarding the State House and on political affairs that there was much crime and disorder in the City.

Many of the force were Negroes, though the majority were white and some were even ex-Confederate soldiers.

The Metropolitan Police cost the City of New Orleans over $800,000 the first year it existed.

After the defeat of the Police on the 14th of September Thomas Boylan was placed in charge by Gov. Penn. When the Kellogg forces regained control they permitted Boylan to remain chief of police for some time, as he was an efficient and honest administrator.

Mrs. Matilda Francis, colored, a daughter of one of the Metropolitan Police, Jordan Adam Allan, twenty-two years old at the time of the battle, states in a letter to the author on Nov. 22, 1953 that her father told her that the Police were instructed to insult and arrest any white Southern woman caught on the streets at night. After the affair of the fourteenth some of the survivors of the Metropolitan Police were given jobs as street cleaners (wearing white suits), but the majority worked on the river front as longshoremen and cotton screwmen where the Federal authorities gave preference to them and to field slaves under whom some white men worked, according to Mrs. Francis.

She states that the "Yankees" instructed them — her father was one of the "bosses" — not to give Irishmen any of the easy jobs at the fabulous pay of four dollars per day. Actually this was not so much even for those who got the jobs. Says Mrs. Francis: "If they were lucky they would sometimes work steady for a whole week or a month. By the time they would save enough to pay up a few over-due debts the mean old ships would not come in, and this meant that these poor unfortunate men were forever at the mercy of the landlords and merchants. The house rent was only four or five dollars, sometimes only three per month, but oh! how hard it was to get this small amount of money together at one time! They managed to exist — only God knows how."

The Arms from the "Mississippi"

What happened to the consignment of arms that arrived in New Orleans on the *Mississippi* and which was the immediate cause of the Battle of the 14th? These arms were taken from the *Mississippi* on Tuesday the 15th after 12 o'clock by Company (or Section) "B" commanded by Capt. George H. Lord. The arms were taken to the Central Police Station. This account is from the *Bulletin* in its Supplement of the 22nd of September giving detailed movements of each company of White Leaguers and Angell's command on the 14th, that night and the following morning.

U. S. Regulars Arrested

From the *Picayune* of the 17th:

A rather amusing scene occurred yesterday, when four or five United States soldiers in undress were arrested by some of the citizen soldiers, and taken to the station, under the impression that they were Metropolitans. The blue coats were not at all alarmed, but appeared to relish it as a good joke, and marched to the station with military precision. On their arrival there they were recognized by the officer in command, who ordered their discharge, reprimanding their captors. The boys apologized, and insisted on taking their late prisoners to a neighboring saloon and treating them to a sumptuous collation, which the boys in blue appeared to relish very heartily.

"They Gazed From Afar"

Under this caption the *Times* pointed out that it was "a rather remarkable fact that during the recent imbroglio, all of the subordinates in direct lineal succession to Governor Kellogg's position were absent from the city, and indeed the State. Those officials are the Hon. Cicero Caesar Antoine, the Lieut.-Governor; the Hon. Charles W. Lowell, Speaker of the House; and the Hon. P. G. Deslonde, Secretary of State."

When Gov. Kellogg learned that Col. Lowell was going to leave the city, he sent for Lowell and told him that grave trouble was impending and that he should remain here. It was reported that Lowell assented, but on the next day took the train for New York City. Gov. Kellogg telegraphed the other two officials to return to the city, but they disregarded the telegrams. They came back when the trouble was over and Kellogg returned to power, with regiments of U. S. soldiers quartered in the city.

White Leaguers Fired on From the Custom House

It was said that there was some firing from the Custom House, and some alleged that this was done not only by the police who had retreated there, but by some of the civilians in the Custom House. The *Bulletin* printed that it had received information from a reliable source that shots were fired from the big granite building and that Judge Dibble was seen shooting from a window, and several stated that he killed a man.

As soon as they knew they were defeated, those policemen who had taken refuge in the Custom House, opened fire from the windows, "Mr. Casey to the contrary notwithstanding." "The wounds of Capt. Wells and others are ghastly proofs against the legal and tax-collecting sharpshooters." Continuing, the *Bulletin* waxed sarcastic:

> "A HORSE! A HORSE! MY KINGDOM FOR A HORSE!"
>
> Alas the day that Prince Henry C. Dibble should have been without a horse! Strange freak of Providence that foiled him in two well laid plans to be mounted in the field! Cruel Providence that forces so brave a Radical leader into the Custom-House and made him shoot unarmed men with a rifle from the window. Brave Henry! Unhappy and unarmed West and Bonzonier! Henry, brave Prince Henry! There was not a White Leaguer who would not have furnished you six horses. Why didn't you send over to our side for a horse? Kellogg was the wrong man to apply to, for he was in the Custom-House as soon as you were. Besides, Kellogg deals in asses.

Judge Dibble, who, as we know, represented Governor Kellogg in the meeting with the citizens committee which had demanded the Governor's abdication on the morning of the 14th, denied emphatically that he had fired on any one. It is hard to believe that a judge, no matter how mean spirited or unscrupulous, would become a franc-tireur, unless he wished to kill a personal enemy, and none such were among those killed or wounded or even among the White Leaguers in front of the Custom House.

But there was undoubtedly some firing from the windows of the Custom House. When the police had been driven from the field, the White League was drawn up in battle line on the neutral ground in Canal Street for a roll call. Here it was that Toledano was killed, shot from behind, and apparently by someone who had taken refuge in the Custom House.

The evidence of John Creblin in a letter to the *Bulletin* is given here.

> Editor *Bulletin*—The statement of the Radicals that they did not fire on our citizens from the Custom-House, Monday afternoon, 14th inst., is an unmitigated lie, for I was an eye-witness to the dastardly act.
>
> About 4 o'clock P. M. on the above day, I was on Magazine street between Common and Canal streets, coming towards this office, when I heard the rattle of

musketry and the booming of cannon in the direction of the levee. I ran to Canal street, and stood with some others on the banquette by Messrs. Tompkins & Co.'s store. In a few minutes we saw Kellogg's metropolitan butchers running at the top of their speed towards the Custom-House.

Naturally enough a cheer burst from our lips, as well as our hearts, at seeing these boasted warriors, who were so extremely anxious to clean out the White Leaguers, fleeing in wild terror before our brave boys. I suppose our cheer drew the attention of the cowardly miscreants in the Custom-House toward us, for directly afterwards they opened fire upon us from the windows. Fortunately they shot too high, as the marks of their bullets on Messrs. Tompkins & Co.'s will show, and only one of our party was shot down. Up to this time I did not see a gun in the hands of a person present. I noticed at the Custom-House windows U. S. soldiers, or men attired as such. I did not see them fire, but other persons in the crowd said they did.

About twenty minutes after this, when the metropolitans had fled from the corner of Peters and Canal streets, where some of them had held their ground for a time, I again attempted to come to this office, but while crossing Canal from Magazine, I was fired at when near the neutral ground. I felt or heard the whistle of the ball close to me. There certainly is not the ghost of an excuse for this, for I was totally unarmed, not having even a pistol about me.

                                                            JOHN CREBLIN.

How the White Leaguers Were Fed

The problem of logistics, while simple compared to the supplying of any armed force of today with necessary food, equipment, arms, etc., was one that the leaders of the citizen-soldiers of the Battle of the 14th had to make an attempt to solve. Fortunately, Maj. E. A. Burke, who was not a member of the White League, volunteered to take charge of the commissary department and served on the staff of General Ogden. An able organizer and an efficient director, Major Burke collected supplies, mainly food, and distributed them to the hungry and tired men who stayed on duty that night and the next morning. Kursheedt and Bienvenu's store on Camp Street became the headquarters, and ammunition and food were distributed from there. Many groups were fed from homes nearby their places of encampment or bivouac.

The *Picayune* of the 16th compliments the grocers, butchers and bakers of the city for patriotic activity in helping to feed the victors of the 14th:

> As was to have been expected, the call for supplies has been most generously responded to by all classes of our citizens. Many of the family grocers have sent in hams, breakfast bacon, butter, coffee and other supplies; the bakers have sent in large donations fresh from their ovens, and the butchers in all our markets have given large quantities of fresh meats. All of these donations were accompanied by the message, "If more is required, send again."
>
> As soon as the fresh meat from the butchers was received, Mr. Ed. Prophet, of the Imperial, volunteered to prepare it for the men, and his ranges have been employed in the good work all the morning.

The *Bulletin* of the 27th printed the following resolution:

HEADQUARTERS SECTION D,
September 24, 1874.

By resolution unanimously passed at the first meeting of the Section D since the last campaign, it has become my duty, as it is my pleasure, to bear grateful testimony in my own name, and in behalf of the men in my command, to those ladies and gentlemen who furnished us so liberally with the most choice viands during the short period we were on duty; a supply so ample that, had we been under arms a week instead of two days, we would probably have had no occasion to draw upon the stores of our efficient commissary.

To the following ladies and gentlemen our thanks are due:

Mrs. William Green,	Mrs. Joseph Robea,
Mrs. Cath. Donnelly,	Mrs. Mary Gill,
Mrs. C. Delmore,	Mrs. W. F. Houston,
Mrs. H. Rennyson,	Mrs. C. Doetling,
Mrs. A. Mitchell,	Mr. S. M. Angell,
Mrs. W. S. Pike,	Mr. A. A. Maginnis,
Mrs. C. J. Leeds,	Mr. F. Cammerden,
Mrs. Mary Stamps,	Mr. J. Machado,
Mrs. D. Mather,	Mr. John McCove,
Mr. L. Sbisa	Mr. S. Sbisa,
Mr. Frank Johnson,	Mrs. Larkin,
Mr. A. K. Finlay,	Mrs. Walker.

ARCHIBALD MITCHELL,
Captain Section D.

NOTE FROM DR. TEBAULT

NEW ORLEANS, Sept. 16, 1874.

To the Editor of the *Picayune*:

In your issue of this evening I observe that you mention the name of Tebault as belonging to one of Kellogg's wounded policemen. Permit me to state that the name mentioned has never served in any such position, nor has it ever faltered in its uncompromising opposition to Kellogg. In proof of this, two bearing that name— B. Rutledge Tebault, of Company B, and William G. Tebault, of Company E, of the Crescent City White League—were where the fighting was hottest and cannons to be taken at the point of the bayonet.

C. H. TEBAULT, M. D.,
Late Asst. Med. Purveyor State Forces.

*   *   *   *   *

E. L. Tinker says that on the morning after the affair of the 14th all the members of the White League and Col. Angell's companies who were not wounded or dead wore a piece of black ribbon in their button holes .

*   *   *   *   *

Much praise is due to Capt. Thos. W. Rea, of the steamer *Belle of Shreveport,* for his very kind and liberal attentions to the company and to young J. M. Henderson, son of our old friend, Capt. Sam Henderson, who fell with a ball through his knee joint, after having discharged his rifle twelve times, and was charging with Capt. Pleasant's Company E, of the White League, on the Gatlin and two Napoleon guns, from which the peelers were driven away.

CHAPTER IX

NEWSPAPER COMMENT

The event of the 14th of September seemed to have produced a thrilling effect throughout the North. Messages of sympathy and encouragement poured in to the *de jure* government of McEnery and Penn and the White League from all over the country.

At St. Louis a large and enthusiastic mass meeting was held on the 15th, attended by ten thousand persons. Resolutions were passed and hearty sympathy extended to the Louisiana people. The *St. Louis Times* approved the action of the White League. A few days later (Sept. 24th) Carl Schurz, famous general of the Civil War, U. S. Senator, writer, statesman and political leader, made a speech before another large crowd in St. Louis in which he denounced Kellogg and his government.

The citizens of Waco, Texas, sent congratulations, as well as numbers of other Southern cities. On the 18th a mass meeting was held in Memphis to express sympathy for the citizens of Louisiana. And on the same day a large meeting at Jackson, Tennessee passed resolutions condemning the interference of Federal authorities in Louisiana affairs and expressing sympathy for its people.

Among the papers approving the efforts of Louisiana to get rid of Kellogg, and which carried favorable editorials on the event of the 14th were:

New York Herald
New York Sun
New York Bulletin
New York Graphic
New York Tribune
Brooklyn Eagle (largest evening circulation of any paper in U. S. carried scathing articles about Kellogg)
St. Louis Globe
St. Louis Amerika
St. Louis Anziger
Cincinnati Enquirer
Boston Post
Philadelphia Enquirer

Some of these journals had hitherto been bitter and vindictive towards the South, or supporters of the radicals in Congress who foisted so-called "reconstruction" on the Southern people. The activities of the White League brought about a change of attitude.

It is impossible here to give many of these expressions of editorial opinion, but a few will suffice to show the tenor of views of the press.

The New York *Tribune,* (Liberal Republican) of the 15th inst. said:

The frightful mismanagement of affairs in Louisiana under the present administration has wrought out its logical result and culminated, according to telegrams received at a late hour last night, in an attempt at revolution on the part of the citizens who, suffering under great and continued wrongs are unable to find any redress.

Unhappily the story of wrongs and misgovernment to which the people have been subjected is in the main true. Whether they are sufficient warrant for a revolution or an attempt at revolution is quite another question. It is not difficult to understand how the people of Louisiana may have been badgered by their oppressors to make this desperate effort to free themselves.

The *Sun* (Sept. 18, 1874) said editorially: The rapid and complete success of Lieut. Gov. Penn and his associates has been followed by the resurrender of Louisiana to President Grant, represented by Major General Emory, having proved that the people of the State are substantially unanimous in their rejection of Kellogg and his usurpation; that in fact there is no party to support that wretched imposition; they have now proved likewise that the uprising was not against the laws or authority of the United States; with the appearance of the army upon the scene they have withdrawn, resigning everything into the hands of the commanding general.

The *New York Post* concluded its editorial with: We believe President Grant's interference in the domestic affairs of the Southern States has been wholly mischievous; through his aid Kellogg has fortified his position on every side by legal barriers. Men do not seek redress with musket in hand when they have a fair chance to obtain redress at the ballot box. Kellogg's hand now covers every ballot box in Louisiana. Like the late Louis Napoleon, he can obtain for his most illegal acts apparent sanction of the people. Even the ballot, the peaceful wagon of free men, has become under his management an instrument of political tyranny, social discord and financial ruin. He ought to be left to the vengeance of the people whose neck's are under his heel.

The *Mail* deplored the outbreak of a conflict of which no man can see the end; earnestly deprecates a war of races, and regrets the necessity for the interference of the Government with the concerns of States.

The *Forum* of Bucyrus, Ohio on Sept. 19th wrote:

The dispatches inform us that the solid, substantial people of Louisiana and New Orleans have risen in their might and deposed from office the usurper, Gov. Kellogg, and his party throughout the State, and inducted Gov. McEnery and the rest of the State officials who were elected into office. There was a bloody collision before Kellogg and his clique surrendered, many lives being lost.

In the meantime President Grant, who instinctively favors all such corruptionists and usurpers as Kellogg, has issued a bombastic proclamation for the dispersion of what he calls a mob, and the reinstatement of Kellogg and his infamous faction to power.

The sympathy of the press generally, throughout the country both South and North, is in favor of the people, who, perhaps should have resorted to the moral power of the ballot box in preference to armed revolution . . . It remains to be seen whether the people of this country will stand idly by and look on with cold, calm indifference, while the goddess of liberty is being slain in her own citadel.

A VOICE FROM THE HOME OF ABRAHAM LINCOLN.

The Springfield (Ill.) *Monitor,* on hearing of the overthrow of the Kellogg Government, places at the head of its first column the American eagle, and thus rejoices:

GLORY TO GOD—AMERICANS STILL POSSESS THE SPIRIT OF 1776.

We hail with unspeakable gladness the news from New Orleans, announcing the overthrow of the most outrageous usurpation and tyrannical exercise of power ever allowed to exist among a free people.

LIGHT BREAKING (from the *Bulletin*)

As the facts are becoming known outside of Louisiana, even our bitterest political opponents begin to realize how greatly deceived they have been as to the state of affairs. Here is what the Pittsburgh *Leader,* a violent Radical paper, has to say about it:

What makes it worse is that the rebels have just enough right and reason on their side to divide public sympathy and embarrass the Government in their efforts to put them down. There is no earthly doubt now that Kellogg is not the legally elected Governor of Louisiana, and that McEnery is—this much was frankly admitted by Mr. Morton's Republican Senate committee last year.

There is no doubt either, that the action of United States Judge Durell in ousting the McEnery board, giving Kellogg the election was a usurpation and an outrage. Grant, himself, we do not doubt, now knows that his action in sustaining Kellogg and Durell, at the instance of his brother-in-law, Casey was rash and wrong. There is no doubt either, that the action of Kellogg (who in many instances has acted quite judiciously), in ordering the disarming of private citizens is directly in violation of the United States Constitution, and is a usurpation that would as surely raise a riot in Pittsburgh as in New Orleans.

WHAT GRANT HAS DONE FOR LOUISIANA—The New York *Tribune* thus shows what Grant has done for this unfortunate State:

He has done (so Grant says) "everything in his power to assist the South." He has given it Spencer, Moses, Brooks, Baxter, Kellogg, Durell, Casey, Patterson, Packard, Pinchback, and Poker Jack. He has filled its Legislatures with thieves, adventurers, barbers, bootblacks, bartenders and confidence men. He has put up its offices to the highest bidder, confiscated its lands, impaired the value of its real property generally, ruined its credit, and brought its business to such a pass that in some of the richest regions of the South nothing can be bought and sold except votes. The highways are scoured by gangs of masked marauders. The bush is filled with armed Negroes in ambush. South Carolina and Louisiana are relapsing into barbarism, and nine years after the close of the war the South is not yet at peace.

A DEAD FAILURE
(Cartoon in Harper's Weekly, Oct. 3, 1874)
— *Courtesy Leonard V. Huber*

"Everything in his power to assist the South—especially Louisiana." He has taken away from Louisiana the right of choosing its own officers, and sent his soldiers down there to put into power the persons whom he deems most fit to rule. He has sustained them while they plundered the State and overturned even the semblance of popular government, and for all the wrongs and sore distress which have attracted for Louisiana the commiseration of mankind, his only remedy is "more troops." And ungrateful Louisiana, after all this kindness, will not be quiet. "The attention, sir," said Mr. Squeers, "that was bestowed upon that boy in his illness—dry toast and warm tea offered him every night and morning when he couldn't swallow anything—a candle in his bedroom on the very night he died—the best dictionary set up for him to lay his head upon—I don't regret it though. It is a pleasant thing to reflect that one did one's duty by him."

A Splendid Exhibition of Character

Editorial from Mobile *Register,* Sept. 16, 1874:

The people of the South are without doubt the most patient people on the face of the Globe. A popular revolution in Paris is always attended by the most revolting scenes of retributive justice as well as of brutal injustice. Monuments are overthrown, archbishops are slaughtered in cold blood, dwellings are burned by infuriated women, and the gutters run with gore. In England we have seen Jeffreys dragged through the streets with a rope about his neck, and suspected like Fawkes and Oates hurried to the block with short shrift.

In the *coup d'etats* of the Napoleons we have seen the highest magnates incarcerated and executed without trial, and the populace shot down unmercifully with grape and canister. In Spain we see to-day the adherents of Serrano and Don Carlos alternately massacred upon the streets of the towns and villages which pass successively under the rule of either combatant. All over the world the rise of a people against tyrants has been marked with those hideous scenes which disgrace humanity.

In New Orleans the other day we saw a spectacle in marked contrast to this universal history of mankind. A people who have been oppressed and plundered for ten years, and who, having at last selected their own rulers, have been doomed for two years longer to see usurpers occupying the seats of government and setting at defiance all the laws of persons and things, rise in their majesty and overthrow the despotism; the armed supporters of the tyranny are dispersed, but beyond the attack upon the civil troops, no one is injured in person or property.

Even when the most infamous of the oppressors lay wounded under the charge of the citizens, he is carefully removed to the hospital, and his wounds attended to. The flying police are not shot down, but simply arrested, disrobed and dismissed to private life. Not a store is sacked, not a negro is molested, not an outrage is committed on public property. In a few hours after the battle is over, ladies and children reappear upon Canal street, the police are actively on duty, perfect order reigns, and nothing is left to mark a great revolution except a few trembling fugitives behind the grim walls of the Custom-House.

No effort was made to intercept Kellogg's flight to the Custom-House. Not a single motion was offered to bayonet a despicable tyrant. Longstreet was permitted to sneak away from his police station unmolested. Newton, who stabbed a citizen in cold blood because he was a leaguer, was not taken from the jail and hanged. The *Republican* newspaper office was not sacked, nor did the mob hang its vile editor, who, from an inpecunious seedy schoolmaster has become by plunder possessed of an immense fortune. No such deeds of violence occurred. This was an American, Anglo-Saxon revolution, led and prosecuted by the descendants of the men who threw the tea overboard in Boston Harbor and who drove Gov. Dinwiddie* to his shipping in the James River. It was marked with justice and moderation. There was nothing of the madness of that New York mob which, resenting the military draft, took vengeance upon the colored race by burning their hospitals— nothing of that retaliatory indignation which recently marked the fury of Plymouth Church as it aimed its blows at a single individual. The people of New Orleans have shown the world how signally they can crush a foreign tyranny, and at the same time preserve the dignity of human nature.

Not Gov. Dinwiddie who died in 1770, but Lord Dunmore. In 1775 Patrick Henry organized a regiment of militia which compelled the Governor to take refuge on board an English man-of-war.

Persiflage

Every newspaper of the day had its Pete Baird, but this disciple of *Punch* was anonymous and his witticisms appeared without a by-line. They were stuck around as "fillers" — on the editorial page, among the personals or after a news item.

The New Orleans *Republican,* the journal of the Kellogg *de facto* government and its apologist, sprung this one:

> Every PENN-urious editor in the country has some smart thing
> to say about the Penn and the sword.

And here is an example from the *New Orleans Bulletin* of newspaper courtliness:

> The consumptive *Times* gaspingly wheezes that Gravier Street
> is unhappy because the *Pic* claims to be a big dog in the White
> League.

The *Bulletin,* under the head of BUTLER FOR NEW ORLEANS, in its issue of Sept. 22nd, assured its readers not to be afraid:

> Some of the Northern Radical papers are threatening us with Butler, and a Terre Haute paper puts his quotation (slightly amended) in our mouths:
>
> > For all the sad word of tongue or Penn,
> > The saddest are these—we may have Ben.
>
> There is no danger of Butler's coming to New Orleans. Our spoons and money are gone, and there is no inducements to bring him down here.

THE FIRST GUN—1861–1874.—[See Page 813.]
"I shall deal with this trouble as I should have dealt with the trouble in 1861."—U. S. Grant

(Cartoon in Harper's Weekly, Oct. 3, 1874)
— *Courtesy Leonard V. Huber*

CHAPTER X

KELLOGG RETURNS TO POWER

In his proclamation of the 15th General Grant gave the citizens of New Orleans five days to lay aside their arms, and the McEnery officials to resign their offices, seized the day before, and turn the government of the State back to Governor Kellogg. Actually they were not accorded that much time. On the 16th the Adjutant General of U. S. wired Gen. Emory not to recognize the insurgent government. Gen. Emory took charge Wednesday morning and placed the government of the State on the 17th in the hands of Gen. Brooke, who turned it over to Governor Kellogg on Saturday the 19th. Thus Acting-Governor Penn served Tuesday and Governor McEnery* assumed office Wednesday, and the anti-Kellogg forces were in power only two days.

In the meantime in the country parishes of Louisiana there was great rejoicing and many Kellogg officials were ousted.

In these parishes there was a change of officers from the Kellogg crowd to the McEnery faction.

Richland Parish on the 16th — McEnery's appointees took over. Cannon were fired at Dellior's — general rejoicing.

Franklin Parish — Installed McEnery men on 17th.

East Baton Rouge, 16th — Turned out Kellogg officials and installed McEnery's commissioned officers in City and Parish.

Livingston — Declared for McEnery on 16th. Adjacent parishes on 17th — no disturbances.

Shreveport, 16th — Last vestige of Kellogg government disappeared from North Louisiana without a word or act of violence to any person, white or black.

New Iberia — Mass meeting of citizens endorsed overthrow of Kellogg government. Grand jubilee — torchlight procession.

St. Mary on 17th — Parish officials installed who were elected in 1872.

---

*Governor McEnery returned to New Orleans on Tuesday evening, the 16th. On the same train was General Emory who was to dispossess him. Governor McEnery had been in Vicksburg, Miss., and Acting-Governor Penn stated in his recollections published later that McEnery's absence had not been due to any pre-concerted arrangement with him. In his talk to the crowd that met him at the train with a brass band, after having been introduced by B. F. Jonas, Governor McEnery expressed his regret that he was not "an actor in the transformation scene, as he was on other fields fighting for the cause."

On the 17th a dispatch to the *Picayune* from Franklin stated that the officers elected in 1872 were installed. Two usurpers gave up their offices voluntarily except the sheriff who insisted that his office be taken from him which was done by a posse of six unarmed men and peacefully disposed citizens. All quiet.

St. Helena)
) on 17th — Kellogg officials ejected.
Tangipahoa)

On the 16th leading business men of New Orleans attempted to influence General Grant to pursue a more meliorative course. They sent this telegram and got Casey, the President's brother-in-law, to endorse it:

To THE PRESIDENT.

To His Excellency U. S. Grant, President U. S. of America, Washington, D. C.:

We, the undersigned, beg leave to inform your Excellency that this city is perfectly quiet and free from all disturbing elements, and business has been resumed as usual.

No further trouble anticipated.
Moses Greenwood, Vice President, President Chamber of Commerce.
Samuel H. Kennedy, Acting President of Clearing House.
Perry Nugent, Acting President of Cotton Exchange.
R. S. Howard, President Merchants' Exchange.

CUSTOMHOUSE
New Orleans, La., Sept. 16, 1874.

I have been asked to sign the above.

The statement that the city is perfectly quiet is true, and business is proceeding as usual. Property and persons are safe from insults or injuries, except from some rowdy or drunken man.

JAMES F. CASEY.

On the 17th. Gen. Emory ordered the McEnery government to vacate the State House, and appointed Col. J. R. Brooke to the military Command of the City.* Brooke took possession of State House and State buildings. He permitted Thomas Boylan to continue to have charge of the police to preserve order until relieved.

---

*"I placed Col. Brooke in command of the city as well as in command of the troops, otherwise there would have been anarchy. Gov. Kellogg did not, and has not, yet called on me for support to reinstate the State government. His Chief of Police was shot down, the next in command also, and the whole force utterly dispersed and hidden away out of sight. For one of them to have attempted to stand on his beat would have been certain destruction, and even now the State authorities represented by Governor Kellogg have asked to defer taking charge for the present."
— Gen. Emory's report to Adj.-Gen. Townsend by telegram.

At 7 P.M. the State House was occupied by U.S. troops — about 200 — with sentinels all around the building and troops with arms stacked in every room. All doors bolted and guarded.

Conferences were held between Gov. McEnery, Lt. Gov. Penn, Dr. Samuel Choppin, Duncan F. Kenner, B. F. Jonas and U. S. Marshal Packard. Also between the presidents of banks and insurance companies headed by Mr. Munson with Gen. Emory.

Later there was another conference at the Custom House between Penn, Ogden, Marr, Packard, Casey and Carter. These conferences came to naught, and according to the *N. O. Times,* wild rumors went all over the City, exciting the populace.

The committee representing the people met at the Boston Club, which was then located on Carondelet Street where the City Bank Branch of the Whitney Bank now stands. The Radical Committee held their meetings at the Custom House.

Efforts were made to compromise but the two committees couldn't get together mainly on the subject of the Returning Board. The conservative or McEnery committee thought that both parties should have equal representation on the Board. Kellogg and the Radicals insisted on three out of five for their side.

The White Leaguers Retire Gracefully

There was a consultation on the 17th at the State House, between the Governor, Lieutenant Governor, and officers of the lawful administration, together with a number of prominent citizens, to receive and consider certain propositions of Gen. Emory. These propositions demanded the retirement of all armed men from the streets, and the return of the arms to the arsenal. These propositions were acceded to, as will be seen by the following orders:

HEADQRS. EXECUTIVE DEP'T. OF LA.
New Orleans, Sept. 17, 1874.

(General Orders No. 7.)

I.

The State troops now under arms will be at once retired to their homes.

II.

The arms captured from the usurpation will be carried and deposited in the Central Station or at the Third Precinct accordingly as they who hold them live above or below Canal street.

III.

The artillery, horses and other public property captured will be carried and deposited at the Central Station.

IV.

All private arms purchased by citizens will be taken to the respective homes of those who bear and own them.

V.

Superintendent Boylan will continue the work of organizing the police and policing the city. He will receipt for the public property, arms, etc., turned over to him.

VI.

Gen. Ogden, commanding the State forces, is charged with the execution of this order.

BY COMMAND OF   JOHN McENERY,
Gov. and Commander-in-Chief.

E. JOHN ELLIS, Col. and A.A.G.

The following communications issued in the late afternoon of the 18th confirmed the re-instatement of Governor Kellogg and his restoration to power.

Department of the Gulf.
New Orleans, La., Sept. 18, 1874.

To the Hon. W. P. Kellogg, Governor of the State of Louisiana:

Sir—In obedience to the orders of the President, I have the honor to inform you of the surrender of the insurgents, lately in arms against the State government, and to afford you the necessary military support to re-establish the State government. Very respectfully, your obedient servant,

(signed)   W. H. EMORY,
Colonel and Brevet Major General Commanding.

Immediately upon receipt of the foregoing, this letter was transmitted in reply:

New Orleans, Sept. 18, 1874.

Major General W. H. Emory, Commanding:

Sir—I have the honor to acknowledge the receipt of your communication of this date informing me that you are prepared to afford me the necessary military support to re-establish the State government. I will promulgate an executive order in the official journal tomorrow morning instructing all officers of the State who have been prevented from performing their duties, to resume their functions at once.

Owing to the disorganization of the police force in New Orleans, resulting from the recent conflict of arms, the Commissioners of the Metropolitan Police will not be able to get their officers on their beats until tomorrow. Therefore, I must request you to assume the maintenance of the peace and order of the city during the coming night.

I have the honor to be, yours, etc.,

WILLIAM P. KELLOGG, Governor.

"Distinguished" Members of the Constitutional Convention
of 1868

Photograph of a print at the Louisiana State Museum. In the center
is O. J. Dunn, Lieut.-Gov. of Louisiana, 1868-1872. Pinchback's picture is at the bottom of the print, and Antoine is at Dunn's left.
(*Reproduced through the courtesy of the Museum*)

KU KLUX KLAN MARCH
Published at Nashville, 1868

Published at New Orleans, 1874

MUSIC OF RECONSTRUCTION DAYS

When the feelings of a people are stirred by great events they express themselves in songs and in music. The success of the White League inspired quite a number of musicians in New Orleans to compose music honoring its leaders and celebrating its victories. William B. Wisdom of New Orleans, well-known book collector, has assembled an unusual collection of sheet music issued during the Reconstruction period. The four title pages reproduced here are from his collection.

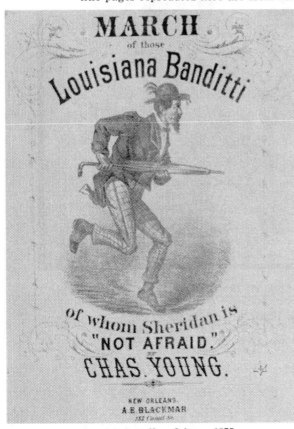

Published at New Orleans, 1875

Published at New Orleans, 1874

(*Above*) Mayor Walmsley, prominent citizens, Commissioners of Liberty Place and White League survivors at the 60th Anniversary celebration on September 14, 1934.

— Photo from Morning Tribune, Sept. 15, 1934.

(*Below*) Veteran White Leaguers at the Liberty Place monument on September 14, 1937. From left to right: James B. Pelitier, G. D. May, J. C. de Armas, Charles D. Smith, E. E. Hooper, Jeff D. Hardin, Sr., Sam Dreyfous, Nicholas Foto and James Wilkinson.

— Times-Picayune, Sept. 15, 1937.

Above — Ceremonies at Liberty Monument, Sept. 14, 1936. (Left to right) Rev. William H. Nes, Dean of Christ Church Cathedral; Arthur A. de la Houssaye, Secretary of the Board of Commissioners of Liberty Place; Rene J. LeGardeur, Chairman of the Commission; Alfred Danziger, Aide to Mayor Maestri; and Rev. J. J. Wallace, S.J.

— *Photo New Orleans States, Sept. 15, 1936*

Above—Three veterans of '74 at the ceremony at Liberty Place on Sept. 14, 1935. (Left to right) S. A. Trufant shaking hands with Charles D. Smith, and James Wilkinson.

— *Times-Picayune, Sept. 15, 1935*

At Left—Col. John G. Angell.

(Executive order.)

New Orleans, Sept. 18, 1874.

All State officers who have been prevented during the recent troubles from performing their duties will immediately resume their official function.

The Board of Metropolitan Police will at once assemble and organize the police
force of New Orleans and assume the maintenance of the peace and order of the
city.

W. P. KELLOGG, Governor.

On the morning of the 19th the Kellogg "dynasty" was restored and the
Times describes the event in its issue of the 20th:

A little before ten o'clock an Saturday morning General Longstreet and his
military staff left the Customhouse unarmed, and on foot proceeded to the State
House, where a TIMES reporter found them occupying the rooms of the Governor.

General Brooke had not yet appeared at the office, but did soon thereafter, and
while he was yet engaged in conversation with General Longstreet, Governor Kellogg walked unattended into the room. A number of persons who were present
congratulated him on his restoration to offcial duty. When this desultory conversation was over, Gen. Brooke approached the Governor and informed him that he
was prepared to turn over to him the State House and all records and public property belonging to the State which had come into his possession at the time of the
surrender of the insurgents to his command. Everything, the General said, would
be found in precisely the same condition as it had come into his hands, except that
in some departments the records and papers had been found scattered on the floor;
these he had caused to be gathered up and placed under lock. The Governor accepted the transfer, and Gen. Brooke thereupon immediately retired.

These events were hardly complete when a carriage arrived with other persons
from the Customhouse, among whom was H. C. Dibble.

How Gov. Kellogg Appeared

Gov. Kellogg appeared quite at ease, as much so as in less troublous times, and
having given orders for the opening and resumption of business in the various departments, returned again to the Customhouse for the purpose of resuming the
conference which had been going on there between his party and the representatives
of the McEnery party.

While General Longstreet and his party was passing along the street, they
very naturally attracted a good deal of attention. There was no guard attending,
but they passed along like other citizens, and reached the State House without incident of any kind.

The Metropolitans. Their Restoration

Saturday morning the interior of the Customhouse presented an unusually lively
aspect, instead of the anxious and subdued looking crowd who had sought refuge
within its granite walls. An air of triumph sat upon the countenances of those
who were so ingloriously defeated on Monday, and this great change, it is of course
understood, has been the outcome of the action of the President and the subsequent
order of Gov. Kellogg.

At an early hour the captains of the various precincts began to muster their
men for the purpose of taking charge of the stations, and from present appearances
it is thought that about one-half of the force can be got together—in all say two
hundred and fifty policemen.

At about 12 o'clock the Metropolitans assembled, and marched in a body to the First Precinct station and Police Headquarters, under command of General Baldy, who, during General Badger's illness, will have control, where Captain Flanagan and the First Precinct men will be placed. From there to the Third Station the Metropolitans will take the line of march, and at that station place Capt. Gray in command, and so on throughout the city.

With the exception of the Third Station, formerly Capt. McCann's, the same officers will be installed.

U. S. REGULARS AT NEW ORLEANS

At the urgent request of Gov. Kellogg the authorities in Washington hastened to send all the troops they could assemble to the rebellious city of New Orleans to maintain peace and order.

According to the *New Orleans Times* army officers protested, saying the Army was not large enough to protect the frontiers (from Indians) and at the same time act as a posse comitatus to aid the judiciary in the South to enforce its edicts, particularly in such extraordinary cases as that of Louisiana. The following dispatch to the *Republican* shows that President Grant, in modern lingo, "threw the book" at New Orleans:

> Washington, September 17.—Additional evidences of the earnestness of the government in dealing with affairs in Louisiana are apparent today in the formal ordering of the Twenty-second Infantry to New Orleans. These troops are scattered in various places, including Detroit, Fort Porter and Fort Gratiot. Some days may elapse before they can be en route for this city.
>
> Orders have also been issued for the troops at Fortress Monroe to hold themselves in readiness for a movement thither.
>
> General McDowell is now engaged in gathering up such forces as can be spared from his department for services in Louisiana.
>
> Should the exigencies require, it is supposed that about 5000 troops can be concentrated in Louisiana within a week or ten days, including those already there or in the vicinity.
>
> This number is about one-third of the active force of the army, which nominally consists of 18,000 men, but allowance must be made for vacancies by casualties, expiration of enlistments and privates on detail duty. Recruiting, however, is in progress to keep the army up to the maximum.

But the Federal authorities did the best they could. On the 19th of September General Emory had under his command in New Orleans 25 companies of infantry, three batteries of 18 guns and four companies of artillery.

On the 20th Captain Wells of the U. S. Navy had five gunboats with guns in working order trained on the city. By the 29th two more U. S. warships had arrived, making seven in the harbor.

Some of these troops were used as a guard for the Governor. According to the *Bulletin* of Sept. 22nd: "Kellogg was at the State House last night guarded by some half dozen Metropolitans. Five companies of U. S. troops guarded the Metropolitans."

GOVERNOR KELLOGG.

Wm. Pitt Kellogg, born in Vermont in 1831, practiced law in Illinois in 1853, appointed Chief Justice of the Territory of Nebraska by Pres. Lincoln in 1861, Col. of 7th Ill. Cavalry, appointed collector of the Port of New Orleans April, 1865, his commission bearing the last official signature of the martyred president. Served two terms in U. S. Senate.

Governor Kellogg's relish for the confines of the Custom House during the hectic days of the week of the 14th made him susceptible to criticism as well as sarcasm and the *Bulletin* of the 19th under the caption, CAN'T TELL THE TRUTH publishes this:

The following dispatch was sent by the *de functo* Kellogg to J. R. West or J. H. Sypher, in Washington.

New Orleans, Sept. 18, 1874.

To Senator West or J. H. Sypher, Member of Congress,

Washington, D. C.:

I see by Western papers that you have severely criticized my leaving the State House. I left the State House Monday at the earnest solicitation of all our friends. The Lieutenant Governor and Speaker being absent from the State, an accident to me, they felt, would have made complication desperate. None but colored militia in the State House, and had they made any resistance they would have been burned out and massacred, the buildings being entirely indefensible. If our friends will come here and help up we shall be very glad.

W. P. KELLOGG.

The "earnest solicitation of all our friends." Why, the fellow has not got a friend in the whole city. "Nothing but colored militia in the State-House;" absolutely and unqualifiedly false. We saw hundreds of them in the State-House while he was cowering in the Custom House. A thousand witnesses can be brought to prove the assertion a lie out of the whole cloth. There were numbers of white and black metropolitans within the building, and hundreds of Negroes about the streets were run in and placed at the windows and along the roof with rifles in their hands.

The *Bulletin,* September 27, 1874, prints this poem by a local wit:

THE NEW ORLEANS CUSTOM-HOUSE

(A poem supposed to have been spoken by a certain usurping Governor.)
Dedicated to the N. O. Daily Republican.

I.

I love the Granite Building,
It is so large and strong,
And from there to the State-House,
The distance isn't long.

II.

When angry people rise in wrath,
And my police stampede,
I fly to that strong citadel,
It is my "friend in need."

III.

Behind its granite pillars
Protection sure I find.
Its walls are proof 'gaint bullets,
And with blue jackets lined!

IV.

Within its secret dungeons
My dearest plans are made;
And when I'm in a muddle
I call on it for aid.

V.

So, glory to the building
Beneath whose roof I'm brave,
But for it I'd have met my end—
Not Governor—but KNAVE.

B. S.

In accordance with the agreement by the leaders of the White League and General Emory, the following circular was issued for the information of parties who may come under the provisions contained in the order:

CIRCULAR
NEW ORLEANS, Sept. 21, 1874.

In accordance with General Order No. 7, Sept. 17th, 1874, all arms, ammunition and ordnance stores belonging to the State of Louisiana should be at once turned over to the United States authorities.

The officers in command of organized troops are herebly instructed to inspect their various commands at once, and cause all State property in their possession to be delivered to the officer of the United States troops in command of the First Precinct Central Police Station, or to the United States officer in command of Third Precinct Station, Jackson Square.

All citizens having in their possession arms or ammunition belonging to the State are earnestly requested to at once deliver the same to the officers above indicated.

Persons delivering arms or ammunition will in nowise be interfered with by the United States or State authorities.

JOHN McENERY
D. B. PENN.

* * * * *

During the week of September 14th to 19th Louisiana had four different governors:

Monday, Sept. 14th — Wm. Pitt Kellogg
Tuesday, Sept. 15th — D. B. Penn
Wednesday, Sept. 16th — John McEnery
Thursday, Sept. 17th — Col. Brooke — in charge
Friday, Sept. 18th — " " " "
Saturday, Sept. 19th — Wm. Pitt Kellogg

CHAPTER XI

AFTERMATH

On September 18, 1874 General Emory notified Governor Kellogg that the "insurrection" was at an end. The next day Kellogg and his officials resumed control.

The White Leaguers accepted the situation, and it seemed that all their efforts were useless and their splendid victory unavailing. But it was far from such. From some of the newspaper comments given in another chapter, it will be seen that the whole United States became awakened to the abnormal situation in the South. Newspapers and magazines day after day printed columns of notes and editorials about the conditions in the Southern States and particularly in Louisiana.

The struggle of the people in Louisiana against inefficient and corrupt government, instituted by fraud and kept in power by Federal bayonets, won the admiration and sympathy of much of the press as well as many of the people of the North. Voices were raised in Congress against President Grant's conduct in handling the situation in Louisiana.

The Republican leaders began to see that they were endangering that party's control of the Congress if they continued to support the administration's "carpet bag" policy in the South.

Six weeks after the affair of September 14th, that is, in the election of November 4 of 1874, the Democrats won a majority of 87 in the House of Representatives — the first time in twenty years that they had control of either branch of Congress.

The change in the political climate was undoubtedly caused by the Battle of Liberty Place, which brought to the attention of the country the difficulties of the people of Louisiana and the unjust rule that was being forced upon them.

In the meantime, the leaders of the White League were not discouraged but became more active than ever. In fact, in January 1875, S. B. Packard, U. S. Marshal at New Orleans, testified that after September 14th many joined the League and in January, 1875 the White League had twice the number of members that it had in September 1874.

All the time the White League was active, it had many members and it watched with eager eye the proceedings and actions of the *de facto* Kellogg officials. In January 1875, when the legislature met, there was another contre-temp, as conservative or Democratic members of the legislature attempted to elect their candidate for Speaker of the House. The radical party sent for a company of Federal troops who prevented the Democratic speaker from presiding. This affair created great excitement and the subsequent events are too involved to be detailed here. But it attracted national attention.

AFFAIRS IN LOUISIANA, BEGINNING OF 1875

The Senate of the United States by resolution on January 8, 1875, requested President Grant to justify his use of the Army in the Federal interference in Louisiana affairs. President Grant complied with a message to the Senate on January 13, 1875 in which he explained why the Federal forces backed up William Pitt Kellogg, whom many Louisianians called a usurper, and justified the use of troops in entering the State House and interfering with the procedure of the Legislature in ejecting its officials. Gen. Philip H. Sheridan on January 5, 1875, from New Orleans wired W. W. Belknap, Secretary of War at Washington.

> I think the terroism now existing in Louisiana, Mississippi and Arkansas could be entirely removed and confidence and fair dealing established by the arrest and control of the ring leaders of the armed White Leaguers. If Congress would pass a bill declaring them banditti, they could be tried by military commission. The ring leaders of this banditti who murdered men here on the 14th of last September, and also more recently at Vicksburg, Mississippi, should in justice to law and order and the peace and prosperity of this southern part of the country, be punished. It is possible that if the President would issue a proclamation declaring them banditti, no further action need be taken except that which would devolve upon me.—Philip Sheridan, Lt. Gen. USA.

On January 10, 1875 Gen. Sheridan wired Secretary of War Belknap his estimate of the murders, riots, etc., in Louisiana since 1866. He reported nearly 3,500 persons (the majority of which were colored) were killed, and that the records showed that 1,844 were killed and wounded, 1,200 of these on account of political sentiments, in the year 1868 alone. Undoubtedly all exaggerated.

Gen. Sheridan's report did not sit well with many people in the North. In fact, on January 19, 1875, the General Assembly of the State of Missouri jointly and concurrently passed a resolution, a copy of which was sent to each Congressman and Senator as well as the President, protesting the use of the Army in the settlement of Louisiana elections. The resolution read in part:

> That one of those fundamental principles of free governments is that the legislature of a state is the sole judge of the election and qualifications of its own mem-

Cartoon by Thos. Nast in Harper's Weekly, March 6, 1875
— *Courtesy Leonard V. Huber*

bers; and that the recent use of Federal troops to expel from the duly organized legislature of Louisiana certain members thereof, on the pretext that they had been wrongfully admitted by that legislature to their seats, is at once a violation of that principle, an outrage upon a helpless people, calculated to insult and bring into public odium the gallant Army of the U. S., intended for nobler purposes than that of upholding an effete local usurpation.

That while the recommendation of Lieut.-Gen. Sheridan that a designated class of people should be declared 'banditti' and tried by court-martial in time of peace, is so absurd as to excite only the derision of every one in the least acquainted with the Constitution and laws of the country, yet such reckless and incendiary language from an officer charged with a delicate mission is abhorrent to the feelings of every friend of humanity and lover of constitutional liberty, and deserves and should receive a stern and prompt rebuke from his official superiors.

CONGRESSIONAL INVESTIGATIONS

In the early part of 1875, two Congressional committees came to New Orleans to investigate conditions here. Their reports, incorporating the testimony of many prominent men on "both sides," aroused the country. They make interesting reading for those who care to wade through two large volumes printed in 8-point type.

In December 1874, the House of Representatives appointed a committee of seven to investigate conditions in Louisiana. A sub-committee of three — Charles Foster, W. W. Phelps (Republicans) and C. L. Potter (Democrat) — began the hearing on December 30. The committee stayed eight days in New Orleans and heard 95 witnesses. In view of the exigency of the situation, the sub-committee did not wait to print all the testimony. But their special report included their examination into the acts of the Returning Board and the operation of the White League.

The report of the special committee of three, representing George F. Hoar's Select Committee on the Condition of the South, filed and signed on January 14, 1875 by Charles Foster, Wm. Walter Phelps and Clarkson N. Potter read in part:

The members of the White League had purchased arms; the police had seized these arms without process of law, taking them forcibly from the merchants who had sold and from the members who had bought them. A consignment of arms was to arrive by the steamer Mississippi. The league were called out on the morning of the 14th to go and take them in a body; the police undertook to seize the arms; the two bodies came into collision on the wharf, with the loss of several killed and wounded. There were then hardly any Federal troops in New Orleans, and the disintegration of the Kellogg party was such that before night Penn and his associates had only to take possession of the executive offices without a struggle. The movement was everywhere quietly accepted by the whites throughout the State until the Federal Government intervened, when Penn and his associates at once surrendered. If Louisiana were a country by itself, McEnery and his associates would at once be installed in power; but the conservatives of Louisiana do not propose to fight the Federal Government. They submit, not because they want to, but because they must; not because they proclaim any enmity against the flag; not because free labor has not been found practicable; not because of any general hostility to the colored people because colored; but because they regard themselves as defrauded out of the election of 1872, and yet more out of this last election, and because the State government to which they have been subjected has been, as they think, to the last degree destructive and corrupt.

Indeed, in our judgment the substantial citizens of the State will submit to any fair determination of the question of the late elections, or to anything by which they can secure a firm and good government. What they seek is peace and an opportunity for prosperity; to that end they will support any form of government that will afford them just protection in their business and personal relations. In their distress they have got beyond any mere question of political party. They regard themselves as practically without government and without the power to form one.

This report did not meet with the approval of many members of the House. Says Charles Nordhoff: "The report of the first New Orleans Committee, though based on evidence not afterwards controverted, was received with so much doubt that a second committee was thought necessary — to investigate the first."

Later in January, 1875, the second committee composed of George F. Hoar, William P. Frye, W. A. Wheeler (Republicans) with Sam Ballard (Democrat) came to New Orleans to see what they could find out. They submitted a report and on February 23, 1875, Congressmen Foster, Phelps, Potter and Marshall submitted minority reports, disagreeing with that of Messrs. Hoar, Wheeler and Frye.*

THE ELECTION OF 1876

In the election held in Louisiana on November 7, 1876, the candidates were: Democrats, Francis T. Nicholls for Governor and Louis A. Wiltz for Lieutenant Governor; Republicans, U. S. Marshal S. B. Packard for Governor and Cicero Caesar Antoine (Negro) for Lieutenant-Governor. At this election members of the White League stood guard throughout the State, while Federal troops watched at the polls also.

The Returning Board composed of three white Republicans and a Negro undertaker, announced on December 6, 1876 that the Republican ticket had been elected.

On the same day, the Nicholls' forces claimed that the Democrats had won a sweeping victory. The Returning Board's decision was upheld by a committee of prominent Republicans who had come to New Orleans to watch the work of the Louisiana Returning Board. On this committee were James A. Garfield, future President of the United States; General Lew Wallace, author of "Ben Hur"; and Senator John Sherman, a brother of General W. T. Sherman. The Democrats also sent a delegation to watch the election and

---

The word "report" means their conclusions or opinions. The evidence upon which they based their conclusions was, of course, the same.

they condemned the Returning Board's verdict as "partial and unfair, illegal and entitled to no respect whatever." Once again Louisiana had two rival governments.

The Democratic State Legislature of Louisiana met on January 1, 1877 at St. Patrick's Hall in New Orleans with Louis A. Wiltz, Lieutenant Governor, presiding over the Senate, while Louis Bush was elected Speaker of the House.

Governor Packard had taken possession of the State House on Royal Street and admitted as members of his Legislature only those who had certificates from the Returning Board. This legislature had as President of the Senate, the Negro Lieutenant-Governor Antoine, while the House elected Michael Hahn as Speaker.

On January 8, there were two inaugurations, Governor Nicholls at St. Patrick's Hall and Packard at the State House, the old St. Louis Hotel. Louisiana again had two governors.

On the next day, on the 9th, the White League in New Orleans came into action once more. It assembled to the number of 6,000, some say, and under the command of Gen. Fred Ogden, took possession of the courts, police station and arsenal. It looked like there would be another September 14th, but Packard's forces surrendered and left the Cabildo.

The Federal troops in New Orleans preserved order between the governments of Nicholls and Packard. Packard had only the State House in his possession. For nearly four months, the White League guarded the courts and police stations and patrolled the streets in the neighborhood of the Cabildo.

On March 1, 1877, Packard pleaded with Gen. Grant to recognize his administration. President Grant told him he did not believe that public opinion would support any longer the maintenance of the State government in Louisiana by the use of United States troops. When this bad news arrived, the carpetbag government began to disintegrate and members of the Packard legislature went over to the Democrats in St. Patrick's Hall.

President Hayes was inaugurated on March 4 and immediately turned his attention to conditions in Louisiana. He sent five commissioners to New Orleans to study affairs. On April 21, the commissioners recommended to President Hayes that he recognize the Democratic government headed by Governor Nicholls. On April 24, 1877, the President ordered the United States troops to move away from the State House on Royal Street. Governor Packard peacefully surrendered the State House to General Ogden and the White League.

Reconstruction was now at an end — a tragic era, an era of humiliation and economic suffering for the South; of hate, greed and injustice on the part of the conquerors.

A chain of events led directly from the Battle of Liberty Place on the 14th of September to the election of President Hayes and his withdrawal of Federal troops from the South. Some have said that this would have come about without the effort of the White League that Hayes would have been elected anyway and that he would have ended Reconstruction just the same. Like many of the other "ifs" of history this theory cannot be proved.

But the troubles in Louisiana, which caused the formation of the White League and made them battle on the 14th of September, were thereby emphasized and brought forcibly to the attention of the country. Its political effect was direct and helped to bring the Democrats back into power in the lower house of Congress. It made the Republicans more tolerant and less arbitrary in their attitude toward the South. It is believed that Tilden really won the election of 1876, but in a manner that does not redown to the credit of the politicians of the time, he was defrauded of his office as President of the United States. Actually the Louisiana affairs and the propaganda emanating therefrom caused so much dissension that it actually elected a Democratic President although he was deprived of the office by a national "returning board."

The Battle of Liberty Place on September 14, 1874, was an important event, and in a careful study of our country's history, we see that it had repercussions almost as great as that of a more famous battle — Jackson's defeat of the British at Chalmette nearly sixty years before.

The effects of the Battle of New Orleans were mostly social. All historians agree that it had no "military value." It would not have made a bit of difference if Packenham had won instead of Jackson.* The main effect of the Battle of New Orleans was to elect Jackson president and bring the western frontier into prominence and to develop further the principles of Democracy. Sad to say, Jackson also instituted the policy of "to the victor belongs the spoils" — a policy which plagued the country for many decades.

It is interesting to know that small affairs such as the White League Battle of September 14th have a way of starting chain reactions to cause explosions that change the face of things. At the Battle of Concord in 1775, there

---

*I realize that this opinion is anathema to many in this section.
My great-grandfather was an officer at the Battle of New Orleans and I had no ancestors at Liberty Place, so I should be prejudiced in favor of the event of January 8th. It was a glorious victory, but as with many other great battles, what was the use?

were only a few hundred Minute Men engaged, and 10 or 12 died across the bridge where stood the "embattled farmers whose shot was heard around the world." More White Leaguers were killed in New Orleans on that fateful day than at Concord. While Concord started the Union on its way, the Battle of Liberty Place did the same for the new South.

More Americans were killed in the Battle of Liberty Place than were killed in the Battle of New Orleans. In the Battle of January 8th, 1815 the Americans on the East bank, that is at Chalmette, lost only seven killed and six wounded. When we include those on the West bank, the total was only 13 killed, 39 wounded and 19 missing. The British reported 291 killed, 1262 wounded and 484 missing, or a total of 2037 on both sides of the river. The White Leaguers lost 18 killed and about 30 wounded. Kellogg forces lost 35 killed and 50 wounded. The exact number will never be known.

The Battle of Liberty Place in 1874 changed the tide of opinion, brought the end of Reconstruction in the South, and started the Southern people on their way to the great prosperity which they now enjoy.

CHAPTER XII

THE SUPREME COURT OF LOUISIANA
AND THE BATTLE OF SEPTEMBER THE FOURTEENTH

As a result of the affair of the Fourteenth of September ten suits were instituted against the City of New Orleans for property damage. This opinion was rendered by Mr. Associate Justice F. P. Poche (32 La. Annual 577):

HENRY STREET et al. vs. THE CITY OF NEW ORLEANS

Henry Street and nine other plaintiffs, joining together, sue the City of New Orleans for damages alleged to have been done to their property in this city, on the 14th, 15th 16th and 17th days of September, 1874, by a body of rioters, who took violent possession of the State House and other public buildings in the city, and used, carried away, destroyed or otherwise illegally disposed of, plaintiffs' property, which is fully described in several statements annexed to their petition.

The city filed a general denial, and urged as special defenses that on the 14th of September the city government was suspended in its functions; that the then existing State Government which had under the law the exclusive control of the police, had been subverted, or had ceased to exercise its authority, and that both State and city governments were, during the days mentioned by Plaintiffs, under the control of a "de facto" government which had supplanted the previous State government, thus rendering the city powerless to hinder or prevent the acts complained of.

The case was tried by a Jury, who returned a verdict in favor of the city, opn which judgment was entered accordingly and two of the plaintiffs, Henry Street and Otto Burauld, have appealed.

The evidence shows that considerable property of plaintiffs was destroyed or lost to them on the occasion referred to, and they claim damages therefor under the provisions of Article 2453 of the Revised Statutes of 1870, under which all municipal corporations in this State are made liable for damages done to property by mobs or riotous assemblages in their respective limits. In order to recover in this suit, plaintiffs must bring their case within the strict provisions of this statute, and they must therefore prove, beyond doubt, that the body of men who took possession of the State House, and in fact of the State government, on the 14th of September, 1874, and held and controlled the same during the three succeeding days, was a mob or riotous assemblage within the meaning of the statute, and in default of such proof they must fall. The record is very voluminous, and the evidence decidedly conflicting, but after a careful perusal of the testimony, we are clear that the body of men, who coöperated in that movement, and on that memorable occasion, was not a mob or a riotous assemblage, nor unruly and wanton destroyers of property.

We are satisfied, on the contrary, that it was a well organized body of citizens and patriots, acting under the orders of, and in obedience to, a State government ordained by the people, and wielding legitimate power, and that those citizens were exercising the sacred rights of resistance to oppression and usurpation, under which their dearest rights were being destroyed.

And, therefore, the property which was destroyed, and the victims who fell, during the conflict were the inevitable results of a collision of arms between organized and contending forces, and under such a state of facts no municipal corporation can legally be held liable in damages for property destroyed.

The occurrences of the 14th of September, 1874, although they failed to bear the fruits which immediately resulted from the events of the 9th of January, 1877, from which the true government of the State sprang into life, were not more than the latter, the deeds of a mob or of a riotous assemblage.

Both are marked epochs in the history of Louisiana, of which we take judicial cognizance; both contributed to the reëstablishment of justice and order in the State; and neither could entail any liability for damages on the City of New Orleans, because, by accident, she happened to be on the scene of the two movements.

And, besides, at that time, the city authorities had no control over the police force, which under the laws, was part of the existing State government. The evidence in this case also shows that, on the 14th of September, the police force of New Orleans had been removed by the State athorities from its post of legitimate duty, that it was converted into a Militia Brigade, and that, armed and equipped and officered as for war, that same police was marched out to disperse the citizens who had assembled to petition and remonstrate against the abuses and outrages perpetrated by the usurping State government. This fact of itself should release the city from all liability in the premises.

Plaintiffs having utterly failed to make out their case, the verdict of the Jury, and the judgment of the lower Court, are therefore correct and are affirmed with costs.

CHAPTER XIII

BIOGRAPHIES

GOVERNOR JOHN McENERY

John McEnery was born in Petersburg, Virginia, on March 31, 1833. His father, Henry O'Neal McEnery, a native of Limerick, Ireland, emigrated to Virginia where he married Carolyn H. Douglas. He was a colonel of the Virginia Militia and later came to Monroe, Louisiana to become a planter. He was also Registrar of the Land Office there for eight years.

His son, John, received his early education in Monroe and later was sent to Hanover College in Indiana. He studied law and later practiced with his brother S. D. McEnery. (Afterwards governor of the State). In 1856 John McEnery married Miss Mary Thompson. He was appointed Registrar of the Land Office in Monroe. In 1857 President Buchanan removed him for supporting Stephen A. Douglas for the presidency. When the Civil War commenced, John McEnery joined the Confederate Army as a captain of infantry. Soon he was promoted to major and subsequently became Lieutenant Colonel, commanding the Louisiana 4th Battalion. He served with distinction in several campaigns in Virginia, West Virginia and Mississippi and was twice wounded. At the close of the war he resumed practice of law. In 1866 he was elected to the lower House of the Louisiana State Legislature. The Reconstruction Acts of Congress caused him to lose his seat in 1867.

In June, July and August 1872, Col. McEnery became the coalition candidate of several groups opposing the Republican Party. In June, July and August 1872, he was nominated for governor by the Democrats, the Democrats and Reformers and the Democrats and Liberals. He was elected by a 10,000 majority, but was counted out by the Republican Returning Board.

Governor McEnery became the *de jure* governor and contested with Kellogg the governorship of the State as has already been told. Governor McEnery spent much of his time in Washington attempting to win the support of senators and representatives as well as the president to have the *de facto* governor ousted and himself and his newly elected state officials given control of the government of the State of Louisiana.

(Harper's Weekly, Oct. 10, 1874)

JOHN F. M'ENERY.

On September 14, 1874 the governor was not in the State, and ever since that time many have accused him of avoiding the issue and absenting himself, perhaps, ingloriously. Historians have arched their eyebrows and made invidious suggestions. It is only by accident that the present writer has found out why Governor McEnery was not in New Orleans or in charge of affairs that day.

In a letter to the *Times-Democrat* published on the 19th of November, 1902, Benjamin Rice Forman, commenting at the time of the death of Governor D. B. Penn on the events of 1874, had this to say about Governor McEnery:

> Gov. McEnery early in 1873, when he had no armed militia and no prospect of being sustained by any armed force, and when he was threatened with arrest, had given his word that he would make no forcible attack on the Kellogg government. He therefore left the State and D. B. Penn became acting governor.

Governor McEnery, a man of honor, kept his promise.

He died March 28, 1891.

GOVERNOR D. B. PENN

David Bradfute Penn was born in Lynchburg, Virginia, on May 13, 1836 at the home of his grandmother. His father, Alfred Penn, came to New Orleans when a young man and became a banker and owner of a cotton press.

Young David attended Springhill College near Mobile and later the Virginia Military Institute at Lexington from which he was graduated in 1856. While there he was honored by the cadets electing him to receive the statue of Washington presented to V.M.I. by Governor H. A. Wise.

Penn studied law at the University of Virginia. He returned to New Orleans in 1858 to conduct a cotton press business. In 1861 he lived at 76 Chippewa Street. When the war broke out he organized a company of his employees and as captain took the men to Camp Moore. There the company became part of the 7th Regiment, and Captain Penn, age 25, was elected major. This regiment was mustered in "for the duration" and was one of the first to reach Virginia. It did yeoman's service at the Battle of Bull Run.

The 7th Regiment later became part of Ewell's Division and took part in many engagements. In the Battle of Cross Keyes and Port Republic the colonel of the Regiment, Hayes, was wounded and Lt. Col. de Choisel was killed, and Major Penn then commanded the regiment. Hayes was made a Brigadier General and Penn was promoted to the colonelcy.

Colonel Penn was wounded twice. The 7th Regiment under his command was active at Gettysburg and was the last to leave the town as it brought up the rear of the infantry in retreat on the fateful day of July 3rd.

Colonel Penn was later made a prisoner and stayed for eleven months at Johnson's Island. Exchanged he was ordered to Dick Taylor's command in the Trans-Mississippi Department. On his way he was captured again at Athens, Georgia, and as the war was now over, he was paroled.

Returning to New Orleans Col. Penn resumed his former business and engaged in cotton and sugar planting. He became active in politics and his party.

Governor Penn was a liberal Republican and was very popular with both the white and Negro voters. If he had been nominated instead of McEnery in 1872 it is probable that his vote would have been so large that the Returning Board would not have dared to throw him out.

At the expiration of Gov. Nicholls' term in 1880 Penn wanted the nomination for the next term, but the Convention gave it to Louis Wiltz. He was offered the Lieutenant-Governorship again, but refused to accept second place

(Harper's Weekly, Oct. 10, 1874)

D. B. PENN.

on the ticket. One of his friends advised taking it, pointing out that Wiltz was in bad health. A year later Wiltz died and S. D. McEnery, the Lt. Gov., became Governor and later U. S. Senator.

Governor Penn was appointed Recorder of Finances in the City of New Orleans in 1893. He represented the State of Louisiana at the World's Fair at Chicago. He was Vice-President of the National Commission in conduct of the Fair, and was active as president of the Commission for 60 days while President Palmer was absent.

Governor Penn died on November 15, 1902 at the Penn Flats on Lafayette Square where the Federal Building now is. This was the residence of his sister, Mrs. Charles Conrad. Those surviving him were: his sisters—Mrs. Charles Conrad and Mrs. W. B. Krumbhaar; his children—Alfred Penn of New Orleans, David B. Penn of New York, Mrs. George W. Nott, Jr. and Misses Evelyn, Lutie and Marie Penn.

When Governor Penn died the newspapers printed abbreviated obituary notices, and this led Benjamin Rice Forman, a lawyer and friend of the Governor's, to complain in a letter to the *Times-Democrat* on November 19, 1902 about this "scant justice done Governor Penn" in the accounts of his life and death. Mr. Forman pointed out that in stirring times when doubt and fear were widespread and the future of the people of Louisiana seemed dismal, Governor Penn assumed the gravest and fullest responsibility. He formulated a plan and did not hesitate to carry it out. Governor Penn was a strategist, a shrewd observer of human nature, as well as a diplomat, and his masterly handling of affairs of the days immediately preceding and following the 14th of September are in accordance with the actions of a great man.

However, at the time Governor Penn's leadership was appreciated as is shown by the following editorial in the *Picayune* in its issue of September 16th, 1874:

THE PEOPLE'S MOVEMENT AND THE PEOPLE'S REPRESENTATIVE

It is the universal understanding throughout the city that to Gov. Penn, Gen. Ogden and the gallant followers who flocked to their call we are indebted for the present hopeful and reassuring condition of affairs. To those who met and swept away the Kellogg janissaries we are bound by everlasting ties of gratitude and love; to D. B. Penn, the modest, manly, honorable gentleman, the worthy citizen and steadfast friend—to him and to his healthful influence is due the enthusiasm, the cordial, unreserved support and encouragement of the entire community, both white and colored.

Gov. Penn possesses, in a higher degree than any man now prominent in our State, the confidence and respect of all classes. A native of Louisiana, reared among the people of New Orleans, of a distinguished and eminent family, and gifted with great personal attraction, he is everywhere esteemed and admired. He was a gallant soldier throughout the war, and since that time, in his capacities of planter and merchant, has been conservative, moderate and impartial of principle. A Liberal Republican in politics, he is recognized among the colored people as a ruler on whom they could securely depend for protection and justice; a gentleman of lofty character and unimpeachable integrity, he is beloved and trusted by all parties of his own race.

He is the only one of the contesting Governors and Lieutenant Governors whose election was conceded by both sides—the only one against whom prejudices, just or otherwise, do not exist, within and without the State. His recent sudden elevation to the head of power has been accepted by the colored people, and greeted with joy and satisfaction by the whites. As the type and central figure of the revolution, and the representative of the complete and peaceful restoration which has ensued, he imparts to both a dignity, and attracts to both a respect and confidence which no one else could have encompassed. Being in no sense of the word a partisan, he expresses faithfully and appropriately the spirit of the movement which has set Louisiana free. It was the uprising of a whole people, and Gov. Penn is unquestionably its best and truest exponent.

It is one of the ironies of history that a man of Governor Penn's standing and influence while he was alive should have had his name traduced long after he was dead by careless historians who wrote that he was a mulatto. This outrageous mis-statement of fact first appeared in "Reconstruction in Louisiana after 1868" by Ella Lonn, published in 1918. Such carelessness on the part of this historian makes one wonder about the accuracy of some of her other statements.

Only two years ago, E. L. Tinker in his book, "Creole City," repeated this grave error. When brought to their attention the publishers corrected the mistake and reprinted the page.

Governor Penn came from one of the oldest and finest families of Virginia. His father was one of the founders of the Boston Club, the third oldest social club in the United States, and Governor Penn himself was an active member for many years. He was socially impeccable.

Let the record stand corrected with the hope that future writers will no longer defame the ancestry of David Bradfute Penn.

————————o————————

GENERAL FRED NASH OGDEN

Fred Nash Ogden, Jr., was born on January 25, 1837 at Baton Rouge, Louisiana. His father was Dr. Frederick Nash Ogden from North Carolina who came to Baton Rouge where he married Carmelite Lopez, of Spanish descent.

The Ogden family were of early American stock, resident in New Jersey, where an ancestor, Robert Ogden II, was Speaker of the Assembly in Revolutionary times. Gen. Matthias Ogden was with Gen. Arnold at Quebec and later on Washington's staff.

At age sixteen Fred Ogden worked in New Orleans for the firm of Hewitt, Norton and Company. When the war started he enlisted in Dreux's (afterward Rightor's) Battalion, which took part in the Peninsula Campaign. When New Orleans was captured Lt. Ogden was stationed at the forts below the city with Pinckney's Battery of heavy artillery.

Escaping, the young lieutenant went to Port Hudson, where he took part in the heavy fighting there. Later as Major of the 8th Louisiana Battalion he participated in the defense of Vicksburg, and was conspicuous for gallantry. There is today at Vicksburg in the National Park a bas relief of Major Fred Ogden. When the war ended he had become a lieutenant colonel, and surrendered with General Forrest in Alabama.

Returning to New Orleans Col. Ogden became associated with W. A. Bell in the bagging and tie business. He was president of the Crescent City Democratic Club in 1868, leader of the attack on the Third Precinct Station in 1872 when he was wounded, and general in command of the White Leaguers on September 14, 1874.

General Ogden was superintendent of the World's Industrial Exhibition here in New Orleans in 1884-85. He was president of the Howard Association for many years. This famous organization gave aid in yellow fever epidemics, and in the great epidemic of 1878, General Ogden was particularly active. General Ogden was also President of the Louisiana Branch of the Red Cross, newly organized about that time.

General Fred Ogden was distinguished for his military capacity and for coolness and courage in battle. His accomplishments during the later Reconstruction period were remarkable. Without arms or money he formed "the incongruous material of what appeared to be a political club into a regiment of disciplined and drilled soldiers." Night after night under his inspiration and drive, the men met secretly and drilled, many without arms or equipment. With indomitable will and without hope of reward he surmounted all difficulties. When the great day of Septebmer 14th came, he was prepared. Placed in command by Governor Penn he conducted the battle of the day with tactical skill and with the energy and decision that make a great general.

General Ogden kept his organization together, and in the Spring of 1877, as we know, patrolled the streets of New Orleans for Governor Nicholls and kept guard over the movements of the usurper, Packard. On the 14th of September, 1877, at a public ceremony Governor Nicholls presented Gen. Fred N. Ogden with a magnificent sword of honor. The scabbard was of solid silver and the top of the handle surmounted with a superb amethyst. The sword cost $1100. This sword was in the keeping of the Louisiana Historical Society in July 1920.

General Ogden died on May 25, 1886. His death brought profound sorrow to the populace and the newspapers printed eulogistic editorials and elaborate obituaries. The funeral was one of the most representative ever held in New Orleans. The leaders of society, of the professions, of business, as well as public officials attended.

Some of General Ogden's papers are at the Howard-Tilton Library.

The following appeared in the *Picayune* on 15 September 1874, the day after the Battle of the 14th:

> Too much credit cannot be awarded Gen. Fred. N. Ogden, commander of the citizens' forces, for the prudence, self-control and admirable power of command exhibited by him throughout the affair of yesterday. Placed over a large body of men burning with ardor and almost wild with indignation, he curbed all excesses, restrained all imprudence, checked all immoderation, and, when the time arrived, he led his soldiers like a gentleman and a hero.
>
> We are glad to know that he suffered but slight injuries when his horse was shot under him, and fell while at full speed. Both on his own account and on that of the community we rejoice in the knowledge of his having escaped serious harm.

COLONEL JOHN G. ANGELL

John Goodrich Angell was born in Jefferson County, Miss. His father was Dr. Richard Angell of a prominent English family from London. Moving to New Orleans Dr. Angell with his sons — Samuel M., a physician; John G., a dentist; and James, an apothecary, who manufactured and sold "Angell's Cough Remedy" (well known to old-timers) — operated what today would be called a "Clinic" at 152 Julia St. after the War.

In May 1861 John G. Angell, 20 years old, left for the front as orderly sergeant, Co. A., Crescent City Guards. Before the end of the year he was elected captain. In 1862 he was frequently in command of his regiment — the Fifth in Hay's Brigade, Army of No. Va. In 1863 he was captured and spent much time in various prisons, including Johnson's Island, enduring many hardships which probably brought on tuberculosis, leading to his early death.

Col. Angell organized the regiment that fought on the Fourteenth. He was promoted to Brig. Gen. afterwards. On Sept. 14, 1876 the militia paraded in front of his house to honor him. The rigors of White League activities hastened his death, August 14, 1877. He was buried in Washington Cemetery, and a great concourse of people attended, including Gov. Nicholls, Gen. Ogden, Gen. Behan and Col. Vaudry. The *Times* and the *Democrat* eulogized him. I. W. Patton, the Adjutant-Gen., as commanded by the Governor, in his order to the 2nd Reg. of Infantry of the La. State Militia to act as the funeral escort said in part:

> . . . . he leaves behind him the record of a career which adorned the organization of which he was a prominent member, and a name which his surviving family may well be proud.

CHAPTER XIV

IN MEMORIAM

THOSE KILLED AND WOUNDED IN THE BATTLE OF SEPTEMBER 14, 1874

It is difficult to obtain an accurate list of the casualties of any battle, particularly as in an affair like that of the Fourteenth where there were thousands of unorganized participants and spectators. In its supplement of Sept. 22nd the *Bulletin* printed a list of the killed and wounded on both sides. On the list of killed are three names that are not found elsewhere and who are not on the monument — Charles Dana, M. Bourse and .... Saganac. Major Wells and Gourdain were put on the wounded list as "mortally" wounded. The *Bulletin* printed these names:

Killed—Citizens.

Wm. C. Robins.
J. M. West, (printer.)
Chas. Dana.
Robt. Bozonier.
S. B. Newman, Jr., son of S. B. Newman, the widely known cotton factor.
M. Bourse.
E. A. Toledano.
Albert M. Gautier.
.... Saganac (in another place Sangemin—may have been a "Met.")
Fred Mohrman, Chief Clerk of Administrator Turnbull's office.
Charles Brulard.
R. G. Lindsey.
John Graval, killed (shot in the head).

Wounded—Citizens.

Major William A. Wells, mortally (since dead.)
Capt. Andrews.
Lieut. Schneidel.
Emanuel Blessey.
R. Aby [Sam Aby in issue of 15th].
Wm. H. Kilpatrick.
Mr. Brown.
H. M. Robinson.
Tom Boyle.
Mike Bettis, driver.
Frank Owen, sailmaker.
J. H. Cross, private watchman.
John Mern, laborer.
James McCabe, blacksmith.
Wm. Ormond, drayman.
Charles Kul, Chinaman [killed in issue of 15th].

J. K. Gourdain, mortally.

Considine Matthewson, employee at Morgan's Railroad offices.

John McCormick, James Davis, both Tenth ward, seriously, and confined to bed.

P. McBride, unattached; wounded in arm, corner Tchoupitoulas and Canal streets.

Francis Pallet, wounded severely through left thigh.

Andrew Close, severely in left leg.

J. R. A. Gauthreaux, leg broken.

Gen. F. N. Ogden, slightly injured; horse shot from under him.

Charles Kit, in arms.

J. H. Keller, in ankle.

D. Soniat, compound fracture of leg.

Martin Lang.

P. Bernos.

R. Swanson, dangerously.

F. Foseetoyn.

*Killed—Policemen.**

Corporals Thornton and O'Keefe, of the metropolitans, and Sergeant McManus, and Corporal D. Fish [Fisher], policeman.

J. H. H. Camp, policeman.

Sergeant J. P. Champagne, fifth precinct.

Corporal J. F. Clermont, first precinct.

Officer J. Hill, seventh precinct.

Officer E. Simonds, third precinct.

Officer J. Shields, first precinct.

Officer H. Ballard, sixth precinct.

Wounded—Policemen.

Gen. A. S. Badger.

Sergt. McCann, in leg.

Wm. Brown, metropolitan.

Corporal Bahncke, of the metropolitans.

Gustavus H. Cochin, metropolitan.

Otto Burandte, metropolitan.

Nelson Woody, sanitary officer.

General Baldy, metropolitan.

Capt. Lawler (police) in stomach.

Wm. Omaud, in breast.

Corp'l William Carleton, mounted precinct, in leg.

Officer J. Coleman, mounted precinct, in head and side.

Officer J. Long, mounted precinct, in head.

Corporal George C. Miller, mounted precinct, in thigh.

Officer John Kennedy, first precinct, mortally.

Officer P. Mallahy, first precinct, in arm.

Officer M. J. Barrett, sixth precinct, in arm.

Officer M. Gonzales, fourth precinct, in knee.

Officer J. Connolly, first precinct, in leg.

Officer S. S. Swan, sixth precinct, in leg.

Corporal J. Ryan, sixth precinct, in body.

Officer L. Backus, sixth precinct, in arm.

There were about thirty-five policemen killed, but it was impossible for us to obtain their names.

Officer L. Desdunes, sixth precinct, in leg.
Officer T. Duffy, sixth precinct, in hand.
Officer T. Dorsey, sixth precinct, in leg.
Officer P. Caesar, fourth precinct, in arm.
Corporal C. Bergeron, fourth precinct, in leg.
Officer A. Pecot, fourth precinct, in leg.
Officer R. Gonzales, fourth precinct, bayonet wound in throat.
Officer J. Gonzales, fourth precinct, in knee.
Officer J. Murta, fourth precinct, in hand.
Officer W. Nichols, fourth precinct, in head.
Officer R. Fouvar, fourth precinct, in head.
Sergeant L. A. Thibault, fourth precinct, in hand.
Officer G. Simpson, sixth precinct, in arm.
Officer C. Elgaro, third precinct, in leg.
Officer C. Davis, fourth precinct, in body.
Officer John Lee, sixth precinct, in arm.
Officer L. Willis, sixth precinct, in knee.
Officer O. Elmore, eighth precinct, in thigh.
Officer W. Brown, leg amputated.
Michael M. McEntee, (since died.)

According to the *Republican* of the 16th, J. H. H. Camp of the police, was a former soldier in the Mexican War and in 1864 he was a Captain in a New York regiment. The same paper stated that General Baldy, Vice-President of the Police Board, received a flesh wound in the arm. When Gen. Badger was wounded he assumed charge of the force and remained in command at the Custom House during the night.

The *Picayune* of the 25th tells of the death of another Metropolitan who had a good record:

> This morning, about 4:30 o'clock, John Kennedy, who was wounded in the battle on Monday evening, died at his residence, corner of Liberty and Gravier streets. The ball which struck Kennedy, entered his mouth, and passed out the back of his neck. Kennedy's history is an eventful one. He was on the New Orleans police force long before the war, went out to Nicaragua with Gen. Walker; was there shot through the lungs; lingered a long time, apparently at the point of death, but finally recovered. He joined the Confederate army when the war broke out, fought gallantly for four years; returned home and subsequently joined the metropolitan police, and was mortally wounded in the late fight.

In its issue of the 15th the *Bulletin* had listed these additional names of citizens as wounded:

Walter J. Butler (spectator) in arm
William Keller (spectator) in leg [was this the same as J. H. Keller on the other list?]
Minor Kenner, in ankle
———— Henderson, son of Sam'l Henderson, Esq., in leg
William Mathison (spectator) slightly, in chest

J. B. Dalury, 184 St. Charles St., cripple on a crutch, dangerously

‑‑‑‑‑‑‑‑‑‑‑ Sauer, 100 First St., over left eye

Walter G. Taylor, dangerously in arm

W. H. Morgan, in the foot

Henry Peel, mortally wounded in the chest

Ernest Buisson, dangerously

Capt. Potts, wounded in the groin

B. P. Mearkay, 151 Poeyfarre St., struck in the left side by a shot fired
from the Custom House about 4:00 P. M. on the 14th.

The *Picayune* in its issue of the 18th mentioned the name of Andrew
Close of 113 Marais Street who was badly wounded in the left leg and in the
left shoulder. He was attended by Dr. Stone.

The *Republican* printed this list of White Leaguers killed:

A. Bozonier	R. G. Lindsey
C. Bruliard	F. M. Mohrman
Charles Dana*	S. B. Newman, Jr.
A. M. Gautier	W. C. Robins
J. K. Gourdain	E. A. Toledano
J. Graval	J. M. West

On the 26th of September the *Times* announced the death of Frank
Owens:

> Last night at 8 o'clock Frank Owens, a native of Ireland, about 29 years old,
> closed his eyes in the sleep of death. During the fight Mr. Owens was engaged in
> mending a tarpaulin under the sugar sheds on the levee, between Crossman and
> Custom House streets, and while thus employed was shot in the left leg above the
> knee. The unfortunate man thirteen years ago had his right leg crushed by a train,
> and it was amputated at the Charity Hospital. By a strange coincidence he was in
> the same ward and the same bed the second time when he died.

One wonders why the name of Frank Owens was left off the monument. It
is true that he was not actively engaged in the battle, but neither was J. M.
West and his name is there. It would seem that a printer is of more importance than a tentmaker, and that since the time of Omar tent and sail makers
have lost caste. In any event, I am glad to do honor to the poor and forgotten
Frank Owens by memorializing him here.

‑‑‑‑‑‑‑‑‑‑

*This name is on the Bulletin's *list also, but it is not on the monument or on lists
made up later on. Perhaps he was a member of Kellogg's forces.*

MICHAEL BETZ

From the *New Orleans Times* we learn that on Friday, September 25th at half past 12 P. M. Michael Betz, a White Leaguer, aged 25 years and a native of Germany, died of traumatic tetanus. Mr. Betz was shot after the charge, in his left thigh.

(See memorial of Washington White League on Sept. 26th to John Graval.)

From the *Bulletin* of September 26, 1874:

IN MEMORIAM

HEADQUARTERS, WASHINGTON WHITE LEAGUE,
New Orleans, September 26, 1874.

The officers and members of the above named league are respectfully requested to assemble at the Engine House of Orleans Fire Company No. 21, corner Claiborne and St. Peter streets, THIS DAY, at half past 2 o'clock P. M., precisely, to pay the last sad tribute of respect to their late member, MICHAEL BETZ, who died from wounds received on Monday, Sept. 14, while in defense of the people's rights.

Sister Leagues in general are respectfully invited to attend.

By order: A. B. PHILLIPS, Captain

H. WUNSCHIG, O. S.

ANTOINE BOZONIER

Listed under *Killed* as Robert Bozonier the *Bulletin* of the 15th said that he lived on the corner of Ursulines Street, corner of St. Claude, and that he was a one-armed man, having lost his arm at the Battle of Bentonville while in the Confederate Army. He was merely a spectator of the Battle of the 14th, and was shot in the groin. He was taken into Lyons' drug store at the corner of Camp and Gravier, where he bled to death in a short time.

Hall of Protector White League, Second District.
New Orleans, Sept. 21, 1874.

Whereas, it has pleased the Almighty to take from our midst three of our most gallant comrades, while in the discharge of a duty which will ever render their memory dear to all lovers of freedom and friends of oppressed Louisiana,

Be it Resolved, That, in the death of ALLEN M. GAUTIER, CHAS. BRULARD and A. BONZONIER, who gave up their lives at the post of honor, on Monday, the 14th September, we lost three of our most cherished friends and Louisiana three of her noblest defenders.

Be it further Resolved, That a copy of these resolutions be forwarded to the families of the deceased, and that we wear the usual badge of mourning for thirty days.

JOHN GLYNN, JR., Chairman,
E. A. GUIBET,
M. J. FORTIER,
CHAS. T. SONIAT,
A. GAMOTIS.

CHARLES BRULARD

This letter published in the *Picayune* of September 17th gives us information about Charles Brulard.

NEW ORLEANS, Sept. 16, 1874.

To the Editor of the Picayune:

You have omitted, in your "Honors to the Dead" the name of Mr. Charles Brulard, who was mortally wounded in the charge at the head of Canal street, Monday evening, and died at 7 o'clock the same day. A more gallant soldier never fell in the cause of his country. A devoted husband, kind father, loving brother or truer friend has never given his life as a sacrifice to his country. He served with gallantry and distinction during the four years war in the Pointe Coupee Battery; was captured at Island No. 10, and remained for six months in a Northern prison. After being exchanged he again joined his command, and was recaptured, and severely wounded at the siege of Vicksburg. Again being exchanged, he served until the last gun was fired for the cause he so dearly loved. He leaves a wife and three young children to mourn his loss, besides two sisters and two brothers, joined by many friends. He was born in the parish of Plaquemines, and resided in this city for the past eighteen years.

A FRIEND.

(See memorial of Protector White League, Second District, on Sept. 21st under Antoine Bozonier.)

JOHN CONSIDINE

The *Picayune* of the 20th printed this paragraph about John Considine. It was too optimistic as Considine died several days later.

Mr. John Considine, who was wounded in the left thigh, near the body, between the bone and principal artery, whilst fighting the metropolitans at the corner of Fulton and Common streets, has been, up to yesterday morning, in a critical condition, but is now better, and the probability is that he will recover. Mr. Considine had a penknife in his pocket, which was shattered to pieces and driven in his thigh by the force of the bullet. He had great loss of blood on the spot, which weakened him considerably.

A. M. GAUTIER

A. M. Gautier was a member of Capt. Glynn's battery and was killed early in the action on Monday afternoon. He was a clerk at Godchaux's Clothing Store, and 26 years old. His funeral was held from his residence on Esplanade Street and was attended by hundreds. Among them were members of Glynn's Battery and the Orleans Boat Club of which he was a member. The *Bulletin* said that he "was a gallant young Creole who nobly sacrificed his life in defense of the rights of his fellow-men."

IN MEMORIAM

Hall Young Men's Gymnastic Club of New Orleans
Meeting of Sept. 16, 1874.

Whereas, our late fellow member, ALBERT M. GAUTIER, met the honorable death of a patriot at his post of duty, while fighting in the defence of the people's rights, on Monday, Sept. 14, 1874, be it

Resolved, That we sincerely feel the loss of his presence from our midst, and do hereby extend our heartfelt condolence and sympathy to his relations. Be it further

Resolved, That our club room be draped and the members wear the usual badge of mourning for thirty days; and be it further

Resolved, That a copy of these resolutions be sent to his relatives.

WM. FRIEDRICK, President.

CHAS. BURKHARDT, Recording Secretary.

(See memorial of Protector White League, Second District, on Sept. 21st under Bozonier.)

MAJOR J. KLEBER GOURDAIN

The *New Orleans Times* on September 22nd reprinted from the *Thibodaux Sentinel* an account of the death of Major J. K. Gourdain.

On Monday Major Gourdain had gone to the meeting near the Clay statute, on Canal street, and it was only after the fight on the levee that he had started down Chartres street with the intent of going to his place of business, 112 Old Levee. As he approached St. Louis street, passing on the right or lower side of Chartres, he came in contact with a fleeing Metropolitan, with whom a struggle took place, it is said, for possession of the gun. Whether the Metropolitan, more powerful than he, had shoved him away, or whether the Major turned to get a stone or some weapon, will perhaps never be known. At all events he was shot in the back, the ball passing through the body and coming out about two inches below the heart. As he fell he was recognized by his slayer, who begged his pardon, saying that had he known who it was he would never have fired. The Major replied that he would freely pardon him, but it was a pardon from a dead man.

Maj. Gourdain was a native of Lafourche Parish, where before the War he held the office of Recorder for many years. He was captain of the Lafourche Guards* and served all through the war. He served with distinction and bravery and was twice wounded, and was discharged as Major in the 18th Louisiana. At the close of the war Maj. Gourdain moved to New Orleans and joined the firm of Sevin & Gourdain, commission merchants. He was 48 years old and left a widow and six children, and was buried at Thibodaux on Wednesday, the 17th. The *Picayune* of the 18th published this card:

My uncle, John S. Billiu, was a first lieutenant in the Lafourche Guards under Capt. Gourdain. He served through the War, and long afterwards his uniform was given to the Confederate Memorial Hall where it has since been misplaced. John Billiu was also a member of the State Legislature in 1875, and on Jan. 4th put the motion to elect Wiltz as Speaker. Federal troops interfered and Kellogg's man became Speaker.

The friends of the late Major J. K. Gourdain, who accompanied that gallant soldier's remains to Thibodaux, desire to tender their sincere thanks through the columns of the Picayune, to the officers of Morgan's Louisiana Railroad, in furnishing them with an extra passenger car, free of charge going and returning and in keeping the ferry in readiness for the recrossing of the river. Thanks are also tendered to Conductor David Hackney of the passenger train, and to Conductor John A. Spahr of the freight train, for their courteous attentions during the trip.

The *Picayune* said: "His uniform courtesy and high integrity, combined with many bright social qualities, gained him hosts of friends." "He was beloved and respected by all who knew him."

The *Bulletin* commented: "Mr. Gourdain was one of Louisiana's most gallant and patriotic sons, and was one of our most honorable and upright citizens."

JOHN GRAVAL

John Graval was an ex-Confederate soldier, having served in the 22nd Louisiana Regiment as a private. He was killed on the afternoon of the 14th. He was the only son of his highly respected parents.

IN MEMORIAM.

HEADQUARTERS COMPANY A, LOUISIANA'S OWN.

Whereas it has pleased Almighty God to take from us, while in the performance of his duty as a citizen-soldier, our gallant and beloved comrade, JOHN GRAVAL, be it

Resolved, That we deeply mourn his loss, and tender our heartfelt sympathies to his family.

Be it further resolved, That a copy of these resolutions be forwarded to his family.

EUCLID BORLAND, JR.,
FRED A. OBER,
W. H. BARNETT,
Committee.

IN MEMORIAM
(*Bulletin,* September 27, 1874)

Hall Washington White League

Whereas, it has pleased the Almighty to take from us our much beloved brother in arms, JOHN GRAVAL, killed in the engagement at the corner of Chartres and Customhouse streets, on Monday, Sept. 14; and

Whereas, it has pleased the Almighty to cause our beloved brother, M. BETZ, to be wounded in the above engagement for our liberty and our rights; and

Whereas, it has pleased the Almighty to take from us the said Brother M. BETZ, after a period of suffering; therefore, be it

Resolved, That we, the officers and members of the Washington White League, bow in humble submission to His will, knowing that He does all things for the best.

And be it further resolved, That in the death of our late brother members, John Graval and M. Betz, we have lost good and steadfast friends, and Louisiana staunch and unflinching defenders, who have given up their lives upon the altar of freedom, not for the furtherance of individual interests, but for the deliverance of Louisiana and her people from the yoke of the tyrant; and be it still further resolved, that the officers and members of the League wear the usual badge of mourning for the period of thirty days.

And be it further resolved, That we transmit a copy of these resolutions to the bereaved families.

Be it further resolved, That these resolutions be published in the N. O. Bulletin and the German Gazette; and be it further resolved, that the foregoing resolutions be spread upon the minutes of our League.

A. A. MOUTON,
GEO. H. TARDY,
PETER HERMANN,
LOUIS HELFRICH,
C. GEHLBACK,
Committee.

Richard G. Lindsey

Richard G. Lindsey (spelled Lindsay in some papers) was a well-known gentleman in New Orleans. "His," said the *Picayune,* "is another name that Louisianians will long remember with emotions of pride and a sad thrill of sorrow. He fell defending the rights of our people." He was the only support of a mother, a great aunt and two sisters. His body was sent to Jackson, Miss., his former home. The Crescent City White League sent an escort of honor.

IN MEMORIAM

Died, Richard G. Lindsey, Sept. 14th, 1874, aged 21 years.

A brave heart was stilled Monday when Richard G. Lindsey yielded up his young life, a willing sacrifice on the altar of patriotism. Accustomed to bear a man's part in the battle of life, doing a man's share manfully while a boy in years, he voluntarily offered his life in support of his State, as he had hitherto devoted it to the loving ones who made his home. Ardent, impulsive, faithful and generous, loving Louisiana as he loved the dear ones dependent on him, he was ever eager to discharge his full duty to them and to her, the community joins the family in lamenting his death. Public sympathy for them is the stronger because the public needs such warm, faithful devotion as his proved. With his relatives grief will be mingled remembrance of the cause in which he lost his life and the gallantry with which he met his end. The faithful and affectionate son and brother has gone to his rest. His precious memory is embalmed in the history of his beloved Louisiana and in the sacred recesses of the breasts of mourning relatives and friends. Peace to his early, noble grave.—*Bulletin.*

IN MEMORIAM

SECTION E, CRESCENT CITY WHITE LEAGUE.
New Orleans, September 21, 1874.

At a meeting of Section E, Crescent City White League, held this day, the following preamble and resolutions were unanimously adopted:

A three-dollar bill circulated in Reconstruction times. Issued in December 1873 by the Merchants and Traders Bank of New Orleans. (*Courtesy Howard-Tilton Library, Dr. Henry D. Ogden Collection*)

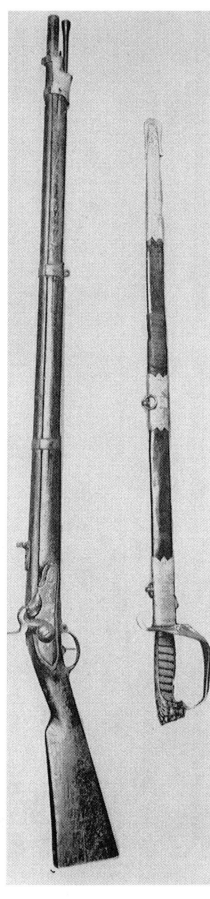

Above: Muzzle-loading rifle, fired with a cap, used in the Battle of the 14th of September by a White Leaguer.

Below: Sword presented to Capt. John Glynn, Jr., by the City of New Orleans for his services on the 14th of September, and later given to the Louisiana State Museum by his grand-nephew. The City likewise presented a sword to Lieut. E. A. Guibet — later promoted to Captain — now in possession of his grandson, Charles P. Carriere.

(*The rifle and sword are in the White League room of the Louisiana State Museum and are pictured here with the Museum's permission. Photo by Frank H. Allen*)

LIBERTY PLACE MONUMENT NEAR THE FOOT OF CANAL STREET

As it looks today (1955) nearly 65 years after its erection. It stands about where the old Iron Building stood and the fighting on the 14th of September was the hottest around this spot. Note the Custom House in the distance. (Photo by Frank H. Allen)

Whereas, on the 14th day of September, 1874, it was the misfortune of our Section to lose our brave and gallant comrade, Richard G. Lindsey, who fell nobly fighting for the liberty of his State, and against the usurpation that had been forced upon her.   Therefore, be it

Resolved, That while we bow in humble submission to the dispensation of an all wise and overruling Providence that has seen proper to remove our comrade from our midst, we are constrained to give expression to our heartfelt sorrow at the loss of one who so nobly yielded up his life in defending his State against the oppression and tyranny of an usurping Government.

Resolved Second, That in the death of Richard G. Lindsey we experience the loss of a christian gentleman, warm-hearted and generous friend, and a brave and chivalrous soldier, whose early death has deprived Louisiana of one of her noblest defenders and the community in which he lived of a promising and useful citizen.

Resolved Third, That we tender to the sorrow-stricken bother and family of our deceased comrade our sincere sympathy in the irreparable loss they have sustained, and assure his bereaved mother that her noble boy died as he had ever lived, in the brave and fearless performance of duty.

Resolved Fourth, That as an expression of sorrow, the officers and members of Section E wear the usual badge of mourning for thirty days.

Resolved Fifth, That a copy of these resolutions be transmitted to the family of our deceased comrade.

By the Committee.

R. B. Pleasants, Chairman.
Wm. Fagan,
W. J. J. Armstrong,
Chas. Palfrey,
J. M. Harding.

FREDERICK M. MOHRMAN

Frederick M. Mohrman* was chief clerk of the Administrator of Commerce in New Orleans. He resided at 960 Magazine Street. He was a private in Capt. C. H. Allen's company Sixth District Protector League. He fell at Capt. Allen's side with rifle in hand while confronting the Metropolitan Police near the corner of Canal and Tchoupitoulas Streets, shot through the heart. A large concourse of friends attended his funeral, and two sections of his former fellow-soldiers marched in the funeral train with reversed arms.

---

*Fred Mohrman died on a mattress furnished by Margaret Haughery, owner of a bakery and famous for her philanthropy. Mohrman was shot from a window in the Custom House. His mother went in a carriage to see him while the excitement was still great, but he was dead when she arrived. These facts were furnished by his niece, Mrs. Julia Walle of New Orleans in July, 1953.

IN MEMORIAM

HEADQUARTERS COMPANY "C", SIXTH
DISTRICT WHITE LEAGUE,
New Orleans, Sept. 23.

At a meeting of this company held last evening, the following preamble and resolutions were unanimously adopted:

Whereas, it has pleased an inscrutable Providence to select out of our band as a sacrifice to liberty, and to teach his associates that such a death is made to ennoble and sanctify the cause in which he fell;

Resolved, therefore, That we, his surviving comrades, humbly accept this lesson of duty and patriotism, and will, with a memory chastened by this dispensation, ever bear in remembrance the manly virtues and heroism of

FREDERICK M. MOHRMAN.

Resolved, That the members of this Company wear an appropriate badge of mourning for thirty days.

C. H. ALLEN, Captain.
Eugene May, Acting Secretary.

SAMUEL B. NEWMAN, JR.

Son of one of the City's oldest and best known cotton merchants, Samuel B. Newman, Jr., was a cotton factor at 171 Gravier St. He was shot through the body while cheering on his men at the foot of Canal Street. He had gone through the great War unharmed and was one of the most popular young men of New Orleans. Newman was buried in Washington Cemetery where the funeral services were preached by the Rev. Mr. Mallard. There was a long line of carriages in the funeral procession and a line of those who walked on foot extended over several squares.

THE HONORED DEAD.

Headquarters Section A,
Crescent City White League,
New Orleans, September 19, 1874.

Whereas, we are assembled on this sad occasion with hearts oppressed with deepest grief for the loss of those who were our truest friends, dearest and bravest soldiers, it becomes our solemn duty to perpetuate the honors of those who have displayed heroic daring and performed deeds that have inspired us with their exalted virtues; therefore be it

Resolved, That while we bow with submission to the decrees of an all-wise Providence, we cannot refrain from expressing our most sincere sorrow for the loss of those gallant patriots S. B. NEWMAN, JR., and E. A. TOLEDANO, members of our organization, who, rather than submit long to the tyranny and wrongs of an infamous usurpation, for the love of their native land, protection of their homes and firesides, and for these alone, bared their breasts upon the field of strife and yielded up their noble lives in a holy cause.

Resolved, That we deeply feel the loss of these brave spirits, endeared to us by every tie of friendly association, in whom were combined all those elements of character essential to true and dignified manhood.

Resolved, That, worthily to show our veneration for these gallant patriots, we will wear the customary badge of mourning for thirty days. Be it further

Resolved, That a copy of these resolutions be transmitted to the afflicted families of our lamented comrades, and we extend to them our profound sympathy in their bereavement.

"For us they fell;
Let history tell
In its page of crimson story,
How they faced the tide
And bravely died
On fields so dread and gory.

"They may crush us low
Neath the iron bow;
They may ruin our Southern land;
But the right to mourn
Is from God alone,
And we mourn our broken band."

W. T. Vaudry,
Harrison Watts,
B. M. Harrod,
R. M. Fouquier, Committee

Major William C. Robbins

Major William C. Robbins (spelled Robins in some papers) was from Philadelphia and was an ex-officer of the U. S. Army, having served with distinction during the late war. At its close he settled in New Orleans as the manager of the agencies of the Louisiana Equitable Life Insurance Company. He was only 30 years old at the time of his death. Major Robbins was one of the marshals of Section "C," Crescent City White League, and was wounded in the leg at the foot of Canal Street. His leg was amputated but he died late Monday afternoon.

The *Picayune* of the 17th gives this account of the funeral:

FUNERAL OF MAJOR WM. C. ROBINS.—A large number of citizens, among whom there were many ladies, gathered at the late residence of this gallant gentleman, to pay the last sad tributes of respect to one who had proved himself a worthy citizen, brave soldier and estimable man in every walk of life. The deepest regret was expressed that a life so full of bright promise of usefulness and distinction, should have been brought to such an early close, and all spoke in the highest terms of praise of the alacrity with which he took up arms in the people's cause and the brave manner in which he discharged the duties of his position.

The funeral services were performed by Rev. Mr. Harris, assisted by Rev. Mr. Granberry, after which the remains were conveyed to the hearse and the funeral cortege moved down Carondelet street to Girod street, and thence to the Girod street cemetery.

The pall bearers were Col. Saml. Manning Todd and Capt. B. T. Walshe on the part of the Louisiana Equitable Life Insurance Company, of which Major Robins was a valued and esteemed officer; Capt. Buck and Lieut. Nixon, on the part of the Crescent City White League, in which Major Robins held the rank of lieutenant, and Messrs. Barker and Johnson, on the part of Quitman Lodge, F. and A. M.

A long line of carriages, with the members of Quitman Lodge and of the Crescent City White League, to the number of six hundred, on foot, followed the remains of their beloved comrade to their last resting place.

E. A. TOLEDANO*

E. A. Toledano, or Capt. Arthur Toledano, as the *Bulletin* lists him among the deaths on the 15th belonged to an old and well-known New Orleans family. He lived on Toledano Street between Prytania and St. Charles. Age 44, he was a large cotton buyer with an office at 186 Gravier Street, and at one time a cotton weigher for Farley, Bright & Co.

IN MEMORIAM

Headquarters Company B,
First Louisiana State Militia.

Whereas, it has pleased the Almighty to take from us Corporal A. E. TOLE-DANO, who was killed in the gallant performance of duty, during the engagement with the metropolitan police, on Monday, the 14th day of September, 1874; and

Whereas, we recognized in the deceased a true gentleman and a gallant soldier, one of those whose loss can never be replaced; and

Whereas, this Company shares with his afflicted family and the whole community their grief over his loss;

It is hereby ordered that the officers and members of this Company do wear mourning in behalf of said deceased brother, for and during a space of thirty days, as a mark of respect for his memory.

FRANK McGLOIN, Capt. Commn'd.
L. A. ARNAULT, 1st Lieut.
C. L. WALKER, 2nd Lieut.
CHAS. B. BOARMAN, 3rd Lieut.

(See In Memoriam for S. B. Newman, Jr., for joint resolution passed by Section "A," Crescent City White League on Sept. 19th.)

MAJOR WILLIAM A. WELLS

Said the *Picayune* in its issue of September 20th:

Another name is added to the list of those who have sealed with their lives their devotion to the liberties of the people of our downtrodden State. Major Wm. A.

Mr. H. C. Mackie of Covington was a little boy at the time, but remembers seeing Toledano's body taken out of a spring wagon and brought into his house that fateful afternoon.

Wells died at his residence yesterday evening from the effects of wounds received in the engagement on Monday last.

Major Wells was a native of Port Gibson, Miss., and was forty years of age at the time of his death. He entered the Confederate Army, in Company C of the Crescent Regiment, and served through the war with great daring and bravery, gaining the rank of Major. He was a gallant soldier, an accomplished gentleman and a good citizen, a warm friend, and a most exemplary husband and father. He leaves a wife and one child, who will receive the sincere condolence of our whole community in this, their gallant affliction.

On the 22nd the *Picayune* described the funeral:

On Sunday evening, at 4 o'clock, a mourning throng had assembled at the Notre Dame Cathedral, on Jackson street, to hear the burial service read over the body of the gallant Major Wells, the citizen soldier, who fell in front of the foremost rank while fighting for the State of his adoption.

When the coffin was borne down the long aisles of the Cathedral, covered with wreaths and white crosses of flowers, it was followed to the hearse by all the members of the numerous congregation. These filled the long line of carriages that were waiting to take them to the cemetery, while many more yet remaining followed the funeral cortege on foot.

Several companies of the Crescent City White League, and the citizens' militia formed in two columns with the hearse between the heads of the columns and marched in procession to the Washington Street Cemetery, where the mortal remains of Major Wells were interred.

IN MEMORIAM.

HALL TENTH WARD CENTRAL DEMOCRATIC CLUB.

Whereas, it has pleased Almighty God to decree that our recent victory over the Kellogg usurpation should be consecrated by the blood of some of our bravest and best; and

Whereas, among those who fell, gallantly fighting for their country's rights, on September 14, 1874, was WILLIAM A. WELLS, a member of this club:

Resolved, That in his death the community has lost a good citizen, this Club an active and earnest member, and his family a loving husband and father, who in freely giving his own life a sacrifice for the rights of the people, has demonstrated that the sons of Louisiana yet know how to fight and how to die for their loved State.

Resolved, That we will ever cherish his name with fond remembrance of his many virtues, and his glorious death, holding ourselves ready, should need arise to imitate his example.

Resolved, That a copy of these resolutions be sent to his afflicted family, and that they be published in the *Picayune, Bulletin* and *Bee.*

WASH. MARKS, Chairman; E. PETTUS, W. H. WATKINS, M. D., J. D. MAHONEY, J. O. NIXON, JR., Committee.

IN MEMORIAM

At a meeting of Tenth Ward White League, held Friday evening Sept. 25th the following preamble and resolutions were adopted:

Whereas, Almighty God has in his infinite wisdom taken from us in the prime and strength of his manhood our comrade and friend, Major WILLIAM A. WELLS, and

Whereas, the same afflicting but Holy Providence that has so sorely stricken the surviving friends and relatives of our late brother, has fallen likewise, in deep affliction upon us, his associates, and upon all this community, before whom we deem it meet to bow in humble submission.

He fell in the noble and manly defence of our liberties, and of the holy principles of freedom and of the righteous cause of legal government.

He was a true and generous friend, a faithful and devoted husband, and a good citizen.

His ability, energy and public spirit made him a pillar of strength and an ornament to the associations with which he was connected.

His death has caused a void in our community which will be long lamented.

Over his grave we tearfully, but proudly, write the epitaph, *"Dulce et decorum est pro patria mori."* Therefore, be it

Resolved, That we hereby express our deep and poignant sense of suffering in this affliction in common with that of the bereaved family of our friend, and in heartfelt and lasting sympathy with them in their irreparable loss. Be it further

Resolved, That a copy of these resolutions be sent to the family of our deceased comrade and friend, and be published in the BULLETIN and *Picayune* papers.

> EDWARD FLOOD, Chairman,
> H. GALLAGHER,
> THAD WATERMAN,
> C. TAYLOR GAUCHE,
> WM. H. HARVEY,
> JAMES D. NUGENT.

From the *Bulletin* Sept. 27, 1874.

J. M. WEST

From the *Picayune* of the 16th we learn that J. M. West was deliberately shot down by the Metropolitans while passing by on Canal Street. The *New Orleans Times* had this to say about "Capt." West the next day:

Among the brave men who fell in the brief but fierce conflict on Monday last, was Capt. J. M. West, an old printer and newspaperman, long and well known in this city. He was on Canal street, in front of Bayly & Pond's grocery, taking notes of the contest for the New Orleans Bee, when a ball, fired from the direction of the Customhouse, it is stated, struck him down. He was a fierce and persistent opponent of Radicalism, and over the signature of "Crescent" had written a series of letters to the *Chicago Times,* in which he relentlessly denounced the corruption and abuses of that party and its leaders in this State. The *Times* of the 16th publishes his last letter, written only two days before his death. It closes with this prophetic paragraph:

"The people generally are greatly incensed at the high-handed outrages committed by Kellogg. Even Republicans condemn his course, and declare that he is carrying usurpation a little too far. His pretorian guard are not feared to the extent he supposes. The people are ready at any moment to rise in their might and hurl him from power. If the committee of seventy would advise such a course, and nominate a leader, Kellogg's usurpation would not last twenty-four hours. That advice may be given at any hour. When it does, the usurper will discover that he has sowed the wind and reaped the whirlwind—that he has relied upon support that only tolerated his service from necessity."

IN MEMORIAM

Resolutions of the Crescent City White League

At a regular meeting of the Crescent City White League, held Tuesday, Sept. 22, a "committee of five members of which the President shall be chairman," was on motion, appointed to prepare resolutions expressive of the feelings of the League concerning the losses which befell them in their struggle for civil freedom on the memorable 14th of September, 1874.

In obedience to and in heartful sympathy with these instructions the committee respectfully report:

That, whereas, the Crescent City White League distinctly and openly proclaimed in their articles of constitution, that the sole objects of their formation were to assist in restoring an honest and intelligent Government to the State of Louisiana, and, by a union of all other good citizens, to maintain, protect and enforce our rights.

And whereas, in no lawless, intemperate, or riotous spirit, but in obedience to a high and holy purpose, and at the unanimous call of their oppressed fellow-citizens, they took up arms as the last remedy left them against measureless wrongs.

Resolved, That the patriotic citizens who fell in the late contest between right and fraud, between the lawful Government of the people's choice and a tyrannical usurpation created and maintained by force alone, were as true martyrs to freedom as any who have ever given up their lives, on any field, for conscience sake or for country.

Resolved, That we will forever cherish their memories and strive to emulate their example, which we hold up as worthy of all imitations by every one to whom the purity and perpetuity of republican institutions and the maintenance of civil liberty are dear.

Resolved, That to their bereaved family and friends we tender our heartfelt and solemn condolence.

> F. N. OGDEN, Chairman.
>
> J. DICKSON BRUNS,
>
> N. T. N. ROBINSON,
>
> W. J. BEHAN,
>
> SAM'L. FLOWER,
>
> Committee.

From the *Bulletin,* September 27, 1874.

FELL IN ACTION

The names on the Liberty Place Monument today read as follows:

Michael Betz	John Graval
A. Bozonier	R. G. Lindsey
Charles Brulard	F. M. Mohrman
James Crossin	S. B. Newman, Jr.
J. Considine	Wm. G. Robbins
Adrian Feuillan	E. A. Toledano
A. M. Gautier	Wm. A. Wells
J. K. Gourdain	J. M. West

THE GRAVES OF THE MARTYRS

The *Picayune* of September 15, 1885 gave a list of the burial places of those who were killed at the Battle of Liberty Place on September 14, 1874. It was the custom every year for the people of New Orleans to put flowers on th graves of these heroes. This custom continued until September, 1898. A list of the names of the martyrs and their places of burial are as follows:

Michael Betz	Fireman's Cemetery
A. Bozonier	St. Louis No. 2
Charles Brulard	St. Louis No. 2
James Crossin	St. Joseph Cemetery
J. Considine	Greenwood Cemetery
Adrien Feuillan	Cypress Grove No. 2
A. M. Gautier	Metairie Cemetery
J. K. Gourdain	Thibodaux, La.
John Graval	St. Louis No. 2
R. G. Lindsey	Jackson, Miss.
F. M. Mohrman	Greenwood Cemetery
S. B. Newman, Jr.	Washington Cemetery
Wm. G. Robbins	to Philadelphia
E. A. Toledano	St. Louis No. 2
Wm. A. Wells	Washington Cemetery
J. M. West	Girod Cemetery

Relief for the Families of Those Who Were Killed

As many of those who were killed in the battle at the foot of Canal Street on September 14th left their families without means of support, public spirited citizens came to their rescue.

The *Bee* on the 17th announced that that newspaper would receive subscriptions for the benefit of the families of those who were killed in the fight with Kellogg's Metropolitans, and the proprietors of that paper headed the list with a subscription of $100. In a few moments $750 was raised at the Cotton Exchange that afternoon.

The Southern Dramatic Club announced that it would give a benefit at the St. Charles Theatre for these families whose breadwinners had lost their lives "while battling for the redemption of the City and State." They put on a performance of the popular drama, "Waiting for the Verdict."

The ladies of the city, wives of the leaders of the White League, and others prominent in society organized a relief association. The *Bulletin* of Sept. 23, 1874 had this squib:

> The Crescent City Benevolent Association, recently organized, since the battle of the 14th inst., for the express purpose of providing for the families of those who fell in the fight, propose to give, on the 29th day of the present month, a grand concert at the Exposition Building.*
>
> The concert will be arranged and conducted by Prof. Colignon, and the best known and most accomplished artists and amateurs in the city will take part.
>
> The object is one that appeals to all, and by no means vanity, for the efforts of the ladies have thus far been crowned with the greatest success.
>
> Mr. Gallagher has tendered the Exposition Hall free of charge, the New Orleans Gas Company will accept no money for light, Armstrong and Benners are doing the printing, and thus far the ladies have not been called on to expend one cent from their fund, and the probability is that they will not have to do so.

The name of the association must have been changed because a few days later — in the *Picayune* and the *Bulletin* of the 25th of September — we find a list of names of the members of the association given here under this caption:

CRESCENT CITY RELIEF ASSOCIATION.
MRS. R. A. WILKINSON, President.
MRS. F. N. OGDEN, Secretary.
MRS. H. E. SHROPSHIRE, Treasurer.

MRS. COLUMBUS H. ALLEN,	MRS. JOHN LALLANDE
MRS. H. S. ARMSTRONG,	MRS. JNO. AUGUSTIN,
MRS. NEWTON BUCKNER,	MRS. ABRAHAM,
MRS. WM. J. BEHAN,	MRS. JAMES BUCKNER,

The Exposition Building was for many years afterward the Washington Artillery Hall; then the home of an automobile company, and now torn down.

MRS. E. A. BURKE,
MRS. JAMES BROOKS,
MRS. J. D. BRUNS,
MRS. J. A. BLAFFER,
MRS. S. H. BOYD,
MRS. D. WARREN BRICKELL,
MRS. W. A. BELL,
MRS. N. COMMANDEUR,
MRS. C. A. CONRAD,
MRS. H. D. COLEMAN,
MRS. S. DUVAL,
MRS. JOSEPH DENEGRE,
MRS. R. FLOWER,
MRS. CID. FOLGER,
MRS. JOS. N. FOLWELL,
MRS. W. H. FOSTER,
MRS. GIVEN,
MRS. L. H. GARDNER,
MRS. LEEDS GREENLEAF,
MRS. FRED HOLYLAND,
MRS. CHAS. HARROD,
MRS. E. J. HART,
MRS. DAVE C. JOHNSON,
MRS. JOHN KREUTZNICH,
MRS. D. M. KILPATRICK,
MRS. FELIX LIMET,
MRS. T. P. LEATHERS,
MRS. CHAS. MACREADY,
MRS. WASH MARKS,
MRS. JOS. MITCHELL,
MRS. EUGENE MAY,
MRS. I. N. MARKS,
MRS. PERRY NUGENT,
MRS. S. OVIATT,
MRS. H. N. OGDEN,
MRS. R. B. PLEASANTS,
MRS. W. S. PIKE,
MRS. JOHN U. PAYNE,
MRS. THEODORE SHUTE,
MRS. WARREN STONE,
MRS. FRED SOUTHMAYD,
MRS. SCHRIEBER,
MRS. MARY STAMPS,
MRS. A. B. SEGAR,
MRS. C. TOBY,
MRS. C. TYLER,
MRS. ULHORN,
MRS. O. F. VALLETTE,
MRS. THAD. WATERMAN,
MRS. ALEX. WALKER,
MRS. I. W. PATTON,
MRS. J. B. COOPER,

MRS. JESSE K. BELL,
MRS. JAMES BOWLING,
MRS. NEUVILLE BIENVENU,
MRS. E. P. BRIGGS,
MRS. AUGUSTUS BLOCK,
MRS. A. FOSTER AXSON,
MRS. WM. BLACK,
MRS. JAS. T. AYCOCK,
MRS. SAMUEL CHOPPIN,
MRS. E. P. COUTTREAUX,
MRS. W. H. CHAFFE,
MRS. J. B. COTTON,
MRS. M. DIETRICH,
MRS. E. JOHN ELLIS,
MRS. WM. FAGAN,
MRS. N. C. FOLGER,
MRS. AM. FORTIER,
MRS. JOHN GLYNN, JR.
MRS. JAS. K. GUTHEIM,
MRS. CHAS. GALLAGHER,
MRS. WM. HUYGHE,
MRS. HOFFMAN,
MRS. A. H. ISAACSON,
MRS. JOS. JONES,
MRS. E. KIRKPATRICK,
MRS. D. C. LABATT,
MRS. JOS. McELROY,
MRS. FRANK McGLOIN,
MRS. ARCH'LD MITCHELL,
MRS. VICTOR MEYER,
MRS. JOHN MYERS,
MRS. JOHN MATTHEWS,
MRS. F. O. MINOR,
MRS. R. PRITCHARD,
MRS. PALFREY,
MRS. FRANK PRESTON,
MRS. D. B. PENN,
MRS. W. C. RAYMOND,
MRS. I. W. STAUFFER,
MRS. T. LEE SHUTE,
MRS. J. M. SEIXAS,
MRS. THOMAS SIMMS,
MRS. W. B. SCHMIDT,
MRS. J. J. TARLETON,
MRS. E. A. TYLER,
MRS. W. V. TUDOR,
MRS. ALBERT VOORHIES,
MRS. EUGENE WAGGAMAN,
MRS. J. B. WOODS,
MRS. C. E. WHITNEY,
MRS. R. H. MARR,
MRS. J. J. MELLON

This association has been organized by the ladies of New Orleans for the purpose of raising a fund for the relief of the families of those who fell in defense of the people's rights on September 14.

The initial effort will be a Grand Concert, to be given at Exposition Hall, on September 29, under the direction of Prof. G. Collignon, assisted by artists and amateurs. Refreshments at the Hall during the Concert.

In the *Picayune* of the 26th we find the following notice:

It has come to the ladies of the Relief Association that there were quite a number of citizens seriously wounded in the fight of the 14th of September, and therefore, prevented from going to work, whose names are unknown to the ladies of the association, and who cannot, therefore, be assisted or properly attended to. The names of all citizens who were wounded fighting in behalf of the people's rights are requested to be sent to Mrs. Stamps,* 187 Magazine street. Immediate attention will be paid to these and all the necessary assistance given.

The papers of the same date carried the names of the Reception Committee for the grand benefit entertainment. The following from the *Bulletin*:

At the meeting of the lady managers of the entertainment to be given on Tuesday, at Exposition Hall, for the relief of the families of the victims of September 14, the following named gentlemen were appointed as a reception committee. The committee is requested to assemble to-day at 1 o'clock P. M., in the gentlemen's parlor of the St. Charles Hotel:

Gov. J. McEnery, Lieut. Gov. D. B. Penn, Gen. Fred N. Ogden, Hon. R. H. Marr, Col. Chas. Roman, J. N. Payne, Octo Ogden, Fred. Southmayd, James Buckner, Capt. Jno. Glynn, Jr., Capt. H. E. Shropshire, Capt. Arch. Mitchell, Capt. R. B. Pleasants, Capt. Borland, Col. W. H. Behan, Felix Limet, Capt. E. John Ellis, R. Weightman, H. N. Ogden, Col. E. Waggaman, Capt. Bosworth, C. E. Whitney, Alf. H. Isaacson, Felix Sauve, Hon. Albert Voorhies, George Hoggshett, Fred Norma, Wallace Wood, S. P. Cottreaux, Dr. John Angell, Col. Marshall J. Smith, Hon. L. A. Wiltz, Capt. Geo. Dupre, Wash. Marks, Paul Waterman, Willie Cautzon, Gus. Micou, Charlie Keep.

The press gave splendid publicity to the grand entertainment of the Relief Association. For instance, the *Bulletin* on the 26th ran the following:

We sincerely trust that all of our citizens will attend the grand entertainment to be held at Exposition Hall on Tuesday evening, September 29th, for the benefit of those who fell on the 14th of September in defense of the people's cause. Everyone should attend and further the good cause. The entertainment will be under the auspices of the ladies committee of seventy, the executive council being Mrs. H. E. Shopshire, Mrs. Gen. F. N. Ogden, Mrs. Eugene Waggaman, Mrs. Wilkinson, Mrs. W. F. Pike and Mrs. A. J. Tarleton.

On the 29th, the morning of the day of the grand event, the *Picayune* stated that the number of tickets sold far exceeded the seating capacity of the hall, and that it had been decided to give a second concert the next evening, Wednesday, with an entire change of program. The *Picayune* also ran the following announcement:

The Mrs. Stamps mentioned was the grandmother of the late Stamps Farrar, a member of the Board of Commissioners of Liberty Place for several years.

TO MERCHANTS AND EMPLOYERS.

On the part of many clerks and employees who are directly interested, we publish the following: Many of the clerks in this city, it is well known, were out on the levee in Monday's fight and did gallant service in the people's cause. Many of these also express a great desire to attend the entertainment at Exposition Hall, on Tuesday night and Wednesday morning. Some of these used up all their ready money in September getting ammunition and arming themselves for the conflict; and as pay day does not come till Thursday, Oct. 1st, after the entertainment, they will not be able to attend unless their employers are willing to pay part of their salaries two days ahead of the customary date. If this were done many clerks and employees would be enabled to enjoy themselves at the entertainment, and the Relief Association would realize more.

On the 30th the *Picayune* mentioned this unusual case:

The attention of the ladies of the Relief Association may well be called to Mrs. Casey, No. 5 Bienville street, corner of Peters. Mrs. Casey was not, of course, in the fight, but her residence was in the very route the peelers pursued in their retreat. Mrs. Casey was standing in her door when the police passed by. Her sympathies were with the citizens. The policemen knew this, and taking her presence as an insult, one of them barbarously stabbed her with a bayonet as he fled past. Mrs. Casey deserves the sympathy and assistance of all. If she did not suffer as others did, fighting in the people's cause, she was made the victim of the hatred and malignity of the people's enemies. She is still in a dangerous condition, as much from the nervous shock she suffered as the real wound given.

Excerpts from the *Picayune's* account on the 30th of the entertainment:

CRESCENT CITY RELIEF ASSOCIATION. THE ENTERTAINMENT.

As the concert of the Crescent City Relief Association has been the talk of the streets for the last few weeks, we could not fail to have the popular opinion of what it would be. Certainly there was much unanimity among the people in this concert as in our men in the fight that gave its birth. Everybody was there.

Some six or eight thousand persons crowded the hall, at one time, and the mighty audience was ever changing, ever renewing itself.

The orchestra was the largest ever heard in this city, and the chorus, particularly that by the German Quartette Club, was charming. The entire selection was admirable, part sentimental, part as it were, a memorial hymn to the fallen.

The large hall of the Exposition Hall was overcrowded, many seeking room in the supper room, next thereto.

About half-past 10 o'clock the concert broke up. The crowd surged on toward the refreshment hall, the ancient "Fine Arts Gallery." The scene was not one easy to be described. Around the wall in all directions stretched tables, covered with dainties and luxuries, and the more substantial things of life.

A voyage around this little city showed but half its charms and curiosities. The older ladies busied themselves in household cares, anxious to supply their guests, while the young ladies, transformed into *garsons,* tempted the gentlemen into an extraordinary display of appetite.

To sum it up, it was the most perfect entertainment of the year. The wreaths, the booths, had all been prepared days before, nothing was behind hand. We are almost afraid to say what are our anticipations of the pecuniary result—a matter which, with all the fun, is not to be neglected—lest some might regard us as Munchausens. We will await the efficial report, convinced that if all the young ladies acted as nobly in the money line as one or two we know, the promised thousands to be reaped will be trebled.

From the *Picayune* of October 1, 1874 are excerpted these paragraphs about the final evening of the entertainment:

CLOSING SCENES OF THE GREAT POPULAR MANIFESTATION.

The second night of the entertainment of the Crescent City Relief Association showed but a small falling off in numbers, nothing in energy. The rooms were not so crowded, and the substitution of dancing for the concert enabled the young ladies to display their dresses to better advantage. Behind the counters and tables were some new faces, taking the places of those who, in their zeal, had overworked themselves.

The dance was found a most agreeable feature; there was the same good music under the direction of Prof. Meyer and his men, who have acted so generously in this matter.

But although the ladies were ever kept busy at the supper-tables, and seemed ladling out punch from inexhaustible bowls, they were not the prominent features of the evening. There was raffling of cakes and wine, and everything imaginable. The ladies seemed to appreciate and admire this sport, and proved good partisans, soliciting votes for their candidates with an energy that was never unsuccessful. As the night wore on the voters became more nervous and exacting, and the votes were more numerous, until the ballot boxes overflowed.

Mr. R. H. Marr and Gov. D. B. Penn were rivals for a fine gold watch, Messrs. E. Jno. Ellis and R. L. Gibson, candidates not only for Congress but for a splendid desk. A golden card dish was voted for by the gentlemen to the favorite married lady of the entertainment. A diamond ring for the pleasantest, most popular and prettiest young lady, was the cynosure of all eyes. Gentlemen gathered there to get some idea of the lady ahead, and to swell the vote with monstrous figures and heavy bank bills, to be rewarded by a glance from bright eyes.

A sword was also to be voted for among the captains of the various companies or sections of the Crescent City White League. No one entered the hall without depositing at least one ballot here. At the latest hour it was the universal question, "Who's ahead " Capts. W. B. Pleasants, Kilpatrick and Buck headed the list. Of these, Capt. Pleasants was the popular favorite and hero, and received a handsome majority and the sword.

Last night presented to us another phase of this heroic philanthrophy. It was the manifestation of the sympathy, the pride, and devotion to country and liberty of the women of New Orleans. In the conflict of the 14th there were brave lives lost. Widows, orphans and parents mourned the sudden taking off of heroic husbands, fathers and sons. Deprived of their support, menaced with destitution and all its humiliations, there arose a most eloquent appeal to the benevolence and charity of our people to relieve their unfortunate bereavement, and the hard condition into which they were cast through the self-sacrificing devotion of the brave men who fell in defense of the rights and liberties of the people.

The response to this appeal was given last night in the form of one of the most brilliant entertainments which ever occurred in New Orleans. It was altogether the work of the ladies of New Orleans. A full description will be found in our morning edition. The proceeds of this entertainment must have exceeded ten thousand dollars. Despite the general poverty of our people, everybody who could scrape together a few dimes repaired to the great Exposition Hall to swell the dense and incessant throng which filed through its vast rooms.

Memorial Exercises

For many years it was the custom of relatives, friends and compatriots to place flowers on the graves of the martyrs of September the Fourteenth on each anniversary date.

As time went by and the living of that day joined the dead, the graves of the heroes were less and less remembered until there came a Fourteenth when there were no flowers to be seen on the tombs of the martyred White Leaguers.

But they are not forgotten. Their names are engraved on the long-lasting granite of the Liberty Monument at the foot of Canal Street. And each Fourteenth of September a group — for a while of their old comrades, now the descendants of those who fought with them — gathers at the monument, where with appropriate ceremonies a wreath is placed at its base in honor of the men who gave their lives to the cause of liberty.*

The exercises commemorating the Battle of the Fourteenth of September are conducted by the Board of Commissioners of Liberty Place, an official body of the City of New Orleans, to which the public is invited. On the same evening a banquet is held at a prominent restaurant, and speakers retell the story of the great battle and toast the memory of the glorious dead.

Until recent years veterans of the battle attended the exercises and the banquet. Now all are gone.

On September 14, 1937 James Wilkinson, a veteran of '74, spoke at the banquet, concluding with the following inspiring words:

> For over sixty years some of the good men and good women of this city have gathered on this anniversary to bless and perpetuate the memories of those whose names are inscribed on the face of the monument before us. As the needle of the compass guides the mariner on his way towards home we trust the shaft of this monument, pointing upward to the skies, may point to where the brave soldiers named there have found happiness and peace.
>
> Few of the comrades of those soldiers are living. Before these few pass on to join the army camping on the farther shore, we have thought it meet and proper to offer and adopt the following resolution.

---

*On September 14th, 1935 Dr. R. A. Mayer of Abbeville, La., wrote a letter to the Commissioners of Liberty Place in which he said: "While paying tribute to the heroes of September 14th, who fell at the foot of Canal Street and gave their lives to restore white supremacy to Louisiana, a few words of praise might be uttered in memory of that patriotic son of Vermilion Parish, the Honorable Adrien Nunez, then a member of the Legislature, who disposed of his entire sugar crop to pay the board and lodging of the white Legislature pending the arrival of arms and ammunition, the first consignment of ammunition having been seized by Governor Kellogg. Without this financial assistance the glorious September 14th would have been indefinitely postponed."

"We, some of the survivors of the memorable 14th of September conflict of 1874, here assembled, in behalf of the dead and living soldiers of that conflict, express our deep and lasting gratitude to those who have gathered year after year at this shrine and there with kindly speech and music and bearing flowers have joined in honoring and blessing the illustrious dead and the cause for which they died.

We revere the members of your association for your good work as men revere those who gathered to do loving service at that sacred tomb on Easter morn nearly twenty centuries ago.

To the living members of your association and to those members, 'long loved but for a season gone,' the veterans here present make due acknowledgment of all their kindly service.

We ask this weak expression of our abiding gratitude and our blessings be recorded in the minutes of your association.

We further ask that when taps have sounded for us and we are no longer able to be here to speak for ourselves, that these resolutions may be read on some future anniversaries to voice our gratitude to you and yours in the years to come."

LAYING THE CORNER STONE OF THE LIBERTY MONUMENT
ON SEPTEMBER 14, 1874
(Reproduced from the Times-Democrat of Sept. 15, 1891)

CHAPTER XV

THE MONUMENT AT LIBERTY PLACE

The idea for the erection of a monument was not long in taking form. On September 16, 1874, the *Picayune* said: "For those who fell fighting so gallantly against our oppressors, the people of Louisiana already propose to erect a monument. The 14th of September 1874, and the devotion of these loyal sons, will long be remembered in the hearts of those who are living; but it is well to commemorate such deeds as they have done, to let those who live after we have passed away, know that in this age of submission to despots there were still a few who dared defy the rod of tyrants."

The *Vicksburg Herald* also suggested erection of a monument and the *New Orleans Bulletin* quotes the *Herald* as follows:

BATTLE MONUMENT.—While our friends in Louisiana are rejoicing over their redemption from the rule of the plunderers, we trust they will not forget their heroic dead. On the spot where they fell, there where the stones were dyed with their blood, let a monument arise to commmorate their courage, their virtues, and their patriotism. Let it tell to future generations how the men of 1874 preferred death to bondage, and as long as the great river flows onward to the sea, so long shall men point to it as evidence of an example to be imitated and honored.

The movement for the erection of a monument spread, and the following monument committee was appointed:

Gen. W. J. Behan, Chairman	Major B. M. Harrod
Capt. A. E. Morphy, Secretary	Fred G. Freret
Gen. John Glynn, Jr.	Col. J. D. Hill
Capt. D. M. Kilpatrick	Major G. LeGardeur
Col. George A. Williams	Capt. D. A. S. Vaught
Capt. P. L. Bouny	Col. Euclid Borland
Major C. H. Allen	Maj. W. E. Huger
Major L. L. Lincoln	

The Ladies Auxiliary Committee, assisting in raising funds for the erection of the Liberty Place Monument, consisted of the following:

Mrs. F. N. Ogden	Mrs. A. B. Griswold
Mrs. Jno. Glynn, Jr.	Mrs. Atwood Violett
Mrs. J. L. Richardson	Mrs. L. P. Reese
Mrs. J. V. Moore	Mrs. F. T. Nicholls
Mrs. W. E. Huger	Mrs. W J. Behan
Mrs. R. A. Wilkinson	Mrs. L. A. Adam
Mrs. A. E. Morphy	Mrs. J. R. S. Selleck

Mrs. W. A. S.Wheeler   Mrs. A. Mitchell
Mrs. J. D. Bruns   Mrs. Sam Flower
Mrs. A. A. Woods   Mrs. J. O. Nixon, Jr.
Mrs. Geo. Dunbar   Mrs. D. A. S. Vaught
Mrs. R. S. Day   Mrs. Alfred Roman
Mrs. D. M. Kilpatrick   Mrs. Rodd
Mrs. S. A. Trufant   Mrs. Sam Logan
Mrs. F. G. Freret   Mrs. J. D. Bruns
Mrs. James Buckner   Miss Kate McCall
Miss Lobrano   Miss Mollie Vaudry
Miss Mary Lincoln   Miss Pinckard
Mrs. G. A. Williams

On November 15, 1882, an ordinance was passed by the Council of the City of New Orleans dedicating that portion of the neutral ground between Wells and Delta Streets, or such part as is necessary for the erection of a monument to be known as Liberty Place "In honor of those who fell in defense of civil liberty and home rule in that heroic and successful struggle of the 14th of September 1874."

The same ordinance appointed as commissioners of Liberty Place:

F. N. Ogden   Frederick G. Freret
J. Dickson Bruns   John Glynn, Jr.

The ordinance was signed by Joseph Shakespeare, Mayor. The vote was— yeas: Fagan, Fitzpatrick, Mealey and Walsh. Absent: Delamare, Guillet, Huger.

The cornerstone of Liberty Monument was laid on September 14, 1891. A vast crowd assembled to witness the ceremonies. There was much oratory and great enthusiasm. Judge R. H. Marr presided. B. F. Jonas was the orator of the day. Rev. B. M. Palmer gave the opening prayer and Very Rev. Father Bogaerts, Vicar-General, gave the benediction. Gen. John Glynn, Jr., laid the cornerstone in the presence of the monument's committee and the Ladies Auxiliary Committee. (The trowel used by Gen. Glynn was later presented to the Louisiana Historical Society.)

Damage To Liberty Monument

From an article in the Louisiana Historical Quarterly by James Renshaw we learn that the Liberty Monument was damaged in the great storm of September 29, 1915. The shaft was blown down from the pedestal and when put back was short a few inches.

COMMISSIONERS OF LIBERTY PLACE

Original Commissioners of Liberty Place — 1882

Gen. F. N. Ogden   Frederick G. Freret
Dr. J. Dickson Bruns   Col. John Glynn, Jr.

The members of this commission died and there is no record of others being appointed to take their places. The Commission became inactive. It was reconstituted in 1932 in accordance with a resolution of the Commission Council of New Orleans as follows:

Mayoralty of New Orleans

City Hall, September 28, 1932

Calendar No. 14,422

No. 13,820 Commission Council Series

Section 1. Be it ordained by the Commission Council of the City of New Orleans that the Mayor be and he is hereby authorized to appoint a Commission to be composed of thirty members and to be known as the Board of Commissioners of Liberty Place. The members of said Board of Commissioners to be appointed from amongst citizens who took part in the Battle for white supremacy at Liberty Place on September 14, 1874, or descendents of said citizens; six of said Commissioners shall be appointed for a term of one year; six for a term of two years; six for a term of three years; six for a term of four years; and six for a term of five years; all vacancies shall be for the unexpired term and all appointments or reappointments at the expiration of terms shall be for five years. The Mayor shall name the Chairman of said Commission. The said Board of Commissioners shall be charged with the care and maintenance of Liberty Place and Monument and to see that the objects and purposes for which Liberty Place was indicated or perpetrated. All improvements, alterations, etc. to said Monument or place shall be upon the approval of the said Board of Commissioners.

Section 2. Be it further ordained etc. that all ordinances or part of ordinances in conflict with the provisions of this ordinance and particularly Ordinance No. 13,681 C.C.S. be and the same are hereby repealed insofar as they conflict with the provisions of this Ordinance.

Adopted by the Commission Council of the City of New Orleans.
September 27, 1932.

THOMAS J. HILL
Clerk of Commission Council

Approved September 28, 1932.

T. S. WALMSLEY,
    Mayor.

Members of the Liberty Monument Commission, as re-constituted, appointed by the Honorable T. Semmes Walmsley, Mayor, September 12, 1932.

Rene J. LeGardeur, Chairman
Arthur A. de la Houssaye, Secretary
James Henry Bruns
Reuben Bush
Henry Chaffe
Duralde Claiborne
John Dart
Philip S. Gidiere
C. H. Hamilton
William E. Huger
D. M. Kilpatrick
Mrs. Stella Levert
Robert L. Levert
Bernard McCloskey, Jr.

Henry L. McLean
Frank H. Mortimer
Richard M. Murphy
Dr. John G. Pratt
E. M. Rea
A. L. Saxon
Charles B. Thorn
S. A. Trufant, Jr.
Ernest C. Villere
S. P. Walmsley, Jr.
A. B. Wheeler, Jr.
Nelson Whitney
William B. Wisdom

Additional list of members of the Board Who Served Between the Years 1933 and 1953

Stamps Farrar
Dr. E. D. Fenner
Frank B. Hayne, Jr.
George C. H. Kernion

Bruns Lawrason
Bernard McCloskey, Sr.
Archie M. Smith
John M. Wisdom

LIST OF MEMBERS OF THE BOARD OF COMMISSIONERS OF LIBERTY PLACE (as of September 14, 1954)

1949-1954

William B. Wisdom
R. J. LeGardeur, Jr.
H. S. Hardin

James Wilkinson
Hughes P. Walmsley
Richard R. Foster

1950-1955

Frank McLoughlin
Henry Chaffe
Bernard J. McCloskey

Walter J. Stauffer
Judge Richard McBride
Fred N. Ogden

1951-1956

Charles P. Carriere
Killian Huger
Jeff D. Hardin, Jr.

James J. A. Fortier
John Dart

1952-1957

Arthur A de la Houssaye
Charles J. Smith
Isaac Davis Stamps Farrar, II

Rene J. LeGardeur
William B. Dreux
William A. Feuillan, Jr.

1953-1958

Hughes Jules de la Vergne, II
Fred A. Toledano
Dr. Henry Ogden

A. J. McEnery
Hugh M. Wilkinson
Dr. Roy E. de la Houssaye

LIST OF THOSE WHO TOOK PART IN THE BATTLE OF
14th OF SEPTEMBER, 1874

It is difficult to get an exact list of the names of those who were on duty on the 14th of September, 1874. The original muster rolls have been lost or misplaced. The list which follows is made up from several sources.

First, the pamphlet, issued by J. Curtis Waldo in 1877, which gives the names of all the members of the White League companies between 1874 and 1877. This pamphlet entitled, "The Roll of Honor — Roster of Citizen Soldiery Who Saved Louisiana. Revised and Complete." It contains several thousand names, but only some of them were in the affair of the 14th and their names are marked with an asterisk.

Second, there is a roster of the "First Crescent City Regiment, Col. W. T. Vaudry commanding, through April 25, 1877." This roster is of companies that were in the Crescent City White League, and the names of those who were in the original companies or who served on the 14th are marked with an asterisk.

Third, in the daily *Picayune* of September 14, 1899, the silver anniversary of the 14th of September, there is a list of participants.

Fourth, the Louisiana Historical Quarterly of October, 1924, contains an article by W. O. Hart which lists again the names of the citizen soldiery of September 14, 1874. Mr. Hart stated that it was a partial list of the men who responded to the call of arms: "Following are the rosters of the companies who engaged in the 14th of September movement. It is necessarily incomplete but has been made as nearly accurate as possible."

In making up the list appended herewith, I have checked these four groups of names against each other. Besides variations in spelling, the lists generally agree. But some names are on each list that were not on others. In this manner I was able to obtain as near a complete list as possible.

There are also names taken from General Ogden's report and the reports of his officers and from newspaper accounts. The list given is believed to be as accurate as is possible to obtain at this late date.

Originally the White League companies were known as the "Protector League" companies or "sections." On the 14th of September they were divided into two groups generally, the Crescent City White League sections and the companies belonging to the Louisiana Field Artillery organized by Colonel John G. Angell.

In addition to checking the names against the lists mentioned, they have been checked against the New Orleans city directory of 1874. This emphasized the difficulty of obtaining an accurate list, for many names are not found in the city directory. Ben Mire, Captain of Company H, Eugene Waggaman, W. R. Stauffer — all well known names — are not listed in the city directory for that year. It is possible they lived in the suburbs.

The name *Tynan* is spelled in some registers as Tynan and in others as *Tinan*. The city directory shows *Tinan*. Captain Tennison's name is spelled with a "y" in some lists — *Tennyson*. There is one James Davis listed as a participant in the Battle of the 14th, and there are ten James Davises listed in the directory of 1874.

There are instances of name transposition. One list shows the name as Thomas O. Nelson, another as Thomas Orrellson and his real name was Thomas Orrell, Sr. One listing shows M. O. Rourke instead of M. O'Rourke.

Captain Joseph P. Macheca and his company of Italians was active on the 14th. There is no roster available showing the membership as of that date, so the members of his valiant group are not listed in the names that follow. The full roster is given in the 1877 pamphlet reprinted on another page.

OCCUPATIONS OF WHITE LEAGUERS

Those who engaged in the White League Movement and the members of the Louisiana Field Artillery belonged to all grades of society with the better class people predominating. There were 24 physicians and surgeons, and the list included lawyers, grocers, furniture dealers, cotton brokers, architects, skilled workmen, saloon keepers, printers, brokers, auctioneers, bartenders, store clerks from Holmes and Godchaux's, bookkeepers and cashiers. Among the group was the sexton of Trinity Church; John W. Tobin, well-known steamboat captain; A. J. Tardy, Deputy civil sheriff; J. W. Patton, Criminal Sheriff for the Parish of Orleans and Charles Roman, President of Salamander Fire Insurance Company. Rev. Stewart, Minister, was mentioned as a participant. Leed's Foundry, of which Captain Archibald Mitchell was the superintendent, furnished more members probably than any other organization.

Some of the leading lawyers, doctors and business men served as privates, including Edward Douglas White, later Chief Justice of the United States. After the Battle of the 14th, many citizens joined the White League, and served in the Spring of 1877. A complete list of the White League membership for the three years is reprinted elsewhere.

The names on the following list are arranged alphabetically and taken from the various rosters mentioned above.

CCWL — Crescent City White League

LFA — Louisiana Field Artillery

1st La. Inf. — First Louisiana Infantry, Col. Angell's Command

W.L. — White League

A

Abat, Valcour—Pvt. Sec. C, 5th Wd. WL

Abbott, J. North—Pvt. Co. A, 1st La. Inf.

Abbott, Wm. M.—Pvt. Co. A, 1st La. Inf.

Aby, R. C.—Pvt. Co. G, CCWL

Ackerman, A.—Pvt. Sec. D, CCWL

Adams, J. S.—Pvt. Co. D, 1st La. Inf.

Addison—Lt. La. Rifles.

Affleck, H. J.—Pvt. Sec. E, CCWL

Agar, Geo.—Pvt. Co. B, 1st La. Inf.

Aleix, L.—Pvt. Sec. A, 5th Wd. League.

Alexander, Gus—Pvt. Co. D, CCWL

Alexander, John—Pvt. Co. D, 1st La. Inf.

Alexius, A. G.—Pvt. Co. B, 6th Dis. WL

Alleman, John—Pvt. Co. C, 1st La. Inf.

Allen, C. H.—Capt. 6th Dis. WL

Allen, C. W.—2nd Sgt. Sec. E, CCWL

Allen, W. M.—Pvt. Co. D, CCWL

Alleyn, M. A.—2nd Lt. Sec. D, CCWL

Andrus, F. M.—Capt. 11th Wd., WL

Angell, John G.—Col. 1st La. Inf., Companies A, B, C and E.

Armstrong, Alex J.—Pvt. Sec. D, CCWL

Armstrong, Frank—Pvt. Co. A, 1st La. Inf.

Armstrong, W. J.—2nd Lt. Sec E, CCWL

Armstrong, R. N.—Pvt. Sec. E, CCWL

Arnauld, L. A.—1st Lt. Co. B, 1st La. Inf.

Arnoult, Christian—Pvt. Co. B, CCWL

Arnoult, J. B. G.—Pvt. Co. B, CCWL

Artigue, J. P.—Pvt. Sec. C, 5th Wd. WL

Audler, Charles—St. John WL

Audler, Adolph S.—Pvt. 7th Wd. WL

Audler, Louis—Enl. Man, 7th Wd. WL

Audler, Louis—St. John WL

Augustin, John—Maj. in command of La. Rifle Club and unattached forces.

Augustin, Joseph Numa—2nd Sgt. Sec. A, 5th Wd. WL

Avegno, Bernard—Pvt. Co. H, 6th Wd. WL

Avenel, Aime—Bat. C, Protector WL

B

Babcock, C. E.—Pvt. Co. B, 6th Dis. WL

Babcock, O. S.—Pvt. Bat. A, L. F. Art.

Bachelot, E. (Bachelor?)—Pvt. Sec. A, 5th Wd. WL

Bachemin, John—Pvt. Co. C, CCWL

Bailey, N. E.—Pvt. Co. A, 1st La. Inf.

Bailey, N. E., Jr.—Pvt. Co. D, 1st La. Inf.

Bailey, R. A.—Pvt. Co. C, CCWL

Bailey, Dr. Walter, Jr.—Pvt. Co. C, CCWL

Baker, Alf. T.—2nd Lt., Bat. A, La. F. Art.

Baker, John P.—Pvt. Co. A, 1st La. Inf.

Baker, H. H.—2nd Cpl. Sec. E, CCWL

Baker, Harry N.—Pvt. Bat. A, L.F.A.

Balfour, C. C.—Pvt. Sec. A, CCWL

Balfour, James R.—1st Lt. Sec. A CCWL

Banister, M.—Pvt. Bat. A, L.F.A.

Bardon, E. N.—1st Lt., Washington WL

Barnett, Alfred R.—Pvt. Co. H, 6th Wd. WL

Barnett, C.—Pvt. Sec. C, 5th Wd WL

Barnett, W. H.—Pvt. Co C, 1st La. Inf.

Barre, J.—Pvt. Sec. A, 5th Wd. League

Barrett, D.—Cpl. Co. G, CCWL

Barrett, James—Pvt. Co. G, CCWL

Barrett, John—Pvt. Co. C, CCWL

Barringer, J. H.—Pvt. Bat. A, L.F.A.

Barringer, L. G.—Pvt. Bat. A, L.F.A.

Barry, John—Pvt. Sec. C, 5th Wd. WL

Bartlett, J. T.—Pvt. Co. C, 1st La. Inf.

Bartlette, O.—Pvt. Co. C, 1st La. Inf.

Barton, ?.—1st Lt. Washington WL

Barton, T. S.—Pvt. Co. C, CCWL

Bateson, C. E.—Pvt. Co. C, CCWL

Bath, T. J.—Pvt. Co. B, CCWL

Baxter, Thos.—Pvt. Sec. E, CCWL

Bayhi, J. R.—Pvt. Washington WL

Bayle, A.—Pvt. Sec. A, 5th Wd. WL

Bayon Dr. Henri—Pvt. Sec. A, 5th Wd. League

Beanham—Sgt. Co. G, CCWL (From re-union dinner list Sept. 16, 1875)

Beattie, G. W.—Pvt. Co. D, 1st La. Inf.

Beattie, W. A.—Pvt. Co. D, 1st La. Inf.

Beaulieu, Ned—St. John WL

Beauregard, James—Pvt. Sev. C, 5th Wd. WL

Bedford, W. D.—Pvt. Co. G, CCWL

Beers, George M.—Pvt. Co. A, 1st La. Inf.

Beggs, James—Pvt. Co. B, 6th Dis. WL

Behan, W. J.—Col. in command of Companies A, B, C, E and G of CCWL and commands of Capts. Flood, Andrus, Allen and Shropshire.

Bein, C. W.—Pvt. Co. C, CCWL

Bell, H. S.—2nd Sgt. Co. C, CCWL

Bell, P. B.—Pvt. Co. A, 1st La. Inf.

Bell, Wm.—Pvt. Co. K, 10th Wd. WL

Bell, Wm. A.—Aide to Gen. Ogden

Bellanger, A, Pvt. Sec. A, 5th Wd. League.

Bender, Frank—Pvt. Co. F, CCWL

Bercegeay, C.—Pvt. Sec. C, 5th Wd. WL

Bergegeay, Emanuel—Pvt. Bat C, LFA

Berg, Fred—Pvt. Co. C, 1st La. Inf.

Berry, W. A.—Pvt. Co. F, CCWL

Berwin, Geo.—2nd Lt. Washington WL

Betz, J. W.—Pvt. Co. C, 1st La. Inf.

Betz, Mike—Pvt. Washington WL

Bezou, Dr. H.—Pvt. Sec. A, 5th Wd. League

Bienvenu (& Kurscheedt)—Mentioned in Gen. Ogden's report

Bienvenu, F. A.—Pvt. Sec. A, 5th Wd. League

Bienvenu, Nemours, 1st Lt. Co. H, 6th Wd. WL

Bienvenu, Neuville—Pvt. Co. H, 6th Wd. WL

Bienvenu, R. H.—Pvt. Co. H, 6th Wd. WL

Bienvenu, William—Pvt. Co. H, 6th Wd. WL

Biers, J. S.—Pvt. Co. B, 6th Dis. W L

Biggar, J. R.—Pvt. Sec. D, CCWL

Birmingham, P.—Pvt. Co. K, 10th Wd. WL

Black, D. C.—Pvt. Co. C, CCWL

Blaffer, J. A.—Pvt. Co. B, CCWL

Blanchard, Dawson A—Capt. Co. C, 1st La. Inf.

Bloch, S.—Pvt. Co. H, 6th Wd. WL

Block, John T.—Pvt. Co. C, CCWL

Bloodgood, C. B.—Pvt. Co. C, CCWL

Boarman, Charles B.—3rd Lt. Co. B, 1st La. Inf.

Boarman, J. R.—Pvt. Co. A, 1st La. Inf.

Bobb, Leslie—Pvt. Sec. E, CCWL

Boisblanc, Chris—Pvt. Bat. C, LFA

Bolton, A.—Pvt. Washington WL

Bond, R. C.—3rd Lt. Sec. A, CCWL

Booth, George—Pvt. Co. A, 1st La. Inf.

Borge, James—En. Man, 7th Wd. WL

Borland, Euclid, Jr.—Capt. Co. A, 1st La. Inf.

Bosworth, M.—Pvt. Sec. E, CCWL

Bosworth, W.—Pvt. Co. C, 1st La. Inf.

Bosworth, Wm.—Pvt. Sec. E, CCWL

Boulet, Wm.—Pvt. 9th Wd. WL

Bouligny, Ed—Pvt. Sec. A, CCWL

Bolllemet, R. H.—Pvt. Co. C, CCWL

Boulware, A, Jr.—Pvt. Co. F, CCWL

Bouny, P. L.—1st Lt. Sec. A, 5th Wd. WL

Bowman, M. M.—Pvt. Sec. E, CCWL

Boylan, T. N.—Pvt. Sec. A, CCWL

Boyle, C. H.—Sgt. Co. K, 10th Wd WL

Bozant, John—1st Lt. Co. B, 6th Dis. WL

Bozonier—A. Bat. C, L. F. Art.

Bradford, Geo. K.—Vaudry's Rifles (see his letter Sept. 9, 1934)

Brandenborg, Thos.—Pvt. Sec. D, CCWL

Braud, E.—2nd Lt. Co. H, 6th Wd. WL

Breedon, Monk—Pvt. Co. D, 1st La Inf.

Breen, Chas. H.—Pvt. Co. B, 6th Dis. WL

Brewer, E. M.—Pvt. Co. A, 1st La. Inf.

Brewster, John—Pvt. Co. H, 6th Wd. WL

Bringier, M.—Pvt. Co. A, 1st La. Inf.

Bringier, M. S.—Pvt. Sec. A, CCWL

Brower, E. M.—Pvt. Co. A, 1st La. Inf.

Brown, And. K.—3rd Cpl. Co. C, CCWL

Brown, D. F.—1st Cpl. Sec. D, CCWL

Brown, D. W.—Pvt. Washington WL

Brown, H. W.—Pvt. Co. C, CCWL

Brown, M. M.—5th Sgt. Sec. E, CCWL

Brown, W.—3rd Sgt. Co. B, CCWL

Brown, W. L., Jr.—1st Cpl. Sec. E, CCWL

Brugier, August—Enl. Man, 7th Wd. WL

Brulard, Chas.—Bat. C, L. F. Art.

Brunnard, Aug.—Pvt. Bat. C, L. F. Art.

Bruns, Dr. J. D.—Surgeon Gen.

Bryan, Henry H.—Pvt. Co. A, 1st La. Inf.

Buck, S. H.—Capt. Co. C, CCWL

Buckley, Thomas—Pvt. Co. H, 6th Wd. WL

Buckner, James—Pvt. Sec. A, CCWL. (On the 14th he was Inspector Gen. on Staff of Gen. Ogden)

Buddecke, Chas. B—4th Sgt. Co. D, 1st La. Inf.

Buddendorf ?.—Volunteer Aide to Gen. Ogden

Budge, Ben.—Pvt. Co. F, CCWL
Buhler, J. R.—Pvt. Sec. A, CCWL
Buisson, Theodule—2nd Lt. Sec. C, 5th Wd WL
Bunce, Wm. F.—Pvt. Sec. E, CCWL
Burckel, Jacob—Pvt. Washington WL
Burke, E. A.—Maj., On Gov. Penn's Staff
Burns, Dan—Pvt. Sec. D, CCWL
Burns, Ed—Pvt. Co. B, CCWL
Burvant, Pascal H.—Pvt. Co. H, 6th Wd. WL
Butterfield, J.—Pvt. Co. F, CCWL
Butts, Wm.—Pvt. Sec. A, 5th Wd. League
Byrd, John G.—1st Cpl. Co. C, CCWL
Byrnes, J.—Pvt. Sec. D, CCWL
Byrnes, Nat—Pvt. Co. C, 1st La. Inf.
Byrnes, Richard—Cor. Bat. C, L. F. Art.

C

Cabochi, L.—Bat. C, La. F. Art.
Cahn, Jos.—Pvt. 9th Wd. WL
Callen, Jas.—Pvt. Sec. D, CCWL
Calongne, W.—Bat C, La. F. Art.
Campbell, M.—Pvt. Sec. D, CCWL
Campbell, Percy—Pvt. Sec. E, CCWL
Campbell, Robt.—6th Dis. WL
(See letter of his daughter Sept. 8, 1934
Campbell, W. S.—Pvt. Co. C, CCWL
Cannon, J. J.—Pvt. Sec. D, CCWL
Cantzon, W. H.—Pvt. Bat. A, L. F. A.
Capedevielle, A.—Pvt. Sec. A, 5th Wd. League
Carey, B. F.—Pvt. Sec. E, CCWL
Carey, Wm.—Pvt. Sec. D, CCWL
Carley, C. J.—Pvt. Co. I, 3rd Wd. WL
Carlisle, Frank—Pvt. Co. B, 1st La. Inf.
Carlisle, S. S.—Pvt. Co. B, 1st La. Inf.
Carman, Allen—Pvt. Co. B, 6th Dis. WL
Carriere, Emile E.—Bat. C, Lt. F. Art.
Carroll, Charles—Pvt. Co. A, 1st La. Inf.
Carroll, D. R., Jr.—Pvt. Sec. A, CCWL
Carter, Prentiss B.—(of Franklinton, La., lived in New Orleans and was in battle according to his daughter)
Carter, Thomas—Pvt. Co. I, 3rd Wd. WL
Cartner, J.—Pvt. Sec. A, 5th Wd. League.
Cary, Geo. W.—Pvt. Co. C, CCWL
Cassard, A.—Pvt. Co. F, CCWL
Cassard, John E.—Co. B, CCWL
Cassidy, Henry—Pvt. Co. B, 1st La. Inf.
Castanedo, Arthur—Pvt. Washington WL
Caufield, Martin—Pvt. Co. B, CCWL
Cellos, J. V.—Pvt. Co. C, 1st La. Inf.
Chaery, Leo—Pvt. 9th Wd. WL
Chaffe, W. H.—Adjutant, 1st La. Inf.
Chalaron, Henry—Pvt. Sec. A, CCWL
Chalaron, James—3rd Cpl. Co. D, 1st La. Inf.
Chaneville, F.—Pvt. Co. C, 1st La. Inf.
Chapman, Ed.—Pvt. Co. C, CCWL
Charbonnet, Lotana—Pvt. Bat C, L.F.A.
Charlton, C. H.—Lt. Co. G, CCWL
Cherbonnier, F. E.—Bat. C, La. F. Art.
Chopin, E.—Pvt. Sec. A, 5th Wd. League
Chopin, Oscar—Pvt. Co. B, 1st La. Inf.
Church, G. W. Jr.—Pvt. Co. A, CCWL
Clague, James—Pvt. Co. K, 10th Wd. WL
Claiborne, F.—Pvt. 6th Wd. WL
Clark, Pat—Pvt. Co. I, 3rd Wd. WL
Clements, Dennis—Pvt. Co. F, CCWL
Clements, E. J.—Pvt. Sec. E, CCWL
Clements, E. S.—Pvt. Co. E, CCWL
Clements, J. B.—Pvt. Sec. E, CCWL
Cleveland, Wm. F.—1st Cpl. Co. D, 1st La. Inf.
Clinchy, Geo.—Pvt. Co. I, 3rd Wd. WL
Cloney, D.—Pvt. Co. I, 3rd Wd. WL
Close, Andrew—Pvt. Co. K, 10th Wd. WL

Colcock, Daniel D.—1st Sgt. Co. D, 1st La. Inf.
Colcock, R. H.—Pvt. Co. D, 1st La. Inf.
Coleman, H. Dudley—Capt. Bat. A, La. Field Art.
Coleman, J. Wood—Jr. Lt. Sec. E, CCWL
Collens, Thos. W.—Pvt. Co. B, 1st La. Inf.
Collins, Conrad—Pvt. 7th Wd. WL
Collins, Jno. W.—Pvt. Co. B, 1st La. Inf.
Collins, Phelps—Pvt. Sec. D, CCWL
Condon, Wm.—Pvt. Co. I, 3rd Wd. WL
Conners, M.—Pvt. Co. B, 6th Dis. WL
Conners, Mortimer—3rd Sgt. Sec. D, CCWL
Conners, Tim—Pvt. Co. F, CCWL
Conrad, J. N.—Pvt. Sec. A, CCWL
Conrad, P. J.—Pvt. Sec. D, CCWL
Conrad, Wm.—Pvt. Sec. D, CCWL
Considine, James Henry—Pvt. Co. C, 1st La. Inf.
Cook, Fred.—Pvt. Co. C, CCWL
Corcoran, John—Pvt. Sec. D, CCWL
Corkery, Edward H.—Pvt. Co. G. CCWL
Cormier, H. A.—Sgt. Co. C, 1st La. Inf.
Cormier, P.—Pvt. Co. C, 1st La. Inf.
Correjolles, Wm. J.—Bat. C, L. F. Art.
Correy, B. F.—Pvt. Co. E, CCWL
Cortie, Charles—Pvt. Sec. D, CCWL
Costa, A.—Pvt. Sec. A, CCWL
Coste, Arthur—Pvt. Bat. A, L. F. Art.
Couturie, Chas. L.—Sgt. Co. H, 6th Wd. WL
Couturie, Edouard—Pvt. Co. H, 6th Wd. WL
Cowperthwaith, J. W.—Pvt. Sec. A, 5th Wd. WL
Coyle, Peter—Pvt. Co. B, CCWL
Craft, August—Pvt. Co. C, CCWL
Crampton, Terence—Pvt. Co. G, CCWL
Crane, Geo. P.—Pvt. Co. C, CCWL
Creevy, Wm., Sr.—Pvt. Sec. D, CCWL
Creevy, Wm., Jr.—Pvt. Sec. D, CCWL
Criswell, Benj. P.—2nd Sgt. Co. F, CCWL
Criswell, Elijah—Pvt. Bat. A, La. F. Art.
Crosby, Jeff—Pvt. Co. F, CCWL
Crosby, W. T.—Pvt. Co. F, CCWL
Crossin, Jas. M.—Pvt. Co. B, CCWL
Crump, Benjamin—Pvt. Co. G, CCWL
Cucullu, S.—1st Lt. Sec. C, 5th Wd. WL
Cullen, Dr. John M.—La. Rifles
Cumberland, J.—Pvt. Co. C, CCWL
Cumberland, W. B.—Pvt. Co. C, CCWL
Cunningham, J. B.—Pvt. Co. G, CCWL
Curry, Thomas—Pvt. Co. B, 1st La. Inf.
Cusick, M. J.—Pvt. Co. D, CCWL

D

Dallas, Madison—3rd Cpl. Sec. E, CCWL
Daly, D. J.—Pvt. Sec. D, CCWL
Dancy, Clifton—Pvt. Co. C, CCWL
Dannoy, A. C.—Pvt. Co. B, 6th Dis. WL
D'Aquin, W. H., 6th Wd. WL
D'Aquin, Dr. H.—Cpl. Sec. C, 5th Wd. WL
Daunoy, P.—Sgt. Co. C, 1st La. Inf.
Davey, R. C.—Pvt. Co. A, 1st La. Inf.
Davey, J.—Pvt. Co. A, 1st La. Inf.
Davis, James—Pvt. Co. K, 10th Wd. WL
Davis, Dr. J. B.—Pvt. Co. B, 1st La. Inf.
Day, R. S.—Pvt. Sec. A, CCWL
De Armas, Charles—Pvt. Sec. C, 5th Wd. WL
Deas, R. J.—Pvt. Co. D, 1st La. Inf.
DeBlanc—A. E.—Acting 2nd Lt. Co. H, 6th Wd. WL
DeBlanc, Gus S.—Pvt. Bat. C, La. Field Art.
DeBlanc, J. A., Jr.—2nd Sgt. 9th Wd. WL

DeBuys, Geo.—Bat. C, La. F. Art.
De Camp, C. M.—2nd Cpl. Co. C, CCWL
De Gruy, Henry—Pvt. Co. B, 6th Dis. WL
Degruy, J. V.—Pvt. Sec. A, CCWL
De Fuentes, C. L.—Pvt. Sec. C, 5th Wd. WL
De La Morinierre, Jules—Pvt. Sec. C, 5th Wd. WL
De Lassus, Charles—1st Sgt. Sec. A, 5th Wd. WL
Deleban, E. T.—Pvt. Co. C, 1st La. Inf.
Delery, Frank—Bat. C, La. F. Art.
Delery, John—Pvt. Co. H, 6th Wd. WL
Delgado, Henry—Pvt. Sec. E, CCWL
Delord, A.—Pvt. Co. C, 1st La. Inf.
Denegre, Henry—2nd Sgt. Sec. A, CCWL
Dennee, R. Stewart—Capt. 2nd Wd. WL
Dennis, Adam—Pvt. Washington WL
Desposito, Robert—Pvt. Co. I, 3rd Wd. WL
Deter, Anthony—Pvt. Co. B, 6th Dis. WL
De Tomes, A.—Pvt. 9th Wd. WL
Devine, A.—Pvt. Sec. D, CCWL
De Went, J. E.—Pvt. Washington WL
Diamond, J.—Pvt. Co. K, 10th Wd. League
Dietrich, C. E.—Pvt. Co. D, 1st La. Inf.
Dillenschneider, Victor—Pvt. Washington WL
Dinken, C. A.—Pvt. Co. G, CCWL
Dodsworth, Wm. E.—Pvt. Co. A, 1st La. Inf.
Doherty, Wm.—Pvt. Sec. D, CCWL
Doize, A. J.—Pvt. Washington WL
Dolan, P.—Pvt. Sec. D, CCWL
Domenech, J.—Pvt. Sec. D, CCWL
Donafort, A.—Pvt. Sec. A, 5th Wd. League.
Donafort, L.—Pvt. Sec. A, 5th Wd. League
Donafort, L., Jr.—Pvt. Sec. A, 5th Wd. League
Donald, Samuel—Sgt. Co. A, CCWL
Donnelly, J.—Pvt. Sec. D, CCWL
Donovan, Alex.—Pvt. Co. C, CCWL
Donovan, John—Pvt. Co. C, CCWL
Doran, W. H.—Pvt. Co. B, 6th Dis. WL
Douglas, James A.—Pvt. Co. F, CCWL
Douk, A.—Pvt. Sec. A, 5th Wd. League
Doussan, G.—Pvt. Sec. A, 5th Wd. League
Dowling, P. M.—3rd Cpl.—Co. I, 3rd Wd. League
Dreters, Henry—Pvt. Co. C, 1st La. Inf.
Driscoll, C.—Pvt. Co. C, CCWL
Driscoll, M.—5th Sgt.—Co. I, 3rd Wd. WL
Drouett, Edward—Pvt. Co. B, 1st La. Inf.
Ducros, Edw. O.—Pvt. Bat. C, La. F. Art.
Dugas, R.—Pvt. Washington WL
Duncan, W. C.—Pvt. Sec. A, CCWL
Dunn, Frank—Pvt. 9th Wd. WL
Dunoy, Clifton—Pvt. Co. C, CCWL
Dupaquier, E.—Sgt. Co. H, 6th Wd. WL
Dupre, Alfred—Pvt. 9th Wd. WL
Dupre, E.—Pvt. Co. H, 6th Wd. WL
Dupre, Geo. W.—Capt. Co. H, 6th Wd. WL
Dupre, Henry—1st Sgt. Bat. A, LFA
Dupre, R.—Pvt. Co. H, 6th Wd. WL
Dupre, W.—Pvt. Co. H, 6th Wd. WL
Durand, Charles—Pvt. Co. C, La. Inf.
Durand, E.—3rd Lt. Sec. A, 5th Wd. League
Durr, Jean Pierre—Pvt. 7th Wd. WL
Durr, Dr. Lafayette G.—Pvt. Sec. E, CCWL
Dwyer, A. J.—Pvt. Co. F, CCWL
Dyer, John—Pvt. Co. A, 1st La. Inf.

E

Eager, C. E. Jr.—Pvt. Sec. E, CCWL
Eager, W. M.—Pvt. Sec. E, CCWL
Eckleberg, J. P.—Pvt. Sec. E, CCWL
Egan, Thomas—Pvt. Co. I, 3rd Wd. WL
Eichorn, Rudolph—Pvt. Co. I, 3rd Wd. League
Ellis, E. John—Adjutant-General under Gov. Penn. Pvt. Co. B, 6th Dis. WL
Ellis, Issac B.—Cpl. Co. G, CCWL
Ellis, L. L.—Pvt. Co. G, CCWL
Eschman, Andrew—Pvt. 7th Wd. WL
Escousse, Victor—Pvt. Co. H, 6th Wd. WL
Estlin, R. W.—Pvt. Co. A, CCWL
Eustis, F.—Pvt. Co. C, CCWL
Evans, Wm. M.—Pvt. Washington WL
Eyle, Fred,—2nd Lt. Jr. Co. F, CCWL
Eyrich, Robert G.—Pvt. Co. F, CCWL

F

Fagan, Wm.—1st Lt. Sec. E, CCWL
Faget, L.—Pvt. Bat. C, L. F. Art.
Fahey, John—Pvt. Co. K, 10th Wd. WL
Fallon, M. J.—Pvt. Co. D, CCWL
Farmer, T. C.—Pvt. Sec. D, CCWL
Farrell, James—Pvt. Sec. D, CCWL
Farrell, John—Pvt. Co. A, CCWL
Farrell, M. J.—Pvt. Sec. A, CCWL
Farrelly, Patrick—Pvt. Co. B, 1st La. Inf.
Farren, D.—Pvt. Co. C, CCWL
Fauquier, R. M.—Pvt. Sec. A, CCWL
Fayssoux, C. I.—Pvt. Co. C, CCWL
Fazende, Lucien—Bat. C, L. F. Art.
Fee, James—Pvt. Sec. D, CCWL
Feehan, James—Pvt. Co. B, CCWL
Feely, Pat—Pvt. Co. I, 3rd Wd. WL
Feicht, P.—Pvt. Co. K, 10th Wd. WL
Feicht, Simon—Pvt. Co. K, 10th Wd. WL
Feindel, Fritz—Pvt. 7th Wd. WL
Fenton, John—Pvt. Sec. D, CCWL
Ferguson, H. B.—5th Sgt. Sec. A, CCWL
Ferguson, E. S.—Pvt. Sec. E, CCWL
Fernandez—Gabriel—Pvt. Co. B, 1st La. Inf.
Ferrigan, Ed.—Mentioned in Gen. Ogden's report
Finan, Mark—Pvt. Co. G, CCWL
Finan, P.—Pvt. Sec. D, CCWL
Fink, J.—Pvt. Sec. A, 5th Wd. WL
Finley, W. W.—Pvt. Co. E, CCWL
Finnegan, E.—Pvt. Co. G, CCWL
Fisher, B.—Pvt. Wash. WL
Fitch, John B.—Pvt. Co. B, CCWL
Fitzhugh, Samuel—Pvt. Bat. A, L. F. Art.
Flanagan, James—Pvt. Sec. D, CCWL
Flanagan, P. J.—Pvt. Co. B, CCWL
Flanner, Joseph—Pvt. Sec. E, CCWL
Flood, Ed.—Capt. Co. K, Wd. WL
Flower, Ives—Pvt. Sec. E, CCWL
Flower, James—Pvt. Sec. E, CCWL
Flower, Jesse—Pvt. Sec. E, CCWL
Flower, Richard—4th Sgt. Sec. E, CCWL
Flower, Samuel—Aide to Gen. Ogden
Foley, Tim H.—Pvt. Co. I, 3rd Wd. WL
Foley, W. T.—Pvt. Co. F, CCWL
Folger, Wm.—Pvt. Sec. E, CCWL
Ford, Thos.—Pvt. Co. K, 10th Wd. WL
Forman, B. R.—Capt. Co. E, 1st La. Inf.* Also listed as Pvt. Co. D.
*According to Frank Richardson's statement, his wife was sick and he turned over the command to 1st-Lt. Richardson
Forno, C. H.—1st Lt. Jr. Bat. A. L. F. Art.
Forno, Lawrence—Pvt. Bat. A, L. F. Art.
Forstall, Felix—Bat. C, L. F. Art.
Fortier, Alcee—Pvt. Sec. A, 5th Wd. WL
Fortier, Gustave R.—Bat. C, L. F. Art.
Fortier, Michel J.—Bat. C, L. F. Art.

Foster, Rush—Pvt. Sec. A, CCWL
Foster, W. K.—Pvt. Sec. A, CCWL
Fox, Wm. G.—Pvt. Co. A, 1st La. Inf.
Francois, M.—Pvt. Sec. D, CCWL
Frank, Lewis—Pvt. Co. E, CCWL
Frellsen, Albert—Pvt. Co. B, 1st La. Inf.
Frellsen, J.—Pvt. Co. C, CCWL
Fremeaux, L. J.—Capt. Sec. C, 5th Wd. WL
Fremeaux, Leon V.—Pvt. Sec. C, 5th Wd. WL
Fremeaux, Paul—Pvt. Sec. C, 5th Wd. WL
Ferert, Gus—Pvt. Co. B, 6th Dis. WL
Freret, F. G.—Pvt. Sec. E, CCWL
Freret, Miles—Pvt. Co. B, 1st La. Inf.
Freret, Wm. A.—Pvt. Co. D, 1st La. Inf.
Fried, Henry—Pvt. 7th Wd. WL
Fried, William—Pvt. 7th Wd. WL
Frisbie, W. R.—Pvt. Co. A, 1st La. Inf.
Frizenreiter, Charles—La. Rifles
Frost, J. M.—Pvt. Co. C, 1st La. Inf.
Fulham, Thos.—2nd Sgt. Co. I, 3rd Wd. WL
Fulham .Wm.—1st Lt. Co. I, 3rd Wd. WL

G

Gaffney, James—Pvt. Sec. D, CCWL
Gaffney, John—Sgt. Co. K, 10th Wd. WL
Gaffney, Peter C.—2nd Lt. Sec. D, CCWL
Gallagher, M.—Pvt. Co. I, 3rd Wd. WL
Gallagher, Scott—3rd Sgt. Sec. A, CCWL
Gamotis, Alphonse—Pvt. Bat. C, L. F. Art.
Gannon, E. H.—Pvt. Co. B, CCWL
Gannon, Thos.—Pvt. Sec. D, CCWL
Ganter, G. B.—Pvt. Sec. D, CCWL
Ganucheau, Henry—Bat. C, L. F. Art.
Garcia, A. E.—Pvt. Sec. A, CCWL
Garcia, Ben—Pvt. Sec. C, 5th Wd. WL
Garcia, Jos.—2nd Lt. Jr. Sec. C, 5th Wd. WL
Garidel, J.—Pvt. Co. B, 1st La. Inf.
Garry, P. M.—Pvt. Co. I, 3rd Wd. WL
Garvey, James—Pvt. Wash. WL
Garvey, John—Pvt. Co. B, CCWL
Garvey, P. M.—Pvt. Co. I, 3rd Wd. WL
Gause, H. C.—Pvt. Co. C, CCWL
Gauthreaux, J. R. A.—Pvt. Sec. E, CCWL
Gautier, Albert M.—Sgt. Mj. Bat. C, L. F. Art.
Gayarre, Chas. Jr.—Pvt. 7th Wd. WL
Geheeb, Charles—Pvt. Bat. A, L. F. Art.
Gehlbach, Charley—3rd Lt. Wash. WL
Generelly, E.—Pvt. Bat. C, L. F. Art.
George, J. R.—Pvt. Co. A, 1st La. Inf.
Gerard, A.—Pvt. Wash. WL
Geron, Louis—Pvt. Bat. C. L. F. Art.
Gernon, Louis—Pvt. Bat. C, L. F. Art.
Gill, T. M.—Pvt. Co. D, 1st La. Inf.
Gilleck, L. G.—Pvt. Sec. D, CCWL
Gilthorpe, Wm. J.—Pvt. Sec. D, CCWL
Gleason, J. P.—Pvt. Co. C, CCWL
Glennon, P.—Pvt. Co. I, 3rd Wd. WL
Glynn, John, Jr.—Chief of Artillery and Capt. Bat. C, La. F. Art.
Gonzales, Nunez—Pvt. Wash. WL
Gordon, Donald—Pvt. Sec. E, CCWL
Gorman, Sol.—Pvt. Co. B, 6th Dis. WL
Gorman, T. W.—Pvt. Co. D, 1st La. Inf.
Gourrier, Clay—Pvt. Co. G, CCWL
Gowland, Wm.—Pvt. Co. A, 1st La. Inf.
Graner, T. H.—Pvt. Co. C, CCWL
Grass, John—Pvt. 7th Wd. WL
Graugnard, J. H.—Pvt. Co. C, 1st La. Inf.
Gravel, John—Pvt. Co. A, 1st La. Inf.
Graval, John—St. John White League
Gray, A. P.—Pvt. Bat. A, L. F. Art.
Greeger, H.—Pvt. Co. C, 1st La. Inf.
Green, Conrad—Pvt. Sec. D, CCWL

Green, George—Pvt. Co. K, 1st Wd. WL
Green, T. H.—Pvt. Co. C, CCWL
Greenleaf, Leeds—Volunteer Aide to Gen. Ogden
Gregory, James—Pvt. Co. K, 10th Wd. WL
Greig, Frank—2nd Lt. Bat. C, LFA
Gresham, Jas. A.—Pvt. Co. B, 1st La. Inf.
Grieff, A. H.—Pvt. Sec. A, CCWL
Griffin, Thos., Sr.—Pvt. Co. I, 3rd Wd. WL
Griffon, Charles—Pvt. Bat. C, L. F. Art.
Grimer, Victor—Pvt. Co. B, 1st La. Inf.
Gros, A.—Pvt. Co. H, 6th Wd. WL
Guel, J.—Pvt. Sec. A, 5th Wd. WL
Guerin, E.—Pvt. 9th Wd. WL
Guerin, M. J.—Ord. Sgt. Sec. C, 5th Wd. WL
Guerin, Paul O.—Capt. 9th Wd. WL
Guibet, E. Achille—1st Lt. Bat. C, La. F. Art.
Guild, J. F.—Pvt. Co. G, CCWL
Guillotte, C.—Pvt. 9th Wd. WL
Guillotte, Henri—Pvt. Bat. C, L. F. Art.
Guillotte, J. V.—1st Sgt. 9th Wd. WL
Guinault, George—Pvt. Sec. A, 5th Wd. WL
Gurley, Charles—Cpl. Co. A, 1st La. Inf.
Guyol, Charles—Pvt. Bat. C, L. F. Art.
Gwathmey, T. F.—Pvt. Sec. A, CCWL

H

Haber, Frank—Pvt. Co. C, CCWL
Hagan, James—Pvt. Sec. A, CCWL
Hailey, Andes Buford—CCWL (Not on any roster but his son reports that he fought on the 14th)
Hall, Frank M.—Cpl. Sec. A, CCWL
Halloway, Peter—Pvt. Co. D, CCWL
Halpin, John—Pvt. Co. B, CCWL
Hambert, Fritz—Pvt. Co. H, 6th Wd. WL
Hamilton, Chas. B.—Pvt. Sec. E, CCWL
Hamilton, Henry A.—4th Sgt. Bat. A, L. F. Art.
Hands, G. T.—Pvt. Co. D, 1st La. Inf.
Hansen, M., Sr.—Pvt. Co. C, CCWL
Hansen, M. Jr.—Pvt. Co. C, CCWL
Harang, E.—Pvt. Bat. C, L. F. Art.
Hardie, Pierce—Volunteer Aide to Gen. Ogden
Harding, J. M.—Pvt. Sec. E, CCWL
Harding, P. M.—Pvt. Sec. E, CCWL
Hardouis, Alfred—Pvt. 7th Wd. WL
Hare, Walter—Aide to Gen. Ogden
Harmon, H.—Pvt. Co. C, 1st La. Inf.
Harnett, John—Pvt. Co. I, 3rd Wd. WL
Harrahan, J. H.—Pvt. Co. C, 1st La. Inf.
Harriman, J. L.—Pvt. Co. D, 1st La. Inf.
Harrod, B. M.—2nd Lt. Sec. A, CCWL
Hart, M. J.—Pvt. Co. F, CCWL
Hart, Wm.—Pvt. Co. I, 3rd Wd .WL
Harvey, James M.—Pvt. Bat. A, L. F. Art.
Harvey, J. M.—Pvt. Co. C, CCWL
Harvey, Wm. H.—Ord. Sgt. Co. K, 10th Wd. WL
Hayes, James B.—Pvt. Co. K, 10th Wd. League
Hays, Patrick—Pvt. Co. B, 1st La. Inf.
Healy, Dan—Pvt. Co. F, CCWL
Heaney, James—4th Sgt. Co. F, CCWL
Helfrich, Louis—Pvt. Wash. WL
Henderson, J. M.—Pvt. Sec. E, CCWL
Hennen, M.—Lt. Co. G, CCWL
Hennessey, James—Pvt. Sec. D, CCWL
Henthorne, A. P.—Pvt. Co. B, 1st La. Inf.
Herbelin, L.—Pvt. Sec. A, 5th Wd. League
Herman, S. E.—Pvt. Co. C, CCWL
Hermann, Andrew—Pvt. Co. B, CCWL
Hermann, Peter—Pvt. Wash. WL

Hernandez, E.—Pvt. Bat. C, L. F. Art.
Higginbotham, H. J.—Pvt. Sec. A, CWL
Hill, J. D.—Maj. 1st La. Inf.
Hinman, M.—Pvt. Co. G, CCWL
Hite, Claiborne McI.—CCWL
   (Name not on any roster, but his son Morgan D. Hite says he was there and helped to save Badger's life)
Hoffman, John—Pvt. 7th Wd. WL
Hogan, G. L.—Pvt. Sec. C, 5th Wd. WL
Hogsett, George—Pvt. Co. B, 6th Dis. WL
Hoggsett, Robert—Pvt. Co. B, 6th Dis. WL
Holland, A.—Pvt. Co. B, 6th Dis. WL
Holland, W. J.—Pvt. Co. C, CCWL
Hollingsworth, L. B.—Pvt. Co. A, 1st La. Inf.
Holloway, Paul—Pvt. Sec. E, CCWL
Holloway, Peter—Pvt. Sec. D, CCWL
Holmes, I. K.—Cpl. Sec. A, CCWL
Holt, Frank S.—Cpl. Co. A, 1st La. Inf.
Holyland, Fred—On Gen. Ogden's staff
Holzhalb, Frank—Pvt. 7th Wd. WL
Holzhalb, Leon—Pvt. 7th Wd. WL
Homes, Warren—2nd Lt. Co. F, CCWL
Hood, J. C.—Pvt. Co. A, 1st La. Inf.
Hooper, Lee—Pvt. Bat. A, L. F. Art.
Hopf, H. (See N. O. Bulletin 9/25/74)
Hopkins,—Pvt. Co. D, 1st La. Inf.
Hough, S. B.—Pvt. Co. B, 6th Dis. WL
Houssand, J. P.—1st Sgt. Co. I, 3rd Wd. WL
Hoyt, C. E.—Pvt. Co. B, CCWL
Huber, Frank—Pvt. Co. C, CCWL
Huber, J. L.—Pvt. Co. A, 1st La. Inf.
Hubert, M.—Pvt. 9th Wd. WL
Huger, W. E.—
Huguet, R. H.—Pvt. Co. F, CCWL
Hunter, H. B.—Pvt. Co. C, CCWL
Hurley, John—1st Sgt. Sec. D, CCWL
Hyams, R. K.—Pvt. Co. A, 1st La. Inf.
Hyatt, A. W.—1st Lt. Co. F, CCWL
Hyde, William—St. John White League
Hyman, Sam E.—Pvt. Co. C, CCWL
Hynson, J. H. Jr.—Pvt. Co. A, 1st La. Inf.

J

Jamison, David—Pvt. Co. D, 1st La. Inf.
Janvier, Charles—Pvt. Sec. A, 5th Wd. League
Jasper, Henry—Pvt. Co. B, 1st La. Inf.
Jaunet, L.—Pvt. Co. C, 1st La. Inf.
Jenkins, J. G.—Pvt. Co. C, CCWL
Jennings, E. R.—Pvt. Bat. A, L. F. Art.
Johnston, W. J.—Pvt. Sec. E, CCWL
Jonas, Hon. B. F.—La. Rifles
Jones, A. C.—Pvt. Sec. E, CCWL
Jones, A. W.—Pvt. Bat. A, L. F. Art.
Joufroid, F.—Pvt. Sec. C, 5th Wd. WL
Jourdan, L.—Pvt. Sec. C, 5th Wd. WL
Jones, Walter—Pvt. Sec. E, CCWL
Jumonville, Chas. F.—Pvt. Sec. C, 5th Wd. WL
Jumonville, Raoul—Pvt. Sec. A, CCWL
Jung, L. E.—Pvt. Sec. C, 5th Wd. WL

K

Kane, T. D.—Pvt. Bat. A, L. F. Art.
Kearns, L. A.—Pvt. Sec. A, CCWL
Kearney, Inskeep—2nd Sgt. Co. B, CCWL
Keenan, P. H.—Pvt. Co. C, CCWL
Keep, C. S.—Pvt. Co. B, 1st La. Inf.
Kelley, Dan—2nd Lt. Co. B, 6th Dis. WL
Kelly, E. C.—Mentioned in Gen. Ogden's report
Kelly, Ed.—Pvt. Co. I, 3rd Wd. WL
Kelly, John H.—Pvt. Co. B, CCWL
Kennedy, Duer—Pvt. Co. D, 1st La. Inf.
Kennedy, F. R.—Pvt. Co. D, 1st La. Inf.
Kennedy, M.—Pvt. Sec. D, CCWL
Kennedy, Dr. T. S.—La. Rifles

Kenney, Chris.—2nd Sgt. Sec. D, CCWL
Kerkel, E.—Cpl. Sec. A, 5th Wd. League
Kernaghan, M. J.—Pvt. Co. I, 3rd Wd. WL
Kerr, Frank—Pvt. Bat. A. L. F. Art.
Kerr, R. H.—Pvt. Bat. A, L. F. Art.
Kilpatrick, Douglas M.—Capt. Sec. G, CCWL
Kilpatrick, Wm. H.—Pvt. Co. G, CCWL
Kilshaw, J.—Pvt. Co. F, CCWL
King, Fred. D.—Pvt. Co. B, CCWL
Kinney, Chris—Sgt. Co. D, CCWL
Kirke, W. E.—3rd Lt. Co. C, 1st La. Inf.
Klar, L. C.—Pvt. Wash. WL
Kleinpeter, W. B.—Sgt. Co. B, 1st La. Inf.
Klotz, Bernard—Pvt. Co. B, 1st La. Inf.
Koch, James—Pvt. Sec. A, CCWL
Kostmayer, John G.—Pvt. Co. A, 1st La. Inf.
Kratz, Dr. Otto—Pvt. Sec. D, CCWL
Kreeger, Sam G.—Pvt. Co. B, CCWL
Krumbhaar, W. B.—Capt. On Gov. Penn's Staff
Kruttschnitt, E. B.—Pvt. Co. B, CCWL
Kurscheedt & Bienvenun—Mentioned in Gen. Ogden's report
Kuntz, John B.—Cpl. Co. A, 1st La. Inf.

L

Labarre, L. V.—Pvt. Co. C, L. F. Art.
Lacantuguy, S.—Pvt. Sec. A, 5th Wd. League
Lacoste, E.—Pvt. Sec. A, 5th Wd. League
Lacoste, Paul—Pvt. Sec. C, 5th Wd. WL
Lacroix, E.—Pvt. Sec. A, 5th Wd. League
Lafon, Philip—Pvt. Co. B, 1st La. Inf.
Lafonta, Ed.—Pvt. Co. I, 3rd Wd. WL
Lahey, James—Pvt. Co. D, CCWL
Lahey, Joseph—Pvt. Co. D, CCWL
Lambert, Louis L.—Pvt. 7th Wd. WL
Lamberton, C. A.—Pvt. Co. C, 1st La. Inf.
Lanaux, Davis—Pvt. Co. C, L. F. Art.
Landry, Dr. A.—Pvt. Sec. A, 5th Wd. League
Landry, A. C.—4th Sgt. Sec. A, 5th Wd. League
Landry, E. A.—Pvt. Co. C, 1st La. Inf.
Landry, Jerome—Pvt. Sec. A, CCWL
Landry, J. Stans—2nd Cpl. Co. D, 1st La. Inf.
Laney, Jos.—Pvt. Sec. D, CCWL
Lang, Emile J.—Pvt. Wash. WL
Lange, F.—Pvt. Co. C, L. F. Art.
Langsdroff, E.—Cpl. Sec. A, 5th Wd. League
Lansing, Geo.—Pvt. Bat. A, L. F. Art.
Larkin, J.—Pvt. Sec. D, CCWL
Laroussini, Hippolyte—Pvt. Co. H, 6th Wd. WL
Laroussini, Urbin—Pvt. Co. H, 6th Wd. WL
Latey, R.—3rd Cpl. Sec. D, CCWL
Lavie, Gus—Cpl. Sec. A, 5th Wd. League
Lawler, H. T.—Pvt. Co. B, 1st La. Inf.
Leary, Dennis—Pvt. Sec. D, CCWL
LeBlanc, C. E.—Sgt. Co. B, 1st La. Inf.
LeBreton, Charles—Pvt. Sec. A, 5th WL
Leche, A.—Pvt. Sec. D, CCWL
Lecollier, Alph.—Pvt. Sec. A, 5th Wd. League
Lee, Oliver H.—Pvt. Co. A, 1st La. Inf.
Leeds, Chas. J.—Pvt. Sec. D, CCWL
Lefevre, Joseph—Pvt. 7th Wd. WL
LeGardeur, Gustave, Jr.—Maj. of Battalion: Sec. C, Fifth Ward League; Sec. A, same Ward (Roman Rifles); 9th Ward League.
Legien, E.—Pvt. Sec. E, CCWL
Lehman, A.—Pvt. Co. H, 6th Wd. WL
Lennox, John—Pvt. Sec. D, CCWL

Lennox, Robert—Pvt. Sec. D, CCWL
Leonard, Martin—Pvt. Sec. D, CCWL
Lerouge, A. E.—Pvt. 9th Wd. WL
Lesseps, A.—Pvt. Co. D, 1st La. Inf.
Letten, F. J.—Pvt. Co. H, 6th Wd. WL
Leverich, Henry—4th Sgt. Sec. A, CCWL
Levy, Albert—Pvt. Co. K, 10th Wd. WL
Levy, Albert M.—Sgt. Co. G, CCWL
Levy, Alex. B.—Pvt. Co. G, CCWL
Levy, E.—Pvt. Bat. C, L. F. Art.
Levy, S. L.—Pvt. Sec. A, 5th Wd. League
Lewis, A. D.—Pvt. Co. G, CCWL
Lewis, B. S.—Pvt. Sec. E, CCWL
Lewis, C. C., Jr.—Pvt. Sec. E. CCWL
Lewis, Frank—Pvt. Sec. E, CCWL
Lewis, H. L.—Pvt. Sec. E, CCWL
Lewis, H. S.—Pvt. Sec. E, CCWL
Lewis, John Pintard—Pvt. Co. G, CCWL
Liberman, Fred.—Pvt. Sec. D, CCWL
Lincoln, L. L.—1st Lt. Co. C, 1st La. Inf.
Lindsay, R. G.—Pvt. Sec. E, CCWL
Livaudais, L.—Pvt. Sec. A, CCWL
Llambias, Tony—Pvt. Co. H, 6th Wd. WL
Lochelle, C.—Pvt. Wash. WL
Logan, Dr. Samuel—Pvt. Sec. D, CCWL
Lonsdale, W. L.—Pvt. Sec. A, CCWL
Lord, George H.—Capt. Co. B, CCWL
Louque, Chas.—Pvt. Co. C. 1st La. Inf.
Lubben, John—Pvt. Sec. D, CCWL
Lucich, A.—Pvt. Sec. D, CCWL
Luminais, Ed. A.—Pvt. Sec. C, 5th Wd. WL
Luminais, Ferdinand—Pvt. Bat. C, L. F. Art.
Lusk, A. A.—Pvt. Sec. E, CCWL
Lusk, James T.—Pvt. Sec. E, CCWL
Lyons, Capt. I. L.—La. Rifles
Lyons, Jos.—Pvt. Co. I, 3rd Wd. WL
Lyons, M.—Pvt. Sec. D, CCWL
Lyons, Mike—Pvt. Co. I, 3rd Wd. WL

McC

McBride, Wm.—1st Lt. Co. D, CCWL
McCabe, James—Pvt. Co. B, CCWL
McCabe, John—Pvt. Co. K, 10th Wd. WL
McCabe, Phil—Pvt. Co. I, 3rd Wd. WL
McCabe, Wm.—Pvt. Co. B, CCWL
McCaffery, John—Pvt. Co. I, 3rd Wd. WL
McCall, J. W.—Pvt. Co. C, CCWL
McCandlish, Coleman—Pvt. Co. F, CCWL
McCardle, Thos.—Pvt. Co. B, CCWL
McCardle, Thos. Jr.—Pvt. Co. I, 3rd Wd. WL
McCarthy, John—Pvt. Sec. D, CCWL
McCartney, J. H.—Pvt. Sec. A, CCWL
McClelland, Jas.—St. John WL
McClelland, John—St. John WL
McCloskey, George—Pvt. Co. D, 1st La. Inf.
McCloskey, Hugh—Pvt. Co. A, 1st La. Inf.
McCloskey, John—Pvt. Co. B, 1st La. Inf.
McCloskey, R.—Pvt. Co. B, 1st La. Inf.
McCormack, John—Pvt. Co. K, 10th Wd. WL
McCullu, N.—Pvt. Co. C, 1st La. Inf.
McDermott, P.—Pvt. Co. I, 3rd Wd. WL
McDonald, Jno. T.—Sgt. Co. K, 10th Wd. WL
McDonald, Sam—Com. Sgt. Sec. A, CCWL
McDonogh, B. A.—1st Lt. Co. K, 10th Wd. WL
McDonough, M.—Pvt. Sec. D, CCWL
McFee, Jas.—Pvt. Sec. R, CCWL
McGeehan, W. J.—Pvt. Sec. E, CCWL
McGloin, Frank—Capt. Co. B, 1st La. Inf.

McIllsley, Charles—Pvt. Sec. A, 5th Wd. League
McIntyre, Thos. L.—Capt. Sec. F, CCWL
McKay, Tim—Pvt. Co. I, 3rd Wd. WL
McKernan, James—Pvt. Co. I, 3rd Wd. WL
McKinney, Pres.—Pvt. Co. C, CCWL
McLaughlin, James—Pvt. Co. I, 3rd Wd. WL
McLaughlin, M.—Pvt. Sec. D, CCWL
McLellan, Orris I.—Pvt. Co. A, 1st La. Inf.
McManus, Hugh—Pvt. Co. I, 3rd Wd. WL
McManus, John—Pvt. Sec. D, CCWL
McMartin, J. A.—Pvt. Sec. E, CCWL
McMullen, J. F.—1st Cpl. Co. I, 3rd Wd. WL
MacMurdo, Charles—Pvt. Sec. A, CCWL
MmNulty, Geo.—Pvt. Co. F, CCWL
McWilliams, A.—Pvt. Co. D, CCWL

M

Macheca, Jos. P.—Capt. Co. B, 1st La. Inf.
Maes, R.—Pvt. Co. C, CCWL
Magnifico, Isidore—Pvt. Bat. C, L. F. Art.
Mahoney, D. P.—Pvt. Co. B, CCWL
Mahoney, John D.—1st Sgt. Co. B, CCWL
Mailhes, John—Pvt. Sec. A, 5th Wd. League
Maitre, F.—Pvt. Sec. A, 5th Wd. League
Mallam, G. H.—Pvt. Co. C, CCWL
Malle', P.—Pvt. Co. C, CCWL
Malochee, Pierre—(according to his son James Malochee)
Mandeville, Chas.—3rd Sgt. Bat. A, L. F. Art.
Mandeville, Dr. W. R.—Pvt. Bat. A, L. F. Art.
Manion, M.—Pvt. Bat. A, L. F. Art.
Manning, John—Pvt. Sec. D, CCWL
Marceau, P.—Pvt. Co. C, 1st La. Inf.
Marie, Jean—Pvt. Co. B, 1st La. Inf.
Marks, Marion H.—Pvt. Co. G, CCWL
Marks, Wash—Pvt. B, CCWL
Marquez, R.—Pvt. Bat. C, L. F. Art.
Martinez, C.—Pvt. Co. F, CCWL
Martinstein, E. O.—Pvt. Sec. A, 5th Wd. League
Mather, A. T.—Pvt. Sec. A, CCWL
Mather, C.—Pvt. Sec. A, CCWL
Mather, E.—Pvt. Sec. A, CCWL
Mather, Jas.—Pvt. Sec. A, CCWL
Mather, L. J.—Pvt. Sec. A, CCWL
Maury, Jules—Pvt. Bat. C, L. F. Art.
Maxwell, J.—Pvt. Sec. E, CCWL
May, A. H., Jr.—Pvt. Co. C, CCWL
Meehan, C.—4th Cpl. Sec. D, CCWL
Mehle, John—Pvt. Sec. D, CCWL
Meilleur, E. M.—Pvt. Sec. A, 5th Wd. League
Meilleur, J. Simon—Pvt. Wash. WL
Mellen, J. P.—Co. B, 6th Dis. WL
Menard, John H.—Ord. Sgt. 7th Wd. WL
Mestier, L. J.—Pvt. Co. B, 1st La. Inf.
Meunier, Eugene F.—Pvt. Bat. C, L. F. Art.
Meunier, Jules F., Jr.—Pvt. Bat. C, L. F. Art.
Meux, John—Pvt. Sec. A, CCWL
Miangolara, J.—Pvt. Sec. A, 5th Wd. League
Micou, Augustin—2nd Sgt. Co. D, 1st La. Inf.
Miles, Dr. A. B.—Sgt. Co. D, 1st La. Inf.
Miller, W. H.—Pvt. Co. C, CCWL
Miltenberger, E.—Pvt. Sec. A, 5th Wd. League
Miltimore, C. J.—4th Sgt. Co. I, 3rd Wd. WL
Minnox, James—Pvt. Co. B, CCWL
Minnox, John—Pvt. Co. B, CCWL

Minor, F. O.—Pvt. Co. C, CCWL
Mire, B. C.—Capt. Co. H, CCWL
Mire, Ben. G.—Pvt. Sec. A, CCWL
Mitchell, Archibald—Capt. Sec. D, CCWL (Also Capt. Co. D, 1st La. Inf.)
Mitchell, Arthur J.—Pvt. Co. B, 6th Dis. WL
Mitchell, Chas. O.—Pvt. Co. A, 1st La. Inf.
Mitchell, Ferd.—Pvt. Co. B, 6th Dis. WL
Mitchell, Frank D.—Sgt. Co. B, 1st La. Inf.
Mitchell, M.—Pvt. Sec. D, CCWL
Mitchell, W. S.—Pvt. Sec. A, CCWL
Mix, Frank—Pvt. Co. B, CCWL
Moffett, A. W.—Pvt. Co. F, CCWL
Mohrmann, Fred—6th Dis. WL
Monaghan, Wm.—Pvt. Co. K, 10th Wd. WL
Moore, Jas.—Pvt. Sec. D, CCWL
Moore, John V.—Volunteer Aide to Gen. Ogden
Moran, Michael—Pvt. Sec. D, CCWL
Moran, Thomas—2nd Lt. Co. I, 3rd Wd. WL
Moran, Wm.—Pvt. Co. I, 3rd Wd. WL
Morel, Charles—Sgt. Sec. C, 5th Wd. WL
Morel, Wm., Jr.—Pvt. Sec. C, 5th Wd. WL
Morgan, Capt. W. H.—Mentioned in Gen. Ogden's report
Morgan, W. T.—Pvt. Sec. A, CCWL
Mornas, P.—Pvt. Sec. A, 5th Wd. League
Morphy, A. E.—1st Sgt. Sec. A, CCWL
Mossy, J.—Pvt. Sec. A, 5th Wd. League
Mount, W. S., Jr.—Cpl. Co. A, 1st La. Inf.
Mouster, T.—Pvt. Sec. A, 5th Wd. League
Mouton, A. A.—Pvt. 6th Wd. Wash. WL
Mouton, Aleck.—Pvt. Sec. D, CCWL
Muir, J. A.—Capt. 2nd Wd. WL
Murphy, J. C.—Pvt. Sec. A, CCWL
Murphy, J. H.—Pvt. Co. D, CCWL
Murphy, John—Pvt. Sec. D, CCWL
Murphy, John, A.—Pvt. Co. K, 10th Wd. WL
Murphy, William—Pvt. Sec. D, CCWL
Murray, J.—Pvt. Co. C, 1st La. Inf.
Musson, A.—Pvt. Wash. WL
Myers, Peter—Pvt. Co. C, CCWL

N

Nelson, J. W.—Pvt. Co. B, 1st. La. Inf.
Newhouse, J. T.—Pvt. Co. C, 1st La. Inf.
Newman, John K.—1st Lt. Co. A, 1st La. Inf.
Newman, S. B., Jr.—Ord. Sgt. Sec. A, CCWL
Newton, A. A.—Pvt. Wash. WL
Nicaud, Fred—Pvt. Sec. C, 5th Wd. WL
Nicholson, W. S.—Pvt. Co. C, CCWL
Nixon, J. O., Jr.—1st Lt. Co. B, CCWL
Nock, L. C.—Pvt. Bat. A, L. F. Art.
Noblon, Jules—Pvt. Sec. A, 5th Wd. League
Norman, Fred.—Pvt. Sec. E, CCWL
Norman, James—Pvt. Sec. D, CCWL
North, Thos.—1st Sgt. Co. F, CCWL
Norton, Geo.—Pvt. Sec. A, CCWL
Norton, Hewitt—Pvt. Sec. A, CCWL
Nozeret, A.—Pvt. Sec. A, 5th Wd. League
Nugent, Matt—Pvt. 7th Wd. WL
Nunez, C. A.—Pvt. Sec. D, CCWL

O

Ober, C. W.—Pvt. Co. A, 1st La. Inf.
Ober, Fred A.—Cpl. Co. A, 1st La. Inf.
Ober, George—Pvt. Co. A, 1st La. Inf.
Ober, G. R.—Pvt. Co. G, CCWL
Ober, J. F.—Pvt. Co. A, 1st La. Inf.

O'Brien, E. E.—Pvt. Co. C, CCWL
O'Brien, Emile J.—1st Lt. Co. C, CCWL
O'Brien, John—Cpl. 10th Wd. WL
O'Brien, John—Pvt. Sec. D, CCWL
O'Connors, T.—Pvt. Co. K, 10th Wd. WL
O'Donahue, J.—2nd Lt. Co. D, CCWL
Ogden, Charles G.—2nd Lt. Co. F, CCWL
Ogden, Fred N.—Maj. Gen, in command of all White League forces on the 14th of Sept.
Ogden, Octo N.—3rd Lt. Co. D, 1st La. Inf. (Also Pvt. Co. F, CCWL)
O'Hara, James—Pvt. Co. B, CCWL
O'Hara, M. J.—Pvt. Bat. A, L. F. Art.
O'Leary, David—Pvt. Co. D, CCWL
Oliver, Chas.—St. John WL
Olivier, Wm.—Pvt. Wash. WL
O'Neil, John—Pvt. Co. D, CCWL
O'Reilley, P. J.—Pvt. Co. B, 1st La. Inf.
Orrell, Thomas, Sr.—Pvt. Sec. D, CCWL
O'Rourke, M.—Pvt. Sec. A, CCWL
Overton, John K.—2nd Lt. Co. D, 1st La. Inf.

P

Pagaud, J. Alphonse—Pvt. Co. G, CCWL
Palfrey, Chas.—1st Sgt. Sec. E, CCWL
Parham, B. B.—Pvt. Co. A, 1st La. Inf.
Parker, C. A.—Pvt. Bat. A, L. F. Art.
Parker, C. H.—Pvt. Co. D, 1st La. Inf.
Parker, Jim—Pvt. Wash. WL
Pascal, Gabriel—Sec. A, 5th Wd. League
Patterson, A. H.—Pvt. Co. C, 1st La. Inf.
Patton, I. W.—Pvt. Sec. E, CCWL
Paul, Albert—Pvt. Co. B, 1st La. Inf.
Payne, John N.—Aide to Gen. Ogden
Peale, Henry—Pvt. Wash. WL
Peck, Ossian F.—1st Lt. Bat. A. L. F. Art.
Peltier, Elime—Pvt. 9th Wd. WL
Pelton, James—Pvt. Co. K, 10th Wd. WL
Percy, Henry—Pvt. Sec. C, 5th Wd. WL
Percy, Joseph L.—Pvt. Sec. C, 5th Wd. WL
Pettingill, W. S.—Cpl. Co. A, 1st La. Inf.
Pettis, Ed.—Pvt. Co. B, CCWL
Peyroux, Albert—Pvt. Co. H, 6th Wd.
Peyroux, Placide—Pvt. Co. H, 6th Wd. WL
Peyroux, P. O.—Capt. Co. D, 1st La. Inf.
Phelps, Ashton—Co. G, CCWL (From re-union dinner list Sept. 16, 1875)
Phelps, Orlando H.—Pvt. Co. K, 10th Wd. WL
Philippi, Jules C.—Pvt. Bat. C, L. F. Art.
Philips, A. B.—Capt. 6th Wd. Wash. WL
Phillips, Isaac—Pvt. Co. B, CCWL
Phillips, Eugene—Pvt. Sec. A, 5th Wd. League
Pichon, Zenon—Pvt. Bat. C, L. F. Art.
Pickford, Thos.—Pvt. Co. F, CCWL
Pierce, H. C.—Pvt. Bat. C, L. F. Art.
Pierson, Jos.—Pvt. 9th Wd. WL
Pilard, A.—Pvt. Sec. A, 5th Wd. League
Pinckard, W. F.—Ord. Sgt. Co. C, CCWL
Pinsard, V.—Pvt. Sec. A, 5th Wd. League
Pitts, Chas.—Pvt. Co. B, 1st La. Inf.
Pleasants, Reuben B.—Capt. Sec. E, CCWL
Pollock, E.—Pvt. Co. C, CCWL
Posey, Lloyd—Pvt. Co. C, 1st La. Inf.
Potts, J. C.—Pvt. Co. C, CCWL
Potts, R. M.—Pvt. Sec. A, CCWL
Poursine, E. Pvt. Bat. C, L. F. Art.

Poursine, F.—Pvt. Sec. C, 5th Wd. WL
Prados, Hy.—Pvt. Sec. C, 5th Wd. WL
Prados, L.—Capt. Co. C, 1st La. Inf.
Pratt, Dr. Geo. K.—Sgt. Co. D, 1st La. Inf.
Pratt, M. F.—Pvt. Sec. A, CCWL
Prendergast, Thomas—Pvt. Sec. A, CCWL
Prevost, L.—Pvt. Sec. A, 5th Wd. League
Pritchett, Geogre D.—Pvt. Co. D, 1st La. Inf.
Puech, Ernest—Pvt. Co. H, 6th Wd. WL
Pursell, Dave E.—Sgt. Co. G, CCWL
Purcell, W. J.—Pvt. Sec. D, CCWL
Putnam, Oscar L.—Pvt. Sec. E, CCWL
Pymer, David—Pvt. Sec. D, CCWL

Quackenbos, F. W.—Pvt. Sec. E, CCWL

R

Rainey, H. H.—Pvt. Co. C, CCWL
Ranlett, Charles—Pvt. Co. B, CCWL
Ranlett, E. L.
Rareshide, George H.—Pvt. Co. C, 1st La. Inf.
Raymond, Ernest—Pvt. Sec. C, 5th Wd. WL
Raymond, Felix—Pvt. Wash. WL
Raymond, Fernand—Pvt. Wash. WL
Raymond, Lewis—Pvt. Wash. WL
Rebenack, Chas.—Pvt. Wash. WL
Rebenack, F.—Pvt. Sec. C, 5th Wd. WL
Reed, James—Cpl. Sec. C, 5th Wd. WL
Reilly, Mike—Pvt. Co. I, 3rd Wd. WL
Reinecke, Henry—Sgt. Sec. C, 5th Wd. WL
Reinecke, John L.—Bat. C. L. F. Art.
Renaud—Lt. La. Rifles
Renaud, Albert—St. John WL
Rennyson, Henry—Pvt. Sec. D, CCWL
Renshaw, Judge Henry—Sgt. Co. D, 1st La. Inf.
Renshaw, Jas. A.—Lt. Co. G, CCWL
Renshaw, W. W.—Pvt. Co. G, CCWL
Reynolds, Ed.—Pvt. Sec. D, CCWL
Reynolds, James—Pvt. Co. B, 6th Dis. WL
Reynolds, M. A.—Sgt. Wash. WL
Reynolds, Thos.—Pvt. Sec. D, CCWL
Reynolds, W. W. H.—Pvt. Co. B, 6th Dis. WL
Rice, Jos. A.—Pvt. Co. C, CCWL
Richards, Newton—Pvt. Sec. A, CCWL
Richardson, Frank L.—1st Lt. Co. D, 1st La. Inf.
Richardson, W. R.—Pvt. Co. F, 1st La. Inf.
Ricketts, Thomas—Pvt. Co. F, CCWL
Rieger, Rudolph—Pvt. 7th Wd. WL
Rightor, N. H.—Pvt. 7th Wd. WL
Rightor, R. H.—Pvt. Wash. WL
Rivarde, John—Pvt. Bat. C, L. F. Art.
Rivivere, L.—Pvt. Sec. A, 5th Wd. League.
Roach John—4th Sgt. Sec. D, CCWL
Robbins, W. C.—2nd Lt. Co. C, CCWL
Robert, A.—Pvt. Sec. A, CCWL
Robert, Edward—Pvt. Sec. A, 5th Wd. League
Roberts, Alonzo, Ord. Sgt. Co. C, 1st La. Inf.
Robinson, Henry—Pvt. Co. I, 3rd Wd. WL
Robinson, N. T. N.—Pvt. Co. C, CCWL
Robinson, W.—Mentioned in Gen. Ogden's report
Robinson, W. C. H.—3rd Sgt. Co. C, CCWL
Rochester, Frank U.—Pvt. Co. A, 1st La. Inf.
Rodenberg, A. G.—Pvt. Sec. E, CCWL
Roemer, Jacob—Pvt. Co. K, 10th Wd. WL
Roesch, D.—Pvt. Sec. D, CCWL
Rohrbacher, Chas.—Pvt. Sec. D, CCWL
Roman, Andre L.—3rd Sgt. Sec. A, 5th Wd. League

Roman, Charles—Capt. Sec. A, 5th Wd. League
Rondeau, J. P.—Pvt. Bat. A, L. F. Art.
Rooney, Jas.—Pvt. Co. F. CCWY
Roper, O. E.—Pvt. Co. D, CCWL
Rosiere, E.—Bat. C, L. F. Art.
Ross, Ambrose—Pvt. Sec. D, CCWL
Roubion, L. B.—Pvt. Sec. C, 5th Wd. WL
Roux, Amilcar—Cpl. Sec. A, 5th Wd. League
Roux, A. P.—Bat. C, L. F. Art.
Roux, E.—Pvt. Co. H, 6th Wd. WL
Roux, Edwin—St. John WL
Royes, Manuel—Pvt. Sec. D, CCWL
Rugan, W. Henry—Pvt. Sec. D, CCWL
Russell, Chris.—Pvt. Sec. D, CCWL

S

Safely, George—Pvt. Co. B, CCWL
St. Rosa, E.—Pvt. Sec. 5th Wd. League
Sanford, Geo.—Pvt. Sec. D, CCWL
Sarrat, Belmont—2nd Lt. Sec. A, 5th Wd. League
Sauvage, R.—Pvt. Sec. A, 5th Wd. League
Sauve, F. A.—Pvt. Sec. E, CCWL
Sauve, Lopez—Pvt. Co. B, 6th Dis. WL
Savage, J.—Pvt. Sec. C, CCWL
Sbisa, John—Pvt. Co. H, 6th Wd. WL
Schneidau, Ed.—Pvt. Co. D, 1st La. Inf.
Schneider, Adam—St. John WL
Schoebel, George—Pvt. Bat. C, LFA
Schwable, T.—Pvt. Wash. WL
Schwaner, A.—Pvt. Bat. A, L. F. Art.
Scott, D. R.—Pvt. Sec. E, CCWL
Scott, Wallace—Pvt. Co. D, 1st La. Inf.
Scott, Walter—Cpl. Sec. A, CCWL
Seehil, John—Pvt. Co. D, CCWL
Seghers, Dr. E.—Pvt. Sec. A, 5th Wd. League
Seguin, E.—Pvt. Sec. E, CCWL
Selleck, J. R. S.—Capt. Co. I, 3rd Wd. WL
Selles, F.—2nd Lt. Co. C, 1st La. Inf.
Selles, G.—Pvt. Co. C, 1st La. Inf.
Selph, Dudley—Sgt. Co. A, 1st La. Inf.
Sere, Leon—Pvt. Co. B, 1st La. Inf.
Sessman, James—Pvt. Co. D, CCWL
Sewell, J. C.—Pvt. Co. I, 3rd Wd. WL
Shanks, Gus—St. John WL
Shanks, Wm.—St. John WL
Shannon, David—Pvt. Sec. D, CCWL
Shay, Wm.—Pvt. Co. D, CWL
Shepard, Sam K.—2nd Sgt. Bat. A, L. F. Art.
Shepard, Will L.—Sgt. Co. B, 1st La. Inf.
Sheridan, Wm.—Pvt. Co. I, 3rd Wd. WL
Sherry, James—Pvt. Co. A, CCWL
Shields, John—Pvt. Co. G, CCWL
Shields, Wilmer—Pvt. Co. G, CCWL
Shropshire, H. E.—Co. B, 6th Dis. WL
Shute, T. Lee—Col. and Adj. Gen. on Gen. Ogden's staff
Sill, George—Pvt. Sec. D, CCWL
Simms, B. J.—Pvt. Co. F, CCWL
Simonin, Gus—Pvt. Co. G, CCWL
Simpson, A. S.—Pvt. Co. D, 1st La. Inf.
Simpson, John—Pvt. Co. D, 1st La. Inf.
Slattery, Matthew—Commisary Sgt. Sec. D, CCWL
Slayden, J. L.—Pvt. Co. B, CCWL
Smith, Chas. D.—Pvt. Sec. A, 5th Wd. League
Smith, Dr. Howard—Pvt. Sec. D, CCWL
Smith, J. H.—Mentioned in Gen. Ogden's report
Smith, John, N.—Pvt. Bat. C, L. F. Art.
Smith, M.—Pvt. Co. G, CCWL
Smith, Marshall J.—Volunteer Co. A, 1st La. Inf.
Smith, Marshall J., Jr.—Pvt. Co. A, 1st La. Inf.
Smith, Percy—Pvt. Co. G, CCWL
Smith, P. F.—Pvt. Sec. E, CCWL

Smith, W. R.—Pvt. Sec. A, 5th Wd. League
Solomon, W. E.—Pvt. Co. I, 3rd Wd. WL
Sombsthay, J.—Pvt. Sec. A, 5th Wd. League
Soniat, Chas. T.—Bat. C, L. F. Art.
Soniat, Edw. J.—Bat. C, L. F. Art.
Sougeron, Jules—Pvt. Sec. A, CCWL
Southmayd, F. R.—Aide to Gen Ogden
Sparrow, Wm.—St. John WL
Spyker, George—Pvt. Sec. E, CCWL
Stannard, Wm.—Pvt. Co. F, CCWL
Stansbury, W. B.—Pvt. Co. B, CCWL
Starks, Chas. A.—2nd Lt. Co. A, 1st La. Inf.
Stauffer, W. R.—Pvt. Sec. A, CCWL
Stein, George—Pvt. Co. B, CCWL
Stem, George—Co. B. CCWL
Stevenson, John—Pvt. Co. K, 10th Wd. WL
Stewart, Rev.—Pvt. Co. B, 1st La. Inf.
Stille, Walker—Pvt. Co. B, CCWL
Stoddard, Thomas—Pvt. Sec. D, CCWL
Stokes, Chas.—Pvt. Co. B, 1st La. Inf.
Stone, Garret—4th Cpl. Co. D, 1st La. Inf.
Stone, Dr. Warren, Jr.—Pvt. Bat. A, L. F. Art.
Story, Wm.—Pvt. Sec. D, CCWL
Stuber, James L.—Pvt. Co. A, 1st La. Inf.
Sullivan, J. J.—Pvt. Sec. D, CCWL
Sully, G. W.—Pvt. Co. C, CCWL
Sutherland, W. R.—Pvt. Co. B, CCWL
Sutton, Joseph—Pvt. Sec. D, CCWL
Swarbrick, George—Pvt. Co. I, 3rd Wd. WL
Swayne, Wm. M.—Pvt. Co. B, CWL
Swift, J.—Pvt. Sec. D, CCWL

T

Tabary, O.—Pvt. 9th Wd. League
Tallon, C. J.—Pvt. 1st La. Inf.
Tardy, A. J.—Pvt. Co. B, 6th Dis. WL
Tardy, George H.—Sgt. Wash. WL
Taylor, J.—Pvt. Co. B, 6th Dis. WL
Taylor, Thomas—Pvt. Co. D, CCWL
Tebault, B. R.—Pvt. Sec. E, CCWL
Tebault, Dr. C. H.—Pvt. Sec. D, CCWL
Tebault, W.—Pvt. Co. B, CCWL
Tell, George—Pvt. Co. B, 1st La. Inf.
Tenbrink, Wm.—Pvt. Co. F, CCWL
Tennison, O. M.—Capt. 7th Wd. WL
Tete, A.—Pvt. Co. H, 6th Wd. WL
Thibaut, James—Pvt. Sec. A, 5th Wd. WL
Thibodeaux, Ben—Pvt. 9th Wd. WL
Thomas, H. O.—Pvt. Sec. A, CCWL
Thomas, John—Pvt. Sec. D, CCWL
Thomas, Wm.—Pvt. Sec. D, CCWL
Thurber, Dr. John A.—Pvt. Co. B, 1st La. Inf.
Thurber, Dr. L. A.—Pvt. Co. B, 1st La. Inf.
Tiller, Ben.—Pvt. Co. H, 6th Wd. WL
Tilford, R. H.—Pvt. Co. F, CCWL
Tilton, James—Cpl. Co. K, 10th Wd. WL
Tobin,—Volunteer Aide to Gen. Ogden
Tobin, Jno. W.—Pvt. Co. B, 1st La. Inf.
Toby, Thos.—Pvt. Co. F, CCWL
Toca, L.—Bat. C, L. F. Art.
Todd, John R.—Pvt. Bat. A, L. F. Art.
Toledano, E. A.—Pvt. Sec. A, CCWL
Toole, Hugh—Pvt. Sec. D, CCWL
Torregrossa, Emile—St. John WL
Tracey, Dennis—2nd Cpl. Co. I, 3rd Wd. WL
Trelford, Aug.—Pvt. Co. I, 3rd Wd. WL
Triest, Fred—Pvt. Co. C, 1st La. Inf.
Trinchard, Lennard A. (according to his grandson, Dr. Percy L. Querens)
Trudeau, L. Z.—Pvt. Sec. A, CCWL
Trufant, Sam A.—Pvt. Co. C, CCWL
Tully, James—Pvt. Co. H, 6th Wd. WL
Tully, John S.—Pvt. Co. H, 6th Wd. WL
Turner, John G.—Pvt. Co. G, CCWL

Turpin, Henry—Pvt. Sec. A, 5th Wd. WL
Tuyes, Jno.—Pvt. Co. B, 1st La. Inf.
Tuyes, John—Ord. Sgt. Co. H, 6th Wd. WL
Twichell, Ben S.—Pvt. Co. D, 1st La. Inf.
Tynan, Andrew—Pvt. Sec. D, CCWL
Tynan, Wm.—Pvt. Co. I, 3rd Wd. WL

U

Uhlhorn, Chas. L.—Pvt. Sec. A, CCWL
Uhlhorn, T. G.—Pvt. Sec. A, CCWL
Uter, Oscar—Gunner, Bat. C, LFA

V

Valeton, A.—Bat. C, L. F. Art.
Van Court, J.—Pvt. Co. I, 3rd Wd. WL
Vatinel, Chas.—Bat. C, L. F. Art.
Vaudry, W. T.—Capt. Sec. A, CCWL
Vaught, D. A. S
Vautier, Chas.—Capt. St. John WL
Vautier, Domminick—Pvt. Wash. WL
Veran, Louis—Bat. C, LFA
Veran, William—Pvt. 7th Wd. WL
Veron, Wm.—St. John WL
Verges, L.—Pvt. Sec. A, 5th Wd. League
Vienne, L. B.—3rd Sgt. Sec. E, CCWL
Vincent, Ed.—Pvt. Co. B, CCWL
Vinet,—Mentioned in Gen. Ogden's report
Vinot, B.—Pvt. Wash. WL
Violet, Atwood—Pvt. Sec. A, CCWL
Voorhies, C. Arthur—Pvt. Co. H, 6th Wd. WL
Voorhies, Paul E.—Pvt. Co. H, 6th Wd. WL
Voorhies, Wm.—3rd Lt. Co. H, 6th Wd. WL

W

Waggamann, Albert—Pvt. Co. B, 6th Dis. WL
Waggaman, Eugene—Pvt. Co. B, 6th Dis. WL
Wagner, A. C.—Pvt. Sec. D, CCWL
Wagner, J. C.—2nd Cpl. Sec. D, CCWL

Wagner, P. K.—Pvt. Sec. D, CCWL
Walker, Clem L.—2nd Lt. Co. B, 1st La. Inf.
Wallen, Patrick—Pvt. Sec. D, CCWL
Walsh, Richard—Pvt. Sec. D, CCWL
Walton, J. B.—On Staff of Gen. Ogden
Ward, J. P.—Pvt. Sec. A, CCWL
Ward, Thos. J.—Pvt. Co. F, CCWL
Warner, Henry—Pvt. Sec. D, CCWL
Watts, Harrison—Capt. Sec. A, CCWL
Weaver, Wm. K.—Pvt. Co. A, 1st La. Inf.
Weber, A.—Pvt. Wash. WL
Weber, L.—Pvt. Sec. D, CCWL
Webre, J. A.—Pvt. Sec. A, 5th Wd. League
Weiman, P. J.—Pvt. Sec. D, CCWL
Weis, John—Pvt. Co. B, 6th Dis. WL
Weisenbourg, Henry—Pvt. 9th Wd. WL
Weiss, Gottlieb—Pvt. Co. B, 6th Dis. WL
Wells, W. A.—Pvt. Co. C, CCWL
Wells, Wm.—Pvt. Co. K, 10th Wd. WL
Welsch. John—Pvt. Wash. WL
West, Edward—Pvt. Co. A, 1st La. Inf.
West, J. Will—Pvt. Co. A, 1st La. Inf.
Whalen, Thomas—Pvt. Co. K, 10th Wd. WL
Wheeler, J. B.—Pvt. Co. C, CCWL
Wheeler, W. A. S.—Pvt. Co. C, CCWL
White, D. Prieur—Mentioned in Gen. Ogden's report
White, Ed.—Pvt. Co. G, CCWL
White, Edw. Douglas—Pvt. Co. D, 1st La. Inf.
Whitney, C. E.—Pvt. Co. D, 1st La. Inf.
Wiendahl, H.—Pvt. Sec. A, 5th Wd. League
Wild, Harry—Pvt. Co. B, 6th Dis. WL
Wilkinson, James—Orderly Sgt. Co. B, 6th Dis. WL
Williams, George A.—Aide to Gen. Ogden
Willis, Ed—Pvt. Co. K, 10th Wd. WL
Wiltz, Geo. L.—Gunner, Bat. C, La. F. Art.

Wiltz, Octave—Pvt. Sec. C, 5th Wd WL
Wiltz, P. S., Jr.—1st Lt. 9th Wd. WL
Winseky, H.—Ord. Sgt. 6th Wd. Washington WL. (This name is spelled Wunschig in memorial published Sept. 26th. Not in N.O. Directory, but find Hugo Winske)
Winslow, W. P.—Pvt. Co. A, 1st La. Inf.
Winter, E.—Pvt. Co. C, CCWL
Winter, F.—Pvt. Co. C, CCWL
Wire, Frank—Pvt. sec. D, CCWL
Wisdom, M. N.—Pvt. Co. C, CCWL
With, Wm.—Pvt. Co. B, CCWL
Woelper, Wm.—Lt., La. Rifles (Sec. to Gov. McEnery)
Wood, Col. Robert—Mentioned in Gen. Ogden's report
Woods, A. A.—Pvt. Co. D, 1st La. Inf.
Woods, Gus—Pvt. Co. B, -st La. Inf.
Woods, John G.—Pvt. Co. F, CCWL
Worth, J. Well—Pvt. Co. A, 1st La. Inf.
Wunschig, Hugo—Ord. Sgt., 6th Wd. Washington WL (This name is given as Winseky in other lists)

X

Ximenes, J. R.—Pvt. Sec. A, 5th Wd. League

Y

Youents, Jos.—Pvt. Sec. A, 5th Wd. League
Young, Geo. W.—Pvt. Co. B, 6th Dis. WL
Yuille, Frank—Pvt. Co. C, CCWL

Z

Zelesky, Felix—Pvt. Co. F, CCWL
Zengel, Fred—Pvt. Co. B, 1st La. Inf.
Zengel, Jos.—Pvt. Co. B, 1st La. Inf.
Zenneck, Adolph—Pvt. Co. B, 1st La. Inf.
Ziegler, George—Pvt. Co. C, 1st La. Inf.

THE END

INDEX

INDEX

CPSIA information can be obtained
at www.ICGtesting.com
Printed in the USA
BVHW010015111021
618647BV00007B/88

9 781565 544432